❧ THE CARE OF THE DEAD
IN LATE ANTIQUITY

A VOLUME IN THE SERIES
Cornell Studies in Classical Philology

Edited by Frederick M. Ahl, Theodore R. Brennan, Charles F. Brittain, Kevin M. Clinton, Gail J. Fine, David P. Mankin, Sturt W. Manning, Alan J. Nussbaum, Hayden N. Pelliccia, Pietro Pucci, Hunter R. Rawlings III, Éric Rebillard, Jeffrey S. Rusten, Barry S. Strauss

VOLUME LIX
The Care of the Dead in Late Antiquity

By Éric Rebillard

A list of titles in this series is available at www.cornellpress.cornell.edu.

THE CARE OF THE DEAD IN LATE ANTIQUITY

ÉRIC REBILLARD

*Translated by
Elizabeth Trapnell Rawlings
and Jeanine Routier-Pucci*

CORNELL UNIVERSITY PRESS
Ithaca and London

Originally published under the title *Religion et sépulture: L'Église, les vivants et les morts dans l'Antiquité tardive,* by Éric Rebillard. © 2003, Éditions de l'École des hautes études en sciences sociales, Paris.

Copyright © 2009 by Cornell University

All rights reserved. Except for brief quotations in a review, this book, or parts thereof, must not be reproduced in any form without permission in writing from the publisher. For information, address Cornell University Press, Sage House, 512 East State Street, Ithaca, New York 14850.

First published 2009 by Cornell University Press
First printing, Cornell Paperbacks, 2012

Printed in the United States of America

Library of Congress Cataloging-in-Publication Data

Rebillard, Éric.
 [Religion et sépulture. English]
 The care of the dead in late antiquity / Éric Rebillard ; translated by Elizabeth Trapnell Rawlings and Jeanine Routier-Pucci.
     p. cm. — (Cornell studies in classical philology ; v. 59)
 Includes bibliographical references and index.
 ISBN 978-0-8014-4677-1 (cloth : alk. paper)
 ISBN 978-0-8014-7795-9 (paper : alk. paper)
 1. Death—Religious aspects—Christianity. 2. Funeral rites and ceremonies, Ancient—Rome—Religious aspects. 3. Funeral rites and ceremonies, Ancient—Religious aspects. I. Title. II. Series: Cornell studies in classical philology ; v. 59.
  BT826.R4313 2009
  265'.850937—dc22
                                                2008052547

Cornell University Press strives to use environmentally responsible suppliers and materials to the fullest extent possible in the publishing of its books. Such materials include vegetable-based, low-VOC inks and acid-free papers that are recycled, totally chlorine-free, or partly composed of nonwood fibers. For further information, visit our website at www.cornellpress.cornell.edu.

Cloth printing   10 9 8 7 6 5 4 3 2 1
Paperback printing 10 9 8 7 6 5 4 3 2 1

Contents

Abbreviations vii
Introduction ix

1. The Problem of the Origins: Christian Burial in Rome and Carthage — 1

2. Burial and Religious Identity: Religious Groups and Collective Burial — 13

3. Voluntary Associations and Collective Burial: The Church, Christians, and the Collegia — 37

4. Violation of Tombs and Impiety: Funerary Practices and Religious Beliefs — 57

5. Christian Piety and Burial Duty: From the Duty to Bury the Dead to the Organization of Burial for the Poor — 89

6. Christian Funerals and Funerals of Christians: The Church and the Death Ritual in Late Antiquity — 123

7. The Church, Christians, and the Dead: Commemoration of the Dead in Late Antiquity — 140

   Conclusion — 176

Primary Sources 179
Secondary Sources 191
Index 213

Abbreviations

CIL   *Corpus inscriptionum Latinarum.* Berlin, 1862–.
CPG   *Clavis Patrum Graecorum.* Edited by M. Geerard. Turnhout, 1983–.
PG   *Patrologia Graeca.* Edited by Jacques-Paul Migne. Paris.
ICVR   *Inscriptiones Christianae urbis Romae.* Rome, 1922–.
ILCV   *Inscriptiones latinae Christianae veteres.* Edited by Ernst Diehl. Berlin, 1961.
PIR   *Prosopographia Imperii Romani Saeculi I, II, III.* Berlin, 1933–.
CJ   *Codex Justinianus. Corpus Iuris Civilis.* Vol. 2. Edited by Paul Krueger. Berlin, 1954.

INTRODUCTION

This book's title, *The Care of the Dead in Late Antiquity,* is directly inspired by the title of a treatise Augustine wrote toward the end of his life.[1] His friend Paulinus of Nola had asked him about the utility for salvation of being buried next to a martyr. It was a difficult question and Augustine offered a carefully balanced answer: burial, whether or not next to a martyr's tomb, is not relevant to salvation and therefore would not matter from a Christian point of view were men not attached to the idea. In this text and a few others, Augustine elaborated a clear distinction between what is relevant for salvation and to be taken care of by the ecclesiastical institution, and what is not relevant for salvation and is left to the care of the family. We will get a better and more nuanced understanding of what is at stake in Augustine's treatise, but for now this brief presentation suffices to introduce the main topic of this book: the role the bishops claimed to play in the relations between the living and the dead in Late Antiquity.

In his *Tod und ritual in den christlichen Gemeinden des Antike,* Ulrich Volp provides a good summary of the scholarly consensus on this topic:

> The universal and totalizing claim that Christianity exercised on the life of the believers was not compatible with leaving death, burial and the commemoration of the dead simply to the families and professional undertakers. The holy Christian texts demanded intervention in this sphere—given, for example, the centrality of the resurrection in the New Testament! Both the functions of the traditional "family religion" and those of the public cults were taken over by Christianity, at least from the fourth century onward, despite not having resources and personnel on a medieval scale (which is why religious funerals, and regular masses for the departed became common practice everywhere only later).[2]

---

1. I must here thank Peter Brown for suggesting it; see chapter 4 for more on this important text.
2. Ulrich Volp, *Tod und ritual in den christlichen Gemeinden des Antike,* Supplements to Vigiliae Christianae 65 (Leiden: Brill, 2002), 270 (English summary).

In this book I argue against this consensus, and claim that burial and commemoration of the dead were left by the bishops out of their sphere of control and to the care of the family. In this sense, my study of the care of the dead contributes to the shifting of the traditional paradigm from a focus on bishops and their regulating role to an emphasis on lay people and their expectations.[3]

The case of the catacombs is typical of the old paradigm: these impressive underground burial structures in the *suburbium* of Rome had to be the result of the entrepreneurship of the bishops and therefore had been understood as communal burial grounds developed exclusively for Christians by the bishops from the beginning of the third century. In chapter 1, I summarize the results of some of my preliminary research on the topic and suggest that the texts archaeologists relied upon were not in fact supporting their interpretation of the material remains. I propose, therefore, to temporarily leave aside the archeological evidence of the Roman catacombs, and with them the assumption that bishops provided for the care of the dead in Late Antiquity since they had organized cemeteries since the third century.[4]

The rest of the book is based on written sources. The blending of written sources and archaeological data too often leads only to circular reasoning, and it is highly difficult—which is not to say impossible—to analyze both with wholly up-to-date criteria.[5] In my study of the written sources, I try to

---

3. This shift characterizes Late Antique studies in the last few years. See the special issue of the *Journal of Early Christian Studies* 15, no. 2 (2007): "Holy Households: Domestic Space, Property, and Power," with contributions by Kim Bowes, Kate Cooper, and Kristina Sessa; see also Kim Bowes, *Private Worship, Public Values, and Religious Change in Late Antiquity* (Cambridge: Cambridge University Press, 2008); Kate Cooper, *The Fall of the Roman Household* (Cambridge: Cambridge University Press, 2007); and Kevin Uhalde, *Expectations of Justice in the Age of Augustine* (Philadelphia: University of Pennsylvania Press, 2007).

4. This assumption has recently been challenged from a different perspective by John Bodel, "From *Columbaria* to Catacombs: Collective Burial in Pagan and Christian Rome," in *Commemorating the Dead: Texts and Artifacts in Context, Studies of Roman, Jewish, and Christian Burials*, ed. Laurie Brink and Deborah Green (Berlin: De Gruyter, 2008), 177–242.

5. See Walter Goffart, *Barbarian Tides: The Migration Age and the Later Roman Empire*, The Middle Ages (Philadelphia: University of Pennsylvania Press, 2006), 9–12. I myself have used the "mixed argumentation" against which Goffart warns us in two papers where I propose a new interpretation of the mission given to Callixtus by Zephyrinus; see Éric Rebillard, "KOIMHTHRION et COEMETERIUM: tombe, tombe sainte, nécropole," *Mélanges de l'École française de Rome. Antiquité* 105, no. 2 (1993): 975–1001; and "L'Église de Rome et le développement des catacombes: à propos de l'origine des cimetières chrétiens," *Mélanges de l'École française de Rome. Antiquité* 109, no. 2 (1997): 741–63. Jean Guyon and Vincenzo Fiocchi Nicolai, "Relire Styger: les origines de l'*area f* du cimetière de Calliste et la crypte des papes," in *Origine delle catacombe romane*, ed. Vincenzo Fiocchi Nicolai and Jean Guyon, Sussidi allo studio delle antichità cristiane 18 (Città del Vaticano: Pontificio Istituto di archeologia cristiana, 2006), 121–61, successfully show on archaeological ground that the *koimeterion* that the bishop of Rome Zephyrinus entrusted to Callixtus could not have been the

discuss pagan, Jewish, and Christian evidence together.⁶ I do not necessarily believe in Late Antique common patterns, but I do not want to passively assume a difference. As long as Christians are considered in isolation, it is tempting to conclude that they were living separately and in opposition to surrounding communities.

On the other hand, it is also important not to prejudge that religious affiliation is a relevant criteria. The numerous groups whose proliferation characterizes the religious life of the Roman Empire from the third century onward do not impose any rule related to burial. This observation, documented in chapter 2, opens the way to other questions—in particular, that of Christians' participation in one of the most typical forms of collective behavior in the Roman Empire: the association or collegium, whose funerary role is reevaluated in chapter 3 in light of recent research.

After the first three chapters, dedicated to forms of collective burial, in chapters 4 and 5 I consider issues involved in burial itself. Chapter 4 looks at the reason why it was important to Christians to be buried. There again, in order not to make assumptions about what might have been specifically Christian, I start from a study of the evidence on tomb violation in imperial laws and in private measures taken to protect tombs (funerary fines and curses in epitaphs). The body seems to become the focus of a new concern, one that leads to the definition of the crime of profanation of cadavers as opposed to damage to the tomb, which was the only crime taken into account prior to the end of the third century. This concern for the body reappears in a number of discussions concerning the best means of disposing of it at death. These took place at a moment when cremation was increasingly abandoned in favor of inhumation as the dominant funerary practice in the Roman Empire. Today it is generally agreed that religious beliefs were far from being the primary factors in this change, and I also emphasize that, contrary to a widely held view, Christian belief in the resurrection does not make burial a religious necessity for Christians.

Chapter 5 is concerned with burial duty and its relative importance among good works. Providing burial to martyrs played a significant role in the construction of a Christian identity throughout the third century and at the beginning of the fourth. In the fourth and fifth centuries, however,

---

so-called Crypt of the Popes, as I suggested, but they cannot prove their case when they contend that it was the whole Area I, and that therefore Zephyrinus was willing to accommodate in a ecclesiastical cemetery the desire of those Christians who wanted to be buried together, because they do not take into account my philological arguments about the meaning of the term *koimeterion*.

6. In retrospect, I wish I had done it more systematically, especially in the last two chapters on the commemoration of the dead.

pastoral discourse on good works devotes little attention to burial. As for the burial of the poor, it is indeed part of the strategy of the bishops to promote "that other city" so well described by Peter Brown;[7] but the continuing role of the state, whether directly through the emperor for Rome and Constantinople or through the city authorities in the rest of the empire, explains why burial of the poor played such a minor part in ecclesiastical sources and why concrete measures are relatively few.

Chapters 6 and 7 address two aspects of the same question: the existence of specifically Christian ritual responses to death in Late Antiquity. Chapter 6 deals with the funerals, and chapter 7 with the commemoration of the departed. The earliest documents describing a Christian ritual for funerals date from the eighth and ninth centuries, as do also the earliest rituals for the blessing of the burial ground,[8] and, while it may be possible to find several elements of these rituals already attested to, it is vain to hope to reconstruct a Christian liturgy of death for the period. The church neither required nor proposed any ritual for a Christian burial in the fourth and fifth centuries. The presence of clergy at funerals and the celebration of the Eucharist were left entirely up to the family. It was also ultimately to the family that the church left the responsibility for remembering the dead. The commemoration of the departed by the universal church was both general and anonymous, concerned only with the baptized and offering no assurance of salvation for sinners. Pastoral documents, however, reveal somewhat different expectations on the part of Christians. The church, in Late Antiquity, seems more concerned with fixing strict limits to the relations between the living and the dead than with taking responsibility for remembering the dead. This might explain not only why Christians continued traditional practices but also why the bishops did not attempt to stop them.

Should we conclude, as does Ramsay MacMullen, that "for centuries, the pagan cult of the dead was a common part of Christianity?"[9] This is too

---

7. Peter Brown, *Power and Persuasion in Late Antiquity: Towards a Christian Empire* (Madison: University of Wisconsin Press, 1992); Peter Brown, *Poverty and Leadership in the Later Roman Empire*, Menahem Stern Jerusalem Lectures (Hanover, NH: University Press of New England, 2001); see also Éric Rebillard, "La conversion de l'Empire romain selon Peter Brown (note critique)," *Annales: histoire, sciences sociales* 54, no. 4 (1999): 813–23.

8. On this topic, see Donald Bullough, "Burial Community and Belief in the Early Medieval West," in *Ideal and Reality in Frankish and Anglo-Saxon Society: Studies Presented to J. M. Wallace-Hadrill*, ed. Patrick Wormald, Donald Bullough, and Roger Collins (Oxford: Blackwell, 1983), 177–201; and Cécile Treffort, *L'Église carolingienne et la mort: christianisme, rites funéraires et pratiques commémoratives*, Collection d'histoire et d'archéologie médiévales 3 (Lyon: Presses Universitaires de Lyon, 1996), 141–43.

9. Ramsay MacMullen, *Christianity and Paganism in the Fourth to Eighth Centuries* (New Haven, CT: Yale University Press, 1997), 111.

schematic a view of the interactions between bishops and lay people. On the other hand, I hope to show that the attempt to locate practices linked to the care and memory of the dead within the continuum from the profane to the religious, as MacMullen proposes to do for other practices, will prove very fruitful.

Only a few changes have been made to the text or notes of the French original. I have added a few items of recent bibliography when they are particularly relevant to the issues I discuss and altered the text where the French original was not satisfactory. I must thank my two translators, Elizabeth Rawlings and Jeannine Routier-Pucci, for their patience with my multiple corrections due mainly to my concerns about the French text.

Translations of primary and secondary sources not listed in the bibliography are by Elizabeth Trapnell Rawlings and Jeanine Routier-Pucci.

THE CARE OF THE DEAD
IN LATE ANTIQUITY

 CHAPTER 1

The Problem of the Origins
Christian Burial in Rome and Carthage

Textbooks on church history or Christian archaeology all contain accounts of the organization of cemeteries by the first Christian communities at Rome and Carthage at the end of the second century. As I have stated in the introduction, the question is actually far from being as simple as one might think from reading the textbooks. In this brief chapter I wish to point out that the question of the origins is now facing an impasse, and thus pave the way for an approach that will take a radically different point of view. The basic account for the organization of the Catacombs of Rome was developed by Giovanni Battista De Rossi (1822–94) and has changed very little since; the case of the *areae* of Carthage has been recently revisited, but also without any significant change. As we shall see, these two aspects of the "dossier of the origins" together present an excellent example of the "philologico-combinatory method" criticized by Arsenio Frugoni in the following terms: "as though dealing with perfect pieces in a mosaic, statements—that is, attested facts—have been connected with utmost confidence to Providence, always so well-disposed to the endeavors of historians."[1] The issue for us is not to reconstruct the biography of a heretic but to examine the organization governing a set of monuments.

---

1. Arsenio Frugoni, *Arnaud de Brescia nelle fonti del secolo XII* (Rome: Nella sede dell'Istituto, 1954), vii.

❧ Was the Catacomb of Callixtus the First Cemetery of the Roman Church?

De Rossi's report on the organization of cemeteries of the Roman Church before Constantine is a consummate example of the art of establishing connections. Indeed, De Rossi strove to make the data he drew from texts fit the archaeological monuments. The central piece of his reconstruction was a recently discovered text that he describes as "a revelation on the Roman Church": the *Refutation of All Heresies*.[2] Attributed to Origen in manuscripts, this pamphlet was actually written by a Roman cleric who refused to recognize the election of Callixtus in 217. It has been identified as a work of Hippolytus.[3] While writing the first volume of *La Roma sotterranea cristiana*, which describes the catacomb of Callixtus, De Rossi gives a thorough archeological commentary on book 9 of the *Refutation* that contains biographical information on Callixtus.[4] In it Hippolytus writes—notably—that Callixtus was called back from exile by Zephyrinus in 199 and appointed *eis to koimeterion* (*Refutatio* 9.12). De Rossi identifies Callixtus's function as that of an archdeacon whose main responsibility would have been the administration of a cemetery. And that cemetery could only be the one still bearing his name today: the famous catacomb of Callixtus on the Appian Way. De Rossi actually claims that Hippolytus's statement must be understood by antonomasia, whether referring to the only cemetery administered by the Roman Church at that time or the first one. He favors the second hypothesis by connecting it with the legislation of the Severi dealing with the collegia. The laws deal with different measures liberalizing the creation of funerary or religious

---

2. Until 1841 when the manuscript Parisinus supplementus graecus 464 was acquired, only book 1 was known. See Hippolytus, *Refutatio omnium haeresium*, ed. Miroslav Marcovich, Patristische Texte und Studien 25 (Berlin: De Gruyter, 1986), 5–7.

3. It is impossible here to go into Hippolytus's question, another convincing illustration of the philologico-combinatory method. The controversy started in 1947 with Pierre Nautin, *Hippolyte et Josippe: contribution à l'histoire de la littérature chrétienne du IIIe siècle* (Paris: Éditions du Cerf, 1947). Two roundtables held at Istituto Patristico Augustinianum have greatly helped the exploration of the question: *Ricerche su Ippolito*, Studia Ephemeridis Augustinianum 13 (Rome: Institutum patristicum Augustinianum, 1977), and *Nuove Ricerche su Ippolito*, Studia Ephemeridis Augustinianum 30 (Rome: Institutum patristicum Augustinianum, 1989). See also Allen Brent, *Hippolytus and the Roman Church in the Third Century: Communities in Tension before the Emergence of a Monarch-Bishop*, Supplements to Vigiliae Christianae 31 (Leiden: Brill, 1995), with the review of Manlio Simonetti, "Una nuova proposta su Ippolito," *Augustinianum* 36 (1996): 13–46.

4. Giovanni Battista De Rossi, "Esame archeologico e critico della storia di s. Callisto narrata nel libro nono dei Filosofumene," *Bullettino di archeologia cristiana* 4 (1866): 1–14, 17–33, 77–99. Most of this memoir is summarized in Giovanni Battista De Rossi, *La Roma sotterranea cristiana*, vol. 1 (Rome: Cromo-litografia pontificia, 1864), 197 ff.

associations for the *tenuiores*.⁵ These legal texts are connected in turn with a passage in which Tertullian defends Christians accused of forming illegal associations.⁶ From this comes the hypothesis that Christians legally organized their communities in the empire on the basis of laws on associations, and De Rossi concludes by presenting Callixtus as the head of a legally registered funerary collegium entitled to possess, corporately, a cemetery.

It was, therefore, at the end of the second century that the Roman Church established its first communal cemetery, at the very time when Tertullian, in describing pagans attacking them, would indirectly attest to the existence of such cemeteries in Carthage.⁷ De Rossi then sketched the development of the institution up to the Peace of Constantine on the basis of two documents. The first is the entry dedicated to Fabian (bishop of Rome from 236 to 250) in the sixth-century *Liber Pontificalis*. It mentions that the ecclesiastical regions were assigned to deacons and that works were done in the *cymeteria* without any explicit connection between the two statements (*Liber Pontificalis* 21.2–3). However, this was all De Rossi needed to find support for his earlier hypothesis: Callixtus was clearly an archdeacon, since, when the number of cemeteries had increased, their administration had become the responsibility of deacons. The entry on Fabian also allowed De Rossi to outline an early system of distribution of cemeteries according to ecclesiastical regions. The second document is a decree of the emperor Gallienus in which he ends, in 260, the persecution begun by Valerian in 257, and allows various bishops to "recover the places containing the so-called cemeteries."⁸ The effect of Gallienus's edict is then confirmed by the passage in the *Liber Pontificalis* (26.2) concerning Dionysius (bishop of Rome from 259 to 268), who is credited with a system of distributing the cemeteries according to the different parishes.

One might add here and there one or two supplemental pieces to the skillful puzzle put together by De Rossi, but this is the basic material: from the birth of the first cemetery of the Christian community in Rome to the creation of parish cemeteries once the church actually possessed an administration.

The thread that runs through all the elements so skillfully combined by De Rossi is the word *cemetery* in its Greek or Latin form; hence, this is where

---

5. The text can be found in *Digesta* 47.22.1. I will return below to this point of legislation concerning collegia and their funerary activities.

6. Tertullian, *Apologeticum* 38–39.

7. Tertullian, *To Scapula* 3.1

8. Eusebius, *Ecclesiastical History* 7.13. Most of the time the expression is simply translated as "places called cemeteries": see Éric Rebillard, "KOIMHTHRION et COEMETERIUM: tombe, tombe sainte, nécropole," *Mélanges de l'École française de Rome. Antiquité* 105, no. 2 (1993): 982.

we ought to begin.[9] The word *cemetery* comes to us from the Greek through the Latin form *coemeterium* and numerous variants. The Greek verb from which the noun is derived means "to lie down," "to sleep," and the noun itself, from its earliest appearances in the fourth century BCE up to the Rules of Byzantine monasteries, where it designates the monastery dormitory,[10] means a place to sleep.

The earliest uses of the word in a funerary context date from the end of the second century of the common era, when Christians appropriated the word with a specific meaning, a usage easily justified by the scriptural imagery of the sleep of death as sleep preceding resurrection.[11] In Greek, the first Christian testimony goes back to the mention in the *Refutation* cited above, but the oldest literary example extant happens to be a Latin one, a text by Tertullian, from the end of the second century. This relates the miracle of a previously buried corpse that made space, *in coemeterio,* for a second body (*On the Soul* 5.17). The meaning of the word leaves no room for doubt: *coemeterium* is used to designate a tomb, and not a common burial ground. The same is true in several early Greek cases: in another text of Hippolytus, the *Commentary on Daniel,* where among the victims of disasters that will accompany the coming of the Antichrist are mentioned the saints whose *koimeteria* will be destroyed and the remains removed from the ground and spread on the plain; in a homily of Origen (185–254), in which are described the faithful who will accompany the martyrs to their *koimeteria;* and in the edict of Gallienus (260), which mentions the restitution of all the places where the so-called *koimeteria* are located.[12] In Greek, moreover, the meaning of tomb or grave is widespread in the epigraphy of many different regions.[13]

---

9. The entry "Cimetière" by Henri Leclercq in the *Dictionnaire d'archéologie chrétienne et de liturgie* can no longer be used; see Antonio Ferrua, "Il Cimitero dei nostri morti," *Civiltà Cattolica* 109 (1958): 273–85, reprinted in *Scritti vari di epigrafia e antichità cristiane,* Inscriptiones Christianae Italiae, Subsidia 3 (Bari: Edipuglia, 1991), 284–96; Josef Krammer, "Was bedeutet κοιμητηρίον in den Papyri?" *Zeitschrift für Papyrologie und Epigraphik* 80 (1990): 269–72; and Rebillard, "KOIMHTHRION et COEMETERIUM."

10. Krammer, "Was bedeutet κοιμητηρίον," 269–70, 271. In the twelfth-century rule of the *Théotokos Kécharitôméné,* ed. Paul Gautier in *Revue des études byzantines* 43 (1985): 5–165, the word *koimeterion* refers both to the dormitory and the "cemetery."

11. John 11:11 (Lazarus' Resurrection), 1 Thess. 4:13f. See Marbury Bladen Ogle, "The Sleep of Death," *Memoirs of the American Academy in Rome* 11 (1933): 81–117; and Alfred Clement Rush, *Death and Burial in Christian Antiquity,* Studies in Christian Antiquity 1 (Washington, DC: Catholic University of America Press, 1941), 12–22.

12. Hippolytus, *Commentary on Daniel* 4.51; Origen, *Homilies on Jeremiah* 4.3.16; Gallienus' decree in Eusebius, *Ecclesiastical History* 7.13. Ferrua, "Il Cimitero," 279, reaches the same conclusion.

13. This is particularly so in Attica (see John S. Creaghan and Antony Erich Raubitschek, "Early Christians' Epitaphs from Athens," *Hesperia* 16 [1947]: 5–6), and in Macedonia (see Denis Feissel, *Recueil des inscriptions chrétiennes de Macédoine du IIIe au VIe siècle,* Bulletin de Correspondance Hellénique, Supplément 8 [Paris: De Boccard, 1983], 116 and in "Sicily to Pontus, to Lycaonia, to

The traditional hypothesis about the evolution of the meaning from an individual tomb into a place of communal burial has been quite rightly dismissed by Antonio Ferrua, who prefers to consider regional variations and therefore the coexistence of the two meanings.[14] However, all the texts in which he thinks that *koimeterion* was used in the sense of a communal burial site are closely related to the specific context of the cult of martyrs. And indeed, with respect to the martyr cult, the word has had a more specific usage designating not so much a place of communal burial as the martyrs' tombs, and also the place where they were located.

In Latin, *coemeterium* has thus been used to refer to the churches located in the Roman *suburbium*. They were erected in honor of the martyrs and might have held burials. In the sixth century, the *Liber Pontificalis* very clearly attests to this usage in the entry on Julius I (bishop of Rome from 337 to 352) that calls *cymeteria* buildings designated as *basilicae* in its source, the *Liberian Catalog*, compiled under Liberius (bishop of Rome from 352 to 366).[15] This usage extends beyond Rome, and a medieval glossary retains as equivalent *caementaria* and *ecclesia*.[16] The shift in meaning is easy to understand: the church was built to be a tomb, on the one hand a cenotaph for the honored martyr and on the other a place erected to shelter the tombs of a few notables. *Coemeteria* seems also to have been used in Rome to designate the *tituli,* those churches that were part of a virtual missionary network around the city and whose titular priests, according to the *Liber Pontificalis* (32.2), were charged with the care of the martyrs' tombs, among other responsibilities.[17]

Corresponding to this well-known, specialized use of the Latin word in relation to martyrs, there is a similar use of the Greek word that has not been studied.[18] Because it involves the earliest texts, it merits particular attention. Indeed, the word *koimeterion* is so often used in connection with *martyrium* as to amount at times to a hendiadys. One example of this is found in the collection of canons assembled at the end of the fourth century and

---

Cappadocia, to Cilicia and to Syria through Greece, Macedonia and Thrace, as well as by Lydia, Bithynia, Phrygia and Galatia" (Louis Robert, "Les inscriptions de Thessalonique," *Revue de philologie* 100 (1974): 189, n. 43). Two Latin inscriptions use *coemeterium* with the meaning of burial: *CIL* 8.7543 of Cirta, in Numidia, could be pagan; *CIL* 11.1700, of Florence. See Antonio Ferrua, *Note al Thesaurus linguae latinae: addenda et corrigenda* (Bari: Edipuglia, 1986), 121.

14. Ferrua, "Il Cimitero," 279–83.

15. See Louis Duchesne's comments in *Liber Pontificalis,* ed. Louis Duchesne, 2nd ed., 2 vols. (Paris: De Boccard, 1955–57), 1:277.

16. See Ferrua, "Il Cimitero," 283–85, which quotes a text from Great Britain, the *Miracles of Thecae;* for the medieval glossary, see *Corpus glossariorum Latinorum,* ed. Georg Goetz, 7 vols. (Leipzig: Teubner, 1888–1923), 5:419.

17. See Charles Pietri, "Régions ecclésiastiques et paroisses romaines," in *Actes du XIe Congrès International d'Archéologie Chrétienne,* (Rome: École française de Rome, 1989), 2:1045–46.

18. See Rebillard, "KOIMHTHRION et COEMETERIUM," 980–88.

called the Council of Laodicea, which retained one rule stating that Catholics are forbidden from going into "*koimeteria* or the so-called *martyria* of heretics, to pray or to celebrate holy services."[19] This text suggests that the word *koimeterion*, when it designates the tomb of a martyr, also designates—by extension—the place of the cult linked to the tomb, and may thus be an equivalent of *martyrium*. This is how, in my view, we should interpret the edict issued by the Emperor Valerian against the Christians in 257: "It is always forbidden for you, or others, to meet in or enter into places known as *koimeteria*."[20] These had to be the tombs of "the very special dead," where we know that Christian communities gathered on the anniversary of their death.[21] We find the same usage in the edict of Gallienus mentioned above, and in that of Maximinus Daia, who in 311 sought to harass the Christians by forbidding "assemblies in *koimeteria*."[22] There is never any question in these texts of forbidding burial; the interdiction only referred to the cult gatherings around the tombs of the martyrs. The word *koimeterion*, in both the singular and plural, does not designate a place of communal burial but a martyr's tomb, or a group of them and, by extension, the place of the cult that developed around them.

While serving as a priest in Antioch (386–98), John Chrysostom devoted the introduction of a Good Friday sermon to explaining why the place where the church of Antioch celebrates the crucifixion is called the *koimeterion*:

> Why do we gather in this *martyrium* and not in another? Indeed, by the grace of God, our city is surrounded on all sides by a shield of saintly relics. So why do our Fathers desire us to assemble here, and not in another *martyrium*? Because it is here that so many of the dead are lying. And as this is the day when Jesus descended among the dead, we gather here. And this is why this place is called *koimeterion:* in order that we should know that the dead, while they may lie here, are not dead, but are asleep and at rest.[23]

---

19. Council of Laodicea canon 9, in Charles Joseph Hefele, *Histoire des conciles d'après les documents originaux*, with translation, corrections, and additions by Henri Leclercq (Paris: Letouzey, 1907), 1/2:1002. For the date of the collection, see Jean Gaudemet, *Les sources du droit de l'Église en Occident du IIe au VIIe siècle*, Initiations au christianisme ancien (Paris: Éditions du Cerf/Éditions CNRS, 1985), 47, and 75, n. 1.

20. Eusebius, *Ecclesiastical History* 7.11.10.

21. See Hippolyte Delehaye, *Les origines du culte des martyrs*, Subsidia hagiographica 20 (Brussels: Société des Bollandistes, 1933), chap. 2, "L'anniversaire et le tombeau," esp. 38–39; and Peter Brown, *The Cult of the Saints: Its Rise and Function in Latin Christianity* (Chicago: University of Chicago Press, 1981).

22. Eusebius, *Ecclesiastical History* 7.13.

23. John Chrysostom, *De coemeterio et de cruce* (= CPG 4337), PG 49, 393.

Context shows that the name *koimeterion* is given to the place of the martyrium where the crucifixion is celebrated, and to no other places. From additional evidence we know that this was the martyrium of Daphne. The appellation by antonomasia can only be understood if the word usually signifies a tomb: the martyrium of Daphne becomes the tomb par excellence, that of the martyrs. In the middle of the fourth century, for the Christians of Antioch, it is clear that the word *koimeterion* does not mean "cemetery."[24]

The note on Callixtus, the starting point of De Rossi's entire argument, thus seems to stand singularly alone, particularly inasmuch as several other texts, especially the imperial edicts that use the word *koimeterion*, have lost their relevance.[25] However, the physical presence of the catacombs also has a strong emotional aspect; they represent the oldest remains of Christianity in Rome and it is only very slowly that the legends about their origins (places of secret cult and the refuges of persecuted early Christians) have been dropped. That helps to explain why, despite harshly critical charges against such important elements as the organization of the Church of Rome or the thesis about Christian collegia, De Rossi's basic theory has lasted this long.[26]

Were the Carthaginian Areae Christian Cemeteries, or Burial Enclosures for Christians?

This is also true of the dossier of the *areae* in Carthage.[27] Yvette Duval summarizes well the claims that are traditionally attached to the term: "The

---

24. The same applies to the *koimeterion* of Alexandria; see Rebillard, "KOIMHTHRION et COEMETERIUM," 985–87. For other texts referring to the *koimeterion* of Antioch, see Pio Franchi de' Cavalieri, "Il κοιμητήριον di Antiochia," in *Note agiografiche*. 7, Studi e testi 49 (Rome: Tipologia vaticana, 1928), 146–53, and the commentary in Rebillard, "KOIMHTHRION et COEMETERIUM," 983–85.

25. See Vincenzo Fiocchi Nicolai and Jean Guyon, "Relire Styger: les origines de l'area I du cimetière de Calliste et la crypte des papes," in *Origine delle catacombe romane*, ed. Vincenzo Fiocchi Nicolai and Jean Guyon, Sussidi allo studio delle antichità cristiane 18 (Vatican City: Pontificio Istituto di archeologia cristiana, 2006), 121–61, for a new examination of the mission of Callixus.

26. About the organization, see Pietri, "Régions ecclésiastiques et paroisses romaines." Regarding Christian colleges, Duchesne was the first one to attack De Rossi in his lectures *Origines chrétiennes* (1878–81); see Duchesne, *Histoire ancienne de l'Église* (Paris: De Boccard, 1906), 1:381–87. We must note here that the kind of monoepiscopal organization De Rossi attributes to the Roman Church is questionable; compare Brent, *Hippolytus and the Roman Church in the Third Century*, with the reserves expressed by Simonetti, "Una nuova proposta su Ippolito," and Éric Rebillard, "L'Église de Rome et le développement des catacombes: à propos de l'origine des cimetières chrétiens," *Mélanges de l'École française de Rome. Antiquité*, 109, no. 2 (1997): 741–63, esp. 743–45.

27. See a first approach to this question in Éric Rebillard, "Les *areae* carthaginoises (Tertullien, *Ad Scapulam* 3.1): cimetières communautaires ou enclos funéraires de chrétiens?" *Mélanges de l'École française de Rome. Antiquité*, 108, no. 1 (1996): 175–89. Since the publication of this article,

appearance of a specific term to designate cemeteries that are uniquely Christian implies that they existed and were actually under the control of the ecclesiastical institution from before the Peace of the Church."[28]

The starting point for this case study is a passage from *To Scapula,* an open letter addressed in 212 to Scapula, proconsul of Africa, by Tertullian to protest measures of persecution. Tertullian warned the persecutor of divine vengeance and evoked, as an example, the episode of 202, when the Carthaginians attacked Christians, violating their tombs: "This is what happened, for example, when Hilarianus was governor: While people were complaining about the ground where our graves were located: shouting 'No grounds for them!' it was actually they who lost their grounds: indeed, they did not harvest their grain" (*To Scapula* 3.1). Tertullian wanted to provide a graphic example of divine vengeance against the pagans' persecution of Christians. He had two "true" facts, or two facts that had at least to be accepted as true if he were to be convincing: the pagans' outrages against the Christian tombs, and the famine that resulted from the lack of harvest. Thus he joins two uses of the word *area:* its most common use, as in threshing ground, and another, well known from epigraphy, as (burial) ground. Use of the word seems to have been determined by the possibility of this double meaning, and not for the purpose of informing historians about the name Christians gave their cemeteries!

Tertullian, on the other hand, confirms in this text the existence of burial enclosures clearly identified as Christian. Stéphane Gsell saw in these enclosures a desire for isolation, noting, "The *areae* are naturally found outside cities, near the pagan tombs but separated from them by fences; to bury a Christian amongst idolaters was considered a great impiety, one to be avoided as much as possible. In contrast, cemeteries where rich and poor rested side by side express with eloquent simplicity the feeling of brotherhood among the faithful."[29] For Hugo Brandenburg and Yvette Duval, Tertullian's letter would show that the population of Carthage was outraged by the recent building of *areae* reserved for Christians.[30] The choice of an enclosure,

---

two other works have been published: Liliane Ennabli, *Carthage: une métropole chrétienne du IVe à la fin du VIIe siècle,* Études d'Antiquités africaines (Paris: Éditions CNRS, 1997), which does not bring any new elements to this particular point; and Yvette Duval, *Chrétiens d'Afrique à l'aube de la paix constantinienne: les premiers échos de la grande persécution,* Collection des Études augustiniennes, Série Antiquité 164 (Paris: Institut d'Études Augustiniennes, 2000) which offers a new approach to the question.

28. See Duval, *Chrétiens d'Afrique,* 448, and also 444.

29. Stéphane Gsell, *Les monuments antiques de l'Algérie,* 2 vols. (Paris: Fontemoing, 1901), 2:397.

30. See Hugo Brandenburg, "*Coemeterium:* der Wandel des Bestattungswesen als Zeichen des Kulturumbruchs der Spätantike," *Laverna* 5 (1994): 206–32, esp. 212–13; and Duval, *Chrétiens d'Afrique,* 450.

however, seems not to have been relevant in itself, for pagans used them as well. Christian enclosures, known and identified as such archaeologically, are rather rare in any case, and appear more than a century after Tertullian. Because too little is known about Carthaginian burial grounds,[31] we have to consider Caesarea of Mauritania (today Cherchel, in Algeria) where there is a combination of tombs along the roads and, in high-density areas, tombs inside enclosures.[32] West of the city, along the city wall and south of the Roman road, trenches have revealed a terrace bordered on the north by a wall running east to west. There are not only individual tombs and funerary monuments, but also three *areae*. Only one of them was complete and suitable for a careful excavation.[33] Construction of this area of seventy-two square meters dates from the years 110–20 and its first period of use extended to 150–60. During this first period, burials (nine or ten incinerations and three inhumations) are placed next to each other, in mutual respect. Thus the space of the enclosure was used quite intentionally, but nothing would link its use to a collegium rather than a family.[34]

Funeral enclosures known from African archaeology therefore allow us to speculate about the ones Tertullian knew and that motivated his pun on the double meaning of *areae*. These spaces, surrounded by walls, could accommodate a certain number of burials and were restricted to those entitled to be buried there. This type of structure was not specifically Christian—in fact, far from it—and reflects no preference for isolation. In Carthage, pagans did not attack enclosures reserved for Christians but enclosures they knew to be

---

31. Archaeologists from the nineteenth century were mostly interested in the inscriptions and did not leave information relevant to the organization of the necropolis. For an inventory map of Carthage's necropolis, see Raymond Lantier, "Notes de topographie carthaginoise: cimetières romains et chrétiens de Carthage," *Comptes rendus de l'Académie des Inscriptions et Belles-Lettres* (1922): 22–28. Ennabli, *Carthage: une métropole chrétienne*, does not really bring new information since recent digs focused on the Byzantine era.

32. For a general description and the bibliography, see Philippe Leveau, "Nécropoles et monuments funéraires à Caesarea de Maurétanie," in *Römische Gräberstrassen: Selbstdarstellung—Status—Standart (Kolloquium in München vom 28. bis 30 Oktober 1985)*, ed. Henner von Hesberg und Paul Zanker, Abhandlungen/Bayerische Akademie der Wissenschaften, Philosophisch-Historische Klasse, n. f. 96 (Munich: Verlag der Bayerischen Akademie der Wissenschaften, 1987), 281–90.

33. Philippe Leveau, "Une area funéraire de la nécropole occidentale de Cherchel," *Antiquités Africaines* 5 (1971–74): 73–152.

34. This is Leveau's hypothesis based on the example of Carthage's *officiales* in "Une area funéraire," 151. See Philippe Leveau, *Caesarea de Maurétanie: une ville romaine et ses campagnes*, Collection de l'École française de Rome 70 (Rome: École française de Rome, 1984), 207. On the other hand, I do not follow Leveau's hypothesis, which proposes that given the large number of burials after this first stage, we should consider it a sacred and privileged area. In any case, nothing justifies such hypothesis during the first stage of utilization.

owned by Christians. In another text Tertullian testifies that attacks against the tombs of Christians were frequent:

> Mad as Bacchanals, they spare not even the Christian dead; no! from the repose of the grave, from what I may call a death's asylum, changed as the bodies may be, or mere fragments—they will have them out, rip and rend them. (*Apologeticum* 37.2)

No allusion is made here to reserved space that would naturally attract the attention of the vindictive populace. Tertullian's vocabulary, particularly his reference to the notion of asylum, shows the Roman devotion to the peacefulness of the tomb; there was no greater offense than the violation of the tombs of the enemy. Also, it is possible that in the eyes of the pagans, the practice of inhumation exclusively, and the belief in the resurrection, had marked Christians as being particularly concerned that the body enjoy an undisturbed rest in the tomb.[35] It is also likely that in Carthage to be a Christian did not imply anything clandestine and that, as a result, the pagans knew which tombs to attack. The *Acts of Felix of Abthugni* show that, in Abthugni, clearly a much smaller city than Carthage, pagans and Christians were friends and neighbors and that even the enforcement of the edict of persecution of 303 could be handled sensitively.[36] However, Tertullian provides evidence that even in Carthage, each and every person knew who converted to Christianity. In fact, he says at the beginning of the *Apologeticum* that conversions to Christianity were cause for talk: "Most...run so blindfolded into hatred of that name, that, even if they bear favorable testimony to a man, they throw in some detestation of the name? 'A good man,' they say, 'this Caius Seius, only that he is a Christian.' Then another says, 'I am surprised that that wise man, Lucius Titius, has suddenly become a Christian'" (*Apologeticum* 3.1). During times of tension and persecution, pagans did not have to look far for targets.[37]

There are a few other African documents in which the word *area* has been understood as designating cemeteries for Christians. First, it must be noted

---

35. See Yvette Duval, *Auprès des saints corps et âme: l'inhumation "ad sanctos" dans la chrétienté d'Orient et d'Occident du IIIe au VIIe siècle* (Paris: Études Augustiniennes, 1988), 23–47.

36. See Claude Lepelley, *Les cités de l'Afrique romaine au Bas-Empire*, vol. 1, *La permanence d'une civilisation municipale* (Paris: Études Augustiniennes, 1979), 338–40.

37. Timothy David Barnes, *Tertullian: A Historical and Literary Study* (Oxford: Clarendon Press, 1971), 89–90, notes, "The ordinary Christians of Carthage were a group who could easily be defined and recognized." Hippolytus, *Commentary on Daniel* 4.51, refers to similar attacks against Christian tombs in Smyrna in 203.

that the use of the word in the sense of a funerary enclosure is not found in African epigraphy. The inscription of Cherchel, cited constantly, does use *area,* but is careful to specify the funerary context. The donor explains that the ground, which he is giving to the church, is intended as a place for burial *(aream a[d] sepulchra contulit).*[38] It is hard to establish, on the basis of this inscription, that in Africa the term *area* has the specific meaning of burial ground of Christians.

There remain a few Carthaginian toponyms that designate the places where several martyrs, victims of the persecution of Valerian, were buried: Cyprian, *in areas Macrobi Candidati procuratoris;* Libosus of Vaga, *in nouis areis;* Successus of Abbir Germaniciana, *in area* (or *areis) Tertulli;* Leucius of Theveste, *in area* (or *areis) Fausti.*[39] Several scholars have tried to identify and locate these "cemeteries"; the *area Tertulli* accordingly would be the cemetery of pious Tertullus who, according to Cyprian *(Letters* 12.2.1), was responsible for the burial of the martyrs in Carthage; the *area Fausti* would originally have been part of the *basilica Fausti,* the Carthaginian basilica where Augustine preached on several occasions; the *areae nouae* would in turn have been originally the *basilica Nouarum.* These connections quickly came to be accepted as fact and are the basis for conclusions about the Christian topography of Carthage.[40] Let us also discuss the case of the *areae maiores.* In 1907 Father Delattre discovered fragments of an inscription bearing the name of the *Vibia* family in what he took to be an *area* in front of the basilica situated on the site called the Mcidfa. He surmised that the family of the famous martyr Perpetua owned, in that region, an *area ad sepulchra* (this was

---

38. *CIL* 8.9585; text and commentary in Yvette Duval, *Loca Sanctorum Africae: le culte des martyrs en Afrique du IVe au VIIe siècle,* 2 vols., Collection de l'École française de Rome, 58 (Rome: École française de Rome, 1982), 1:380–83, no. 179. About the translation of *aream at sepulcra...contulit,* see the discussion in Rebillard, "Les *areae* carthaginoises," 178–79.

39. See Duval, *Chrétiens d'Afrique,* 450–51. About Cyprian, see *Acta proconsularia Cypriani* 4.3. For the other three martyrs, the information comes from marginal notes in Cyprian's *Codex Veronensis,* in which are copied the *Sententiae Episcoporum,* protocol from Carthage's synod in September 256; see Giovanni Mercati, "D'alcuni nuovi sussidi per la critica del testo di S. Cipriano," *Studi e documenti di storia e diritto* 19 (1898): 321–63, and 20 (1899): 61–88 (repr. in idem, *Opere minori.* 2, Vatican City: Biblioteca apostolica vaticana, 1937, 152–267). See also Pierre Petitmengin, "Le *Codex Veronensis* de saint Cyprien: philologie et histoire de la philologie," *Revue des études latines* 46 (1968): 330–78, which, thanks to new elements, develops and confirms Mercati's argument. See Hermann von Soden, ed., "*Sententiae LXXXVII Episcoporum:* das Protokoll der Synode von Karthago am 1. September 256, textkritisch hergestellt und überlieferungsgeschichtlich untersucht," *Nachrichten von der Königlichen Gesellschaft der Wissenschaften zu Göttingen, Phil.—hist. Klasse* (1909): 247–307; Successus, no. 16 (257); Libosus, no. 30 (262); Leucius, no. 31 (263).

40. For the bibliography, see Ennabli, *Carthage: une métropole chrétienne,* 17–21. Noël Duval, "Études d'architecture chrétienne nord-africaine. 1, Les monuments chrétiens de Carthage: études critiques," *Mélanges de l'École française de Rome. Antiquité* 84 (1972): 1071–125, prudently favors archaeological data.

the expression on the inscription of Cherchel) where the martyr and her companions are supposed to have been buried. These *areae* had to be the *areae maiores*, the old ones as opposed to the more recent ones, called *nouae areae*, where Libosus of Vaga was buried. The basilica itself was therefore the *basilica Maiorum* (supply *arearum*, as in "the basilica of the old cemeteries") where Augustine had preached several times.[41] This suggestive reconstruction, apart from the speculative nature of its assumptions based on ancient sources, runs into difficulties even on archaeological grounds. In fact, there is no assurance that the rectangular enclosure in front of the basilica was a burial area; it might simply have been an atrium, dating from the time when the basilica was constructed, in the fifth century, or from a remodeling.[42]

Although Duval is very circumspect about these hypotheses, and while she seems to concede in the end that the word *area* is not reserved exclusively for Christian burial places, she remains convinced that the existence of places of burial reserved for Christians is not in doubt and that their institutional nature can be inferred from the testimony of Hippolytus about the mission entrusted to Callixtus.[43]

This brings us back to where we started. It is easy to realize that with studies such as these the debates will continue endlessly, returning constantly to the same sources, which in themselves prove nothing but must be combined in mutual support to make an argument that goes, therefore, in circles. I am not going to attempt to propose another interpretation of every aspect of the Roman or Carthaginian dossiers, nor am I going to try to substitute for this a recombination of the same elements, for every project of this type must necessarily be a captive of its own starting point. I would actually like to launch a resolutely different approach and to study, first, different types of collective and voluntary burial in the Roman Empire when the earliest groups of Christians formed there. This approach consists of a systematic comparison of Christians and other groups of Greco-Roman society, without positing a priori anything as specifically Christian, as the focus of the study is on social practices.

---

41. For a summary and the bibliography, see Ennabli, *Carthage: une métropole chrétienne*, 19, 132–35.

42. See Duval, "Études d'architecture chrétienne nord-africaine. 1," 1119; see also Noël Duval, *Les églises africaines à deux absides: recherches archéologiques sur la liturgie chrétienne en Afrique du Nord*, vol. 2, *Inventaire des monuments. Interprétation*, Bibliothèque des Écoles françaises d'Athènes et de Rome 218 bis (Rome: École française de Rome, 1973), 72.

43. Duval, *Chrétiens d'Afrique*, 452–54.

 CHAPTER 2

Burial and Religious Identity
Religious Groups and Collective Burial

In *Les Origines du culte des martyrs,* Hippolyte Delehaye writes, "The custom that quickly spread of not mingling Christian tombs with pagan ones, but instead setting aside separate areas, was hardly unprecedented. Other associations or groups had introduced this type of solidarity in death into their practices."[1] This statement needs verification, for, besides the obvious relevance to Christianity, it raises the issue of the social behavior of religious groups whose differentiation is one of the characteristics of late antiquity.

Religious development in Late Antiquity is often described as an inevitable movement toward monotheism, according to a point of view that approaches religion on the basis of beliefs. By adopting a point of view based instead on social practice, we shift the emphasis to the development of religious pluralism.[2] Without attempting to go back to the origins of this phenomenon, we can say with confidence that in the third century the Roman Empire was a true "marketplace of religions." Not only were Jews, Christians, and pagans competing with each other but, within paganism,

---

1. Hippolyte Delehaye, *Les origines du culte des martyrs,* Subsidia hagiographica 20 (Brussels: Société des Bollandistes, 1933), 30.
2. This is the point of view adopted in *The Jews among Pagans and Christians in the Roman World,* ed. Judith Lieu, John North, and Tessa Rajak (London: Routledge, 1992).

a plurality of religious groups appeared, weakening the monopolistic position of civic religion.

From this standpoint, John North has noted that one of the most sensitive criteria for evaluating the impact of these groups in traditional Greco-Roman society involves tracing areas of conflict with members' families.[3] Here, the study of funerary practices is decisive. Statistical studies regarding burial inscriptions of civil populations in the Western Roman Empire have shown that, when the relationship was mentioned, 80 percent of commemorators were wives, parents, children, or cousins of the deceased individual honored in the epitaph. This percentage increased in the fourth century, but the samples used for Late Antiquity were all Christian and therefore less representative.[4] Even if commemoration with an epitaph did not extend to every level of Roman society, the numbers allow us to conclude that it was traditional in the Roman Empire for the family, in fact the nuclear family, to maintain the tombs of its members. Did the appearance of new cults and subsequent religious groups lead to tensions between a family and a religious group over the choice of a grave?

Mystery Cults, Oriental Cults, and New Cults

The success of the oriental cults in the Roman Empire has often been viewed as preparation for the rise of Christianity. Because of their common origin in the East, of the mystery surrounding their rites, and of the initiation that separated their members from the rest of society, the comparison was appealing. The cults and their beliefs, as well as their organization, have long been analyzed through the reference system of Christianity. Walter Burkert, who constantly emphasizes the discontinuity between oriental cults and Christianity, has thus attacked the causal relationship between eschatological beliefs and collective burial grounds postulated by Franz Cumont at the beginning

---

3. John North, "The Development of Religious Pluralism," in Lieu, North, and Rajak, eds., *The Jews among pagans and Christians*, 184.
4. See Richard Saller and Brent D. Shaw, "Tombstones and Roman Family Relations in the Principate: Civilians, Soldiers and Slaves," *Journal of Roman Studies* 74 (1984): 124–56; and Brent D. Shaw, "Latin Funerary Epigraphy and Family Life in the Later Roman Empire," *Historia* 33 (1984): 457–97. Dale B. Martin, "The Construction of the Ancient Family: Methodological Considerations," *Journal of Roman Studies* 86 (1996): 40–60, questions the counting method of Saller and Shaw; yet this does not affect the part of their research I use here. See Jonathan S. Perry, *A Death in the 'Familia': The Funerary Colleges of the Roman Empire*, (PhD diss., University of North Carolina–Chapel Hill, 1999), 170ff., for a thorough discussion of the topic.

of the twentieth century.⁵ Of the mysteries of Mithras, Cumont wrote, "In these closed churches, where everyone knew and supported each other, there reigned the intimacy of a large family.... In death, probably, all rested in a common graveyard. Although no one has yet discovered a single Mithraic cemetery, the special beliefs of this sect about the afterlife and its very distinctive rites make it very likely that, like most of the Roman *sodalicia,* it formed not only religious associations but also burial ones."⁶

The origin for claims of this type is to be found in a document dating from the fifth century BCE that has remained the necessary starting point for all discussion of the funerary practices of these cults. It is the famous inscription of Cumae (today Cuma, in Italy), which seems to reserve a burial place for initiates of a cult of Bacchus. The text announces in fact that it is forbidden for a noninitiate to repose there, using a vocabulary that exceeds human law and evokes a religious sanction. Many scholars, after Cumont,⁷ have seen in it proof that Dionysian associations had their own cemeteries. Recent discussions have attempted to determine if this document concerned a Dionysian or Orphic cult; for our purposes, that debate is less important than trying to reconstitute the archaeological context of the inscription.⁸ Actually, this inscription was not carved on a stele but on the inner face of a stone slab that must have been used to cover a tomb. This means that the inscription could not have been read from the outside. The inscription of Cumae, despite its strong religious defense, thus probably did not have a function very different from the Orphic inscriptions on gold tablets whose primary purpose was to proclaim salvation. Rather than an interdiction, this inscription, notes Jean-Marie Pailler, is like "a hyphen between initiation and afterlife."⁹ Moreover, archaeology has provided cases showing that a separate tomb was not the

---

5. Walter Burkert, *Ancient Mystery Cults* (Cambridge, MA: Harvard University Press, 1987), chap. 1.

6. Franz Cumont, *Les mystères de Mithra,* 3rd ed. (Brussels: Lamertin, 1913), 181. See also Franz Cumont, *Textes et monuments figurés relatifs aux mystères de Mithra,* vol. 1, *Introduction* (Brussels: Lamertin, 1899), 328.

7. See, for instance, Franz Cumont, *Lux perpetua* (Paris: Geuthner, 1949), 253, 405–6.

8. The inscription unearthed in 1903 by Antonio Sogliano (*Notizie degli scavi di antichità,* 1905, 380) is published in Franciszek Sokolowski, *Lois sacrées des cités grecques. Supplément,* École française d'Athènes. Travaux et mémoires 11 (Paris: De Boccard, 1962), 202–3, no. 120. Robert Turcan, "Bacchoi ou bacchants? De la dissidence des vivants à la ségrégation des morts," in *L'association dionysiaque dans les sociétés anciennes,* Collection de l'École française de Rome 89 (Rome: École française de Rome, 1986), 227–46, proposes to read it as an orphic document, while Jean-Marie Pailler sustains the traditional interpretation of a dionysian document; see Pailler, "Sépulture interdite aux non bachisés: dissidence orphique et vêture dionysiaque," in *Bacchus: figures et pouvoirs,* Histoire (Paris: Les Belles Lettres, 1995), 111–26. See Angelo Bottini, *Archeologia della salvezza: l'escatologia greca nelle testimonianze archeologiche,* Biblioteca di archeologia 17 (Milan: Longanesi, 1992), 58–62.

9. Pailler, "Sépulture interdite aux non bachisés," 118.

rule; on the site of Hipponium (today Vibo Valentia, in Italy), for example, the tomb of an Orphic initiate was found among tombs of noninitiates in the same necropolis.[10] It has similarly been thought that a cluster of some one hundred tombs at Tarentum (today Taranto, in Italy) laid out regularly and very simply, constituted the cemetery of a Pythagorean community. Archaeologists thought they had found at the center of this necropolis the tomb of Archytas, a Pythagorean general at Tarentum in the fourth century BCE. It has now been proven that this was a woman's tomb from the beginning of the second century BCE; there is nothing to suggest a connection between this cluster of tombs and Pythagorism.[11] This very early evidence does not support the notion of the separation of the dead by religion.

As for the cult of Mithras, Cumont considered it highly likely that places of collective burial existed, even though none are known. At Gross-Krotzenburg, near Hanau in Germany, the tombs that were discovered very near the Mithraeum cannot be the remains of a Mithraic cemetery organized around the sanctuary as they reuse stones from the sanctuary's walls and postdate its destruction.[12] Some epitaphs of Mithriasts are known in Italy or Gaul, but they contain no prescription specific to the cult of Mithras, and the dedicators were always relatives of the deceased.[13]

Worshippers of the Thracian god Sabazius also did not specify their religious affiliation in their epitaphs.[14] Nevertheless, they may have formed associations that provided tombs for their members. A first century BCE stele from Rhodes is dedicated to one Aristo of Syracuse and honors him for his devotion and the care he took of the tombs of the association. This was found in a small funerary monument consisting of two adjacent rooms that might well have belonged to this Sabazian association.[15] Still, there is not

---

10. See Bottini, *Archeologia della salvezza*, 51–58.

11. For the traditional hypothesis, see Pierre Wuilleumier, *Tarente des origines à la conquête romaine*, Bibliothèque des Écoles françaises d'Athènes et de Rome 148 (Paris: De Boccard, 1939), 548–49. Pier Giovanni Guzzo, "Altre note tarantine," *Taras* 12 (1992): 135–41, esp. 135–36, excludes the possibility of it being Archytas's tomb. See Enzo Lippolis, *Catalogo del Museo nazionale archeologico di Taranto. 3, 1, Taranto, la necropoli: aspetti e problemi della documentazione archeologica tra VII e I sec. A.C.* (Taranto: La Colomba, 1994), 58.

12. This is noted in Franz Cumont, *Textes et monuments figurés relatifs aux mystères de Mithra*, vol. 2, *Textes et monuments* (Brussels: Lamertin, 1896), 353. See Maarten Jozef Vermaseren, *Corpus inscriptionum et monumentorum religionis Mithriacae*, vol. 2 (The Hague: Nijhoff, 1960), no. 1148.

13. Vermaseren, *Corpus inscriptionum et monumentorum religionis Mithriacae*, vol. 1 (The Hague: Nijhoff, 1960), nos. 113–15, 206, 511, 623–24, 708, 885.

14. See the inscriptions gathered in Eugene N. Lane, *Corpus cultus Iovis Sabazii*, vol. 2, *The Other Monuments and Literary Evidence*, Études préliminaires aux religions orientales dans l'Empire romain 100, no. 2 (Leiden: Brill, 1985).

15. Lane, *Corpus cultus Iovis Sabazii*, vol. 2, 22, no. 46. See especially the thorough commentary of Vassa Kontorini, *Inscriptions inédites relatives à l'histoire et aux cultes de Rhodes au IIe et au Ier s. av. J.-C. 1*,

sufficient evidence to allow us to assume that Sabazian cemeteries as such existed. Nothing there indicates any particular concern for a separate burial. Another piece of evidence attests that an association of Sabazians at Teos in Asia Minor (today Sigacik in Turkey) also provided tombs for spouses of members although they were not members of the cult themselves.[16]

The cult of Cybele has provided more evidence. It was neither a new cult nor a true oriental one, since it was officially introduced as a public cult in Rome in 204 BCE. The cult, closely linked to that of Attis, was organized around priests attached to the sanctuary (the *galli*), as well as associations with official roles in the large annual festival held in March (*dendrophori* and *cannophori*). The epitaphs are for the most part those of *galli*, or members of the associations, but some inscriptions indicate that worshipers of Cybele and Attis sometimes marked their affiliation by identifying themselves as *religiosi*.[17] Of particular interest is one inscription from Pozzuoli in Campania and dating from around the second century CE. It mentions a "field of believers" (*ager religiosorum*) in which Gaius Julius Aquilinus built a portico and benches at his own expense.[18] What exactly does this expression *ager religiosorum* mean? It could designate one of those funerary gardens, known from epitaphs, in which there stand, beside the funerary monument, various structures intended for the cult of the dead or simply for social gatherings.[19] However, the term could just as well designate a meeting place, where porticos and benches are frequently mentioned.[20] As the inscription was found out of any context, we simply cannot know for certain.

Another inscription at Pozzuoli mentions a field of seven *jugeri* (more than one hectare) belonging "to members of the association of followers of Jupiter Heliopolitanus." Here again, the funerary purpose of the land is not

---

Rhodiaka, Archaeologia transatlantica 6, Publications d'histoire de l'art et d'archéologie de l'Université catholique de Louvain 42 (Louvain-la-Neuve: Institut supérieur d'archéologie et d'histoire de l'art, Collège Erasme, 1983), 71–79, and illustrations X–XI.

16. Lane, *Corpus cultus Iovis Sabazii*, vol. 2, no. 28 for the inscription and Eugene N. Lane, *Corpus cultus Iovis Sabazii*, vol. 3, *Conclusions*, Études préliminaires aux religions orientales dans l'Empire romain 100, no. 3 (Leiden: Brill, 1985), 45, for male membership in Sabazius's cult.

17. See Maarten Jozef Vermaseren, *Corpus cultus Cybelae Attidisque*, Études préliminaires aux religions orientales dans l'Empire romain 50 (Leiden: Brill, 1977–89), vol. 3, no. 337 (Rome), vol. 4, no. 105 (Larinum), vol. 5, no. 142 (Sitifis).

18. Ibid., vol. 4, no. 16. See also Vincent Tam Tinh Tran, *Le culte des divinités orientales en Campanie en dehors de Pompéi, de Stabies et d'Herculanum*, Études préliminaires aux religions orientales dans l'Empire romain 27 (Leiden: Brill, 1972), 107, no. C9 (= *CIL* 10.1894).

19. See the data gathered in Jocelyn M. C. Toynbee, *Death and Burial in the Roman World* (Baltimore: John Hopkins University Press, 1996), 94–100.

20. See the inventory of meeting places owned by collegia in Jean-Pierre Waltzing, *Étude historique sur les corporations professionnelles chez les Romains depuis les origines jusqu'à la chute de l'Empire d'Occident*, 4 vols. (Louvain: Peeters, 1895–1900), 4:447ff.

explicit; the inscription mentions a cistern and taverns and, notably, specifies the conditions for access to the field, but says nothing of the use that could be made of it. To call it a "private cemetery" is questionable.[21] On the strength of this inscription, Felix Hettner postulated a similar cemetery for the worshipers of Jupiter Dolichenus (from Doliché, today Dülück in Turkey) on the Aventine in Rome, where a temple has provided a great deal of evidence. The only inscription that he related to this cemetery cannot, however, be explicitly linked to this cult. The force of his entire argument thus depends upon the example of Pozzuoli.[22] No epitaph of a simple follower of Jupiter Dolichenus is known, and the three extant epitaphs of priests contain no indication on the location of the grave.[23]

It is thus clear that among the documents attesting to the presence or the spread of a particular cult, epitaphs are very few and most often refer to priests, not to simple followers. Walter Burkert has concluded that "individual distinctiveness prevailed over group identity."[24] I would like to add that membership in this type of cult does not seem to have been relevant information for the wording of epitaphs, which in turn suggests that the new cults did not lead to conflict with families over the burial choices of their members. No document relating to the new and rapidly multiplying cults in the empire indicates a religious preference in burial practices.

❧ The Jews

That Jews were buried together and apart from non-Jews has long been considered beyond discussion. Jewish studies basically described the Jews of the Diaspora as living in total isolation from, and in opposition to, the surrounding communities. It is only recently that Jewish documents and monuments have begun to be compared systematically to other, contemporary, documents and monuments; as long as these were studied in isolation,

---

21. This is contra Tam Tinh Tran, *Le culte des divinités orientales en Campanie*, 133; see pages 149–50 for the text of the inscription (= *CIL* 10.1579) and its translation. For Waltzing, *Étude historique sur les corporations*, 4:448, it was a meeting place.

22. Felix Hettner, *De Iove Dolicheno* (Bonn: 1877), 17. This inscription is not listed in the inventory of Monika Hörig, *Corpus Cultus Iovis Dolicheni*, Études préliminaires aux religions orientales dans l'Empire romain 106 (Leiden: Brill, 1987).

23. Hörig, *Corpus Cultus Iovis Dolicheni*, nos. 3, 67, and 123. Pierre Merlat, *Jupiter Dolichenus: essai d'interprétation et de synthèse*, Publications de l'Institut d'art et d'archéologie de l'Université de Paris 5 (Paris: Presses universitaires de France, 1960), 190–210, gives no indication about funerals and burials for the followers of Jupiter Dolichenus.

24. Burkert, *Ancient Mystery Cults*, 48.

historians necessarily concluded that the Jews were isolated. Today it is possible to have a more nuanced view on the degree of integration of Jews in the Roman Empire and on the degree of interactions with other groups.[25] Whenever some degree of interaction has been considered, close examination reveals that the Jews did not live in isolation. Tessa Rajak has thus shown that the Jewish system of honorary titles functioned in the same way as the patronage system in any Greco-Roman city, which made it possible, as she emphasizes very provocatively, to attract non-Jewish patrons to the synagogue.[26] Leonard V. Rutgers, with a very different perspective, has tried to show that artifacts found in Jewish catacombs in Rome had come from workshops that also made artifacts for non-Jews, pagans as well as Christians.[27] Such examples show clearly that Jews in the Roman Empire were not living in ghettos as the nineteenth-century historians had tended to imagine.[28]

What do we know about funerary practices of the Jews of the Diaspora and of the organization of their burial?[29] To start, we must consider the practice of being buried in Palestine. There are cases, at Beth She'Arim, of wealthy Jews from Asia Minor having their remains repatriated to the land of their ancestors.[30] Rabbinical teachings on this subject are not found before the third century and the practice, if only for logistical reasons, was rather marginal.[31] Most Jews in the Diaspora were buried where they lived. Archaeologists, as well as epigraphists, are more prudent than in the past about

---

25. See Judith Lieu, John North, and Tessa Rajak, "Introduction," in Lieu, North, and Rajak, eds., *The Jews among pagans and Christians,* 1–8; and Martin Goodman, ed., *Jews in a Graeco-Roman World* (Oxford: Clarendon Press, 1998).

26. Tessa Rajak, "Archisynagogoi: Office, Title and Social Status in the Greco-Jewish Synagogue," *Journal of Roman Studies* 83 (1993): 75–93.

27. Leonard Victor Rutgers, "Archeological Evidence for the Interaction of Jews and Non-Jews in Late Antiquity," *American Journal of Archaeology* 96 (1992): 101–18. See also Leonard Victor Rutgers, *The Jews in Late Ancient Rome: Evidence of Cultural Interaction in the Roman Diaspora,* Religions in the Greco-Roman World 12 (Leiden: Brill, 1995).

28. About Jewish historiography, see Rutgers, *The Jews in Late Ancient Rome,* chap. 1.

29. See the general introduction in Rachel Hachlili, *Ancient Jewish Art and Archaeology in the Diaspora,* Handbuch der Orientalistik. 1, Nahe und Mittlere Osten 35 (Leiden: Brill, 1998), 263–310. The discussion was opened by Margaret H. Williams, "The Organization of Jewish Burials in Ancient Rome in the Light of Evidence from Palestine and the Diaspora," *Zeitschrift für Papyrologie und Epigraphik* 101 (1994): 165–82. See Noy, "Where Were the Jews of the Diaspora Buried?" in Goodman, ed., *Jews in a Graeco-Roman World,* 75–89.

30. Tessa Rajak, "The Jewish Community and Its Boundaries," in Lieu, North, and Rajak, eds., *The Jews among Pagans and Christians,* 16; see Moshe Schwabe and Baruch Lifschitz, eds., *Beth She'arim,* vol. 2, *The Greek Inscriptions* (Jerusalem: Massada, 1974), 219.

31. See Isaiah Gafni, "Reinterment in the Land of Israel: Notes on the Origin and Development of the Custom," *Jerusalem Cathedra* 1 (1981): 96–104. See also Noy, "Where Were the Jews of the Diaspora buried?" 78–79.

identifying a Jewish tomb or inscription.[32] These efforts, and the removal of prejudices about Jewish isolationism, have revealed that the mixing of Jewish and non-Jewish tombs in the same burial areas was very common.

In the case of Italy, with the exception of Rome, data are scattered. At Venosa, Jewish and Christian hypogea are dug into the same hillside.[33] At Taranto, as at Syracuse and Agrigento in Sicily, Christian and Jewish objects have come from the same cemeteries.[34] One inscription from Ostia, dated from the second century, would attest to a funeral enclosure owned by Jews but situated among non-Jewish enclosures.[35]

In Asia Minor, where Jewish communities are well known,[36] no Jewish cemetery has yet been identified. An inscription discovered at Tlos, in Lycia, dating from the first century, makes a point of mentioning the gift from a certain Ptolemy of the funerary monument, which he built at his own expense for himself and his son, to all the Jews of the city. This kind of evergetism is rare, though attested elsewhere, and does not necessarily evince a communal burial area. Through this gift, the Jewish community simply took ownership of an individual tomb.[37] The private and familial nature of Jewish tombs is clear when fines are stipulated in the epitaph against the burial of an unauthorized body, a practice that was also common among non-Jews. A good example of this practice is the epitaph of Rufina in Smyrna that dates from the third century, at the earliest: "Rufina, a Jewish woman, built this

---

32. See Rutgers, "Archeological Evidence," 110–11; Ross Shepard Kraemer, "Jewish Tuna and Christian Fish: Identifying Religious Affiliation in Epigraphic Sources," *Harvard Theological Review* 84 (1991): 141–62; and Jan William van Henten and Alice J. Bij de Vaate, "Jewish or Non-Jewish?: Some Remarks on the Identification of Jewish Inscriptions from Asia Minor," *Bibliotheca Orientalis* 53 (1996): 16–28.

33. See Harry J. Leon, "The Jews of Venusia," *Jewish Quarterly Review* 44 (1954): 267–84, and Cesare Colafemmina, "Saggio di scavo in località 'Collina della Maddalena' a Venosa," *Vetera Christianorum* 18 (1981): 443–51. See also Eric M. Meyers, "Report on the Excavations at the Venosa Catacombs 1981," *Vetera Christianorum* 20 (1983): 445–59; Rutgers, "Archeological Evidence," 112; and David Noy, *Jewish Inscriptions of Western Europe*, vol. 1, *Italy (Excluding the City of Rome), Spain, and Gaul* (Cambridge: Cambridge University Press, 1993), xv–xxi.

34. See Rutgers, "Archeological Evidence," 112–13 and bibliography.

35. Noy, *Jewish Inscriptions of Western Europe*, vol. 1, no. 18; see also Noy, "Where Were the Jews of the Diaspora buried?" 80–81. The first part of the inscription, in which it says that the society (*synagoga?*) of the Jews bought some land and then gave it to C. Iulius Iustus, who built a tomb, is solely a montage of hypothetical restitutions.

36. See Paul R. Trebilco, *Jewish Communities in Asia Minor*, Monograph series, Society for New Testament Studies, 69 (Cambridge: Cambridge University Press, 1991).

37. See the text and translation by Jean-Baptiste Frey, *Corpus inscriptionum iudaicarum: recueil des inscriptions juives qui vont du IIIe siècle avant Jésus-Christ au VIIe siècle de notre ère. 2, Asie—Afrique*, Sussidi allo studio delle antichità cristiane 3 (Vatican City: Pontificio Istituto di archeologia cristiana, 1952), n. 757 (= *Tituli Asiae minoris. 2, Tituli Lyciae linguis Graeca et Latina conscripti. 2*, ed. E. Kalinka (Vindobonae: Hoelder, 1930), n. 612). See Trebilco, *Jewish Communities in Asia Minor*, no. 71, 227.

tomb for her servants and slaves raised in her house. No one shall have the right to bury others here. Anyone doing so shall pay a fine of 1,500 *denarii* to the sacred treasury and 1,000 *denarii* to the Jewish people. A copy of this inscription has been place in the public archives."[38] Tombs were usually reserved for the nuclear family, though sometimes, as in this example, enlarged to include freedmen and slaves, but without any explicit religious restrictions. These fines were sometimes to be paid to the Jewish community under a variety of names: *synagogue, Jewish nation, Jewish colony*. This might lead us to think there was a kind of community organization controlling and overseeing Jewish burials were it not that, in the same inscriptions, these fines were also directed to the *fiscus,* or the sacred treasury.[39] That tells us that respect for tombs is as much the responsibility of the city and its institutions as it is for a more limited group of coreligionists.

Still, in Asia Minor, whenever identification is possible, we find that Jewish tombs are mixed with non-Jewish ones. That is the case, for example, at Hierapolis or at Corycus.[40] At Acmonia, the great number of epitaphs containing curses against violators of tombs has been used to argue in favor of the existence of a Jewish cemetery there.[41] As these curses actually refer to "curses written in Deuteronomy" or, more generally, to the vengeance of divine justice, they were unlikely to be deterrents for non-Jews.[42] However,

---

38. Frey, *Corpus inscriptionum iudaicarum,* vol. 2, no. 741 = *Die Inschriften von Smyrna. 1,* ed. Georg Petzl (Bonn: Habelt, 1982), no. 295.

39. More examples: Frey, *Corpus inscriptionum iudaicarum,* vol. 2, nos. 775, 776, 799, etc. About the Jewish inscription of Hierapolis, see Elena Miranda, "La comunità giudaica di Hierapolis di Frigia," *Epigraphica Anatolica* 31 (1999): 109–55, esp. 148 (for funerary fines).

40. About Hierapolis, see Tullia Ritti, "Nuovi dati su una nota epigrafe sepolcrale con stefanotico da Hierapolis di Frigia," *Scienze dell'antichità* 6–7 (1992–93): 41–68, esp. 41–43, and Miranda, "La comunità giudaica di Hierapolis di Frigia," 146, which mentions only one case of contiguity between two Jewish sepultures, while the rest of them are scattered along the road. For Corycus, see Joseph Keil, ed., *Monumenta Asiae Minoris antiqua. 3, Denkmäler aus dem rauhen Kilikien* (Manchester: Manchester University Press, 1931), 120–22, where there is a description of the necropolis along the coast and a map (illustration 46). Jewish inscriptions were found in the three areas arbitrarily designated by the editors as A, B, and C. See Margaret H. Williams, "The Jews of Corycus: A Neglected Diasporan Community from Roman Times," *Journal for the Study of Judaism* 25 (1994): 274–86, esp. 278 and notes 23–24.

41. Johan H. M Strubbe, "Curses against Violation of the Grave in Jewish Epitaphs of Asia Minor," in *Studies in Early Jewish Epigraphy,* ed. Jan Willem van Henten and Pieter Willem van der Horst, Arbeiten zur Geschichte des antiken Judentums und des Urchristentums 21 (Leiden: Brill, 1994), 101–2; this is contra Trebilco, *Jewish Communities in Asia Minor,* 227, n. 71. Margaret H. Williams, "The Meaning and Function of *Ioudaios* in Graeco-Roman Inscriptions," *Zeitschrift für Papyrologie und Epigraphik* 116 (1997): 256 and n. 69, stresses the weakness of Strubbe's arguments; we find the same comment in Noy, "Where Were the Jews of the Diaspora Buried?" 81, n. 30.

42. Trebilco, *Jewish Communities in Asia Minor,* 67–68, 83, 100, implies that people in cities like Acmonia had some knowledge of Jewish law.

the curse was engraved more for its own performative value than for the fear it would arouse in a tomb violator who might read it.[43]

Two Jewish inscriptions from Asia Minor also record funds bequeathed to associations, but there is no indication that these were exclusively Jewish. In one of them, from Hierapolis, P. Aelius Glykon gives money to two associations for the placing of wreaths on his tomb—to the purple dyers for the festival of Passover, to the carpet weavers for the festival of Pentecost, and for the Calends.[44] In the other, from Acmonia, Aurelius Aristeas gives land to a neighborhood association, the neighborhood of the First Gate, "on the condition that each year they deck with roses the tomb of [his] wife."[45] To celebrate the *rosalia* or to crown tombs were two traditional commemorative practices in the Greco-Roman world. Their adoption by Jews suggests once again a degree of integration that has often been denied them and would make little sense if funerary segregation were the rule.[46]

The city of Tukrah, Libya (ancient Teucheira in Cyrenaica) provides another interesting example, with a total of 440 inscriptions drawn mostly from chamber tombs cut in the sides of ancient quarries located east and west of the city. Shimon Applebaum was able to identify as Jewish 109 inscriptions, to which he added 144 others from chamber tombs in which other Jews have been identified. That presupposes that within any one chamber, only Jewish graves would be found; there is no reason to think otherwise. However, and contrary to the old view, Applebaum can show that if one of these quarries seems to have been almost exclusively used as a burial place for Jews, others reveal almost no Jewish graves and still others reveal small pockets of Jewish graves among those of non-Jews.[47]

As these examples show,[48] Jews usually buried their dead in the same areas as pagans and Christians. Was that also true in the large cities of the empire?

---

43. This is noted in Strubbe, *Curses,* 100.

44. Frey, *Corpus inscriptionum iudaicarum,* vol. 2, no. 777 (incomplete); new edition in Miranda, "La comunità giudaica di Hierapolis di Frigia," 131, no. 23, with a detailed commentary, 140–45. See also Ritti, "Nuovi dati."

45. See the text, English translation, and commentary in Trebilco, *Jewish Communities in Asia Minor,* 78–81.

46. According to Trebilco, the association of the Neighborhood of the First Gate would be a Jewish association; as for P. Ailios Glykon, he was not Jewish but a "sympathizer." In both cases, the arguments are hardly convincing; neither is the hypothetical reading of Aphrodisias's inscription proposed in Margaret H. Williams, "The Jews and Godfearers Inscription from Aphrodisias: A Case of Patriarcal Interference in Early 3rd Century Caria?" *Historia* 41, no. 3 (1992): 297–310.

47. Shimon Applebaum, *Jews and Greeks in Ancient Cyrene,* Studies in Judaism in Late Antiquity 28 (Leiden: Brill, 1979), 144–160. See also Shimon Applebaum, "The Jewish Community of Hellenistic and Roman Teucheira in Cyrenaica," *Scripta Hierosolymitana* 7 (1961): 27–52, esp. 34–35.

48. Note the case of villages in the Golan Desert, where a mixed population shared the same burial area; see Robert C. Gregg, "Marking Religious and Ethnic Boundaries: Cases from the Ancient Golan Heights," *Church History* 69, no. 3 (2000): 519–57, esp. 547–48.

The larger and stronger Jewish communities have often been credited in the past with their own separate burial places. However, the ancient "Jewish necropolis" at Alexandria, found at El Ibrahimiya, seems to have been a place where Jews and some non-Jews, somehow connected to each other, were buried together.[49] In Carthage, the necropolis of Gammarth is less extensive than it was thought to be and includes actually about two hundred tombs. It thus cannot be the sole "Jewish necropolis" of Carthage but simply a small group of hypogea used by Jews.[50]

The situation at Rome is both better documented and more complex.[51] Six Jewish catacombs are known: the catacomb of Monteverde, on the Via Portuense, which has yielded the most abundant harvest of inscriptions but is now destroyed; the catacomb of the Villa Randanini, situated between the Via Appia and the Via Appia Pignatelli; the two catacombs of the Villa Torlonia on the Via Nomentana; and two smaller hypogea, that of the Villa Labicana on the route of the same name and that of the Vigna Cimarra on the Via Appia.[52] These catacombs are located in areas where there are also pagan and Christian tombs, but there is general agreement that they were used exclusively by Jews. While it is impossible to prove, there is no strong

---

49. Compare William Horbury and David Noy, eds., *Jewish Inscriptions of Graeco-Roman Egypt: With an index of the Jewish Inscriptions of Egypt and Cyrenaica* (Cambridge: Cambridge University Press, 1992), 4; against the old hypotheses proposed in Charles Simon Clermont-Ganneau, "L'antique nécropole juive d'Alexandrie," *Comptes rendus de l'Académie des Inscriptions et Belles-Lettres* (1907): 236–39, 375–76.

50. See Alfred Louis Delattre, *Gamart ou la nécropole juive de Carthage* (Lyon: Mougin-Rusand, 1895); Stéphane Gsell, "Chronique archéologique africaine," *Mélanges d'archéologie et d'histoire* 15 (1895): 829. See Yves Le Bohec, "Inscriptions juives et judaïsantes de l'Afrique romaine," *Antiquités africaines* 17 (1981): 168, and 180–89 (for the inscriptions). Delattre initially thought that Jews and Christians were buried together in Gamart before excluding such theory; see the history of the excavations in Erwin R. Goodenough, *Jewish Symbols in the Greco-Roman Period*, vol. 2, *The Archaeological Evidence from the Diaspora*, Bollingen series 37 (New York: Pantheon Books, 1953), 63–68. For a very cautious evaluation of the basis for Jewish burial groupings in North Africa, see Karen B. Stern, *Inscribing Devotion and Death: Archaeological Evidence for Jewish Populations of North Africa*, Religions in the Graeco-Roman World 161 (Leiden: Brill, 2008), esp. 259–60 and 280–84.

51. Beside the pioneering study of Harry J. Leon, *The Jews of Ancient Rome*, 1st ed., 1960, updated ed. by Carolyn A. Osiek (Peabody: Hendrickson, 1995), see Rutgers, *The Jews of Late Ancient Rome*. See also Tessa Rajak, "Inscription and Context: Reading the Jewish Catacombs of Rome," in *Studies in Early Jewish Epigraphy*, ed. Jan Willem van Henten and Pieter Willem van der Horst, Arbeiten zur Geschichte des antiken Judentums und des Urchristentums 21 (Leiden: Brill, 1994), 226–41.

52. For a detailed description of these catacombs, see Cinzia Vismarra, "I cimiteri ebraici di Roma," in *Società romana e impero tardoantico. 2, Le merci. Gli insediamenti*, ed. Andrea Giardina, Collezione storica (Bari: Laterza, 1986), 351–89, and Leonard Victor Rutgers, "Überlegungen zu den jüdischen Katakomben Roms," *Jahrbuch für Antike und Christentum* 33 (1990): 140–57. For an English revised translation, see Leonard Victor Rutgers, "Dating the Jewish Catacombs of Ancient Rome," in idem, *The Hidden Heritage of Diaspora Judaism* (Leuven: Peeters, 1998), 45–47. Rajak, "Inscription and Context," 228–30, insists on the very limited knowledge we have of these catacombs.

evidence to the contrary. Some epitaphs use the pagan formula *Dis Manibus* in its abbreviated form *D.M.*, but those found in context are very few. The same reasoning may apply to some tombs with a pagan decor. Rooms I and II of the Villa Randanini catacomb are painted with explicitly pagan motifs, but they could originally have belonged to an independent hypogeum.[53] That would mean that at Rome, toward the end of the second century when these catacombs began to be used, Jews preferred to be buried together.

Harry J. Leon posited that the choice of a catacomb for burial was determined by membership in a particular synagogue.[54] However, Margaret H. Williams has recently shown that there was only one case of a synagogue of which all known members were buried in the same catacomb, and that the members of at least three synagogues used several catacombs.[55] Moreover, there are no inscriptions attributing a role in the choice or assignment of a tomb to any synagogue. Inscriptions mention a synagogue only to indicate that the dedicatee held an office there. It is therefore unlikely that membership in a synagogue determined the choice of burial site; it is even more difficult to imagine a centralized system.[56]

Williams offers the hypothesis that Jews, like their pagan contemporaries, bought their tombs from funerary merchants who built these underground burial grounds at their own expense, then sold them in parcels consisting of large or small burial chambers, or of simple tombs.[57] This may in fact be how the catacombs of Beth She'Arim in Palestine were organized. The city is set on a plateau; into its slopes were dug the catacombs, used mainly in the third and fourth centuries. In general, a hallway descends to the heart of the hill, pierced by entryways into halls that consist of one or two connecting burial chambers. Numerous inscriptions preserved in situ give us a fairly precise idea about the organization of the space. These inscriptions are generally deeds of ownership: Aidesius, an official of Antioch, owned—in hall B of catacomb 12—chamber iv that contains, an inscription tells us, six places; hall C of catacomb I was entirely owned by one Thymus; another burial chamber was jointly owned by four people. No inscription ever mentions the act of purchase itself. The only indication about the role of a funerary enterprise is an inscription discovered in the synagogue that was meant to

---

53. See Rutgers, *The Jews of Late Ancient Rome*, 269–72, for the formula *Dis Manibus*; 77–81, for sarcophagi; and 53–55, for rooms I and II in Villa Randanini. Rajak, "Inscription and Context," 239, decides to leave the question open.
54. Leon, *The Jews of Ancient Rome*, 54, and chap. 7, *passim*.
55. Williams, "The Organization of Jewish Burials," 165–70.
56. Ibid., 179–81. See also Noy, "Where Were the Jews of the Diaspora Buried?" 87.
57. Williams, "The Organization of Jewish Burials," 181–82.

mark the benches of two people who were responsible for preparing and placing the body.[58] In Rome, however, no Jewish inscriptions mention the sale of a tomb or its title deed in any way that attests to the intervention of a funerary trade. In general, very little is known of these funeral consortia.[59]

According to the traditional view, the fact that Jews were buried among Jews was not even open to discussion: the synagogue was held to be responsible for the organization of the burial of Jews. According to Williams's view, the question has to be framed differently: Why did Jews choose to be buried among Jews if they were buying their tombs from consortia? Does the answer imply that the consortia themselves were Jewish?

At the beginning of the twentieth century, Jean Juster held that "religious segregation of the dead" was characteristic of Jews. The only justification given to support this statement were a few inscriptions whose wording finds numerous parallels in both Christian and pagan inscriptions relating to *ius sepulchri* and not "religious segregation."[60] In rabbinical teaching, there are no rules about the separation of Jews and non-Jews in burial. *Semahot*, a treatise that seems to have been published in the third century and entirely dedicated to burial and mourning, contains no such proscription. At most, it prescribes that "for pagans or slaves, no rite shall be observed, but [that] there shall be an expression of mourning."[61] The issue is about adopting no ritual signs of mourning and not about refusing burial to a non-Jew. In addition, the *Tosefta* (third and fourth centuries) and the *Jerusalem Talmud* (fifth

---

58. Important precision is brought in Tessa Rajak, "The Rabbinic Dead and the Diaspora Dead at Beth She'arim," in *The Talmud Yerushalmi and Graeco-Roman culture*, ed. Peter Schäfer, Texte und Studien zum Antiken Judentum 71 (Tübingen: Mohr Siebeck, 1998), 349–66. For excavations and inscriptions, see Benjamin Mazar, ed., *Beth She'arim*, vol. 1, *Catacombs 1–4* (Jerusalem: Massada, 1973); Moshe Schwabe and Baruch Lifschitz, eds., *Beth She'arim*, vol. 2, *The Greek Inscriptions* (Jerusalem: Massada, 1974); and Nachman Avigad, ed., *Beth She'arim*, vol. 3, *The Archaeological Excavations during 1953–1958: The Catacombs 12–13* (New Brunswick, NJ: Rutgers University Press, 1976). The inscriptions referred to are *Beth She'arim*, vol. 2, nos. 141–43, 11, 83, and 202 respectively.

59. Susan D. Martin, *The Roman Jurists and the Organization of Private Building in the Late Republic and the Early Empire*, Collection Latomus 204 (Brussels: Latomus, 1989), 48–49, assumes on the basis of *Digesta* 17.2.52.7 that there were small businesses specializing in the development of land for resale as tombs. On the sale of tombs and loculi in *columbaria*, see Stefan Schrumpf, *Bestattung und Bestattungswesen in Römischen Reich: Ablauf, soziale Dimension und ökonomische Bedeutung der Totenfürsorge im lateinischen Westen* (Göttingen: Bonn University Press, 2006), 202–10.

60. Jean Juster, *Les juifs dans l'Empire romain: leur condition juridique, économique et sociale*, vol. 1 (Paris: Geuthner, 1914), 480, and n. 4, which cites the three following inscriptions: Noy, *Jewish Inscriptions of Western Europe*, vol. 2, no. 378 = Frey, *Corpus inscriptionum iudaicarum*, vol. 1, no. 220, where a wife chooses a *loculus* next to her husband's; *Tituli Asiae minoris. 2, 2*, no. 612 = Frey, *Corpus inscriptionum iudaicarum*, vol. 2, no. 757, where a funerary monument is given to the Jews of Tlos; and *CIL* 6.10412, which is no longer identified as Jewish.

61. *Semahot* 1.9. See, Dov Zlotnick, *The Tractate "Mourning": (Semahot): (Regulations Relating to Death, Burial and Mourning)*, Yale Judaica Series 17 (New Haven, CT: Yale University Press, 1966).

century) recommend that in cities where Jews live in the midst of pagans they should take care to bury the poor whether Jewish or not, but give no detail about the place of burial.[62] No impurity seems to have been attached to the tombs of gentiles, either; their homes, however, could be a source of impurity as aborted fetuses could be buried nearby.[63] In a discussion about the Sabbath, it seems that if a gentile dug a tomb for a Jew on the Sabbath, the Jew could not use it, but if the tomb were dug for a gentile, a Jew could use it.[64] Thus a Jew could not require a gentile to work for him on the Sabbath, but nothing would stop a Jew from being buried in a tomb intended for a gentile. Even though the *Mishna* and the *Tosefta* cannot be used as documents relating directly to the relations between Jews and non-Jews,[65] there is every indication that segregation in burial was not the rule.[66]

Ultimately, the choice of a tomb seems to have been a family matter, as it is taught in the Old Testament. The purchase of the Tomb of the Patriarchs by Abraham at Hebron (Gen. 23) is an important model, and the desirability of possessing a family tomb for the burial of the dead is a recurring theme in the Old Testament. This is Jacob's wish in Genesis 49:29–31: that he be buried with his fathers, where he himself buried his wife Leah, in the field where Abraham and Sarah as well as Isaac and Rebecca lie buried. Joseph makes his family promise to take his body back to the land of Abraham when they are able to do so (Gen. 50:25). Gideon and Samson also were buried in their fathers' tombs (Judg. 8:32 and 16:31). David gathers the bones of Saul, of his son Jonathan, and of the seven hanged men, in the tomb of Kish, Saul's father (2 Sam. 21:12–14).

Thus, there was no specific religious ruling about the choice of a tomb; the model is simply that of family burial. Moreover, it should be noted that, for Jews, contrasting family and community did not have the same significance

---

62. *Tosefta. Gittin* 5.5; *Jerusalem Talmud. Demai* 1.4; and *Jerusalem Talmud. Aboda zara* 1.3. See *Babylonian Talmud. Gittin* 61a, where no burial place is indicated either (contra Rutgers, "Archaeological Evidence," 114).

63. *Michna. Ohalot* 18.7–8. See Jacob Neusner, *A History of the Mishnaic Law of Purity*, vol. 4, *Ohalot: Commentary*, Studies in Judaism in Late Antiquity 6, no. 4 (Leiden: Brill, 1974), 340–41; Gary G. Porton, *Goyim: Gentiles and Israelites in Mishnah-Tosefta*, Brown Judaic studies 155 (Atlanta: Scholars Press, 1988), 16–17, 274.

64. *Michna. Shabbat* 23.4, and *Tosefta. Shabbat* 17.14–15. See Jacob Neusner, *A History of the Mishnaic Law of Appointed Times*, vol. 1, *Shabbat: Translation and Explanation*, Studies in Judaism in Late Antiquity 34, no. 1 (Leiden: Brill, 1981), 200–201; Porton, *Goyim*, 28–29, 208.

65. See the important methodological points in Porton, *Goyim*, 4–5.

66. Leonard V. Rutgers, in a review of the French version of this book, states that "the sources do not forbid explicitly the burying together of Jews and non-Jews simply because it was self-evident from the beginning that this was not normal procedure" (*Vigiliae Christianae* 59, no. 2 [2005]: 214). This is the kind of assumption I am challenging in this book.

as for followers of the cults of Mithras or of Isis; burial with family and burial among Jews were one and the same thing. How then are we to explain the groupings of family tombs in the same catacombs at Rome? Was it a desire to distinguish themselves from non-Jews?[67] That seems to be contradicted by the absence of parallels, elsewhere, in Jewish communities of the Diaspora. But the size of the city might explain different social practices.[68]

Christians

The precedent of Jewish communities has often been used as an argument supporting the thesis of burial segregation among Christians. Particularly in Rome, the development of Jewish and Christian catacombs has been attributed to the same religious necessities in the two communities. Yet the case of Jewish catacombs shows that there was no community organization responsible for the burial together of Jews, that this was largely the result of family choice.

The Teaching of the Church

There is no known Jewish teaching that can be cited to support a ban on mixing Jewish and non-Jewish graves. Does Christian teaching contain any new elements? This is assuredly not the case in the New Testament, where even a familial obligation to provide burial for relatives is contested.[69] Christian texts have been closely examined, however, in order to find any trace of a rule against mixing the graves of Christians and non-Christians in one place.[70]

---

67. Noy, "Where Were the Jews of the Diaspora Buried?" 88–89, mentions such desire without giving specific examples. See also David Noy, "Writing in Tongues: The Use of Greek, Latin and Hebrew in Jewish Inscriptions from Roman Italy," *Journal of Jewish Studies* 48 (1997): 300–311, which suggests that using Greek for the epitaph (in about 74 percent of the cases) coincided with choosing a specific formula, a Jewish one therefore, by opposition to Latin epitaphs whose formula was more in accordance with contemporary pagan inscriptions.

68. About the implications of the status of *megapolis*, see Claude Nicolet, Robert Ilbert, and Jean-Claude Depaule, eds., *Mégapoles méditerranéennes: géographie urbaine rétrospective: actes du colloque organisé par l'École française de Rome et la Maison méditerranéenne des sciences de l'homme (Rome, 8–11 mai 1996)*, L'atelier méditerranéen, Collection de l'École française de Rome 261 (Paris: Maisonneuve et Larose/Rome: École française de Rome, 2000). A study of social practices in those large cities has not yet been undertaken.

69. See Matt. 8:25, "Let the dead bury the dead," which is, surprisingly, rarely commented on by the Fathers of the Church, unless allegorically; see Hilary of Poitiers, below, note 73.

70. See Éric Rebillard, "Église et sépulture dans l'Antiquité tardive (Occident latin, 3e–6e siècles)," *Annales: histoire, sciences sociales* 54, no. 5 (1999): 1029–32. See Mark J. Johnson, "Pagan-Christian

As a result, a phrase from Tertullian (c. 160–225) has been taken out of context: "We may live with the heathens, die with them we may not" (*De idololatria* 14.5). Tertullian comments upon the verses of 1 Corinthians in which Paul explains that idolatry must be shunned, but not so as to offend the pagans; thus, one is allowed to accept an invitation to dinner from a pagan and to eat what is served without question, but if meat is offered as a meat of sacrifice, it must be refused. Tertullian concludes, "While it is inevitable that we live and mingle with sinners, we may also sin with them. Where there is social intercourse, which is permitted by the apostle, there is also sinning, which is permitted by no one. We may live with the heathens, die with them we may not." *Death* in that sense means sin, so the second phrase repeats the first and cannot be understood as an interdiction for Christians to be buried among pagan tombs.

A letter from Cyprian of Carthage (d. 258) has also often been interpreted in this sense. The letter is a response by Cyprian and his African colleagues to the Spanish communities of Legio, Astorica, and Emerita on the subject of the bishops Basilides and Martialis. They had obtained false certificates of sacrifice that testified that they had conformed with Decius's edict (250) but they did not themselves actually sacrifice. Nevertheless, their churches deemed their conduct unworthy of bishops and deposed them. The Spaniards appealed to their African colleagues, for Basilides requested and received support from Stephen, bishop of Rome. The offense of the two bishops was not simply their obtaining of certificates of sacrifice. Martialis's case, in particular, was aggravated by his membership in a collegium. Not only did he participate in the banquets of the collegium, but also had buried his sons in the collegium burial place. Cyprian's indignation is clear in the words he used: "his own sons he had buried in the manner of pagans as members of that same sodality, interred in the company of strangers among heathen graves."[71] We must take note of his insistence on describing pagan rites as foreign to Christians, but the key to understanding his indignation is found in the role played by the collegium. Martialis, in effect, not only turned to the collegium for the burial of his sons but obtained for them tombs in the *locus sepulturae* of the collegium—in other words, in the monument or the ground owned by the collegium, where its members could be buried.[72] The choice of such a place had religious implications, for members

---

Burial Practices of the Fourth Century: Shared Tombs?" *Journal of Early Christian Studies* 5, no. 1 (1997): 37–59, for a list of similar testimonies and a critique of the way they have been used.

71. Cyprian, *Letters* 67.6. See Graeme W. Clarke, *The Letters of Cyprian*, vol. 4, Ancient Christian Writers 47 (New York: Newman Press, 1989), 139–42, for the circumstances and the bibliography.

72. See Anna Cafissi, "Contributo alla storia dei collegi romani: i *collegia funeraticia*," *Studi e ricerche dell'Istituto di Storia, Facoltà di Lettere e Filosofia, Università di Firenze* 2 (1983): 89–111; and

of a collegium commemorated their dead together and on those occasions offered libations and sacrifices that were forbidden to Christians. Cyprian's letter therefore contains no general condemnation of the mixing of pagan and Christian tombs, but condemns specifically the recourse to a pagan association for funerals and burials of Christians.

A passage from Hilary of Poitiers (d. 367) has also been misunderstood. It is a commentary on Matthew 18:22: "He did not therefore forbid to honor a father with a decent burial, but by adding, 'let the dead bury the dead,' he urged him not to associate with the memory of the saints (*memoriis sanctorum*) dead nonbelievers, and also to consider as dead those who live without God." The *memoriae sanctorum* have sometimes been understood as the tombs of the saints, but the last part of the sentence shows that death there is used metaphorically, which caused the last editor of the text to conclude that "the wording does not reflect a liturgical usage relative to burials, but is relevant to the rule on excommunication."[73]

Finally, sometimes cited is a text in which Theodoret of Cyrus (d. 458/466) refers to pagan concerns that Christian burials were a source of pollution (*The Cure of Greek Maladies* 8:29). The object of the criticism was actually the veneration of the martyrs. Theodoret dealt with the objection easily by alluding to the cult of the tombs of ancient heroes; their tombs, like those of the martyrs, were intermingled among the living. There was never an issue of the mixing of pagan and Christian tombs.

The first proscription against the mixing of pagan and Christian tombs seems to have been made by Charlemagne in 782 in the *Capitulatio de Partibus Saxoniae*, a collection of measures taken against the Saxons, who had just been defeated: "We order, he said, that the bodies of Christian Saxons be buried in the church cemeteries and not in the pagan *tumuli*." Charlemagne's law was not meant to enforce Christian practice, but to undermine the Saxon aristocracy by banning its traditional burial customs.[74]

In any case, it is impossible to affirm that the exclusive character of Christian burial places was a very ancient regulation. The church clearly wanted to leave the question of burial to the discretion of the family and not interfere in this sphere.

Waltzing, *Étude historique sur les corporations*, 4:487–95, for an inventory of *locus sepulturae* known through epigraphy. See chapter 3 of the present volume for the funerary activities of the collegia.

73. Hilary, *In Mattheum* 7.11, with commentary by Jean Doignon, Sources chrétiennes 254 (Paris: Éditions du Cerf, 1978), 192–93, and n. 15. Johnson, "Pagan-Christian Burial Practices," 44, understands that it is forbidden to bury nonbelievers in the tomb of a martyr, but that the statement does not concern private burials.

74. *Capitulatio de partibus Saxoniae*, 22; see also the analysis of Bonnie Effros, "*De partibus Saxoniae* and the Regulation of Mortuary Custom: A Carolingian Campaign of Christianization or the Suppression of Saxon Identity?" *Revue belge de philologie et d'histoire* 75, no. 2 (1997): 267–86.

The Behavior of Christians

In Christian epitaphs, the place of the nuclear family and even the "conjugal family" is even greater than in pagan inscriptions, even though Christians tended not to note the relationship between the deceased and the commemorators. This change in epigraphic formulae, however, was due to other factors than those that concern us here: it was the vertical relationship of the deceased to God that received the attention, not the horizontal relationships of kinship.[75] Christians did not introduce religious restrictions on the right to burial in their family or hereditary tombs. There are, however, two apparent exceptions that warrant our attention. The first is an inscription, published by Giovanni Battista De Rossi in 1865, which opened the tomb to freedmen and their descendants on condition that they belonged to the same religion (*at religionem pertinentes meam*) as their patron, Valerius Mercurius. On paleographical grounds the inscription is dated from the end of the second century. As it was found among other pagan inscriptions or fragments of inscriptions in the Villa Patrizi, on the Via Nomentana, and out of any specific archaeological context, its Christian character is difficult to determine. For De Rossi the use of *religio mea* was sufficient evidence. But, as we have seen, followers of Cybele, and also those of Isis, use the word *religio* to speak of their cult and called themselves *religiosi*.[76] Be that as it may, membership in the same religion was subordinate to membership in the first category, that of the freedmen of Valerius Mercurius and his wife and their descendants. So this monument was a simple family tomb. The same is true of the tomb that Marcus Antonius Restitutus says was constructed for "himself and his household faithful in the Lord." This epitaph comes from the catacomb of Domitilla in Rome, but we do not know the exact context in which it was found; it may have been simply a *cubiculum* or part of a larger group. It is difficult to say whether the expression "faithful in the Lord" had a restrictive meaning, signifying "on condition that they be faithful in the Lord," or if it was a declaration of faith.[77]

---

75. Shaw, "Latin Funerary Epigraphy and Family Life," 481–83.
76. See Giovanni Battista De Rossi, "Le iscrizioni trovate nei sepolcri all'aperto cielo nella villa Patrizi," *Bullettino di archeologia cristiana* (1865): 53–54 (= *CIL* 6.10412; *ICVR* 8.20737). See Gaston Boissier, *La religion romaine d'Auguste aux Antonins* (Paris: Hachette, 1878), 1:383, n. 5, for the use of *religiosi*. Inscriptions of *religiosi* are now compiled in M. de Souza, *Religiosus ou les métamorphoses du "religieux" dans le monde romain, de la fin de la République à l'Empire chrétien (IIe siècle av. J.-C.-début du Ve siècle apr. J.-C.)* (PhD diss., Université François Rabelais, Tours, 2001), 471–85.
77. See Giovanno Battista De Rossi, "Le varie e successive condizioni di legalità dei cemeteri, il vario grado di libertà dell'arte cristiana, e la legalità della medesima religione nel primo secolo

Burial foundations intended for adherents of Christianity were not very numerous. There was the case of Faltonia Hilaritas, "who built at her own expense this tomb (*coemeterium*) and gave it to her religion (*huhic* [sic] *religioni*)." The inscription was discovered on a tomb, in reuse, near a small funerary basilica at Solluna, on the territory of the ancient *Velitrae*, not far from Rome, on the Via Appia.[78] The discoverer seems to think that the inscription, whose marble plaque bears the marks of hooks, was originally hung at the entrance to the small burial basilica, which Faltonia was supposed to have given to her coreligionists. While it has some appeal, this hypothesis is a fragile one; the context of the inscription cannot be taken as confirmed. Even if it were the case, Faltonia would simply have opened to her coreligionists a funerary basilica built at her expense for her own burial rather than establish a place of communal burial.

A famous inscription from Caesarea (today Cherchel, in Algeria) mentions a gift to the church of a funerary enclosure by a pious benefactor, the *clarissimus* Severianus.[79] What has been preserved is not the original inscription, but that engraved by the Church of Caesarea celebrating the gift. Paleographically, the inscription is from the fourth century, but the gift of Severianus might be earlier. The archaeological context of the inscription is unknown;[80] the description of the enclosure comes entirely from the inscription. Severianus, poetically described by the term *cultor uerbi*, bought some land to be used for burial and built there at his expense a *cella*. The whole is then designated by the word *memoria*—in other words, a (monumental) tomb. The term *cella* is imprecise. We can rule out the idea of a chapel devoted to the

---

verificate dalle recenti scoperte nel cemetero di Domitilla," *Bullettino di archeologia cristiana* (1865): 89–99 (= *ICVR* 3.6555). See, more recently, Philippe Pergola, *Les cimetières chrétiens de Rome depuis leurs origines jusqu'au neuvième siècle: le cas du "praedium Domitillae" et de la catacombe homonyme sur la "Via Ardeatina"* (PhD diss., Université d'Aix-Marseille, Aix-en-Provence, 1992), 305–6. Antonio Ferrua (*ICVR* 3.6555) compares the formula to 2 Cor. 1:9: *non simus fidentes in nobis sed in deo qui suscitat mortuos.*

78. See Gioacchino Mancini, "Scoperta di un antico sepolcreto cristiano nel territorio veliterno, in località Solluna," *Notizie degli scavi di antichità* (1924): 341–53, esp. 345–46 (= *ILCV* 3681). See *Supplementa Italica*, vol. 2 (Roma: Ed. di storia e letteratura, 1983), no. 66.

79. *CIL* 8.9585, with commentary in Yvette Duval, *Loca Sanctorum Africae: le culte des martyrs en Afrique du IVe au VIIe siècle*, Collection de l'École française de Rome 58 (Rome: École française de Rome, 1982), 1:380–83, no. 179.

80. Contrary to what was thought; see, for instance, Stéphane Gsell, *Les monuments antiques de l'Algérie* (Paris: Fontemoing, 1901), 2:398–400, and Paul Monceaux, *Histoire littéraire de l'Afrique chrétienne: depuis les origines jusqu'à l'invasion arabe* (Paris: Leroux, 1901–23), 1:14 and 2:125–30. Actually, Cardinal Lavigerie excavated in the area where the inscription was found, but the excavation did not fulfill his expectations since he discovered a pagan enclosure. See the publication of the excavation in Philippe Leveau, "Fouilles anciennes sur les nécropoles antiques de Cherchel," *Antiquités africaines* 12 (1978): 93–95.

martyrs, for these would be mentioned in the commemorative inscription. *Cella* designates either a tomb or the edifice to house it and intended also for the holding of funerary rites.

Gifts, like those of Faltonia or of Severianus, did not come from a desire to separate Christians and non-Christians in death, but were benefactions comparable to those of contemporary pagans. This is again the case in a second inscription from Cherchel, this time that of a priest, Victor, who built an *accubitorium* in order to house several tombs, including that of his mother Rogata, and who made it a gift "to all the brothers";[81] and in a Lydian inscription dated from the fourth century that relates how Gennadius bought "with what God gave him" a monument and made it a "tomb for Christians of the Catholic Church."[82] We will have to return to this role of the church as an intermediary, in a way, between the donor and eventual beneficiaries. But nothing should lead us to see behind these gifts a Christian duty to be buried together and apart from others; no tension with the family is evident. To open one's funerary monument to other Christians was not even an expression of a preference for "Christian" burial.

❧ The Case of the Catacombs

Is such preference supported by archaeological evidence? We must be cautious; to identify a burial area—or a tomb within such an area—as Christian on the basis of epigraphic formulae or iconographic motif is a delicate business, at least for material dated before the middle of the fourth century. In spite of these difficulties, recent excavations or the reexamination of old ones have led to a number of examples of the mixing of Christian and non-Christian tombs.[83] Rather than attempt to establish an inventory across the provinces of the Roman Empire, which could only be incomplete, I prefer to focus on the situation in Rome. There are many reasons for this choice, principal among them the historiographic importance of the catacombs to the studies of the origins of Christian cemeteries. Because of the antiquity and strength of Christian settlement in Rome, and because of the size of the city itself, this example is appropriate for illustrating the complexity of the issues at stake.

---

81. *ILCV* 1179 = *CIL* 8.9586.
82. Peter Hermann, *Neue Inschriften zur historischen Landeskunde von Lydien und angrenzenden Gebieten,* Denkschriften/Österreichische Akademie der Wissenschaften, Philosophisch-Historische Klasse 77, no. 1 (Vienna: Rohrer, 1959), 13, no. 10 (= *SEG,* 19, 1963, no. 719).
83. See Johnson, "Pagan-Christian Burial Practices," 51 ff.

While it has long been thought that the origins of the catacombs were exclusively Christian, today there is a growing awareness, despite some obvious ideological obstacles, of the fact that they may have had pagan origins.[84] The catacomb of Domitilla is one of the best-known examples, thanks to the work of Philippe Pergola.[85] He has shown how difficult it is, in a number of cases, to determine the religious affiliation of the owners. The neutrality of the epigraphic formulae may suggest a Christian identity, whereas iconography—borrowing its motifs from the traditional repertoire—would suggest pagan sponsors, since Christian iconography, unlike epigraphy, was already clearly defined in the third century. Of the seven pre-Constantine hypogea, only two belong to individuals who are known with certainty to have been Christians: the so-called area of the *scalone* of 1897, with 135 meters of galleries and about four hundred tombs, where inscriptions have been found in situ with the characteristic formulae, and the hypogeum of "the martyrs," where Nereus and Achilles were buried. What is known as the hypogeum of the Flavii, where De Rossi thought he had identified the tomb of Christian members of the family of Flavia Domitilla, niece of the emperor Domitian, is actually a pagan hypogeum from the end of the second or beginning of the third century; it was not used by Christians until the second half of the third century. The Ampliatus after whom is named another hypogeum was, far from being the Ampliatus mentioned in the *Epistle to the Romans,* actually a pagan freedman; the iconography in the two burial chambers of the primitive area contains no explicitly Christian elements. The same is true of the hypogeum of the Good Shepherd, from all evidence a family tomb with a central gallery leading to the burial chamber of the owner and lateral corridors pierced with *loculi* for other members of the *familia*. Finally, the religious affiliation of the owners of the two hypogea known as the Flavii Aurelii cannot be determined: the one with some fifteen tombs was familial; the other, which included about 250 burials, may have belonged to a collegium. What can be seen through the example of the catacomb of Domitilla is that in the second and third centuries in Rome, pagans and Christians were buried together: this pagan hypogeum became Christian in the space of one generation; that area was mixed; and so on. The primitive hypogea do not have an exclusively familial character (250 tombs for the

---

84. See Philippe Pergola, *Le catacombe romane: storia e topografia, catalogo a cura di P. M. Barbini,* Argomenti 8 (Rome: Carocci, 1998), 57–71.

85. See status quaestionis and bibliography in Pergola, *Le catacombe romane,* 211–13, and idem, *Les cimetières chrétiens de Rome depuis leurs origines jusqu'au neuvième siècle.* I would like to thank the author for granting me access to his work before publication.

hypogeum of the Flavii Aurelii A, 400 for that of the *scalone* of 1897), but nothing suggests that the grouping of tombs followed religious prescriptions in the largest areas.

Besides the large catacombs, there are also some fourth-century hypogea of more modest size whose religious affiliation is hard to define.[86] They are sometimes referred to as "private catacombs" as opposed to "communal catacombs," which would have been managed by the church. This concept, which has no legal basis, was used by Antonio Ferrua to explain the presence of certain representations, in the famous catacomb of the Via Latina (Dino Compagni) discovered in 1956,[87] that he believed no ecclesiastical authority would have tolerated. This point of view, like the view that these were the catacombs of heretics,[88] has slowly been abandoned; these hypogea may have escaped ecclesiastical control—which, for the time being, remains to be proven for other catacombs—but primarily they are evidence of pagans and Christians continuing to use the same burial areas in the fourth century in Rome. For instance, the catacomb of the Via Latina, which seems at first to have been used exclusively by Christians, later received pagan burials in the second half of the fourth century, as we know from rooms with pagan iconography located next to rooms with Christian iconography.[89] In other hypogea, such as that of the Aurelii on the Via Labicana or of the Via Livenza, figured scenes have sometimes been interpreted as the result of philosophical and religious syncretism, since pagan and Christian motifs seem to have been juxtaposed in the same spaces.[90] Such a notion supposes a form of synthesis that is far from being documented and thus should be abandoned. In any case, the mixing of pagans and Christians in Rome up to the second half of the fourth century is clear, and hardly exceptional.[91] What about the

---

86. See Pergola, *Le catacombe romane*, 89–93, where he insists on the need to clearly distinguish fourth-century hypogea from those from the end of the second and beginning of the third centuries.

87. Antonio Ferrua, *Le pitture della nuova catacomba di via Latina*, Monumenti di antichità cristiana 2, no. 8 (Vatican City: Pontificio Istituto di Archeologia Cristiana, 1960), 89–91. See De Rossi, *La Roma sotterranea cristiana*, 1:84, on the distinction between common and private burial places; and Pasquale Testini, *Le catacombe e gli antichi cimiteri cristiani in Roma*, Roma cristiana 2 (Bologna: Cappelli, 1966), 141–43.

88. About "cemeteries for heretics" in Rome, see Éric Rebillard, "L'Église de Rome et le développement des catacombes: à propos de l'origine des cimetières chrétiens," *Mélanges de l'École française de Rome. Antiquité* 109, no. 2 (1997): 755–59.

89. See status quaestionis and bibliography in Pergola, *Le catacombe romane*, 171–74.

90. See Fabrizio Bisconti, "L'ipogeo degli Aureli in viale Manzoni: un esempio di sincresi provata," *Augustinianum* 25 (1985): 889–903.

91. For more Roman and Italian examples, see Johnson, "Pagan-Christian Burial Practices," 53–55.

so-called communal catacombs that are interpreted as places of Christian burial exclusively, and that became quite large? Before the beginning of the fourth century, galleries in the catacomb "Ad duos lauros," for example, extended two kilometers and contained some thirty *cubicula;* Jean Guyon estimates that there might have been 11,000 burials there, to which must be added 6,000 surface tombs. He extrapolates from these numbers a population of some 9,000 souls having used the catacomb in the first forty years.[92] The number of Christians living in Rome is estimated between 30,000 and 50,000 for that period. If we accept the traditional thesis, holding that the church managed the catacombs, the question of why Christians chose to be buried together is not an issue; it was imposed upon them by their religious affiliation. But, as I have shown, there is no evidence of any such obligation during the period under consideration. The administration of the catacombs by the church in turn raises a number of problems, as I have already shown in emphasizing the fragility of De Rossi's system. Actually, the only known authority responsible for these burial areas is that of the *fossores*,[93] who were technically responsible for developing the catacombs: digging the galleries, furnishing the tombs, connecting different areas, ensuring their safety. They sold the spaces and received payments. These grave diggers were skilled workers who might have been previously employed in the digging of cisterns and sandpits that catacombs often reused. Charles Pietri has proven that they were not members of the clergy.[94] The epigraphical record of the sales of tombs in catacombs, studied by Jean Guyon, shows, moreover, that their activity was autonomous and independent of the clergy. Of slightly more than one hundred inscriptions, only three texts involve a member of the clergy: in one, a priest witnesses a sale, and in two cases, the priest's involvement concerns the sale of an especially valuable space. Yet, Pietri maintained that the church entrusted these various duties to the fossores.[95] I will show

---

92. Jean Guyon, *Le cimetière aux deux lauriers: recherches sur les catacombes romaines,* Bibliothèque des Écoles françaises d'Athènes et de Rome 264 (Rome: École française de Rome, 1987), 101.

93. About the *fossores* see, in particular, Guyon, *Le cimetière aux deux lauriers,* 98–100; and Jean Guyon, "La vente des tombes à travers l'épigraphie de la Rome chrétienne (IIIe–VIIe siècles): le rôle des *fossores, mansionarii, praepositi* et prêtres," *Mélanges de l'École française de Rome. Antiquité* 86 (1974): 549–96. Elena Conde Guerri, *Los "fossores" de Roma paleocristiana: estudio iconografico, epigrafico y social,* Studi di antichità cristiana 33 (Vatican City: Pontificio istituto di archeologia cristiana, 1979), is mainly valuable for its catalog of figured scenes. See Pietri, *Roma Christiana,* 131–34 and 659–67, and Charles Pietri, "Appendice prosopographique à la Roma Christiana (311–440)," *Mélanges de l'École française de Rome. Antiquité* 89 (1977): 398–406.

94. Pietri, *Roma Christiana,* 659–67.

95. Guyon, "La vente des tombes," 574–76. See Pietri, *Roma Christiana,* 134: "Very pragmatically, the Church entrusts to the *fossores,* who are laymen, the tasks associated with the care and burial of the dead."

that, in fact, it was the emperor who entrusted the control of the grave diggers to the church.

The choice of a burial was not dictated to Christians by the church, and not even suggested as an alternative to family practices. Nor could the grouping of Christians in burial areas as vast as the catacombs have been the result of a "Christian community"; what sort of organization would it have had, outside the church? Was the service of the fossores available exclusively to Christians? We have seen that this was not the case, either in the hypogea later incorporated in the largest catacombs or in the small, independent fourth-century hypogea. Was it, however, the case for the so-called communal catacombs? The question has never been asked; it may be that we should reconsider the cases one by one, now that we can no longer presume to know the answer in advance.[96] Let us also point out that, as in the case of the Jews, there are no Christian burial areas anywhere in the empire comparable to the Roman catacombs; we should not rule out the possibility that the very exceptional size of the city itself played a role in the choice local Christians made to be buried together.

The conclusion is still tentative, but it does seem that Christians, like other religious groups, did not have religious reasons for favoring some form of communal burial over family burial. Funerary practices and, specifically, the choice of burial place does not appear to have been, in the Roman Empire, an important element in the constructing of religious identity. Although membership in a cult, synagogue, or church was not a determining factor in the choice of burial place, we have often seen that membership in an association, or collegium, was. It is this form of social relationship, typical of the Greco-Roman world, that we must now explore.

---

96. John Bodel, "From *Columbaria* to Catacombs: Collective Burial in Pagan and Christian Rome," in *Commemorating the Dead: Texts and Artifacts in Context, Studies of Roman, Jewish and Christian Burials*, ed. Laurie Brink and Deborah Green (Berlin: De Gruyter, 2008), 183–85, uses calculations of mortality rate, estimations of the number of Christians, and the number of excavated graves to suggest that it is very unlikely that the catacombs contain exclusively Christian dead.

# Chapter 3

Voluntary Associations and Collective Burial

The Church, Christians, and the Collegia

Greco-Roman collegia have often been compared to, or contrasted with, the church. An old theory, but one that is constantly repeated, holds that the first Christian communities created collegia in order to enjoy legal status in the Roman Empire. Another theory holds that collegia disappeared when the church assumed the social activities they had performed. Paradoxically, however, Christian membership in collegia, which were omnipresent in the life of cities, is never explicitly considered. We must therefore reexamine the evidence, particularly since our knowledge of the collegia themselves and their transformation in the late Empire has increased considerably.

Funerary Activities of the Collegia

Funerary activity is the most documented aspect of the life of the collegia in the epigraphic evidence. As a result, it has naturally enjoyed the greatest attention and has too often been studied in isolation. Since the work of Theodor Mommsen, scholars have believed that some collegia, the *collegia funeraticia*, could only perform funerary activities and that their purpose was to ensure an honorable burial for those who could not otherwise have afforded one. The high cost of funerals, the expense of burial plots, and the demographics of a large city like Rome where many people lived without family, made burial by a collegium a necessity rather than a choice.[1] Now, however, recent research allows us to correct this view.

In the first place, the very category of *collegia funeraticia* has been called into question.[2] We should remember that the term itself is an invention of Mommsen and that there is no evidence it was used in antiquity. Mommsen believed he was justified in defining this category on the basis of evidence found in a text of Marcianus (*Digesta* 47.22.1) a jurisconsult of the time of the Severans, who refers to a ban on associations passed between 49 and 44 BCE and gives one exception, made for the *tenuiores,* who were authorized to meet once a month and collect fees. The tenuiores (*tenuis* means weak, of little importance) were not the poor, but were in contrast to the *honestiores;* the distinction was a social one rather than an economic one. No specific activity is ascribed to these collegia by Marcianus. However, Mommsen thought he had found an epigraphical record of the law that Marcianus comments upon. At the beginning of an inscription recording the regulations of the *cultores Dianae et Antinoi* who constituted a collegium in 133 at Lanuvium (present-day Lanuvio, Italy), one can read: "Clause from the Decree of the Senate of the Roman People: the following are permitted [to assemble], convene and maintain a society: those who wish to make monthly contributions [for funerals] may assemble in such a society, but they may not [assemble] in the name of such a society except once a month for the sake of making contributions to provide burial for the dead."[3] Unfortunately, the text of the inscription is fragmentary, and Mommsen's interpretation depends upon conjectural restorations of it. Where Mommsen suggests restoring *[in fune]ra,* "for funerals," Frank M. Ausbüttel preferred to restore *[ad facienda sac]ra,* "to perform sacred rites." Thus the monthly contributions would not have been exclusively intended for funerals and burial of members of the collegium. This is the restoration that ought to be accepted, as much for epigraphical reasons (the c of *sacra* is partly visible on the stone) as for the logic of the

---

1. After Theodor Mommsen, *De collegiis et sodaliciis Romanorum* (Kiel: Libraria Schwersiana, 1843), the two classical works on Roman collegia are Jean-Pierre Waltzing, *Étude historique sur les corporations professionnelles chez les Romains depuis les origines jusqu'à la chute de l'Empire d'Occident,* 4 vols. (Louvain: Peeters, 1895–1900) and Francesco Maria de Robertis, *Storia delle corporazioni e del regime associativo nel mondo romano,* 2 vols. (Bari: Adriatica, 1973). On the historiography of Roman collegia, see Jonathan S. Perry, *The Roman Collegia: The Modern Evolution of an Ancient Concept,* Mnemosyne Supplements 277 (Leiden: Brill, 2006).

2. I depend here on Frank M. Ausbüttel, *Untersuchungen zu den Vereinen im Westen des römischen,* Frankfurter althistorische Studien 11 (Kallmünz: Lassleben, 1982), 22–29.

3. *CIL* 14.2112, I, l.10–11, translated by Mary Beard, John North, and Simon Price in *Religions of Rome,* vol. 2 (Cambridge: Cambridge University Press, 1998), 292–93.

text, which thus does not repeat twice that contributions should be used for funerals. So the category of *collegia funeraticia* must be dropped and with it the idea that collegia might have existed exclusively for burial purposes.

The associative phenomenon actually tends to be considered increasingly in its entirety. Jean-Marc Flambart has spoken forcefully about the Italian collegia:

> An overwhelming majority of the *collegia* inextricably combined:
> —occupational data (individuals practicing the same trade or related trades, although certain associations admitted to membership individuals in different professions);
> —geographic data (the *collegae* were often neighbors, living more or less in the same area);
> —religious data: our statistics are rather imprecise, as they usually are based on dedications to particular divinities or on the theonyms borne by the associations, which in no way implied the religious affiliation of each of the members individually. We notice, however, that the *collegae* often shared the same religious convictions and that they practiced the same cults, with variations, which need to be evaluated case by case;
> —burial data: the *collegia*, whatever their main purpose, if they have one, were responsible for the funerals of their members.
> —social data, finally, since, in every case, the great preoccupation of the *collegae* always consisted of various festivals and communal gatherings. Thus it is preferable not to try to classify associations by activities or according to what one might guess from the names they took.[4]

Finally, we have every reason to think that it was less a matter of necessity than choice that members' burials were arranged by the collegia. Onno M. Van Nijf, in the case of the Greek East, and John R. Patterson, in the case of imperial Rome, have shown that members of the collegia were not poor but belonged to that social fringe just below the elites: they were the *plebs media* of merchants and artisans, relatively comfortable: employers rather than employees.[5] It is therefore important to ask about the social value of being

---

4. Jean-Marc Flambart, "Éléments pour une approche financière de la mort dans les classes populaires du Haut-Empire: analyse du budget de quelques collèges funéraires de Rome et d'Italie," in *La mort, les morts et l'au-delà dans le monde romain: actes du colloque de Caen, 20–22 novembre 1985*, ed. François Hinard (Caen: Université de Caen, 1987), 210.

5. Onno M. Van Nijf, *The Civic World of Professional Associations in the Roman East*, Dutch Monographs on Ancient History and Archaeology 17 (Amsterdam: Gieben, 1997), esp. 18–23, and John R. Patterson, "Patronage, *Collegia* and Burial in Imperial Rome," in *Death in Towns: Urban Responses to the Dying and the Dead, 100–600*, ed. Steven Bassett (Leicester: Leicester University Press, 1993), 15–27. See also Beate Bollmann, *Römische Vereinshäuser: Untersuchungen zu den Scholae der römischen*

buried by a collegium. The first element to be noted was the obligation of members of the collegium to attend the funerals of their colleagues. The funerary procession and the number of people in it were an obvious indication of social distinction: thanks to a collegium, the members of the plebs media could aspire to processions almost as grand as those of members of the elite.[6] This was equally true of the funerary monument: collective ownership made it possible to imitate once again the example of the elite. Van Nijf goes even further in this direction, finding models in studies of urban social life and the role of guilds and associations particularly in the Middle Ages and the modern era. He thus suggests, in his study of the documentation from the Greek East during the Roman Empire, that collegia created social identity. For instance, the collegia used funerary practices both to negotiate the status of individuals within the group and to promote a collective identity within the public sphere. Within the group, the hierarchy between different members, marked by the use of titles, may have been manifest in the organization of burial space as well, but evidence of it is rare in the archaeological record.[7] Possessing its own funerary monument or a place in the monument of a patron, as was sometimes the case, situated the collegium in the public sphere. Similarly, the responsibility for collecting funerary fines or for ensuring the commemoration of the dead designated the associations as fully integrated members of the social structure and also helped to articulate their role with other social groups.[8] Beside the funerary activities, participation of the *collegia* in banquets and public processions, as well as the assignment of reserved seats in theaters, amphitheaters and stadia, established their position in the ceremonial life of the cities and gave them a sense of civic importance.[9]

The social identity that membership in a collegium helped create in a society as strongly hierarchical as that of Greco-Roman times implied, therefore, some collective funerary practices: funerary processions, collective tombs, commemoration of the dead. Can we say, however, that these collective funerary practices construct a group identity that could lead to a conflict with the family? Actually, the collegium substituted for the family only in cases where there was none. The money to cover the funeral costs,

---

Berufs-, Kult—und Augustalen-Kollegien in Italien (Mainz: von Zabern, 1998), 27–31; and now Nicolas Tran, *Les membres des associations romaines: le rang social des collegiati en Italie et en Gaules sous le Haut-Empire,* Collection de l'Ecole française de Rome 367 (Rome: Ecole française de Rome, 2006).

6. See Commodianus's text quoted below regarding the importance of the procession.
7. Van Nijf, *The Civic World of Professional Associations in the Roman East,* 43–49.
8. Ibid., 55–68.
9. Ibid., 131 ff.

the *funeraticium,* was normally paid to the heir named by the deceased. In most cases, according to inscriptions, that meant a member of the immediate family.[10] Moreover, if a collegium possessed one, the communal funerary monument was open to members' families: that explains the presence of women in these tombs, despite their having been excluded from membership.[11] Membership in a collegium therefore does not seem to have been in itself a factor challenging the general practice we pointed out above: even for members of a collegium, typically the family was the natural community that looked after the burial of the dead.[12]

The idea that collegia were sought primarily for the funeral arrangements they provided must thus be carefully qualified. Accordingly, the collegia helped the plebs media to find its place in the social order of the city rather than constituting an institution that would compensate its members for their reduced participation in this social order. So the collegia did not constitute a model of communal burial that Christians could have copied. However, they certainly provided a model for Christians once Christians began to organize in groups. This model could lead, as we have just seen, to funeral practices of a collective nature.

Greco-Roman Associations and Christian Churches

In a comparison of Christian Churches and Greco-Roman associations, we must carefully distinguish between two propositions: one that saw in the analogy to associations a means of reconstructing what the early Christian organizations might have been like, and one that saw in associations, particularly so-called funerary collegia, the legal form used by the churches in order to grow and become property owners.

The analogy with Greco-Roman associations was primarily the work of scholars of the New Testament.[13] The approach that saw in the collegia a point of comparison for understanding the organization of early Christian

---

10. Examples in Waltzing, *Étude historique,* 4:523; see also 1:268–69.
11. Ibid., 1:277, 286 ff. See the case of Martialis's sons in Cyprian's letter, as noted above.
12. For an interesting discussion about the relationship between families and collegia, see Jonathan S. Perry, *A Death in the Familia: The Funerary Collegia of the Roman Empire* (PhD diss., University of North Carolina–Chapel Hill, 1999).
13. See *Voluntary Associations in the Graeco-Roman world,* ed. John S. Kloppenborg and Steven G. Wilson (London: Routledge, 1996), and its extensive bibliography; see esp. in that volume Wayne O. McCready, "Ekklesia and Voluntary Association," 59–73.

groups began with Carl Friedrich Georg Heinrici (1844–1915) and Edwin Hatch (1835–89) and has for a long time run up against the prejudice that refused to accept the idea of pagan origins for Christian institutions.[14] Today the comparison is a frequent and fruitful one, even though, on the whole, Christian churches shared only a small number of characteristics in common with the Greco-Roman associations and were quite different from them on a number of key points. Among these, it is important to note the exclusive character of the Christian cult, a much wider social recruiting base, and interregional links among the churches.[15] Thus Wayne A. Meeks has emphasized the differences among the churches described in the Epistles of Paul and the collegia, also pointing out that the very absence of any reference to the organization of Christian burials was enough to cast doubt on any direct identification.[16]

Marta Sordi, however, has recently proposed to identify a collegium as one of the domestic Roman churches mentioned by Paul.[17] Some twenty inscriptions, dating from the beginning of the second century, inform us of a collegium attached to the *domus* of Sergia Paulina and of its burial place located in the area of Piazza dei Navigatori in Rome. The designation of the collegium in some of these inscriptions—*collegium quod est in domo Sergiae Paulinae*—recalls the way in which Paul designates domestic churches in Rome—*ten kat'oikon auton ekklesian*—but also finds parallels in pagan epigraphy.[18] At least one inscription contains an explicitly pagan symbol,[19] which led Sordi to consider only inscriptions containing the formula *collegium quod*

---

14. See John S. Kloppenborg, "Edwin Hatch, Churches and *Collegia*," in *Origins and Method: Towards a New Understanding of Judaism and Christianity: Essays in Honour of John C. Hurd*, Journal for the Study of the New Testament, supplement series 86, ed. Bradley H. McLean (Sheffield: JSOT Press, 1993), 212–38.

15. For an attempt to lessen the differences between associations and churches on this particular point, see Richard S. Ascough, "Translocal Relationships among Voluntary Associations and Early Christianity," *Journal of Early Christian studies* 5, no. 2 (1997): 223–41.

16. Wayne A. Meeks, *The First Urban Christians: The Social World of the Apostle Paul* (New Haven, CT: Yale University Press, 2003), 77–80.

17. Marta Sordi and Maria Luisa Cavigiolo, "Un'antica 'chiesa domestica' di Roma? (Il *collegium quod est in domo Sergiae L. F. Paullinae*)," *Rivista di Storia della Chiesa in Italia* 25 (1971): 369–74. Maria Bonfioli and Silvio Panciera have reviewed all the inscriptions in two articles; See Bonfioli and Panciera, "Della cristianità del *collegium quod est in domo Sergiae Paullinae*," *Atti della Pontificia Academia Romana di Archeologia*, Rendiconti 44 (1971–72): 185–201; and "*In domo Sergiae Paullinae*. Nota Aggiuntiva," *Rendiconti* 45 (1972–1973): 137–138; they have concluded that it was a pagan collegium. Marta Sordi defends her interpretation in "Sergia Paulina e il suo *collegium*," *Rendiconti dell'Istituto Lombardo, Scienze e Lettere* 113 (1979): 14–20; see also Sordi, *I cristiani e l'Impero romano* (Milan: Jaca Book, 1984), 192–96, "I *collegia* romani e l'organizzazione ecclesiale."

18. See Bonfioli and Panciera, "Della cristianità," 196.

19. See inscription 21 in Bonfioli and Panciera, "*In domo*," 135; the dedication *Dis Maribus* can be found on most of these inscriptions, yet it also appears in some Christian inscriptions.

est in domo Sergiae Paulinae as belonging to a domestic church and to acknowledge that the same burial place was also used by non-Christian members of the Sergia Paulina *familia*. The only indication of Christianity for the family of the Sergi Pauli is the proconsul of Cyprus, Sergius Paulus, who was converted by Paul (Acts 13) and whose granddaughter was Sergia Paulina.[20] Through her husband, Cn. Cornelius Severus, she was also related to the family of the Acilii Glabriones, but the Christianity of the famous consul Manlius Acilius Glabrio, who was condemned to death by Domitian in 91, is not accepted anymore.[21] Given the weakness of the case, the identification proposed by Marta Sordi can be rejected definitively. However, the analogy between the associations of the great domus and the first churches is certainly a most productive one, since several collegia of this type are known and well documented.[22]

We also need to examine the position defended by Giovanni Battista De Rossi, who argued that churches adopted the status of funerary collegia in order to achieve legal status. More specifically, this hypothesis allowed him to resolve the question of the Christian cemeteries before ecclesiastical property was officially established.[23] The starting point of De Rossi's hypothesis is a passage from the *Apologeticum* in which Tertullian denies that Christians

---

20. Of Sergius Paulus, proconsul of Cyprus (*PIR¹* S 376), we actually know very little. A very fragmentary inscription in Cyprus (*IGR* 3.935) mentions a Quintus Sergius, but it is from Claudius's time. Is he the L. Sergius Paulus, curator of the Tiber between 42 and 47 (*CIL* 6.31545)? See Laura Boffo, *Iscrizioni greche e latine per lo studio della Bibbia*, Biblioteca di storia e storiografia dei tempi biblici 9 (Brescia: Paideia, 1994), 242–46. Marie-Thérèse Raepsaet-Charlier, *Prosopographie des femmes de l'ordre sénatorial (Ier-IIe siècle)* (Louvain: Peeters, 1987), 1:562–63 and vol. 2, stemma 2, claims that the two men are siblings and that therefore Sergia Paulina would be the niece of the proconsul converted by Paul. But the brick stamps published in Bonfioli and Panciera, "Della cristianità," 197, now establish that she is the granddaughter of the proconsul of Cyprus.

21. See Monique Dondin-Payre, *Exercice du pouvoir et continuité gentilice: les Acilii Glabriones du IIIe siècle av. J.-C. au Ve siècle ap. J.-C.*, Collection de l'École française de Rome 180 (Rome: École française de Rome, 1993), 205–10, 252–54. See also William H. C. Frend, *Martyrdom and Persecution in the Early Church: A Study of Conflict from the Maccabees to Donatus* (Oxford: Oxford University Press, 1965), 214–17.

22. See the very suggestive study by Bradley H. McLean, "The Agrippinilla Inscription: Religious Associations and Early Church Formation," in McLean, ed., *Origins and Method*, 239–70. For an inventory, see Waltzing, *Étude historique*, 4:153–76, and 1:263–64.

23. Giovanni Battista De Rossi, "Dei sepolcreti cristiani non sotterranei," *Bullettino di archeologia cristiana* 2 (1864): 25–32. See Giovanni Battista De Rossi, *La Roma sotterranea cristiana* (Rome: Cromo-litografia pontificia, 1864), 1:101–8. Louis Duchesne was the first to attack De Rossi's thesis, in his *Origines chrétiennes* (1878–1881); see Duchesne, *Histoire ancienne de l'Église* (Paris: Fontemoing, 1906–10), 1:381–87. An important refutation comes from Jean-Pierre Waltzing; see, in particular, "La thèse de J.-B. De Rossi sur les collèges funéraires chrétiens," *Bulletin de l'Académie royale de Belgique (Classe des lettres, etc.)* 6 (1912): 387–401, and *Dictionaire d'archéologie chrétienne et de liturgie*, s. v. "Collegia." For an account of the controversy after this initial sparring, see De Robertis, *Storia delle corporazioni*, 2:64, n. 1, which supports De Rossi's views.

are an illegal faction.[24] In the second part of his treatise, Tertullian defends Christians against charges of the crime of *majestas*. He had first stressed that Christians, even those who refused to sacrifice for the emperor, included him in their prayers to God, and now he wants to reject the label *factio illicita*. The term actually means "seditious association," and with it Tertullian alludes explicitly to the context of the *Lex Iulia* that banned *factiones* in order to avoid divisions at the heart of the city.[25] Associations were never safe from such charges. For instance, at Pompeii in 59, after the bloody incidents that occurred during gladiator fights at the amphitheater, not only were these spectacles outlawed for ten years, but the illegal collegia were dissolved.[26] These were the types of charges Tertullian challenged by pointing out that Christians avoided these spectacles and the potential excesses they occasioned.

According to De Rossi, Tertullian then wants to show that Christians constituted a legal collegium. It is pointless to repeat that it is necessary to drop the category of *collegia funeraticia,* but recently, and in connection with Christianity, another specific category of association, the *collegia religionis causa*, has been proposed. Francesco Maria de Robertis has suggested that the text of Marcianus previously mentioned is a résumé of the existing legislation on the *collegia tenuiorum*. There would be three elements: the *senatus-consultum* also present in the inscription of Lanuvium; a rescript of Septimius Severus extending the measure to Italy and the provinces; and another rescript of Septimius Severus ruling on the collegia religionis causa, which has also been preserved in some Byzantine scholia. De Robertis saw in the second rescript of Severus a refinement of existing legislation, since most collegia known from inscriptions involved religious activities.[27] Silvia Reseghetti suggests we see in this a different type of association: the *collegia religionis causa*, a category that would include the Christian associations described by Tertullian.[28] All these hypotheses actually try to do is to bring together with the legal categories what we know from the epigraphic record about the diverse activities of the collegia. However, once Mommsen's distinction between the collegia tenuiorum and collegia funeraticia is eliminated, these hypotheses become

---

24. Tertullian, *Apologeticum* 38–39. This kind of accusation is fully attested to: for instance, it is one of Celsus's main criticism of the Christians (Celsus, in Origen, *Against Celsus* 1.1 and 8.17).

25. Compare Tertullian, *Apologeticum* 38.2, with Suetonius, *Divus Augustus* 32. Tertullian refers to the same antifactions laws in *On Fasting* 13.5.

26. Tacitus, *Annals* 14.17.

27. De Robertis, *Storia delle corporazioni*, 1:308–9.

28. Silvia Reseghetti, "Il provvedimento di Settimio Severo sui collegia 'religionis causa' e i cristiani," *Rivista di Storia della Chiesa in Italia* 42 (1988): 357–64.

irrelevant; the single category of *collegia tenuiorum* suffices to explain the multiple facets of the life of Roman associations.

To return to Tertullian, did he wish to show, as De Rossi believed, that Christians, far from forming seditious factions, were simply using the laws allowing the collegia tenuiorum? If that were so, Tertullian would have mentioned the laws, as he does in other cases.[29] He describes, using the vocabulary of the associations, Christian practices that could recall those of the collegia: their meetings (*coetus, congregatio*), their president (*praesidere*), the collection of money (*honoraria, summa, arca*), but in each case he emphasizes the differences: Christians meet to pray, and not for banquets; honorary positions cannot be bought; and the money collected is used to help the poor, widows, and orphans—in short, those who are not contributors![30] In the eyes of Romans, such collegia would have lacked anything to make them attractive.

De Rossi's hypothesis, moreover, is useless given what we know about the relations of the church with imperial power. The edicts of the emperor Valerian, in 257, marked a decisive turning point in that they no longer attacked Christians as individuals, but the church as a hierarchy and an organization.[31] The emergence of the church from its clandestine status might actually date from the reign of Commodus (180–92) when his concubine Marcia asked Victor, the bishop of Rome, to give her the list of Christians deported in order to obtain their pardon from the emperor.[32] The knowledge Roman authorities had about the organization of the church after Commodus's reign thus makes recourse to a legal fiction like that of the collegia tenuiorum highly unlikely.[33]

One last case should be mentioned. According to the *Historia Augusta*, Christians and innkeepers conflicted in Rome over the use of a *locus publicus*, a public place, and the Emperor Severus Alexander intervened in favor of the former.[34] This passage is one of a series of six that combine to show Severus

---

29. In *Apologeticum*, Tertullian recalls, for instance, Pliny's letters to Trajan and alludes to antifactions laws. This is contra Reseghetti, "Il provvedimento di Settimio Severo," 362–63, which tries to establish close similarities with Septimius Severus's edict, recorded in *Digesta* 47.22.1. The internal critique of Tertullian's text is already Waltzing's best argument against De Rossi: see Waltzing, "La thèse de J.-B. De Rossi," and Jean-Pierre Waltzing, *L'Apologétique de Tertullian* (Louvain: Peeters, 1911).

30. Tertullian, *Apologeticum* 39.

31. See Marta Sordi, *I cristiani e l'Impero romano*, 117–27, and Paul Keretztes, *Imperial Rome and the Christians*, vol. 2, *From the Severi to Constantine the Great* (Lanham, MD: University Press of America, 1989), 67–81.

32. Sordi, *I cristiani e l'Impero romano*, 83–84, quoting Hippolytus, *Refutation of all heresies* 9.12.10.

33. The point was made already in Duchesne, *Histoire ancienne de l'Église*, 1:381–87.

34. Scriptores Historiae Augustae, *Severus Alexander* 49.6. See discussion and bibliography, Enrico dal Covolo, "Una '*domus ecclesiae*' a Roma sotto l'impero di Alessandro Severo?" *Ephemerides Liturgicae* 102 (1988): 64–71.

Alexander as a philo-Christian. This view is not specifically contradicted by what we know from other sources, but it is still difficult to determine the degree of authenticity of such passages. The *Historia Augusta* was written at the end of the fourth century, when paganism had been outlawed and itself fell victim to persecution. Hence, the tolerance attributed to Severus Alexander, model of the good emperor in the *Historia Augusta,* would serve as a lesson to the Christian emperors who were persecutors of paganism.[35] An anecdote that attributes a locus publicus to Christians thus assumes an entirely different meaning when viewed in the context of the expropriation of places once used by pagan cults.[36]

However, a number of historians have attempted to show that these passages were not without some historical basis. Santo Mazzarino recalled that public places were rented to collegia, as we know from other sources, and suggested that Severus Alexander's decision in favor of the Christians against the innkeepers made sense from an economic point of view, as the innkeepers were probably not solvent.[37] The nonsolvency of the innkeepers remains to be proven, but in any case Severus's decision was dictated, according to the *Historia Augusta,* by very different aims: "Alexander rendered the decision that it was better for some sort of a god to be worshipped there than for the place to be handed to the keepers of an eating-house."[38]

It is not enough that the anecdote seems true for it to have historical value, although it still has some documentary value. Marta Sordi, for her part, recalls that Hippolytus dedicated a treatise on the resurrection to Julia Mammaea, the mother of Severus Alexander, and that Julius Africanus dedicated the *Cestes* to Severus Alexander himself.[39] She also finds confirmation of Severus's philo-Christian leanings in the fact that philo-Judaism, also attributed to him by the *Historia Augusta,* was better documented.[40] Arnaldo Momigliano believed he had found external evidence corroborating the *Historia*

---

35. See Johannes Straub, *Heidnische Geschichtsapologetik in der christlichen Spätantike: Untersuchungen über Zeit und Tendenz der Historia Augusta,* Antiquitas 4, Beiträge zur Historia-Augusta-Forschung 1 (Bonn: Habelt, 1963), 190–91. See Cécile Bertrand-Dagenbach, *Alexandre Sévère et l'Historia Augusta,* Collection Latomus 208 (Brussels: Latomus, 1990), 186–88.

36. See Andreas Alföldi, "Der Rechtsstreit zwischen der römischen Kirche und dem Verein der Popinarii: (Ein Beitrag zur Beurteilung der 'Historia Augusta')," *Klio* 31 (1938): 252 [= *Studien zur Geschichte der Weltkrise des 3. Jahrhunderts nach Christus* (Darmstadt: Wissenschaftliche Buchgesellschaft, 1967), 431–35].

37. Santo Mazzarino, *Il pensiero storico classico,* 2 vols., Collezione storica (Bari: Laterza, 1968), 2:238.

38. Scriptores Historiae Augustae, *Severus Alexander* 49, 6.

39. See Sordi, *I Cristiani e l'Impero romano,* 99.

40. Marta Sordi, in *Storia di Roma,* vol. 9, *Il Cristianesimo e Roma* (Bologna: Cappelli, 1965), 239–46.

Augusta on this point. He thought that a Jewish inscription from Rome mentioned the "synagogue of Arca" and that, as Arca was the emperor's birthplace in Lebanon, Severus Alexander had built this synagogue for his compatriots and was its *archisynagogus* conforming to the title he is given in the *Historia Augusta*.[41] Harry J. Leon, however, showed that the inscription refers to no synagogue, but only to the city of Arca.[42] Severus's philo-Judaism is thus no better documented than is his philo-Christianity, and, as a result there is considerable doubt about the authenticity of the anecdotes in the *Historia Augusta*.

Even if it cannot be taken as proof of the philo-Christianity of Severus, does the passage about the locus publicus still have any documentary value because of its plausibility? We have seen that even the issue of the dispute between the Christians and the innkeepers was no doubt chosen quite intentionally; therefore, it would seem impossible to follow the speculation that located the locus publicus in the Trastevere.[43] Similarly, to deduce from the account in the *Historia Augusta* that Christians, like the innkeepers, were members of a collegium is simply unwarranted.

Therefore, we must reject once and for all the thesis that churches were officially organized as collegia in order to acquire a legal status in the empire, and particularly in order to administer their cemeteries.

❦ Christians and the Collegia

However, that leaves unanswered the question about the extent to which Christians did individually organize into collegia, or participate in existing collegia to which they may have belonged at the time of their conversion—in which case, as John Scheid quite correctly argues, their collective behavior would have been like those of all other inhabitants of the Greco-Roman world.[44] The question is rarely phrased in these terms, and yet there is no a priori reason for dismissing the possibility. One reason why the hypothesis has

---

41. Arnaldo Momigliano, "Severo Alessandro *archisynagogus*: una conferma alla *Historia Augusta*," *Athenaeum* 12 (1934): 151–53.

42. Harry J. Leon, *The Jews of Ancient Rome*, 1st ed., 1960, updated ed. by Carolyn A. Osiek (Peabody: Hendrickson, 1995), 163–65. His interpretation is followed by David Noy, in *Jewish Inscriptions of Western Europe*, vol. 2, 451–52.

43. See Dal Covolo, "Una '*domus ecclesiae*' a Roma," 70–71.

44. John Scheid, "Communauté et communauté: réflexions sur quelques ambiguïtés d'après l'exemple des thiases de l'Égypte romaine," in *Les communautés religieuses dans le monde gréco-romain. Essai de définition*, ed. Nicole Belayche and Simon C. Mimouni, Bibliothèque de l'École des Hautes Études, Sciences Religieuses 117 (Paris: Brepols, 2003), 61–74.

not been considered arises from some confusion between the church, churches, groups of Christians and Christian communities. At this point in our reflections, it might be helpful to try to refine the vocabulary somewhat.

Christian Groups and Communitas

Sociologists and anthropologists often use the term *community* quite vaguely to refer to "local groups"—in other words, groups belonging to a defined area, which itself is part of a larger unit: a neighborhood within a city, a city within a state, and so on. Community, in this sense, designates nothing more than "an area of common living." It is not possible to speak of Christian communities in this sense, because in antiquity, Christians did not have specific common areas, but shared their space with others. However, community may also have a more limited meaning, which does not mean that it is easy to define. Victor Turner noted that in 1955 an American scholar had been able to review ninety-four different definitions of this specific modality of social relationship. He himself suggested an approach to the concept that seems useful. He preferred to use the Latin word *communitas* to mark a distinction between this use and that of the word *community*, meaning an area of common living. The main characteristic of communitas is its contrast to structure. Turner defined two principal models of human relations. The first is of society as a "structured, differentiated, and often hierarchical system of politico-legal-economic positions with many types of evaluation, separating men in terms of 'more' or 'less.'" The second is of society as an "unstructured or rudimentarily structured and relatively undifferentiated *comitatus*, community, or even communion of equal individuals."[45] He then proposed a series of binary oppositions or discriminations that allow us to better perceive how communitas and structure function in reciprocity: homogeneity/heterogeneity; equality/inequality; anonymity/systems of nomenclature; absence of property/property; absence of status/status; sexual continence/sexuality; minimization of sex distinctions/maximization of sex distinctions; absence of rank/distinctions of rank; sacredness/secularity; suspension of kinship rights and obligations/kinship rights and obligations.[46] It is not necessary to lengthen the list or to comment on the different elements; simply enumerating them is enough to grasp what characterizes communitas as antistructure. Victor Turner followed up his analysis by observing that the spontaneity and immediacy of communitas, in stark

---

45. Victor Turner, *The Ritual Process: Structure and Anti-structure* (Chicago: Aldine, 1969), 96.
46. Ibid., 106.

contrast to structure, limits its sustainability and quickly leads to the creation of structure. He thus distinguished between three types of communitas: the existential, or spontaneous, communitas; the normative communitas in which "where, under the influence of time, the need to mobilize and organize resources, and the necessity for social control among the members of the group in pursuance of these goals, the existential *communitas* is organized into a perduring social system"; and finally, the ideological communitas, meaning "a variety of utopian models of societies based on an existential *communitas*."[47]

We return now to the groups formed by Christians. Their organization in the first century, as it can be described based on the Epistles of Paul, fills the criteria of a normative *communitas*. According to Wayne A. Meeks, the use of the terms *brother* and *sister,* the emphasis on loving each other, the role of the spirit and its gifts, set Christian groups apart from the highly structured and hierarchical Greco-Roman society that surrounded them. While these groups already had a certain level of organization, the communitas remained the basic principle of their organization. Their structuring was done on the model of the domus, a patron offering hospitality to other members of the group. Every group thus was structured independently while claiming for itself a kind of universality.[48] By the end of the second century, the emergence of a monarch-bishop and the resulting professionalization of the clergy meant that Christian groups and the ecclesiastical structure no longer coincide.[49] It would be wrong to say that the ideal of communitas disappeared entirely, but clearly that was no longer the organizing principle of the church. An indication of this evolution might be found in the use of the words *frater* and *fraternitas*.[50] According to the analyses of Hélène Pétré, in the second century fraternitas was undeniably recognized as a Christian characteristic, as we know from the attacks on it by the enemies of Christianity, such as Lucian, who railed against Christians "convinced that they were all brothers."[51] In the *Apologeticum,* Tertullian also defends the Christians against

---

47. Ibid., 132.
48. Meeks, *The First Urban Christians,* 84–107.
49. See Allen Brent, *Hippolytus and the Roman Church in the Third Century: Communities in Tension before the Emergence of a Monarch-Bishop,* Supplements to Vigiliae Christianae 31 (Leiden: Brill, 1995) and Gregor Schöllgen, *Die Anfänge der Professionalisierung des Klerus und das kirchliche Amt in der Syrischen Didaskalie,* Jahrbuch für Antike und Christentum, Ergänzungsband 26 (Münster: Aschendorff, 1998). See a review of the different issues in Alexandre Faivre, *Ordonner la fraternité: pouvoir d'innover et retour à l'ordre dans l'Église ancienne,* Histoire (Paris: Cerf, 1992).
50. See Hélène Pétré, *Caritas: étude sur le vocabulaire latin de la charité chrétienne,* Études et documents 22 (Louvain: Spicilegium Sacrum Lovaniense, 1948).
51. Lucian, *Peregrinus* 13.

such critics; for him, and it is still the case for Cyprian, the word *fraternitas*, beyond its moral and spiritual meaning, can refer specifically to the Christian groups. Pétré showed that such use disappeared after the middle of the third century, however, and that the term *frater* also lost its specificity.[52] She also showed how the precept "love thy neighbor" came to acquire an increasingly universalist exegesis.[53] In a half century, the feeling among Christian groups of belonging to a community had declined markedly. A century later, by roughly 350, almost nothing separated a Christian from his pagan counterpart in Roman society, as Robert Markus has written.[54]

This evolution, too briefly outlined, nevertheless shows that, beginning at the end of the second century when this study begins, it was becoming difficult to refer to a group of Christians as a community, even in the very narrow sense proposed by Victor Turner, because, although the ideal of communitas had not disappeared, it was no longer the organizing principle for Christian groups. Thus, there may have been some communities of Christians that were not necessarily Christian communities; in other words, the principle of communitas that governed their organization was not the result of shared religion, and we can assume that Christians participated in communities that included non-Christians. We will see that we can find some confirmation of these inferences in the evidence.

ℐ Christian Collegia, and Collegia of Christians

We must begin by noting the surprising silence of Christian texts concerning an aspect of social life so widespread in the empire. There are only two explicit references to collegia, both dealing with their funeral activities.[55] The first is Cyprian's letter about the Spanish bishop Martialis, who used a collegium for his son's funeral. Cyprian found this to be an aggravating circumstance added to the prior offense of having obtained a certificate of sacrifice. I have suggested above that Cyprian condemned the burial in the tomb of a pagan association owing to the participation in religious rites that

---

52. Pétré, *Caritas*, 118 ff. See Adolf von Harnack, *Die Mission und Ausbreitung des Christentums in den ersten drei Jahrhunderten* (Leipzig: Hinrichs, 1902), 417–19, which considers that *frater* stopped being used by the end of the second century.

53. Pétré, *Caritas*, 141 ff.

54. Robert A. Markus, *The End of Ancient Christianity* (Cambridge: Cambridge University Press, 1990), 27.

55. Bernhard Kötting, "Genossenschaft. Christlich," in *Reallexicon für Antike und Christentum* (Stuttgart: Hiersemann, 1978), 10:150, mentions the canons from the Council of Elvira about priestly collegia, but it is a different kind of associations.

it entailed, and not out of a principle of religious segregation of the dead. The second reference is found in one of the *Instructions* of Commodianus, probably composed in Africa around 250–60: eternal damnation, he warns, awaits those who use a collegium for funerals.[56] The excesses of funerals are morally condemned as proof of vanity unworthy of a Christian. These two texts prove that not all Christians considered their religious beliefs to be incompatible with membership in a collegium.

The dividing line between the sacred and the profane is quite naturally a source of tension. Already in the first century, Paul is confronted with the problem of meat offered in sacrifice, as we know from chapters 8 and 10 of the First Epistle to the Corinthians. In Corinth, some Christians believed that eating meat from a sacrifice was irrelevant because they knew that idols did not exist and that there is only one God (1 Cor. 8:4). For Paul, it was not simply a matter of knowing whether one should or should not eat the meat of a sacrifice, but to what extent it was possible to share a meal with pagans when the food that was served had certainly come from a sacrifice. Paul's answer, and the difficulty it poses for his interpreters, derived from the importance he gave to the interaction inherent in the consumption of food. He did not condemn the consumption of meat sacrifice as such and thus agreed with "those who know" among the Christians of Corinth, but he still recommended declining to share meals with pagans because those who were newly converted knew from experience that the meat came from a sacrifice; thus it offended them to eat food they knew to have been consecrated to idols (1 Cor. 8:7).[57] However, Paul says, it was permissible to buy meat sold in the market even if it was probably meat sacrifice (1 Cor. 10:25). Two "decrees" in Revelation show that John had confronted the same difficulties in applying principles that had not been thoroughly discussed: at Pergamum

---

56. Commodianus, *Instructions* 2.29.12–13. See Jean-Michel Poinsotte, "Commodien dit de Gaza," *Revue des études latines* 74 (1996): 270–81.

57. See Meeks, *The First Urban Christians,* 97–100; and Gerd Theissen, "Die Starken und die Schwaren in Korinth: soziologische Analyse eines theologischen Streites," *Evangelische Theologie* 35 (1975): 155–72, translated into English in *The Social Setting of Pauline Christianity: Essays on Corinth,* ed. John Howard Schütz (Philadelphia: Fortress Press, 1982), 121–43; and Peder Borgen, "'Yes,' 'No,' 'How Far?' The Participations of Jews and Christians in Pagan Cults," in *Early Christianity and Hellenistic Judaism* (Edinburgh: T and T Clark, 1996), 15–43, esp. 48–54, for the discussion about the notion of *syneidesis.* See also Derek Newton, *Deity and Diet: The Dilemma of Sacrificial Food at Corinth,* Journal for the Study of the New Testament, Supplement series 169 (Sheffield: Sheffield Academic Press, 1998). Mark Reasoner, *The Strong and the Weak: Romans 14:1–15:13 in Context,* Monograph series, Society for New Testament Studies 103 (Cambridge: Cambridge University Press, 1999) shows that Rom. 14:1–15, and esp. 13 does not depend on 1 Cor. 8–10 and therefore raises the question of meat consumption in the Roman communities.

and at Thyatira, Christians thought they could participate in pagan cults and still remain Christian.[58]

Contemporary Jewish sources, and in particular Philo of Alexandria, broached these questions of participation in pagan society in a much more thorough manner. Philo often mentions the associations, their festivals and banquets, but as a foil to describe Jewish gatherings: these passages may have been meant as warnings for his coreligionists.[59] More interesting is a passage from *De ebrietate* in which he comments on Deuteronomy 21:18–21. He summarizes the four accusations against the bad son: "disobedience, contentiousness, payment of contributions for riotous feasting and drunkenness" (*De ebrietate* 15). The third accusation quite unequivocally is a reference to dues for a collegium. Contrary to what one might expect, Philo does not denounce the membership in an association, but simply the bad activities it may entail: "As for contributions or club...possessions, prudence, such payments are praiseworthy and profitable; but when they are paid to obtain that supreme evil, folly, the practice is unprofitable and blameworthy" (*De ebrietate* 20). Philo seems to say that a Jew may belong to a (non-Jewish) association on condition, obviously, that he not join any activity contrary to Jewish Law.[60]

The same tensions are portrayed in Tertullian's *De idololatria*.[61] The date of this treatise is still debated, but it is no longer perceived as "Montanist" and thus extremist.[62] It is a reflection on the profane and the sacred, in the form of a series of responses to questions from Christians concerned about breaking social ties with non-Christians. The tone is clear from the

---

58. Revelation 2:12–14, 18–20. See Borgen, "'Yes,' 'No,' 'How far?'" 37–39; and Philip A. Harland, "Honouring the Emperor or Assailing the Beast: Participation in Civic Life among Associations (Jewish, Christian and Other) in Asia Minor and the Apocalypse of John," *Journal for the Study of the New Testament* 77 (2000): 99–121. See also Philip A. Harland, *Associations, Synagogues, and Congregations: Claiming a Place in Ancient Mediterranean Society* (Minneapolis: Fortress Press, 2003).

59. See the texts gathered in Torrey Seland, "Philo and the Clubs and Associations of Alexandria," in Kloppenborg and Wilson, eds., *Voluntary Associations in the Graeco-Roman World*, 114–17.

60. For this interpretation of Philo's passage, see Borgen, "'Yes,' 'No,' 'How far?'" 45–46; and Seland, "Philo and the clubs," 117–25.

61. For the exegesis of 1 Cor. 8 and 10, see John C. Brunt, "Rejected, Ignored, or Misunderstood? The Fate of Paul's Approach to the Problem of Food Offered to Idols in Early Christianity," *New Testament Studies* 31 (1985): 113–24. He notices that the commentators followed the "apostolic decree" of Act 15 that forbids any consumption of meat sacrifice.

62. See discussion and bibliography in Tertullian, *De Idololatria*, ed. Jan Hendrik Waszink and J. C. M. van Winden, Supplements to Vigiliae Christianae 1 (Leiden: Brill, 1987), 10–13, in which a dating close to 197 seems to be ascertained. See Marie Turcan, Introduction to *De spectaculis*, Sources chrétiennes 332 (Paris: Éditions du Cerf, 1986), 37–43. For an analysis of *On Idolatry* see Timothy D. Barnes, *Tertullian: A Historical and Literary Study* (Oxford: Clarendon Press, 1971), 96–100, esp. 99–100, which suggests that Tertullian speaks to a group of recent converts.

beginning: "Most people think idolatry exists only in the following cases: burning of incense, offering sacrifice, organizing a sacrificial feast, performing a religious act or the duty of a priest" (*De idololatria* 2.2). Such a limited definition is not acceptable to Tertullian. More interesting than his ideas about idolatry are the series of objections Tertullian finds it necessary to refute. This cannot be a simple rhetorical trick: it would be awkward to furnish arguments that run counter to his own teaching. Thus we learn indirectly that in Carthage at the beginning of the third century, Christians felt free to practice the profession of idol maker or astrologer, to teach classical literature and mythology, to sell incense to the temples.[63] Tertullian mentions that idol-makers were even found among the clergy (*De idololatria* 7.2–3). When he comes to traditional Roman religious festivals, Tertullian discusses not only cases of Christians who claim to be able to celebrate them together with pagans (*De idololatria* 13.2–14.5) but also those who celebrate the festivals on their own (*De idololatria* 14.6–15.11). In defense of their point of view, Christians cited Paul: "Just as I please everybody in everything" (1 Cor. 10:32–33); "Otherwise, you should have to go out of the world" (1 Cor. 5:10). Only private ceremonies were acceptable in the eyes of Tertullian (*De idololatria* 16.1–17.1): betrothals, weddings, *nominalia* (in which children are officially named) or the "white toga" ceremony (a rite of passage to adulthood for boys). It was not important that sacrifices were associated with these ceremonies—it sufficed simply to refrain from participating in them, because "one should consider the reasons that social duties are fulfilled" (*De idololatria* 16.2). Therefore, we must note that, far from living in isolation or in closed communities, Christians continued to participate in social life and thus to be in permanent contact with non-Christians. Tertullian does not address it, but Christians may well have thought it normal to continue their membership in an association while declining to participate in sacrifices.

It must be stressed that contrary to a widely held view, associations did not disappear during the fourth century. One can no longer make that argument based on the quasi-disappearance of inscriptions mentioning the collegia after the fourth century. That phenomenon must be considered in light of what we know about the general evolution in the number of inscriptions in the empire. As drawn by Stanislaw Mrozek, the general curve of chronological distribution of inscriptions shows that, after peaking around the year 250, the number of inscriptions fell at the end of the third century to the same level it reached under Tiberius. It is thus difficult to draw any conclusions based

---

63. Tertullian, *On Idolatry* 3 (idol maker), 9 (astrologer), teacher (10), incense dealer (11).

on the decreasing number of inscriptions.[64] Another explanation offered for the disappearance of collegia is their religious activity and hence their direct ties to pagan cults, which were soon to be forbidden in the empire. Scholars have thus stressed the parallelism between the disappearance of the collegia and the increasing number of Christians.[65] We have seen throughout this chapter that the religious activity of the collegia should not be singled out. Jean-Marie Salamito, in his study of the *dendrophori* in the Christian Empire, has even suggested that the law of 415 ordering confiscations targeted the revenues used for the cult exclusively and therefore did not necessarily imply the suppression of the common treasury: in particular, "the confiscation spared the funds destined for burial of the *collegiati*." He refutes quite convincingly the thesis of the suppression of the dendrophori and concludes that "the internal life of the associations of *dendrophori* was diminished, probably limited simply to a role in funerals."[66] Finally, De Robertis argued against the thesis of the disappearance of the collegia, citing the conservation of legislative documents concerning them in the *Digesta* and later in the *Basilica*.[67] In fact, it is the *Digesta* that has preserved for us the commentary of Marcianus on the Severan legislation on collegia (*Digesta* 47.22.1). One of the stated purposes for the publication of the *Digesta* was the elimination of obsolete laws (*CJ*, 1.17.1, Cont. *Deo auctore*). So we have no good reason to think that the collegia and their internal life, beyond strictly religious activities, undergo a change as the empire became Christian.[68] The presence of Christians in the collegia is also proven by the fact that the collegia quickly found new and powerful patrons in the bishops.[69]

---

64. See Stanislaw Mrozek, "À propos de la répartition chronologique des inscriptions latines sous le Haut-Empire," *Epigraphica* 35 (1973): 113–18 with the methodological remarks in Ramsay MacMullen, *Paganism in the Roman Empire* (New Haven, CT: Yale University Press, 1981), 184 and n. 493. See also Ian Morris, *Death-Ritual and Social Structure in Classical Antiquity*, Key Themes in Ancient History (Cambridge: Cambridge University Press, 1992), 167–68.

65. Anna Cafissi, "Contributo alla storia dei collegi romani: i *collegia funeraticia*," *Studi e ricerche dell'Istituto di Storia, Facoltà di Lettere e Filosofia, Università di Firenze* 2 (1983): 92. See Jean Gagé, *Les classes sociales dans l'Empire romain*, 2nd ed., Bibliothèque historique (Paris: Payot, 1971), 312–13, 319 ff.; Lelia Cracco Ruggini, "Le associazioni professionali nel mondo romano-byzantino," in *Artigianato e tecnica nella società dell'alto Medioevo occidentale*, Settimane internazionali di studio del Centro italiano di studi sull'Alto Medioevo 18 (Spoleto: Centro italiano di studi sull'Alto Medioevo, 1971), 80.

66. Jean-Marie Salamito, "Les dendrophores dans l'Empire chrétien: à propos de Code Théodosien, XIV, 8, 1 et XVI, 10, 20, 2," *Mélanges de l'École française de Rome. Antiquité* 99 (1987): 1015–16.

67. De Robertis, *Storia delle corporazioni*, 2:58–59.

68. Waltzing, *Étude historique*, 2:357–58, showed that the collegia kept their common funds; see De Robertis, *Storia delle corporazioni*, 2:66–168.

69. On this topic see Cracco Ruggini, "Le associazioni professionali nel mondo romano-byzantino," 166–71; Ramsay MacMullen, *Enemies of the Roman Order: Treason, Unrest, and Alienation in the Empire* (Cambridge, MA: Harvard University Press, 1966), 178 and n. 17; and Peter Brown,

For Jean-Pierre Waltzing, the collegia experienced a twofold development in the later empire: the professional associations were transformed into corporations in the service of the state (*corpora*), and the collegia tenuiorum disappeared, their charitable functions assumed by the church.[70] We have seen that the collegia should not be categorized according to their purpose, but considered as a global phenomenon. As for the *corpora* we now know that not all the professional associations became obligatory after the third century. That concerned only a few professions involved in the *annona*, the transportation and processing of supplies for imperial distribution in the two capitals. As Jean-Michel Carrié has written, "in fact, the entire field of professional life must be reexamined, ignoring the legal documents relative to the *corpora* involved in the *annona*."[71] The same would seem to be true for the life of the collegia generally during Late Antiquity.[72]

I will cite here only one example, but a particularly interesting one: an association of *mensores* in Rome. According to the hypothesis developed previously by Josef Wilpert and recently corrected and more solidly based by Philippe Pergola,[73] the association of the mensores was in fact the owner, in the second half of the fourth century, of a sector of the Catacomb of Domitilla. The *cubiculum*, mistakenly called the cubiculum of the *pistores*, or crypt of the Great Apostles, is famous for its series of paintings depicting the professional activities of its owners: according to Pergola, these were mensores, in charge of the controlling and the weighing grain for the annona. But more interesting still are the conclusions Pergola reached in his topographical analysis of the sector. He was able to show that this cubiculum, itself containing only four tombs, was actually the central part of a small homogeneous area, around which the whole sector was organized.

Power and Persuasion in the Late Antiquity: Towards a Christian Empire (Madison: University of Wisconsin Press, 1992), 143–45.

70. See Waltzing, *Étude historique*, 1:153–54 for a summary.

71. Jean-Michel Carrié and Aline Rousselle, *Nouvelle histoire de l'antiquité. 10, L'Empire romain en mutation: des Sévères à Constantin (192–337)*, Points. Histoire 221 (Paris: Seuil, 1999), 691; see also 687–92 for his argument deriving in part from Adrian Johan B. Sirks, *Food for Rome: The Legal Structure of the Transportation and Processing of Supplies for the Omperial Distributions in Rome and Constantinople,* Studia Amstelodamensia ad epigraphicam, ius antiquum et papyrologicam, pertinentia 31 (Amsterdam: Gieben, 1991).

72. This is mentioned in Jean-Michel Carrié, "Les associations professionnelles à l'époque tardive: entre *munus* et convivialité," in *Humana sapit: études d'Antiquité tardive offertes à Lellia Cracco Ruggini*, Bibliothèque de l'Antiquité tardive 3 (Turnhout: Brepols, 2002).

73. See Josef Wilpert, "Ein unbekanntes Gemälde aus der Katakombe der hl. Domitilla und die coemeterialen Fresken mit darstellungen aus dem realen Leben," *Römische Quartalschrift* 1 (1887): 20–41; and Philippe Pergola, "*Mensores frumentarii christiani* et annone à la fin de l'Antiquité (relecture d'un cycle de peintures)," *Rivista di archeologia cristiana* 66 (1990): 167–84. For the sector of the cubiculum of the mensores, see Pergola, *Les cimetières chrétiens de Rome*, 287–89.

By concluding with this example,[74] I wish to suggest that the Christians who seem to be grouped together in Roman catacombs were possibly grouped in the same manner as other members of the plebs media in the empire.[75] The argument based on numbers—several thousand tombs in the catacombs, whereas there were rarely more than a hundred members in the collegia[76]—collapses once we are ready to envision catacombs as composed of sectors or small units that were more or less independent of each other. This is a hypothesis that should be checked archaeologically.

The importance of associations in the social life of the empire can no longer be underestimated. They show that collective burial might reflect a choice unrelated to membership in a religious group. We also have seen that religion had little bearing on the choice of a burial place. The church would have been obliged to justify itself in imposing such a constraint on Christians. Moreover, the very idea of Christian isolation in Greco-Roman society depends to a great extent on the fact that Christian groups are studied as sects; this must be revised and, fortunately, that is beginning to happen. The history of the interaction of Christians and non-Christians remains to be studied in detail, but it is a good bet that the isolation of Christians is, like that of the Jews, the product of modern prejudice.

---

74. For more examples, see Éric Rebillard, "Les formes de l'assistance funéraire dans l'Empire romain et leur évolution dans l'Antiquité tardive," *Antiquité tardive* 7 (1999): 280–282.

75. John Bodel now arrives at similar conclusions in "From *Columbaria* to Catacombs: Collective Burial in Pagan and Christian Rome," in *Commemorating the Dead: Texts and Artifacts in Context, Studies of Roman, Jewish and Christian Burials,* ed. Laurie Brink and Deborah Green (Berlin: De Gruyter, 2008), 226–33. See also Alison C. Poe, *The Third-Century Mausoleum ("Hypogeum") of the Aurelii in Rome: Pagan or Mixed-Religion Collegium Tomb* (PhD diss., Brown University, 2007), esp. 124–36 for further suggestive evidence for Christian membership in Roman collegia.

76. See Hugo Brandenburg, "Überlegungen zu Ursprung und Entstehung der Katakomben Roms," in *Vivarium: Festschrift Theodor Klauser zum 90. Geburtstag,* Jahrbuch für Antike und Christentum. Ergänzungsband 11 (Münster: Aschendorff, 1984), 15.

CHAPTER 4

Violation of Tombs and Impiety
Funerary Practices and Religious Beliefs

As religion imposed no rules fixing the choice of burial place that might have conflicted with choices determined by kinship and family, it must now be asked whether burial itself was a religious necessity. It is very often said that Christians gave particular importance to burial owing to their belief in resurrection. The body had to be protected in anticipation of resurrection and therefore placement in a tomb was, if not indispensable for salvation, at least preferable. Augustine alone would have argued against such beliefs and wanted to impose a more spiritual understanding of the care for the dead.[1] To avoid a somewhat sterile discussion, one involving the interpretation of the same few texts that deal with the issue explicitly, I would like to follow the path suggested by John Scheid: "To escape the trap or impasse that we run into in embarking on a study that focuses on positive religious facts, the pious acts, we prefer to approach facts from a different angle, from the point of view of impiety. This unusual approach, studying piety by beginning with its opposite, can be very productive, because we are able to observe how our sources, so cold and silent when they are describing normal acts of piety, react violently when they confront religious offenses."[2]

---

1. For such a reading, see Yvette Duval, *Auprès des saints corps et âme: l'inhumation "ad sanctos" dans la chrétienté d'Orient et d'Occident du IIIe au VIIe siècle* (Paris: Études Augustiniennes, 1988), 3–21.
2. John Scheid, *Religion et piété à Rome* (Paris: Édition La Découverte, 1985), 22.

In a similar way I will attempt to outline the feelings and beliefs about burial by studying the discourse on tomb violations. By taking this approach I do not run the risk of studying Christian representations in isolation and thus will avoid a priori assumptions about their singularity.

Tomb Violation in Late Roman Law

In the archaic period, tombs and the bodies they held were protected both by religious and civil laws. Cicero's exposition in *De legibus* established a clear distinction between the two. Pontiffs determined the conditions for a tomb to become *res religiosa* and the rituals to be performed. It was also they who decided what was or was not compatible with the *religio sepulchrorum*, the rules regulating burial in the tomb; only they could authorize the transfer of a body or reparations of a tomb. And finally, they prescribed expiations when the religious rules were not respected. Civil law, on the other hand, prescribed the penalty in cases involving tomb violations. It thus seems that the *Twelve Tables* included the bans on the destruction of tombs and on the introduction of alien corpses into a tomb and set the penalty for these crimes.[3] It is important to emphasize the strict separation between pontifical law, which did not include the judicial penalty for tomb violations, and civil law. As Yan Thomas notes, "the law simplifies, rationalizes, and makes autonomous the criteria defined by religion."[4]

During the historical period, burial was regulated by the "Edict of the praetor." Tomb violations resulted in specific actions, because a tomb, as *res religiosa*, was excluded from legal transaction and thus was not protected by property laws. The action on tomb violation was a popular one since, in addition to the person who had the right to be buried in the tomb and the right to bury other dead in it, anyone else could bring charges. One fine was set for any damage to a tomb, all forms of which are defined in the *Digesta* (47.12.3).[5]

---

3. See Cicero, *De legibus* 46–57 for pontifical laws, and 58–68 for civil laws. The basic account remains Fernand de Visscher, *Le droit des tombeaux romains* (Milan: Giuffrè, 1963), 142–50; see also Arthur Darby Nock, "Tomb Violations and Pontifical Law," *Journal of Biblical Literature* 60 (1941): 88–95 (review of André Parrot, *Malédictions et violations de tombes* [Paris: Geuthner, 1939], reprinted in *Essays on Religion and the Ancient World*, ed. Zeph Stewart (Cambridge, MA: Harvard University Press, 1972), 2:527–33.

4. Yan Thomas, "*Corpus aut ossa aut cineres:* la chose religieuse et le commerce," *Micrologus* 7 (1999): 79. About those distinctions, see Scheid, "Le délit religieux dans la Rome tardo-républicaine," in *Le délit religieux dans la cité antique: Table ronde, Rome, 6–7 avril 1978*, Collection de l'École française de Rome 48 (Rome: École française de Rome, 1981), 117–71, esp. 135–37, about burial desecration.

5. See Visscher, *Le droit des tombeaux romains*, 139–42. The text of the edict can be reconstructed from Ulpian's commentary, of which large passages are kept in the *Digesta* (47.12: *de sepulchro*

Two important developments characterize the laws on tomb violation in the imperial period: tomb violation became a public offense (*crimen*) and profanation of cadavers a specific crime. The second of these developments took place during Late Antiquity and thus raises the question of the influence of Christianity.

Laesae Religionis Crimen

Traditionally it has been thought that tomb violation did not become a public offense (*crimen*) until the time of Septimius Severus who, according to the *Digesta* (47.12.3.7), made it punishable by death. Fernand de Visscher has opposed this view, and introduced a distinction between damage to the tomb and damage to the body, with the latter being a public offense since Augustus.[6] However, Thomas has recently argued that the body was not protected as such by the law until after the turn of the fourth century.[7] A new interpretation of the controversial "Edict of Nazareth" has also revived the question by suggesting that it is an edict of Augustus and that therefore it had universal validity.[8] It is not for me to settle such questions, but we must acknowledge the issues in order to analyze properly late imperial legislation.

The text commonly called the "Edict of Nazareth" is a Greek inscription, first brought to the attention of historians in 1930 by Franz Cumont and debated ever since in the context of laws on tomb violation. Here is a translation:

> Edict of Caesar
>
> It is my pleasure that graves and tombs which anyone has prepared as a pious service for forebears, children, or members of his household are to remain forever unmolested. But if any person shows that another either has destroyed them, or in any other way has cast forth the persons buried there, or with malicious deception has transferred the bodies elsewhere to the dishonor of the dead, or has removed the inscribed or other stones, I command an action to be instituted against such person, protecting the pious services of men, just as if they were concerned with the gods. For it shall be by far more proper to do honor to the dead. No one whatsoever shall be permitted to remove them. If anyone

---

violato). See O. Lenel, *Das Edictum perpetuum: ein Versuch zu seiner Wiederherstellung,* 3rd ed., (Aalen: Scientia Antiquariat, 1956), 228 for a reconstitution.

6. Visscher, *Le droit des tombeaux romains,* 150–53.
7. Thomas, *Corpus aut ossa aut cineres,* 95–96, 103.
8. Adalberto Giovannini and Marguerite Hirt, "L'inscription de Nazareth: nouvelle interprétation," *Zeitschrift für Papyrologie und Epigraphik* 124 (1999): 119–20.

60 CHAPTER FOUR

does so, however, it is my will that he shall suffer capital punishment on the charge of desecration of graves.[9]

The precise provenance of this text is not known: the inscription was sent from Nazareth to Wilhelm Fröhner, the collector who gave it to the Cabinet des Médailles in Paris; it was probably carved in the province of Syria-Palestine, or possibly in Asia. It contains nothing that dates it precisely, but a date from the reign of Augustus or at the latest from that of Nero is generally accepted. The nature of the text, and thus its validity, are subject to much debate. The punishment declared in the last line is most problematic: capital punishment is to be applied to a crime that, until then, had been considered a private offense and was, as a result, punishable by a simple fine.[10] An early hypothesis restricted its importance considerably. Cumont basically considered it a rescript—in other words, the emperor's reply about an individual case, which means that it was to be applied only to this individual case. Cumont also suggests that the circumstance for the rescript might well have been the resurrection of Christ, on the basis of what is said in the Gospel of Matthew (28:12–15), that Christians were accused of having taken the body from the tomb. A number of historians have rushed to embrace this view.[11] De Visscher proposed a variation on this hypothesis, one that is not widely held: the inscription, carved on the tomb as a protection, repeated an imperial rescript in its first part, then added the threat of a punishment decided by the tomb's founder. In that case, the inscription loses all importance in the history of legislation on tomb violations.[12] A second hypothesis, recently supported in two articles with very different conclusions, held that it was indeed an edict, hence a text with widespread application. Erhard Grzybek and Marta Sordi interpret it as an edict of Nero denouncing the robbing of Christ's body by Christians and threatening to punish by death any new crime of that type.[13] This hypothesis as the one defended by Cumont is ingenious, but weak.

---

9. "Edict of Nazareth," trans. Clyde Pharr, in *Ancient Roman Statutes,* ed. Clyde Pharr (Austin: University of Texas Press, 1961), 133.

10. I cannot mention here all the problems raised by the text. For a description of the different thesis, see Giovannini and Hirt, "L'inscription de Nazareth"; and Laura Boffo, *Iscrizioni greche e latine per lo studio della Bibbia,* Biblioteca di storia e storiografia dei tempi biblici 9 (Brescia: Paideia, 1994), 319–33.

11. Franz Cumont, "Un rescrit impérial sur la violation de sépulture," *Revue historique* 163 (1930): 241–66. See also Boffo, *Iscrizioni,* 328, for a list of historians who followed Cumont's suggestion.

12. Fernand de Visscher, "L'inscription funéraire dite de Nazareth," *Revue internationale des droits de l'antiquité* 2 (1953): 285–321, reprinted in *Le droit des tombeaux romains,* 161–95.

13. Erhard Grzybek and Marta Sordi, "L'Édit de Nazareth et la politique de Néron à l'égard des chrétiens," *Zeitschrift für Papyrologie und Epigraphik* 120 (1998): 279–91.

The thesis defended by Adalberto Giovannini and Marguerite Hirt is much less costly: the edict is attributed to Augustus and placed in the context of his policy of reestablishing moral and religious standards. In the first part, the edict concerns punishment of past acts, and claims for them more severe penalties than were currently in use; after the "For," the verbs are in the future and indicate therefore what ought to be, in the future, the punishment for such a crime.[14]

If we accept this new interpretation, we must date to the time of Augustus the moment when tomb violation became a crime, and was judged under the new procedure of the *cognitiones extra ordinem*. This procedure, in which the emperor or one of his officers exercised direct judicial authority, slowly replaced earlier procedural practices under the Roman Empire. Among the offenses annexed to the new procedure, all matters of public interest and those related to sacred rites, seemed to have particular importance. So it should not be surprising to find that laws about graves were, at a very early stage, included among them.[15] In any case, we know that tomb violation was a public offense from the reign of Septimius Severus, and a law of Gordian, from 240 and retained in the Justinian Code (9.19.1), qualified it as "a crime against religion." That the tomb violation qualified as a public offense is an important indication of the status of the dead in Roman society.

❦ *Violatio Sepulcri* and the Profanation of Cadavers

Using the testimony of Macer, a jurist from the beginning of the third century, Visscher has determined that damage to the body, as opposed to damage to the tomb, became a public offense as early as the first century: "The offense of violating a tomb can be said to come under the *lex Iulia de vi publica*, falling within that part of the statute wherein it is provided that nothing shall be done to prevent a person being buried and entombed; for one who violates a tomb does prevent the occupant from being entombed" (*Digesta* 47.12.8). As Visscher has noted, the jurist stated clearly that that is a "broad interpretation, one pushed to the limit of the law."[16] We cannot therefore rule out the possibility that this interpretation reflects jurisprudence of the third

---

14. Giovannini and Hirt, "L'inscription de Nazareth."
15. For a summary, see Ignazio Butti, "La 'cognitio extra ordinem': da Augusto a Diocleziano," in *Aufstieg und Niedergang der römischen Welt: (ANRW): Geschichte und Kultur Roms im Spiegel der neueren Forschung. 2, Principat. 14, Recht* (Berlin: De Gruyter, 1982), 29–59, and Max Kaser, *Handbuch der Altertumswissenschaft. 10, Rechtsgeschichte des Altertums. 3, 4, Das römische Zivilprozessrecht*, 2nd ed. by Karl Hackl (München: Beck, 1996), 451, 458–59, for the law regarding burial.
16. Visscher, *Le droit des tombeaux romains*, 152.

century. Whether it does or not, Augustus's law *de vi publica*—defining when the use of violence (*vis*) constitutes a crime against the state—does have a clause on the correct celebration of funeral rites as attested in Marcianus (*Digesta* 48.6.5 pr.), another jurist of the third century, and in the contemporary collection of the *Opinions of Paul* (5.26.3), but nothing about the protection of tombs or about bodies held in them. For Thomas, it is important to distinguish between "a direct damage to [the bodies]" and "an interruption of the process of burying them."[17] The body, as such, does not have greater legal standing once it is buried than it did during the burial process. It is the tomb the law protects by ensuring the burial of the body, since that is the legal condition for the tomb to become res religiosa. The law also ensures that the body remain buried, for exhumation would terminate the status of res religiosa. Exhumation was forbidden only in as much as it abolished the special status of the tomb, and not because of the pollution it brought to the living or for the offense done to the dead. Thomas insists on the separation between institutions and beliefs: "in Rome, the Law and laws were in no way a reflection of taboos."[18] Even pontifical law does not enjoin an *expiation* except in the case of *locus religiosus:* the exhumation of illegally buried bodies, either because they were buried in a public place, or because they were buried without the consent of the owner of the place, is not cause for expiation.[19] Thomas's evidence is convincing and we can only regret that he stops his analysis with the turn of the fourth century at a time when the profanation of cadavers as such begins to be punished.

The first law to protect the body specifically from profanation of any kind of damage is contained in the collection *Opinions of Paul*. This collection of opinions attributed to Paul, the great Roman jurist who worked between 170 and 230, was probably compiled in Africa around 295.[20] One law, from 327 or 328, preserved in the *Theodosian Code* (1.4.2), grants full authority to these opinions: they are thus valid evidence of the law between the end of the third century and the beginning of the fourth. One of the first opinions defines the crime of tomb violation in a traditional way as damage to the tomb and punishes it, according to the individual's status, with exile to an island or deportation to the mines (1.21.5). Other opinions specified what type of damages were punished: opening of a tomb, with or without

---

17. Thomas, *Corpus aut ossa aut cineres*, 97.
18. Ibid., 97–98.
19. See Thomas, *Corpus aut ossa aut cineres*, 99–101.
20. See *Nouvelle histoire de la littérature latine. 5, Restauration et renouveau: la littérature latine de 284 à 374 après J.-C.*, ed. Reinhart Herzog, trans. Gérard Nauroy (Turnhout: Brepols, 1993), 73–74.

breaking in, in order to introduce the body of a stranger; vandalizing inscriptions, damaging statues, stealing columns and other materials (1.21.8); introducing a body without authorization (1.21.9). Another opinion in the same chapter protects the body specifically, stating, "Anyone who strips a body permanently buried, or which has been deposited temporarily in some place, and exposes it to the rays of the sun, commits a crime, and therefore, if he is of superior station he is usually sentenced to deportation to an island, and if he is of inferior rank, he is condemned to the mines (1.21.4)." Noticeable here is the use of the religious term *piaculum* for a crime, a term which was not found in previous legal texts. As the emperor is also *pontifex maximus* the distinction between religious law and civil law is irrelevant. The opinion does not qualify this crime as tomb violation (it even applies to a temporary deposition), but subjects it to the same penalty. Another opinion (5.19a) also preserved in the *Digesta* (47.12.11), this time qualifies the act of unearthing a body or stealing bones as tomb violation and imposes the death penalty for persons of inferior status (*humiliores*).

Thus, by the end of the third century, damages to human remains were fully considered as a crime; the law did not subsume them under the sole protection of the tomb. Yet it seems difficult to explain this development or to connect it to any specific circumstance. Imperial constitutions of the fourth and fifth centuries, which are slightly more explicit about the principles they wish to establish, will allow us to make a few hypotheses.

Imperial Constitutions of the Fourth and Fifth Centuries

One full section of the *Theodosian Code* (9.17) is devoted to tomb violations. A constitution (9.17.1), issued by Constantius to the prefect of the city on June 25, 340, has no statement of principle and simply defines the penalties that apply in cases of destruction of a tomb: the law is aimed at the pillaging of marble and other precious elements for reuse. The penalties are the same as those in the *Opinions of Paul:* deportation to the mines or exile on an island. A second constitution (9.17.2), again by Constantius and addressed to the Praetorian prefect in 349, rescinds the severity of the penalty and reduces it to a fine. The purchasers of stolen material are punished by the same penalty as those who despoil monuments, "for if it is contrary to divine law (*nefas*) for anything to be touched, it cannot be purchased without pollution." The vocabulary of a religious offense reappears with words such as *piaculum* and *nefas*. Moreover, it was still the pontiffs alone, both in Rome and the provinces, who had the authority to determine the expiations.

A constitution in 356 (9.17.3), bearing the names of Constantius and of Julian Caesar and that again addresses only the question of the demolition of tombs and the reuse of materials, seems to revert to the earlier penalties. This may have been simply a temporary measure: that constitution is not found in the Code of Justinian. However, that same year, or the next, the same individuals offered a constitution at Milan (9.17.4) that was more specific:

> Those persons who violate the habitations of the shades, the homes, so to speak, of the dead, appear to perpetrate a twofold crime. For they both despoil the buried dead by the destruction of the tombs, and they contaminate the living by the use of this material in building. If any person, therefore, should take away from a tomb, stones or marbles or columns or any other material for the purpose of building or if he should do this for the purpose of selling such material, he shall be compelled to pay ten pounds of gold to the fisc.

This is followed by considerations on different ways of prosecuting the guilty, and the law adds, "this penalty is added to the severity of the ancient laws, for nothing has been derogated from that punishment which is known to have been imposed on violators of tombs. Moreover, those persons also who disturb buried bodies or the remains of the dead shall be subject to the same penalty." As Visscher has suggested, only the profanation of cadavers is considered a tomb violation in this law and to the former penalties that punished it is now added the fine that punishes the material damage to the tomb.[21] What motivates the law is clearly stated here: the destruction of the tomb, as well as the profanation of its cadaver, is an offense against the dead. In contrast to classical law as Thomas interprets it, beliefs here are blurred with the institutions. Not only must the dead be protected, but the living must be protected against contact with them. Let us note also that the allusion to the *Manes* did not bother the compilers of the *Theodosian Code,* whereas the compilers of the *Digesta* carefully avoided it. This law has sometimes been attributed to Julian, who was associated with Constantius as Caesar, and presented as a forerunner of the edict of Antioch on funerals and burial.

This edict, as it has been preserved in the *Theodosian Code* (9.17.5), includes two parts: the first concerns tomb violations, while the second concerns the

---

21. Visscher, *Le droit des tombeaux romains,* 156.

ban on diurnal funerals. A Greek text, published today among the *Letters* of Julian, would be the original edict of which the *Theodosian Code* provides only a summary.[22] Julian alluded to ancient laws (*maiores*) that considered tomb violation a sacrilege. The ban on "disturbing the earth or tearing up the sod" has an archaic ring and evokes a tomb that is a simple earthen mound. The allusion to the looting of tombs to decorate dining rooms and porticos reminds us however of the concerns expressed in earlier imperial constitutions. Julian means to restore the very earliest Roman customs regarding funerals, according to the first lines of the Greek text. In the second part, the emperor also evokes the ideas of impurity and pollution connected with cadavers. However, the state of preservation of the documents does not allow us to confirm positively that the recalling of the current laws against tomb violations followed the reasons developed for the ban on diurnal funerals. There is no mention of the profanation of cadavers in the summary preserved in the *Theodosian Code*, but to remove them or to come into contact with them constituted the same type of pollution. What do such notions owe to strict Neoplatonic orthodoxy? The question should be asked, for it also raises another about the singularity of the edict of Julian. Joseph Bidez has stressed that Julian's horror at the pollution associated with cadavers echoes through other passages of his work and in Neoplatonic theories.[23] However, Rowland Smith is justifiably cautious about a view of Julian as a fanatical theurgist and about overinterpreting measures he took as emperor. It seems that avoiding pollution owes at least as much to traditional religious practices as it does to theurgy and purification rites.[24] Similarly, Christians do not seem to be the direct target of such a law, contrary to what has sometimes been said.[25] Its conservation, even as a summary, in the *Theodosian Code* is an indirect confirmation of that.

The last two constitutions that have been preserved do, however, concern Christians. The first (9.17.6), adopted by Gratian, Valentinian, and Theodosius

---

22. Julian, *Epistulae*, 136. For the relationship between the two texts, see Julian, *Œuvres complètes. 1, 2, Lettres et fragments*, ed. Joseph Bidez, Collection des universités de France (Paris: Les Belles Lettres, 1960), 131.

23. Ibid., 129–30. See Joseph Bidez, *La vie de l'empereur Julien*, Collection d'études anciennes (Paris: Les Belles Lettres, 1930), 297–98.

24. Rowland B. E. Smith, *Julian's Gods: Religion and Philosophy in the Thought and Action of Julian the Apostat* (London: Routledge, 1995), 111–13.

25. This is contra Bidez, in Julian, *Œuvres complètes.* 1, 2, 130–31. The Greek text does not mention the Christians and the law applies to everyone. In the fourth century, neither Christians nor non-Christians engaged in night burials. The customs Julian wants to impose are not attested since the beginning of the republic. See the commentary in Cumont, "Un rescrit impérial sur la violation de sépulture," 258–59.

in 381, signals that the law against inhumation within the city limits is also valid in the case of a martyr: it does not deal strictly with tomb violation. The second (9.17.7) given by the same emperors in 386, begins by forbidding the transfer of any buried body, the dismembering of martyrs, and the sale of relics,[26] then creates an exception to the law on tomb violation: in the case of a martyr, it is permissible to embellish a tomb in order to prepare it for the cult.

Another legal text addresses tomb violation: the Novel 23 of Valentinian III, dated to March 13, 447. The law seems to be directed against the activities of the clergy around the tombs of martyrs.[27] In a long preamble,[28] the emperor exposes, in terms he presents as commonly accepted ("For who does not know that…" he begins), the reasons for the severity of the laws against tomb violation and the profanation of cadavers. He invokes both Christianity and traditional wisdom, in other words, Roman legal and religious tradition:

> For we know, and our faith is not vain, that souls which have been freed from their bodies have sensation and that the celestial spirit returns to its original source. This fact is made clear by the ancient books of wisdom, by the mysteries of the religion which we venerate and worship. Although the divine spirit does not undergo the necessity of death, still the souls love the abode of the bodies which they have left, and for some kind of mysterious reason, they rejoice in the honor of their tomb. So great concern for such tombs remains throughout all times that we see the precious minerals of the mountains transferred to such uses at an excessive expense and ponderous masses erected, even though the patrimony suffers thereby. Certainly, the intelligence of prudent men would refuse such actions if they believed that there was nothing after death. It is an excessively barbarous and insane cruelty to begrudge this last service to those who are deprived of the light of life and to destroy their tombs by an inexpiable crime and thus reveal the remains of their buried bodies to the heavens.

---

26. Jill Harries, "Death and the Dead in the Late Roman West," in *Death in Towns: Urban Responses to the Dying and the Dead, 100–1600*, ed. Steven Bassett (Leicester: Leicester University Press, 1992), 63, proposes the hypothesis that the law is an answer to the scandal provoked by the "invention" of Gervasius and Protasius by Ambrose of Milan.

27. See Harries, "Death and the Dead in the Late Roman West," 64.

28. This law, posterior to the Theodosian compilation, came to us in its complete version, with all its circumstantial elements, unlike the laws we previously analyzed. About the work of compiling the *Code*, see John F. Matthews, *Laying Down the Law: A Study of the Theodosian Code* (New Haven, CT: Yale University Press, 2000).

The language Valentinian uses has parallels in the pagan tradition as well as in Christian teaching.[29] The condemnation of impiety is here indeed an occasion for confirming certain principles: souls, though separated from their bodies, are aware of the body's fate, and in particular of the fact that it has a tomb. This edict offers even an attempt at a positive justification of the honors given the dead: the belief that there is something after death. It is a possible allusion to resurrection, but in itself that does not constitute, in Valentinian's eyes, a particular reason for caring for the body of the deceased. However, the place Valentinian reserves for the body is noticeable: all the damages against funeral monuments are directly aimed at the body. Such a position is very different from traditional law that took into account only the ownership of goods.

The repetition of these laws has been interpreted as proof of a growing sense of insecurity in Late Antiquity and also a growing number of tomb violations, as well as an indication of the impotence of the imperial power to stop them. However, repetition of laws cannot always be looked at as the failure or inefficacy of previous laws: above all such repetition proves that the laws remain in effect. These laws are often actually the response to a request for confirmation of previous laws.[30] In the case of tomb violations, the new severity of the punishments and the definition of a specific crime of profanation of the cadavers suffice to explain the repetition of these laws and the increasing justifications offered.

The rising of the cult of martyrs and relics, and the exhumation and dismemberment of the bodies of martyrs that thus became common practice, cannot alone explain the defining of a new crime of profanation of the cadavers, or the repeated measures against tomb violations, even though these activities aroused an undeniable reaction and led to statements or reminders of principles.[31] The laws that have been preserved mention martyrs very rarely: before the Novel of Valentinian, only the constitution of 386 contains any explicit reference. The measure contained in it was a rather positive one, for it even authorizes improvements that modified the material structure

---

29. See the philological commentary in Karl Leo Noethlichs, "Spätantike Jenseitsvorstellungen im Spiegel des staatlichen Gräberschutzes: zur Novelle 23 Kaiser Valentinians III," in *Jenseitsvorstellungen in Antike und Christentum: Gedenkschrift für Alfred Stuiber* (Münster: Aschendorff, 1982), 47–54.

30. See the analysis and examples in Jill Harries, *Law and Empire in Late Antiquity* (Cambridge: Cambridge University Press, 1998), 82 ff.

31. This is contra Visscher, *Le droit des tombeaux romains*, 157; see Nicole Herrmann-Mascard, *Les reliques des saints: formation coutumière d'un droit*, Collection d'histoire institutionnelle et sociale 6 (Paris: Klincksieck, 1975), 28–32. See also Harries, "Death and the Dead in the Late Roman West," 62–65.

of the tomb. Valentinian was trying only indirectly to protect the bodies of martyrs. He was above all denouncing the pollution attached to the profanation of a cadaver and the contamination that resulted from it in the celebration of Christian mysteries.[32] Although practices linked to the martyr cults and to their relics provoked a legislative reaction, imperial constitutions show no direct Christian influence in the justifications offered for the severity of the laws against tomb violation.

The Church and Violators of Tombs

What was the attitude of the church toward tomb violators? What was the response of the church, as an institution, to the crime? There must have been rules about the fate reserved for tomb violators when they came to church: what was the appropriate penance imposed upon them before admitting them back into Communion? We notice two things: this crime is rarely mentioned in the abundant documentation that has come down to us and, when it is, it is usually in reference to civil laws.

The first penitential canons regarding tomb violators were issued by Basil of Cesaerea (c. 329–79) and by Gregory of Nyssa (c. 335–94). Basil stipulated denying tomb violators Communion for ten years. Gregory of Nyssa, however, repeated the distinction present in civil laws between damage to tombs and damage to the body:

> a. Grave-robbing is divided into what is pardonable and what is not pardonable. If someone spares what deserves respect and leaves the interred body intact, so that the shame of our nature is not exposed to the sun, and only makes use of stones from the facing of the tomb in order to build something else, this is of course not commendable. Custom however treats it as pardonable, and when the material has been transferred to something more important and of common benefit.
>
> b. But raking through the ash of the body returned to dust and shifting the bones in the hope of finding some valuable buried along with them, this is condemned with the same sentence as simple fornication, according to the distinction set out in the foregoing discussion. The dispenser of course may shorten the time of the penalty fixed in the canons if he observes from his life the healing of the one undergoing treatment.[33]

---

32. *Novellae Valentiniani* 23.1. See the same preoccupation in Gregory Nazianzen, *Epitaphia* 196.
33. Greek Penitential literature is gathered in Petros-Perikles Joannou, *Discipline générale antique. 2, Les canons des pères grecs (IVe–IXe s.)*, Fonti/Pontificia commissione per la redazione del codice

The reference to civil laws is not explicit, but, other than the distinction already mentioned, we must notice the evocation of the sun, a traditional image in legal language to indicate that human remains have been exhumed. As is the case in civil law, Gregory means to punish more severely those who damage the body. He excuses, however, the damage to funeral monuments; the clause on reuse that he adds is incomplete, for there is no provision about damages made for purely private reasons. Whereas the penitential legislation is in general extremely repetitive, neither the canon of Basil nor that of Gregory is found in later Eastern collections.[34]

In the West, penitential texts dealing with tomb violation are relatively late. A letter from Pope John II (532–35) reports that, according to the Council of Marseille, in 533, tomb violators must be excommunicated: "As for tomb violators, even though they are condemned to death by the august emperors, they must be deprived of the communion of the church if they should survive this crime, because participation in the Christian community is forbidden to those who, from bold audacity, have dared to deprive of their peace the remains of those who were buried."[35] It is interesting to note that their punishment is normally left to the civil power and to find in such a text the notion of the peace of the dead also present in the *Novel* of Valentinian III. At the Council of Mâcon, in 585, the authority of the civil laws still prevailed; as we read in canon 17, "We notice that many have opened the tombs of the dead whose bodies have not yet decomposed in order to add their own dead or those of others. It is forbidden to use religious places for the dead without at least the agreement of the owner of the tombs. This is why we rule that no one should do so. If it should happen, then by the authority of the law, the added bodies will be removed from those tombs."[36] The council added nothing to the Roman legal concepts of *locus religiosus* and *ius sepulchri*, but the bishops were now in charge of the enforcement of the secular law.[37]

---

di diritto canonico orientale 9 (Grottaferrata: Tipografia Italo-Orientale S. Nilo, 1962). For Basil, see canon 66.148, from the third letter to Amphilochus on canons (= *Ep. 217*). For Gregory of Nyssa, see *Epistola canonica* 7, in Gregory of Nyssa, *The Letters*, ed. Anna M. Silvas, Supplements to Vigiliae Christianae 83 (Leiden: Brill, 2007), 224–25.

34. See Petros-Perikles Joannou, *Discipline générale antique. 3, Index analytique aux CCO, CSP, CPG*, Fonti/Pontificia commissione per la redazione del codice di diritto canonico orientale 9 (Grottaferrata: Tipografia Italo-Orientale S. Nilo, 1964), for Greek penitential canons until the ninth century.

35. Pope John, *Letters* 3 (ed. C. de Clercq, *Concilia Galliae. A. 511-a.695*, Corpus Christianorum. Series Latina 148A, Turnhout: Brepols, 1963, 95).

36. Council of Mâcon, canon 17 (ed. C. de Clercq, 246).

37. See Friedrich Prinz, "Die Bischöfliche Stadtherrschaft im Frankenreich vom 5. bis zum 7. Jahrhundert," *Historische Zeitschrift* 217 (1974): 1–35; Ian N. Wood, *The Merovingian Kingdoms, 450–751* (London: Longman, 1993), 75–77. See also Peter Brown, *The Rise of Western Christendom: Triumph and Diversity, 200–1000 A.D.*, 2nd ed. (Oxford: Blackwell, 2003), chapter 6, for the context.

It is in this same context that we must interpret the account by Sidonius Apollinaris of the violation of the tomb of his grandfather in 469. When he arrived at Clermont by the road from Lyons, Sidonius saw grave diggers engaged in work at the site of his grandfather's grave: "The field of burial itself had for a long time been so filled up both with ashes from the pyres and with bodies that there was no more room for digging; but the earth which it is customary to pile upon the buried had spread out until the surface resumed its original flatness, the various heaps having gradually sunk down owing to the weight of snow and a long exposure to downpours of rain" (*Letters* 3.12.1). Sidonius considers the action of the grave diggers nothing less than a crime against the laws of the state (*publicum scelus*) and proceeds to punish them on the spot. Later, he explains that he should not have taken this initiative, but have handed the guilty men over to the bishop. It was, however, only as a representative of the civil authority that the bishop could punish the grave diggers.

The references to violation of tombs in ecclesiastical documents does not reveal any particular interest or responsibility on the part of the church with regard to protection of tombs and the bodies in them. In fact, the crime as such is punished by civil law and the church did not seek to add to the legislative arsenal of public law, or to define the crime of tomb violation in a specific way, even when it took over some of the responsibilities of the civil government, as in the cases analyzed above. According to penitential measures taken against him, the tomb violator apparently did not violate a law against Christianity itself. Let us consider now the point of view of the Christians themselves, by looking at what measures they took to protect their tombs.

Epitaphs and the Protection of the Tomb

Tomb violation is denounced in numerous funerary inscriptions. A number of formulas are designed to protect the tomb and reveal something about the fears attached to tomb violation: sometimes the epitaph is rather chatty and adds an anathema or a curse against the violators. These formulas are not unique to Christians, and it is important to compare their inscriptions with those of pagans and Jews.

The most complete inventory to date includes 3,500 Greek and Latin inscriptions that are meant as a warning, using one formula or another, against tomb violation. The total number of inscriptions preserved is estimated to be about 500,000, which means that the number under consideration is less than one percent of the whole. Chronologically, these inscriptions are difficult to date, but most are from the second to the fourth centuries CE. Moreover, about two-thirds of these 3,500 inscriptions come from Asia Minor.[38] We must not consider these inscriptions as representative of the feeling and attitudes of all the inhabitants of the empire. Nevertheless these characteristics are common to pagan, Jewish, and Christian inscriptions, so that their comparison remains relevant.

The Object of Concern

Most inscriptions contained clauses aimed at restricting the use of the tomb.[39] However, a violation of the restrictions did not break any laws, except in the cases of criminal tomb violation by a third party who did not have the *ius sepulcri*, the right to bury a dead person in a grave. Actually, everyone entitled by the ius sepulcri was free to place whomever he wanted in the tomb.[40] That is why it was important to choose carefully the type of tomb: a family tomb or a hereditary tomb (which can pass out of the family). The second type is rare and is based on rules of hereditary succession as defined by law. The status of the family tomb is the one requiring additional guarantees.[41] Owners tried to protect family tombs from two types of violation: introduction of the body of a stranger, and sale of the tomb, which might *in fine* be construed as one type, since a sale (which must, in any case, respect the funerary purpose protected by law) could become another way of allowing the burial of individuals outside the group for which the tomb was originally intended by the founder.[42]

It is difficult to assess what is meant by the desire to limit the use of a tomb to a family group or other small group designated by its founder. These inscriptions tell us nothing directly about the motivations of their dedicators.

---

38. John S. Creaghan, *Violatio Sepulcri: An Epigraphical Study*, (PhD diss., Princeton University, 1951), 1:2, and annexes in vol. 2 for a description of the corpus. See Johan Strubbe, "Cursed Be He that Moves My Bones," in *Magika Hiera: Ancient Greek Magic and Religion*, ed. Christopher A. Faraone and Dirk Obbink (New York: Oxford University Press, 1991), 33–59.

39. See the analysis of the different forms in Creaghan, *Violatio sepulcri*, 1–38.

40. In this paragraph, I summarize chapters 6 and 7 of Visscher, *Le droit des tombeaux romains*, 93–123.

41. See Sergio Lazzarini, "Tutela legale del sepolcro familiare romano," *Antichità altoadriatiche* 43 (1997): 83–97.

42. The formulas used in these inscriptions present several variants that are distributed all over the empire; see Anna Maria Rossi, "Ricerche sulle multe sepolcrali romane," *Rivista di storia dell'antichità* 5 (1975): 127. Inscriptions that condemn the opening of a tomb without further qualification belong to the same group; they are common in Asia Minor, and also in the West—particularly at Ravenna, and nearby at Concordia Sagittaria; see Creaghan, *Violatio sepulcri*, 1:24–26.

Is it to perpetuate family solidarity in the communal tomb, or a fear of contact with the body of an outsider? More pragmatically, the organization of the family tomb is one of the responsibilities of a pater familias, and that implies control of the burial space even after the founder's death. In any case, we should note that Christians conformed to the same habits and that there is no reason to believe a priori that they had motivations any different from those of non-Christians.

Funerary Fines

Beginning in the second century, respect for the clauses not guaranteed by law was sometimes enforced through a system of funerary fines, which I should describe briefly since the church is sometimes found among the institutions that collect the fines and are therefore responsible for enforcing these clauses.[43] Theodor Mommsen's hypothesis of a law giving the founders of tombs the right to set fines is not supported today, nor is the one that held that the will was the legal basis for this right. The founder of a tomb, like any property owner, was able to determine its allocation and to take any measure necessary to protect the allocation as long as there is no infringement of the law. The fine was to be paid to one or several institutions designated in the epitaph and with which the founder of the tomb had previously registered. This process is well documented in Asia Minor, and can be extended to the rest of the empire. The different institutions that benefited from these fines have often been listed. Beginning in the third century, it was the *fiscus,* or treasury, that was most often designated as the recipient of the fine, but it could also be directed to a variety of agencies: *municipia,* associations, sanctuaries, the local Jewish community (in the institutional sense of the word), or the local Christian church. Clearly the devolution of fines and their ultimate distribution between different institutions were entirely up to the tomb's founder.

No Christian inscription designates the church as recipient of a funeral fine before the last third of the fourth century.[44] The epitaph of Lemnos,

---

43. On funerary fines, compare Giuseppe Giorgi, *Le multe sepolcrali in diritto romano* (Bologna: Beltrami, 1910), with the review of Emilio Albertario, "A proposito di un nuovo studio sulle multe sepolcrali," *Zeitschrift der Savigny-Stiftung für Rechtsgeschichte. Romanistische Abteilung* 32 (1911): 386–90, reprinted in *Studi di diritto romano. 2, Cose, diritti reali, possesso* (Milan: Guiffrè, 1941), 61–67. See Theodor Mommsen, *Le droit pénal romain,* trans. Jean Duquesne, Manuel des antiquités romaines 19 (Paris: Fontemoing, 1907), 130–38; see also Creaghan, *Violatio sepulcri,* 1:96–119; Visscher, *Le droit des tombeaux romains,* 112–23; Rossi, "Ricerche sulle multe sepolcrali romane"; and Max Kaser, "Zum römischen Grabrecht," *Zeitschrift der Savigny-Stiftung für Rechtsgeschichte. Romanistische Abteilung* 95 (1978): 82–89.

44. About funerary fines in Christian inscriptions, see Jean-Pierre Caillet, "L'amende funéraire dans l'épigraphie chrétienne de Salone," *Vjesnik za arheologiju i historiju dalmatinsku* 81 (1988): 33–45.

dated from the third century by Gabriel Millet on the basis of the letter forms, was not earlier than the fourth century, or possibly the fifth, as demonstrated by a study of the use of the epithet *catholic* as an official designation of the Christian Church.[45] Such inscriptions have been found in Asia Minor, in Thrace and in Macedonia; in the West, the only evidence of that practice is in Concordia Sagittaria and at Salona in Dalmatia.[46] Jewish and pagan parallels and the fact that the church was not necessarily the sole recipient of the fines is enough to dispel the idea that the church might have owned the cemetery where tombs protected in this way are found.[47] Christians were only following a practice that was usually a local practice well established before the church also became involved in collecting fines.[48]

Maledictions and Anathemas

The same type of continuity is documented with epitaphs containing maledictions against tomb violators.[49] Pagans, Jews, and Christians used this method of protecting their tombs, sometimes using the same expressions and anathemas, but each also using anathemas more specific to their religious group. I am interested in examining not so much the anathemas themselves, which have been closely studied,[50] but what they say about the nature of the impiety they target.

However, we should note that this practice was most common in Asia Minor. Johan Strubbe, who has collected a body of some 350 texts from Asia

---

45. Gabriel Millet, "Recherches au Mont-Athos," *Bulletin de correspondance hellénique* 29 (1905): 55–141, esp. 55–72. On the use of the expression "Catholic Church," see Paul Lemerle, *Philippes et la Macédoine orientale à l'époque chrétienne et Byzantine* (Paris: De Boccard, 1945), 94–101.

46. Jean-Pierre Caillet, "L'amende funéraire," 36; see also Denis Feissel, *Recueil des inscriptions chrétiennes de Macédoine du IIIe au VIe siècle,* Bulletin de correspondance hellénique, Supplément 8 (Athens: École française d'Athènes, 1983), 69.

47. This is contra Caillet's hypothesis in "L'amende funéraire," 37, which recognizes that the church is not the only one to receive funerary fines.

48. For a comparison between pagan and Christian inscriptions in a local context, see Massimo Tosi, "*Multae, comminationes, dirae* nelle iscrizioni funerarie transpadane pagane e cristiane," *Rivista archeologica dell'antica provincia e diocesi di Como* 175 (1993): 189–241.

49. André Parrot, *Malédictions et violations de tombes* (Paris: Geuthner, 1939), explores Eastern antecedents of this practice (in Mesopotamia, Syria-Phoenicia, Egypt, etc.). Creaghan has gathered and commented on a vast amount of material in *Violatio sepulcri,* 1:39–95. See also Strubbe, "Cursed Be He that Moves My Bones."

50. See Dr. Münz, "Anatheme und Verwünschungen auf altchristliche Monumenten," *Annalen des Vereins für Nassauische Altertumskunde und Geschichtsforschung* 14 (1877): 169–81; Antonio Ferrua, "Gli anatemi dei padri di Nicea," *Civiltà cattolica* 108, no. 4 (1957): 378–97; Denis Feissel, "Notes d'épigraphie chrétienne. 2," *Bulletin de correspondance hellénique* 101 (1977): 224–28 about an epitaph from Argos and Dennis Feissel, "Notes d'épigraphie chrétienne. 4," *Bulletin de correspondance hellénique* 104 (1980): 459–72 about curses in epitaphs from Attica.

Minor, knows of only about 20 in the rest of the Greek world. Of the 205 known Christian texts, more than 100 come from Asia Minor. The same is true of Jewish texts. It also appears that these inscriptions date, for the most part, from the second to fourth centuries, but, outside Asia Minor, the Christian texts are later, often later even than the sixth century.[51]

In Asia Minor, Jews adopted the very ancient custom, later continued by Christians, of threatening with a curse anyone who violated a tomb. Near Eastern, and more exactly Anatolian, traditions have been considered to be at the origin of the practice, but we should be prudent about these genealogical theories.[52] The damage most frequently denounced is the introduction of an outsider into the tomb: the fears of Jews and Christians seem to have been no different from those of their non-Christian neighbors. They distinguished themselves from them, but not in a systematic way, by the use of expressions borrowed from the Bible or by threatening violators of the last judgment. Formally, the practices were thus the same: to what extent can we then hypothesize different beliefs to explain them?[53] Most of the inscriptions were actually concerned with respect for the limits imposed by the founder on the use of the tomb, and not with the necessity of the body to remain buried or with the tranquility of the dead in their graves. There are a few references to the profanation of cadavers, but they are rare and quite comparable to those that non-Christian inscriptions contain.[54]

The later Western Christian texts seem to denounce the violation of the tomb in the most general terms, often by means of the verb *uiolare* without further precision.[55] Only one example, no earlier than the sixth century, adds an explanation: "I beg you, Christians all and my guardian, most favored Julian, [to make sure that] no one ever violate this tomb, so that it be preserved until the end of the world so that I may come back to life without

---

51. Pagan inscriptions from Asia Minor have been gathered in Johan Strubbe, *Arai epitymbioi: Imprecations against Desecrators of the Grave in the Greek Epitaphs of Asia Minor: A Catalogue*, Inschriften griechischer Städte aus Kleinasien 52 (Bonn: Habelt, 1997). For Jewish inscriptions, see Johan Strubbe, "Curses against Violation of the Grave in Jewish Epitaphs of Asia Minor," in *Studies in Early Jewish Epigraphy*, ed. Jan Willem van Henten and Pieter Willem van der Horst, Arbeiten zur Geschichte des antiken Judentums und des Urchristentums 21 (Leiden: Brill, 1994), 70–128; for Christian inscriptions, see Myla Perraymond, "Formule imprecatorie ('APAI) nelle iscrizioni funerarie paleocristiane," *Quaderni dell'Istituto di lingue e letteratura latina. Università degli studi di Roma La Sapienza, Facoltà di magistero* 2–3 (1980–81): 115–45.

52. See Strubbe, "Cursed Be He that Moves My Bones," 37–41, which makes some rather dangerous generalizations about Anatolians' beliefs.

53. Strubbe, "Curses against Violation of the Grave in Jewish Epitaphs of Asia Minor" 71–72, is once again rather imprudent.

54. Creaghan, *Violatio sepulcri*, 28.

55. See Perraymond, "Formule imprecatorie," nos. 1–20 in the epigraphic appendix.

impediment when He comes who will judge the living and the dead."[56] This came from the epitaph of one Guntelda, buried with her son and grandson in the church of St. Julian at Como in Lombardy. The link between the resurrection and the integrity of the corpse in the grave is explicit, but it is only one isolated and late text.[57] A few inscriptions threaten the violator with not resurrecting. One text found in the Cemetery of Saint Agnes contains a whole series of curses: "May whoever violates this tomb die a terrible death, lie unburied, never rise again, and share the fate of Judas."[58] The threat of never rising again is also found in the epitaph of a priest of the Church of San Vitale in Ravenna.[59] The threat of not resurrecting is addressed to the tomb violator and says nothing about the fate of the dedicator if his tomb were violated.[60] The relative singularity of the later inscriptions might be explained by the specific archaeological context of inhumation in churches: space being there limited by definition, there was a fear of reuse of those tombs. However, it is in any case impossible to confirm that that is indeed the case of these inscriptions, since their archaeological context has unfortunately been lost.

The epigraphic evidence shows that it is necessary to define the nature of the tomb violation before making assumptions about fears and beliefs. It appears that the primary function of these inscriptions is to enforce the rules set by the founder of a tomb about its use. In this respect, Christians were acting no differently than pagans or Jews, regardless of their respective religious beliefs.

❦ The Epigrams of Gregory Nazianzen

Notwithstanding their literary character, the epigrams of Gregory Nazianzen show a similar continuity. Nearly 100 epigrams, out of a total of 254,

---

56. *CIL* 5.5415 = *ILCV* 3863: *Adiuro uos omnes xpiani et te custode beati iuliani [...] tremenda die iudicii ut hunc sepulcrum numquam ullo tempore violetur sed coseruet usque ad finem mundi ut posim sine impedimento in uita redire cum uenerit qui iudicaturus est uiuos et mortuos....*

57. Duval, *Auprès des saints corps et âme*, 179–80, 196–97, gives too much importance to this testimony that she compares with some audacity to the text of Lactantius about Christ's burial (see chapter 5 for a commentary). All the texts quoted in Ferrua, "Gli anatemi dei padri di Nicea," are posterior to the sixth century. In "Anatheme," Münz compares these late inscriptions to second- and third-century polemics about resurrection. See Creaghan, *Violatio sepulcri*, 1:76–77.

58. *ILCV* 3845 = *ICVR* 8.21396: *Male pereat insepultus iaceat non resurgat cum Iuda partem habeat si quis sepulcrum hunc uiolarit.*

59. *ILCV* 3850 = *CIL* 11.322.

60. This is contra Ferrua, "Gli anatemi dei padri di Nicea," 378, and Duval, *Auprès des saints corps et âmes*, 44 and 213, who does not notice the very small number of such threats.

are imprecations against tomb violators (*tumboruchoi*).[61] Louis Robert had suggested that these epigrams, for the most part, might have been simply variations on a single event: the violation of the tomb of Antiochus I of Commagene at Nemrod Dag (a mountain sanctuary situated in southeastern Turkey). Reexamining the evidence, Georg Petzl has been able to show that, as appealing as it was, this hypothesis was very weak: Gregory makes no direct reference to the monument of Antiochus I; the few descriptive elements contained in the epigrams could apply equally to several tombs in the region; and finally, the comparisons with the inscription of the Antiochus monument are too vague. The question about the literary character of these texts thus remains intact.[62]

It is unlikely that the epigrams of Gregory, the epitaphs as well as the invectives against the tumboruchoi, were ever intended for engraving in stone. However, the epitaphs relate to explicit circumstances: they refer to a specific death and mention the deceased and his tomb. This is not the case for the invectives, which show a combination of pagan and Christian themes and owe a great deal to literary traditions.[63] Yet the theme of tomb violation does not seem to be part of the traditional genre of funerary epigrams. These poems might thus contain some valuable indications about the beliefs and attitudes of Gregory.

The tomb is sacred; to disturb it is a sacrilege. The vocabulary of impiety is abundant in Gregory's invectives:

As I journeyed I saw an impious thing, a gaping tomb. This is the work of deceitful gold. If you did find gold, you have acquired an evil, but if you went away empty you have got for yourself an empty impiety. (180)

So have you opened this great tomb with impious hands (and in vain). (214.3)

---

61. Gregory's *Epitaphia* are collected in Book VIII of the *Greek Anthology;* nos. 104, 170–72, and 176–254 are imprecations against tomb violators.

62. Although he often announced it, Louis Robert never gave a full treatment of the question: see *Bulletin épigraphique* 1970, nos. 618–19; *Opera minora selecta. 4,* 396. See now Georg Petzl, "Die epigramme des Gregor von Nazianz über Grabräuberei und das Hierothesion des kommagenischen Königs Antiochos I," *Epigraphica Anatolica* 10 (1987): 117–29. About the literary aspect, see Rudolph Keydell, in *Reallexicon für Antike und Christentum,* s. v. "Epigramm"; Justin Mossay, *La mort et l'au-delà dans Saint Grégoire de Nazianze,* Recueil de travaux d'histoire et de philologie, 4e série 34 (Louvain: Publications universitaires de Louvain, 1966), 216–20.

63. See Keydell, "Epigramm," for parallels to pagan epigrams.

But if you dig up a tomb, a solemn trust, and this for the sake of gold, say of what are you worthy? (194.2–4)

The violation of a tomb is, above all, the destruction of the tomb, and it seems that the body is only mentioned through the contrast between the bones contained in the tomb and the gold sought by the looters:

Why do you disturb me, an empty tomb? I contain nothing for those who attack me, but bones and dust. (229)

Why do you heave up my stones? I contain nothing but the feeble dead. The tomb's sole riches are bones. (233)

I am not a house of gold. Why am I broken? The tomb you hack to pieces is but a tomb. All my wealth consists of corpses. (238; cf. 191, 193, 251)

The suffering of the dead is psychological; the dead loves the tomb, for it is a resting place; it is all that is left:

This man, in vain hope, pillaged my dear tomb, the only one of my possessions I carried away with me. (208.1–2)

This was my home after death, but iron attacked my tomb. (225)

You have all you wish, you living, but I, the dead, only my few dear stones. (237)

Strictly speaking, there is nothing in these texts about the sensibility of the body: it is, rather, the personification of the dead as the speaker of the epitaph's words that gives it feeling. It is not certain that there are well-articulated beliefs behind these statements.[64]

There is also mention of the attack on corporal remains. Two epigrams evoke the cadaver stripped bare:

Show not to men the naked corpse, or another shall strip you. Often gold is but a dream. (241)

---

64. On personnification, see Keydell, "Epigramm." Duval, *Auprès des saints corps et âme*, 37–39, does not take into account the literary dimension of these texts and reads them as the expression of "the suffering of the dead."

Who exhibited me to men, the poor corpse hidden for ages by undisturbed stones? (244)

Another epigram wishes that the body of the violator also be thrown "afar from the tombs of his fathers" (208.4); several express their outrage that gold should be sought from bodies:

Was it not enough for men to lay hands on men, but from the dead, too, you strive to get gold? (242; cf. 204)

We should note that, while exhumation of the body is lamented, there is no mention of the eventual consequences for the salvation of the dead. Gregory even claimed to find it preferable to remain without burial than to risk seeing the tomb violated:

I beseech you, if I die, throw my body into a river or to the dogs, or consume it in the all-devouring fire. That is better than to perish by hands greedy of gold. I am in dread as I look on this tomb which has met with this fate. (213)

It appears that in the violation of a tomb what is really feared is not being left unburied but the idea that the body, bones or ashes, should be touched or disturbed.[65] There is no reason to see in that a fear linked to the belief that the preservation of the physical integrity of the dead is necessary for the resurrection. Dismemberment by dogs or reduction to ashes by fire are more drastic forms of destruction. The feelings expressed in Gregory's epigrams, like those of the epitaphs of simple believers, do not necessarily betray religious beliefs.

The study of attitudes toward tomb violation makes it possible to eliminate certain assumptions, especially about the link between belief in the resurrection and Christian care for burial. However, the most characteristic evolution in tomb violation law is that profanation of cadavers became a specific crime at the turn of the fourth century. This crime carried the most severe penalties and was explained by the most elaborated justifications. Thus from the "point of view" of impiety, burial is important because of the body. Burial

---

65. See Jean-Marie Mathieu, "Horreur du cadavre et philosophie dans le monde romain: le cas de la patristique grecque du IVe siècle," in *La mort, les morts et l'au-delà dans le monde romain: actes du colloque de Caen, 20–22 novembre 1985,* ed. François Hinard (Caen: Université de Caen, 1987), 311–20, on the attitude toward the corruption and decomposition of corpses.

duty is always about the body, but that does not mean that burial is done for the body in itself as a component of the human being. The next question is therefore to see whether the evolution of tomb violation law reflects a more general shift in the attitudes towards the body and burial.

Disposal of the Body: The Discussions of the Second and Third Centuries

According to a notice from Pliny the Elder (23–79), inhumations are more vulnerable to tomb violation than cremations: "Cremation was not actually an old practice at Rome: the dead used to be buried. But cremation was instituted after it became known that the bodies of those fallen in wars abroad were dug up again. All the same, many families kept on the old ritual; for instance, it is recorded that nobody in the family of the Cornelii was cremated before Sulla the dictator, and that he had desired it because he was afraid of reprisals for having dug up the corpse of Gaius Marius" (*Natural History* 7.187). The greater vulnerability is the only reason Pliny offers to explain abandoning inhumation for soldiers who die in foreign lands as well as for Sulla fearing to see his own body dug up out of revenge. Could, therefore, the definition of a specific crime for the profanation of the cadaver be the result of the new preference for inhumation that started at the end of the first century CE?

Although recent archaeological discoveries have brought out many exceptions,[66] it is still a fact that in the first century, cremation was the norm in burial practice (Pliny is clear on that point), whereas inhumation had become the norm by the fourth century, as attested by Macrobius, who confirms that the practice of burning bodies had disappeared (*Saturnalia* 7.7.5). We must keep in mind that the law, when punishing tomb violation, does not specify how the body was disposed of and that the measures apply equally to a buried body and a cremated one. The constitution of Constantius and Julian Caesar explicitly includes *corpora sepulta* and *reliquiae*, as does the constitution of Gratian, Valentinian, and Theodosius that mentions urns and sarcophagi; in the Novel of Valentinian, the expression *corporum reliquiae humatorum* may

---

66. There are many regional syntheses and a general discussion in *Incinérations et inhumations dans l'Occident romain aux trois premiers siècles de notre ère: actes du Colloque international de Toulouse-Montréjeau (IVe Congrès archéologique de Gaule méridionale), 7–10 Octobre 1987*, ed. Michel Vidal (Toulouse: Association pour la promotion du patrimoine archéologique et historique en Midi-Pyrénées, 1991).

also implicitly refer to ashes. There is both some conservatism in the legal formulation and the necessity to protect all existing monuments.

Despite the masterful paper by Arthur Darby Nock in 1932,[67] archaeologists and historians have never stopped explaining the progressive adoption of inhumation as the consequence of new religious or eschatological beliefs. Recently, Ian Morris has again reminded us of the methodological impasse to which that could lead.[68] The texts these scholars have scrutinized undoubtedly show that the disposal of the body was a new object of concern.[69]

Objections to Cremation

A first belief, a form of cult of the fire, must be considered. According to Herodotus (*Histories* 3.16), the Persians forbade the burning of bodies. An epigram in the *Greek Anthology* (7.62), composed by Dioscorides (third century BCE), refers to the same prohibition: "Burn not Euphrates, Philonymus, nor defile Fire for me. I am a Persian as my fathers were, a Persian of pure stock, yea, master: to defile Fire is for us bitterer than cruel death. But wrap me up and lay me in the ground." Joseph Bidez and Franz Cumont wonder if there is a reference to this same Mazdean taboo in a fragment of the historian Nicholas of Damaschus (first century BCE) concerning the miracles that saved Croesus from the pyre.[70] Robert Turcan finds traces of the same beliefs in a fragment of the rhetor Apollonius of Athens, a contemporary of Septimius Severus, cited by Philostratus in his *Lives of the Sophists*.[71] Titled "Callias Tries to Dissuade the Athenians from Burning the Dead," this short piece of eloquence attests to the relevance of the question at the end of the second century:

> Lift the torch on high, man! Why do you do violence to its fire and abase it to the earth and torment it? Fire belongs to the sky, it is ethereal, it tends towards that which is akin to itself. It does not lead the dead down below, but leads the gods up to the skies. Alas, Prometheus,

---

67. Arthur Darby Nock, "Cremation and Burial in the Roman Empire," *Harvard Theological Review* 25 (1932): 321–59, reprinted in *Essays on Religion and the Ancient World*, ed. Zeph Stewart (Cambridge, MA: Harvard University Press, 1972), 1:277–307.

68. Ian Morris, *Death-Ritual and Social Structure in Classical Antiquity*, Key Themes in Ancient History (Cambridge: Cambridge University Press, 1992), 31–69.

69. Cinzia Vismara, "L'apport des textes antiques," in Vidal, ed., *Incinérations et inhumations dans l'Occident romain*, 107–47, usefully collects a large number of texts.

70. Joseph Bidez and Franz Cumont, *Les mages hellénisés: Zoroastre, Ostanès et Hystaspe d'après la tradition grecque. 1, Introduction* (Paris: Les Belles Lettres, 1938), 98–99.

71. Robert Turcan, "Origines et sens de l'inhumation à l'époque impériale," *Revue des études anciennes* 60 (1958): 337–40.

torch-bearer and fire-bringer, see how your gift is insulted! It is polluted by the senseless corpse. Come to its help, give it aid, and, if you cannot, even from where you are steal this fire!

These beliefs, linked to a cult of the fire, condemned cremation as a source of pollution for the fire put in contact with corpses. However, they cannot have had much influence and do not really imply a greater respect for the body once it is buried.

A second set of beliefs links the rejection of cremation and the preservation of the soul. In his treatise *On the Soul,* Tertullian, who held that at death a separation of body and soul occurs, attacked doctrines that held, in one form or another, that the soul remained attached to the body after death. He observed:

And yet even this partial survival of the soul finds a place in the opinions of some men; and on this account they will not have the body consumed at its funeral by fire, because they would spare the small residue of the soul. There is, however, another way of accounting for this pious treatment, not as if it meant to favour the relics of the soul, but as if it would avert a cruel custom in the interest even of the body; since, being human, it is itself undeserving of an end which is also inflicted upon murderers. (*De anima* 51.4)

I will return to what this testimony tells us about Christian beliefs. Robert Turcan has compared to this passage from Tertullian a commentary by Servius (*In Aeneid* 3.68) in which the belief that the soul endures as long as the body is credited to the stoics. Servius contrasts this belief with the practice of cremation, which allows the soul to be reunited directly with the universal soul. Turcan reconstructs from these elements an eschatological system that borrows from the stoic Panaetius the principle that body and soul are one entity and to Pythagorism the notion of partial survival of this entity after death and the ban against cremation that it entails.[72] The religious objections of Pythagorism against cremation are well documented and Iamblichus, at the end of the third century, seems to confirm that inhumation remains the rule for practitioners of the sect (*Life of Pythagorus* 154).

This group of texts shows that in the third century CE the choice of inhumation might have obeyed certain religious beliefs. Such beliefs concern

---

72. Turcan, "Origines et sens de l'inhumation," 340 ff.

the soul more than the body; inhumation is preferred because it saves from destruction not only the body but whatever part of the soul remains attached to it after death. However, by placing the emphasis on the survival of the human entity, these beliefs encourage a respect for the tomb, since to preserve the buried body is to preserve the soul as well. Yet it is unlikely that they ever extended outside certain philosophical circles.

Christians and Inhumation

Even if no one today still credits Christianity alone with the adoption of inhumation, almost everyone acknowledges that the spread of Christianity was a factor that reinforced the shift in that direction.[73]

The belief in the resurrection has often been connected with an obligation to bury the dead.[74] It is in any case certain that the manner of disposing of bodies adopted by Christians, at a moment when it was far from being the norm, aroused controversy. Actually, pagans attributed to Christians, as a way of ridiculing them, a belief that cremation, or any other form of corporal destruction, would suffice to prevent resurrection. Nothing, however, in the Christian responses to these attacks confirms that they had any such belief.

The *Octavius*, written by Minucius Felix in the second half of the second century, is a clear case. The pagan Caecilius Natalis rejects belief in the resurrection as absurd, then pretends to wonder if that is why Christians shun cremation:

> I presume this is supposed to be why they abominate funeral pyres and condemn cremation. But of course every body, withdrawn from the flames or not, is eventually reduced to earth in the course of the passing years; it makes no difference if it is torn apart by wild beasts or swallowed up by the seas or covered over with earth or taken away by the flames. If corpses have sensation, any kind of interment causes them suffering; if they have none, speedy dispatch is the most salutary treatment. (11.4)

In his response, the Christian Octavius Januarius denies very simply the belief attributed to Christians: "And it is not true, as you believe, that we fear

---

73. See Morris, *Death-Ritual and Social Structure*, 68.
74. Alfred C. Rush, *Death and Burial in Christian Antiquity*, Studies in Christian Antiquity 1 (Washington, DC: Catholic University of America Press, 1941), 249 ff. See also Turcan, "Origines et sens de l'inhumation," 323. Zbigniew Suchecki, "La cremazione nella legislazione della Chiesa," *Apollinaris* 66 (1993): 653–728, contains no pertinent elements for antiquity.

to suffer any harm from cremation, but our practice is to adhere to the old, and therefore the preferable, custom of inhumation." The "old and therefore preferable custom" refers to Jewish custom and the entombment of Christ. But Octavius Januarius also explains that Christians do not fear the destruction of their bodies: "Something may be removed from our feeble eyes; do you believe it therefore is lost to God as well? A corpse may dry into dust or dissolve into liquid or reduce into ashes or fade into smoke; however it is, every corpse is withdrawn from us but its elements are preserved in the safekeeping of God" (34.10). Christians very clearly rejected any connection between the preservation of the body in a tomb and the resurrection as a simplistic argument on the part of pagans to ridicule their doctrine.[75] The same type of argumentation appears also in treatises on the resurrection written against the Gnostics.[76]

The connection made in the minds of pagans between inhumation and resurrection is also attested to in the *Letter of the Churches of Lyons and Vienna*, transmitted by Eusebius of Caesarea in the *Ecclesiastical History* but written shortly after 177. The governor wished at all costs to prevent Christians from burying martyrs who had just died. For six days, the bodies were exposed to the air, guarded night and day, then burned and thrown into the Rhône river, with the intention of thus preventing their resurrection: "And this they did as though they could conquer God and take away their rebirth in order, as they said, 'that they might not even have any hope of resurrection, through trusting in which they have brought in strange and new worship and despised terrors, going readily and with joy to death; now let us see if they will rise again, and if their God be able to help them and to take them out of our hands'" (Eusebius, *Ecclesiastical History* 5.1.63). There is a direct echo here of the polemics of the first apologists: the power of God is opposed to all efforts to destroy the body. The belief that it could prevent the resurrection is merely the propaganda of the persecutors.

Caroline W. Bynum has placed the development of the doctrine of bodily resurrection in the first apologies and the first treatises on the resurrection in the context of the persecutions, suggesting that belief in resurrection could well have emerged as a compensation for the absence of a burial.[77] She links the anxieties about the necessity of a burial with the belief in the resurrection

---

75. Minucius Felix is following very closely the text of Tatian, whose *Discourse to the Greeks* was written slightly earlier.
76. See, for instance, Athenagoras, *De resurrectione* 4.1, with parallels in Athenagoras, *Sur la résurrection*, ed. Bernard Pouderon, Sources chrétiennes 379 (Paris: Éditions du Cerf, 1992), 226–27, n. 2; Tertullian, *De resurrectione mortuorum* 32.
77. Carolyn W. Bynum, *The Resurrection of the Body in Western Christianity*, Lectures on the History of Religions, new series, 15 (New York: Columbia University Press, 1995), 47–51.

by showing that resurrection is in part a response to the threats that weighed on the possibility of being buried during the persecutions. But it is something very different from attributing to Christians a belief that resurrection depends upon burial.[78] Pagans attacked belief in resurrection by claiming that the integrity of the body was indispensable to such operation. The *Letter from the Churches of Lyons and Vienna* attributes to persecutors the desire to prevent the resurrection of the martyrs by denying them burial. But the Christian response is always that the power of god is such that nothing will prevent him reassembling the martyrs' bodies. No Christian testimony attests the belief that burial is a condition for resurrection.

Tertullian, in the treatise *On the Crown,* confirms that Christians shun cremation. He enumerates different practices imposed on soldiers that seem to him incompatible with being a Christian: "Shall he be disturbed in death by the trumpet of the trumpeter, who expects to be aroused by the angel's trump? And shall the Christian be burned according to camp rule, when he was not permitted to be burned, as to him Christ had remitted the punishment of fire?" (11.4). If he offers no justification in favor of inhumation, Tertullian nevertheless rejects the practice of cremation on numerous occasions. In his treatise on resurrection he reverses the mockery of pagans. The latter believed that nothing exists after death and yet they make sacrifices for the dead: "I however shall with better reason mock at the multitude, especially on occasions when they savagely burn up those very deceased whom they presently supply with gluttonous meals, with the same fires both currying favor and provoking hostility. Thus does piety toy with cruelty. Is it sacrifice, or insult, to cremate the cremated?" (*De resurrectione mortuorum* 1.3). The same accusation of cruelty reappears in the treatise *On the Soul* (51.4). There he criticizes, as we have seen, those who think that after death the body retains some part of the soul. It is not for this reason that Christians refuse cremation, but "to avert a cruel custom in the interest even of the body, since, being human, it is itself undeserving of an end which is also inflicted upon murderers." It is not, therefore, for the soul, but for the body, that inhumation is preferred.

When Origen (c. 185–254) answers, some seventy years later, to the criticism of the pagan Celsus, a contemporary of the previously mentioned apologists, he uses very similar arguments.[79] In order to criticize the belief in

---

78. One should not jump to such a conclusion, as do Donald G. Kyle, *Spectacles of Death in Ancient Rome* (London: Routledge, 1998), 242 ff., and Duval, *Auprès des saints corps et âme,* 24–29.

79. Celsus wrote his treaty around 178; see Michel Fédou, *Christianisme et religion païenne: dans le Contre Celse d'Origène,* Théologie historique 81 (Paris: Beauchesne, 1988), 39–41.

bodily resurrection, Celsus quotes a verse of Heraclitus: "Corpses ought to be thrown away as worse than dung." To this disdain for the body Origen opposes the soul that inhabited it: "For according to good customs [human bodies] are thought worthy of burial with all the honor possible appropriate to their character so that, as far as possible, we may not insult the soul that has dwelt within by casting out the body when the soul has gone out of it, as we do with the bodies of beasts" (*Against Celsus* 5.24). Origen thus explicitly defends the honor of burial that is due the body. More than belief in the resurrection, in his eyes, it is the respect for the body in which the soul has dwelled that explains the care Christians give to the burial of their dead.

From these different texts it appears that, when Christians are constrained to explain why they practice inhumation exclusively, they do not talk about their belief in bodily resurrection. Rather, they stress that resurrection has nothing at all to do with the physical integrity of the body, nor with the type of funeral ritual followed. Tertullian, like Origen, refers to the body and the respect it is due. It seems difficult, however, to see in that a reason specific to Christians for demanding respect for the tombs and the bodies they contain. That confirms why it is useless to explain changes in funerary rites by new religious beliefs. However, the very existence of all these debates, between the end of the second and the middle of the third centuries, signals a new attention to the disposal of the body, which the law, after a slight delay, comes to echo by making profanation of cadavers a specific crime.

✤ Augustine, the Love of the Body, and Care of the Dead

Love of the body is also, in the only early Christian treatise devoted to burial, offered as the reason why it is necessary to care for the dead and particularly to provide for burial. This is a human feeling; it is also the teaching of the Scriptures, as Augustine attempts to show in the treatise *On the Care of the Dead*.

In the *City of God* (1.12–13), Augustine answers the insults of the pagans on the subject of corpses left unburied when Rome was sacked in 410. Pagans said that God should have spared Christians the suffering caused by the lack of a burial. Augustine attempts to show that the lack of burial is not the suffering that pagans thought it to be, and in particular that burial is not at all indispensable for the resurrection of the body. He stresses, however, that one should never neglect burial, which Scripture describes as a good work.

In *De cura pro mortuis gerenda,* Augustine repeats that, from the perspective of salvation and of faith, only prayer can bring help to the dead who earned it during their lives. Thus, to be buried near a holy martyr is useful only to the extent that the proximity might encourage the prayers of their loved ones. Burial is thus, in itself, useless for salvation, which is confirmed by the example of the martyrs who did not receive one (6–8). However, Augustine adds that burial is important: "Yet from that love of the human heart, because of that which 'no one ever hated his own flesh (Eph. 5:29),' if men believe that anything would be lacking to their bodies after death which in their own people or country the solemnity of burial demands, they become sad like men, and before death they fear for their bodies that which has no effect on them after death" (9). Augustine finds in Scripture a double example of the connection between love of the body and the care for burial. The story is a little complicated. A prophet received from God an order neither to eat nor drink at Bethel where he had come to pronounce that Josiah, king of Judea, would exhume the bones of a great many dead in order to burn them upon altars raised to idols. However, he was fooled by another prophet, accepted his hospitality and learned his own punishment from his mouth: "your dead body will not be brought into the sepulcher of your fathers" (1 Kings 13:22). The prophet was killed by a lion not far from Bethel: his body was buried by the prophet who had tricked him in the monument that he had built for himself. When the prophecy about Josiah was realized, around three hundred years later, this only tomb was spared (2 Kings 23:17–18). As Augustine interprets the episode, "From this fact, then, because each one naturally loves his own flesh, it was punishment for him to learn that he would not be in the tomb of his fathers. So he took care that his bones be spared by burying them next to him whose tomb no one would violate" (9). It is Augustine who grants the deceitful prophet the hope that his body would be spared along with that of the first prophet if he lay beside him. In the Scriptures there is no mention that the tomb of the prophet will alone be spared when the prophecy is realized. This emphasizes that it is important for Augustine to establish in the Scriptures the human aspiration of each and every one to have a decent burial.

The verse from the epistle to the Ephesians, "No one ever hates his own flesh" (Eph. 5:29), is used again later in order to explain further what prompts a person to seek a burial place for a fellow human:

> Why, then, are those men said to have done an act of mercy in burying Saul and his son, and blessed by good King David for this, unless it be that the hearts of the compassionate are favorably affected when

they are concerned over the well-being of other bodies of the dead? Or is it because of that love which keeps 'one from ever hating his own flesh' that they do not wish such things to happen after their own death to their own bodies, so that what they wish to be done for them when they shall have no feeling they care to do for others who now have no feeling, while they themselves still have feeling? (11)

This is also repeated at the end of the treatise, where we read, "Regardless of what is spent for burying the body, it is not an aid to salvation, but a duty of our humanity according to that love by which 'no one ever hated his own flesh'" (22).

This verse has played an important role in Augustine's meditation on the body. At the time he wrote *De cura,* Augustine had come to put a full emphasis on humankind's love of the body. What he wrote about the importance of burial, therefore, took on even greater importance.[80]

For Augustine, humankind's care for burial and the horror felt about the idea of its profanation are sentiments of the human heart, not primarily a matter of belief. The duty for burial is not done because it would be necessary for the resurrection, but it may be done as a testimony of the faith in the resurrection: "And if they do this who have no faith in the resurrection of the body, how much more ought we who have faith that a duty of this kind is due to a dead body which shall rise again and live forever? And this is in some way a testimony of one's faith." (22) In conclusion, Christians are less pressed by Augustine to abandon their beliefs in the sensibility of the body in the tomb than to accomplish their burial responsibilities as an act of faith in the resurrection, and not simply out of the human sentiment that causes them to do so naturally.

My reading of *De cura* departs from the traditional one. Far from it being a treatise on the uselessness of burial, I believe, on the contrary, that the treatise offers a Christian explanation of the importance of burial.[81] This reading is much more consistent with what we know from other sources about the

---

80. About Eph. 5:29, see Tarsicius J. Van Bavel, "No One Ever Hated His Own Flesh: Eph. 5:29 in Augustine," *Augustiniana* 45 (1995): 45–93. About Augustine's change of attitude toward the body, see Margaret Miles, *Augustine on the Body,* Dissertation Series, American Academy of Religion 31 (Missoula, MT: Scholars Press, 1979); see also Peter Brown, *The Body and Society: Men, Women, and Sexual Renunciation in Early Christianity* (New York: Columbia University Press, 1988).

81. A good example of a traditional reading of Augustine's treatise is to be found in Yvette Duval's book about inhumations near martyrs' tombs; see Duval, *Auprès des saints corps et âme.* A specialist of the cult of martyrs in Africa, Duval built her work on the opposition between the church official doctrine expressed by Augustine in *De cura,* and popular beliefs expressed in anathema against tombs violators. For Augustine, the tomb is useless to the dead, while simple Christians believe that

general attitude of Augustine toward the body, and even death.[82] The teaching that he offers is not unusual or far from the belief of the faithful; it seems to me, rather, to be an effort to rationalize in Christian terms feelings that are hard to describe and that are not easily reduced to beliefs in the hereafter.

This detour through impiety, specifically tomb violation, has proven rather fruitful. The study of the laws highlighted the emergence of a new crime at the end of the third century: the profanation of the cadaver, as opposed to damage to the tomb alone. At the same time, numerous discussions were taking place concerning choices about ways of disposing of the body that revealed once again a more specific attention to the future of the body after death. The detour through impiety also allows us to compare the attitudes of Christians and non-Christians: the church did not define tomb violation as a religious crime, but insisted on the punishment of it by civil laws; in their epitaphs, Christians, like non-Christians, sought above all to guarantee the use of their tomb and do not bring to bear any specific belief to defend the integrity of their graves. When Christians had to defend their preference for inhumation, in a society where cremation remained, or had been, the norm for a long time, they did not stress their belief in the resurrection, but the respect for the body. Augustine, in the first Christian treatise devoted to burial, is careful to show that this attachment has a basis in Scripture.

The necessity to receive a proper burial answered to no particular religious beliefs, particularly eschatological ones, but rather to a sentiment that is finding a new form of expression: the care for the body. Some scholars have actually suggested that the discovery of the body and of its importance is a characteristic of Late Antiquity, even if it was through the promotion of new ways of controlling it.[83] This chapter is thus also a contribution to the history of the body that inextricably links the study of human behaviors and the analysis of ideas and representations.

---

the dead body retains some "traces of the soul," according to a beautiful expression borrowed from a Roman epitaph (*ICUR* 7.18944: *animae uestigia*).

82. See Éric Rebillard, *In hora mortis: évolution de la pastorale chrétienne de la mort aux IVe et Ve siècles dans l'Occident latin*, Bibliothèque des Écoles françaises d'Athènes et de Rome 283 (Rome: École française de Rome, 1994), 63–66.

83. See, in particular, Aline Rousselle, *Porneia: On Desire and Body in Antiquity*, trans. Felicia Pheasant (Oxford: Blackwell, 1988); Michel Foucault, *The History of Sexuality*, vol. 3: *The Care of the Self*, trans. Robert Hurley (New York: Vintage, 1990); and Brown, *The Body and Society*.

❧ CHAPTER 5

Christian Piety and Burial Duty
From the Duty to Bury the Dead to the Organization of Burial for the Poor

"Why do we not observe that it is their benevolence to strangers, their care for the graves of the dead and the pretended holiness of their lives that have done most to increase atheism?" These are the words of Julian, around 360 CE, on the Christian Church (*Epistulae* 22.429d) in a programmatic letter to restore paganism as the state religion. The moderns, having fully accepted the idea put forth by his Christian critics that Julian tried to imitate the best of Christian practices,[1] failed to notice that his vocabulary and his intentions were not so transparent. The piety of Christians is "pretended." The term *necroi,* cadavers, is rather negative; Julian often uses it to designate martyrs, and speaks scornfully of the cult that developed around their tombs.[2] In the rest of the letter, indeed, Julian does not

---

1. The theory of Julian's imitation of Christian institutions derives from contemporary Christian texts—in particular, Gregory of Nazianzus, *Orationes* 4.111; see Sozomen, *Ecclesiastical History* 5.16. Still fundamental on Julian's projects is W. Koch, "Comment l'empereur Julien tacha de fonder une église païenne," *Revue belge de philologie et d'histoire* 6 (1927): 123–46; 7 (1928): 49–82, 511–50, 1363–85; see more recently, Oliver Nicholson, "The 'Pagan Churches' of Maximinus Daia and Julian the Apostate," *Journal of Ecclesiastical History* 45 (1994): 1–10. The authenticity of Letter 22 (Bidez 84) has recently been questioned, but there seems to be no serious ground for this: see Jean Bouffartigue, "L'authenticité de la Lettre 84 de l'empereur Julien," *Revue de philologie* 79, no. 2 (2005): 231–42.

2. On Julian and the martyrs, see Pierre de Labriolle, *La réaction païenne: étude sur la polémique antichrétienne du Ier au VIe siècle* (Paris, 1900), 419; for the use of the term *nekroi,* see Julian, *Misopogon* 33.361b (corpse of Babylas), and *Contra Galilaeos* 335b.

prescribe any measures aimed at imitating Christians' attention to the dead. Hence, it is not possible to use Julian's letter as a document on the Christian duty to bury the dead, which would shed some light on the organization of cemeteries by the church,[3] but we should nevertheless investigate the object of his scorn.

Burial Duty and the Construction of a Christian Identity

Numerous pagan epitaphs confirm that one of the duties of the *pietas* is to provide a tomb for the dead.[4] Burial of abandoned bodies is an obligation. To assure the dead peace in the afterlife, it is necessary to throw at least a handful of earth over the body.[5] This common view is expressed, for instance, in one of the *Major Declamations* attributed to Quintilian: "From this source [fear of similar misfortunes] also arises that feeling of sympathy which causes us to put soil on corpses, though they are unknown to us. No one is in such a terrible hurry that he would pass by any corpse whatever and pay it due respect with a little pile of dirt, however small."[6] In the jurisprudence on the action for the recovery of funeral expenses (*Digesta* 11.7.14.7), acting out of a sense of duty is fully taken into consideration and usually bars one from claiming reimbursement. Alciphron, in the third century, recounted the remarks of sailors waiting out a storm: "And so, while we wait for the surf to subside and the weather to clear, we'll take a turn around the shores right up to Caphareus in order that, if any corpse cast up from a wrecked ship is found anywhere, we may compose its limbs and bury it. For a good deed is not unrewarded, even though the recompense for the benefaction

---

3. This has been done by many scholars; see, for instance, Adalbert Hamman, *La vie quotidienne des premiers chrétiens (95–197)* (Paris: Hachette, 1971), 163; Hans Brandenburg, "Überlegungen zu Ursprung und Entstehung der Katakomben Roms," in *Vivarium: Festschrift Th. Klauser zum 90. Geburtstag*, Jahrbuch für Antike und Christentum. Ergänzungsband 11 (Münster: Aschendorff, 1984), 48, n. 106; Jean-Marie Salamito, "La christianisation et les nouvelles règles de la vie sociale," in *Histoire du christianisme des origines à nos jours. 2, Naissance d'une chrétienté (250–430)*, ed. Charles and Luce Pietri (Paris: Desclée/Fayard, 1995), 689; and Michel-Yves Perrin, "L'invention du cimetière: le cas romain," *Communio* 20 (1995): 105.

4. See Angelo Brelich, *A halálszemlélet formái a római birodalom sírfeliratain = Aspetti della morte nelle iscrizioni sepolcrali dell'Impero romano*, Dissertationes Pannonicae 7 (Budapest: Magyar Nemzeti Múzeum, 1937), 67–68; Richmond A. Lattimore, *Themes in Greek and Latin Epitaphs*, Illinois Studies in Language and Literature 28, nos. 1–2 (Urbana: University of Illinois Press, 1942), 220–24.

5. See the testimonies gathered in François de Visscher, *Le droit des tombeaux romains* (Milan: Giuffrè, 1963), 32 ff.

6. Pseudo-Quintillian, *Major Declamations* 5.6.

does not appear immediately. And over and above the hoped-for rewards, the consciousness of a good deed done sustains men and warms their hearts" (*Epistulae* 1.10.4). Servius, commenting on *Aeneid* 6.156 ff., in which the pious Aeneas offers the last rites to Misenus, whose body lies unburied on the beach, notes that "while it is forbidden for Pontiffs to see a corpse, it is even more forbidden to leave it unburied once they have seen it," and he concludes "Those who have written about all the forms of piety have put burial duty first" (*In Aeneid* 6.176).

However, the Christian Lactantius (c. 250–325) formally charged the philosophers with having passed over that duty in silence: "The last and greatest duty of piety is burial of strangers and paupers, something which those experts in justice and virtue have never discussed." (*Divine Institutes* 6.12.25). Even worse, he added, "There have even been people who treated burial as superfluous, saying there was no harm in lying unburied and discarded.... They don't dare to say that it is not to be done; rather, that if it weren't, there is no harm done" (6.12.28). Although none of the treatises mentioned by Servius have come down to us, and the theme of the uselessness of burial is a commonplace amply illustrated in philosophical literature,[7] the few texts cited above show that the duty to bury the dead was hardly neglected in Greco-Roman society. Lactantius's declaration should thus be read in the context of the construction of a Christian identity, or of its defense.[8]

Burial of the Poor in Christian Apologies

The earliest documentation of the care taken by Christians to provide for burial of the poor actually appears in texts that present themselves as apologies. This immediately raises the question of the importance of this theme in the definition of Christian identity in relation to other religious groups in the Roman Empire. At the same time, it calls for a careful analysis of the issues that necessarily underlie the effort to forge an identity.[9]

The oldest document is the *Apology* of Aristides, a text written in the first quarter of the second century, but whose original Greek version, with the exception of a few fragments, has come to us only through the *Life of Barlaam*

---

7. Cicero, *Tusculanae disputationes* 1.43.102–45; 1.43.109 presents the main philosophical positions on death; see Pseudo-Seneca, *De remediis fortuitorum* 5 (the text is known to Lactantius).

8. For a reading of the *Divine Institutes* in the context of the Great Persecution, see Elizabeth DePalma Digeser, *The Making of a Christian Empire: Lactantius and Rome* (Ithaca, NY: Cornell University Press, 2000).

9. See Judith Lieu's sharp analysis in "The Forging of a Christian Identity," *Mediterranean Archaeology* 11 (1998): 72–82.

and Joasaph, a Greek novel of the eleventh century, long attributed to John Damascene. There it has been reworked in the form of a speech meant to convert an Indian king to Christianity and was, for this purpose, abridged and slightly adapted. The fourth century Syriac translation is most faithful to the original.[10] Aristides distinguishes between two pairs of races: barbarian and Greek, Jewish and Christian, and presents in succession their conception of the divine and their way of living. The image he gives of Jews is quite positive, first because they worship one God, creator of all things, and second because "they imitate God by reason of the love which they have for man; for they have compassion on the poor and ransom the captive and bury the dead, and do things of a similar nature to these: things which are acceptable to God and are well-pleasing also to men, things which they have received from their fathers of old" (14.3).

When he comes to the Christians, Aristides elevates the virtues he has just attributed to the Jews even higher:

And he who has gives to him who has not, without grudging; and when they see the stranger they bring him to their dwellings, and rejoice over him as over a true brother; for they do not call brothers those who are after the flesh, but those who are in the spirit and in God: but when one of their poor passes away from the world, and any of them sees him, then he provides for his burial according to his ability; and if they hear that any of their number is imprisoned or oppressed for the name of the Messiah, all of them provide for his needs, and if it is possible that he may be delivered, they deliver him.

And if there is among them a man that is poor or needy, and they have not an abundance of necessaries, they fast two or three days that they may supply the needy with their necessary food. (15.6–7)

Burial of the poor, ransom of prisoners: these are the same good works on both sides. Aristides, however, seems to mean that Christians have a more acute sense of belonging to a community in which everyone, rich and poor, and even slaves, contribute to the relief of the sufferings of their "brothers."[11] The burial of the poor, in this context, is not particularly singled out: it is

---

10. Aristides, *Apology*, ed. Bernard Pouderon and Marie-Joseph Pierre, Sources chrétiennes 470 (Paris: Éditions du Cerf, 2003), 107 ff. The second extract quoted is preserved in its original Greek version in a papyrological fragment. The translation is that of J. R. Harris, *The Apology of Aristides* (Cambridge: Cambridge University Press, 1891).

11. See Judith M. Lieu, *Image and Reality: The Jews in the World of the Christians in the Second Century* (Edinburgh: T and T Clark, 1996), 174.

part of what one does out of compassion or love for his neighbor; it matters equally whether it is done for Christians or for the poor. In the *Apology*, the duty to bury the dead is thus one element of the ideal community that Aristides sought to promote or defend in order to forge a Christian identity.

In the *Apologeticum* of Tertullian, written in Carthage at the beginning of the third century, burial duty is also of secondary importance. As noted above, Tertullian rejects the charge that Christians formed illegal collegia, and contrasts the life of the groups they formed with that of the collegia: "You might call them [these offerings] the trust funds of piety. For they are not spent upon banquets nor drinking-parties nor thankless eating-houses; but to feed the poor and to bury them, for boys and girls who lack property and parents, and then for slaves grown old and ship-wrecked mariners; and any who may be in mines, islands or prisons, provided that it is for the sake of God's school, become the pensioners of their confession (39.6)."

Burial of the poor figures among other charitable acts. The context is comparable in every way to that in Aristides's *Apology*, as Tertullian's point is more generally that Christians support one another.

Other Apologists make no mention of the burial of the poor. Justin, who lived among the Christians in Ephesus and Rome in the middle of the second century, attests to the existence of a common fund, for example, but says nothing about burying the poor when he enumerates charitable works (*First Apology* 67.6). Thus, Christians take care to bury their own, particularly the poor, but this duty is probably not at the heart of what defines them.

❧ Christians, Non-Christians, and the Plague

Between 251 and 266, the plague struck again in the Roman Empire, an epidemic that was as ravaging as the one that occurred between 165 and 180.[12] While these epidemics generally resulted in a strengthening of narrow self-interest, which has been described many times, Christians seem to have maintained their solidarity and cared for one another. Without speculating on the concrete consequences of this mutual support,[13] it is clear that bishops praised this solidarity in order to reinforce the sense of Christian identity.

---

12. William H. McNeill, *Plagues and People* (New York: Doubleday, 1989), 103–5.

13. Some scholars supposed a higher rate of survival, which might in turn explain the increase in the number of Christians: see McNeill, *Plagues and People,* 108–9; Rodney Stark, "Epidemics, Networks, and the Rise of Christianity," in *Social Networks in the Early Christian Environment: Issues and Methods for Social History,* ed. L. Michael White, Semeia 56 (Atlanta: Scholars Press, 1992), 159–75; and Rodney Stark, *The Rise of Christianity: A Sociologist Reconsiders History* (Princeton, NJ: Princeton University Press, 1996), 73–94.

Pontius, Cyprian's biographer, ended the chapter in which he praises the conduct of the bishop of Carthage by comparing him to Tobit, whose piety he surpassed. Indeed, Cyprian called on Christians to direct their efforts toward Christians as well as non-Christians, whereas Tobit buried only Jews. Pontius did not provide concrete data about the actions of Christians: the important thing was that everyone participated, the poor by offering service in lieu of money, and that even pagans benefited from their care (*Life of Cyprian* 8–9).

Denis, the bishop of Alexandria, gave a more complete description of what happened in his city in a letter that Eusebius quoted in the *Ecclesiastical History* (7.22.7–10):

> The most, at all events, of our brethren in their exceeding love and affection for the brotherhood were unsparing of themselves and clave to one another, visiting the sick without a thought as to the danger, assiduously ministering to them, tending them in Christ, and so most gladly departed this life along with them.... In this manner the best at any rate of our brethren departed this life, certain presbyters and deacons and some of the laity, receiving great commendation, so that this form of death seems in no respect to come behind martyrdom, being the outcome of much piety and strong faith. So, too, the bodies of the saints they would take up in their open hands to their bosom, closing their eyes and shutting their mouths, carrying them on their shoulders and laying them out; they would cling to them, embrace them, bathe and adorn them with their burial clothes.... But the conduct of the heathen was the exact opposite. Even those who were in the first stages of the disease they thrust away, and fled from their dearest. They would even cast them in the roads half-dead, and treat the unburied corpses as vile refuse.

The difference between Christians and pagans could not have been more striking; the latter avoided the sick, while the former died to help others. Self-sacrifice, comparable to martyrdom, was clearly more important than burying the dead. When Eusebius of Caesarea describes the plague raging at the end of the reign of Maximinus Daia, he also mentions the role of Christians in organizing the burial of the dead:

> The proofs of the Christians' zeal and piety in every respect were manifest to all the heathen. For example, they alone in such an evil state of affairs gave practical evidence of their sympathy and humanity: all day

long some of them would diligently persevere in performing the last offices for the dying and burying them (for there were countless numbers, and no one to look after them); while others would gather together in a single assemblage the multitude of those who all throughout the city were wasted with the famine, and distribute bread to them all. (9.8.14)

The Christians' actions are clearly presented as an organized public service, comparable to that which Pontius referred to in Carthage. The zeal shown by Christians in burying the dead, a hygienic measure that was indispensable for halting the epidemic, as well as their solidarity and organization during the plague, certainly helped to define their group identity, even, as Eusebius suggested, in the eyes of non-Christians.

Providing Burial for the Martyrs

The *Acts of Martyrs* contain numerous accounts illustrating the care taken to bury martyrs. They thus provide important evidence of the significance Christians attached to the duty to bury the dead, not only at the time they were written, but also for centuries to come, for they were read during liturgical commemorations on the anniversary of the martyrs' death.[14] The role that persecution itself played in the construction of Christian identity does not need to be emphasized further.

According to the law, bodies of criminals condemned to death could not be denied burial. Provision was made even for the collecting of the bones and ashes of those burned at the stake. However, the *Acts of Martyrs* stressed that Christians made an effort to remove the martyrs' bodies secretly, though they do not say whether this had to be done secretly because authorities refused to render them, or in order to avoid being taken themselves.[15] In the Greek version of the *Martyrdom of Saints Carpus, Papylus, and Agathonicê*, Christians collected the remains of their burned bodies "furtively." In the same way, the

---

14. See Baudouin de Gaiffier, "La lecture des Actes de martyrs dans la prière liturgique en Occident: à propos du passionnaire hispanique," *Analecta Bollandiana* 73 (1954): 134–66 and Baudouin de Gaiffier, "La lecture des Passions de martyrs à Rome avant le IXe siècle," *Analecta Bollandiana* 87 (1969): 63–78.

15. Legal texts and *Acts of Martyrs* have been analyzed in Valentino Capocci, "Sulla concessione e sul divieto di sepoltura nel mondo romano ai condamnati a pena capitale," *Studia et documenta historiae et iuris* 22 (1956): 266–310; see also Giannetto Longo, "La sepoltura dei cristiani giustiziati," *Annali della Facoltà di Lettere e Filosofia, Università di Macerata* 22 (1958): 75–98, reprinted in *Ricerche romanistiche* (Milan: Giuffrè, 1966), 241–58.

ashes of Fructuosus and his companions were collected at night, and the body of Cyprian was removed for burial.[16] We should not exclude the possibility that the motivation for this was to imitate the circumstances of the laying of Christ's body in the tomb: Joseph had gone to Pilate secretly, and placed the body in the tomb at night (Matt. 27:57–61).

The *Acts of Martyrs* also relate several episodes showing that the persecutors deliberately denied martyrs the right to burial. We have already discussed the case of the persecutor of the martyrs in Lyons who wanted to prevent their resurrection. However, this motivation remains an isolated case in the *Acts of Martyrs,* and other examples show that the reason for denying burial was to prevent a cult from developing around the tomb. The earliest example is the martyrdom of Polycarp of Smyrna: "The jealous and envious Evil One, who is the adversary of the race of the just, realizing the greatness of his testimony, his unblemished career from the beginning, and seeing him now crowned with the garland of immortality and the winner of an incontestable prize, prevented us even from taking up the poor body, though so many were eager to do so and to have a share in his holy flesh" (*Martyrdom of Polycarp* 17.1).

And the text adds that the alleged reason of the persecutor for not giving up the body was that "Otherwise they may abandon the crucified and begin to worship this man (17.2)." There seemed to have been some disagreement in Smyrna about the right attitude, and the letter, which gives an account of Polycarp's martyrdom, tries to impose clear boundaries to the devotion to the martyrs.[17] Then it resumes its account:

> And so, when the centurion noticed the conflict caused by the Jews, he put the body out before everyone and had it cremated, as is their custom. Thus at last, collecting the remains that were dearer to us than precious stones and finer than gold, we buried them in a fitting spot. Gathering here, so far as we can, in joy and gladness, we will be allowed by the Lord to celebrate the anniversary day of his martyrdom, both as

---

16. *Martyrium sancti Carpi, Papyli et Agathonicae* 47; *Passio sanctorum martyrum Fructuosi episcopi, Auguri et Eulogi diaconorum* 6.1–2; *Acta proconsularia sancti Cypriani* 6; see *The Acts of the Christian Martyrs*, ed. Herbert Musurillo (Oxford: Clarendon Press, 1972), 28–29, 182–83, and 174–75, respectively.

17. The authenticity of the passages where the cult of the martyrs is mentioned has been seriously questioned. See status quaestionis and bibliography in Boudewijn Dehandschutter, "The Martyrium Polycarpi: A Century of Research," in *Aufstieg und Niedergang der römischen Welt (ANRW): Geschichte und Kultur Roms im Spiegel der neueren Forschung.* 2, Principat. 27, Religion. 1 (Berlin: De Gruyter, 1993), 492–97, 502–3. See also Gerd Buschmann, *Martyrium Polycarpi: eine formkritische Studie: ein Beitrag zur Frage nach der Entstehung der Gattung Märtyreakte*, Beihefte zur Zeitschrift für die neutestamentliche Wissenschaft und die Kunde der älteren Kirche 70 (Berlin: De Gruyter, 1994).

a memorial for those who have already fought the contest and for the training and preparation of those who will do so one day. (18.1–3)

The Church of Smyrna, author of the letter, thus gathered and buried the remains of its martyred bishop. Still, there is more here than a pious burial duty, as indicated by the desire "to have a share in his holy flesh" (17.1).[18] It was the miracles they witnessed during the martyrdom that made the body of Polycarp so precious in the eyes of the Christians of Smyrna.[19] The expression "in a fitting spot" seems to be in contrast to abandoning the body "out before everyone"—in other words, without a tomb. Nothing would indicate that the lack of burial affected the martyr in any way; rather, Christians wanted to provide a tomb for Polycarp for the purpose of commemoration and the cult.

This was exactly what the persecutors wanted to prevent. In a passage that seems to allude to Galerius (*Divine Institutes* 5.11.6), Lactantius writes that the persecutor was "not just pulling humans limb from limb, but grinding up their very bones and raving at their ashes so that no place of burial even exists—as if the aim of those who confess God were to have lots of visits to their own tombs, rather than go to God themselves!" Valerian, in his first edict promulgated in August 257, forbade Christians "assembling or entering what are called cemeteries." Gallienus canceled these measures in 260 CE and restored to the Christians the places where "what people call cemeteries" were found. I have shown above that the "cemeteries" were in fact the tombs of martyrs and that the imperial edicts were therefore aimed at the cult that took place at their tombs.[20] Eusebius of Caesarea even reports the case of an exhumation at Nicomedia at the beginning of Diocletian's persecution in 303: "As to the imperial servants, whose bodies after death had been committed to the ground with fitting honors, their reputed masters, starting afresh, deemed it necessary to exhume them and cast them also into the sea, lest any, regarding them as actually gods (so at least they imagined), should worship them as they lay in their tombs" (*Ecclesiastical History* 8.6.7). Thus, to provide the martyrs with a place of burial was an undertaking fraught with a very specific meaning.

---

18. On the meaning of this expression, see *Das Martyrium des Polykarp,* ed. Gerd Buschmann, Kommentar zu den Apostolischen Vätern 6 (Göttingen: Vandenhoeck und Ruprecht, 1998), 329.

19. See Willy Rordorf, "Aux origines du culte des martyrs," *Irenikon* 65 (1972): 315–31, reprinted in *Liturgie, foi et vie des premiers chrétiens: études patristiques,* Théologie historique 75 (Paris: Beauchesne, 1986), 363–79.

20. For Valerian's edict, see Eusebius, *Ecclesiastical History* 7.11.10 (see *Acta proconsularia Cypriani* 1). For Gallienus's edict, see Eusebius, *Ecclesiastical History* 7.13.

The *Letters* of Cyprian provide evidence that the clergy were responsible for ensuring that martyrs and confessors were not left unburied.[21] In April or May 250, when he was forced to hide outside Carthage, Cyprian urged his clergy to take care of all Christians who died in prison (*Epistulae* 12.1.2): "You should pay special care and solicitude also to the bodies of all those who, without being tortured, nevertheless die in prison, departing this life in glory."

The special mention made here of confessors shows that martyrs were the object of attention not given to all Christians.[22] The reason for this is explained later when Cyprian asks his clergy to note the day of the confessors' deaths so that the anniversary can be celebrated like that of the martyrs. This fact is a necessary precaution, he adds, even if "our most faithful and devoted brother Tertullus, besides all the other services of charity which he performs with his customary zeal and concern—and that includes equal diligence concerning the bodies of the dead in Carthage—has written and continues to write, letting me know the days on which our blessed brothers in prison depart in glory from this life and enter into immortality" (*Epistulae* 12.2.1). Much has been written about the status of Tertullus: was he a deacon, a grave digger, or a simple layman? It seems that Cyprian considers him a pious layman, when he contrasts his work with that which was expected of members of his clergy.[23]

More ambiguous is the testimony found in a letter preserved among the letters of Cyprian, but that was actually written by the clergy of Rome. After stressing that the members of the clergy must remain in their churches during persecutions, in order to keep Christians from faltering and in order to give communion to the penitents and the catechumen who are threatened, the letter adds, "And in particular, if the bodies of the martyrs or of the

---

21. See Victor Saxer, *Vie liturgique et quotidienne à Carthage vers le milieu du IIIe siècle: le témoignage de saint Cyprien et de ses contemporains d'Afrique,* 2nd ed., Studi di antichità cristiana 29 (Vatican City: Pontificio Istituto di archeologia cristiana, 1984), 285–86. On the circumstances and the chronology, see Luc Duquenne, *La chronologie des lettres de S. Cyprien: le dossier de la persécution de Dèce,* Subsidia Hagiographica 54 (Brussels: Société des Bollandistes, 1972).

22. It is more convincing to read *propensior* as an intensifier than as a comparative; therefore we cannot deduce that such care was granted to every Christian. Cyprian compares the confessors to martyrs, to stress that the merit of the former is similar to that of the later. This is contra Saxer, *Vie liturgique et quotidienne à Carthage,* 286.

23. See Graeme W. Clarke, *The Letters of St. Cyprian of Carthage,* vol. 1, Ancient Christian Writers 43 (New York: Newman Press, 1984), 250, n. 13; for the *fossor,* see Saxer, *Vie liturgique et quotidienne à Carthage,* 285–86. Yvette Duval, *Auprès des saints corps et âmes: l'inhumation "ad sanctos" dans la chrétienté d'Orient et d'Occident du IIIe au VIIe siècle* (Paris: Études Augustiniennes, 1988), 25, n. 7, makes him a bishop. I will not mention the discussion about the hypothesis that identifies Tertullus as the same who gave his name to the *area Tertulli;* see chapter 1 of the present volume.

others are left unburied, severe danger threatens those whose duty it is to do this work. Accordingly, whoever amongst you on whatever occasion carries out this task, he is accounted, we are sure, a good servant and, therefore, as he has been faithful over little, he will be set in authority over ten cities" (*Letters* 8, 3, 2). Once again, "those responsible for this task" have been identified as deacons or grave diggers, but the following sentence, with its allusion to Luke 19:17 ("Well done, good servant! Because you have been trustworthy in a very small thing, take charge of ten cities") suggests that this was not a regular and specific function of any one in the clergy.

A final text, by a contemporary witness in Alexandria, can also be added to the record. In a letter from Denis, bishop of Alexandria, cited by Eusebius of Caesarea, we learn that a deacon was charged with assisting confessors who were imprisoned: "As to the deacons, they who survived those that died in the island are Faustus, Eusebius, Chaeremon: that Eusebius, whom from the beginning God strengthened and prepared to render with all energy the services to the confessors that were in prison, and at no small risk to perform the task of laying out the corpses of the blessed and perfect martyrs" (*Ecclesiastical History* 7.11.24). The service that Eusebius gives does not appear to be related to his status as a deacon: Denis describes this service rather as his particular mission, the one God intended for him.

It is useless to try, on the basis of these documents, to determine that the clergy, and in particular deacons, were responsible for providing burial for the martyrs. Cyprian shows very clearly that recovering the body was above all a family matter when he reports the case of Numidicius whose daughter requested the return of the body from Roman authorities only to learn that he was not dead (*Letters* 40.1.1).

Even if anniversary celebrations should not be linked to the tombs too exclusively,[24] it is undeniable that the Christians' concern for martyrs' burial and therefore for their tombs are crucial elements in the representation of Christian identity. However, nothing in these texts indicates that the church's commitment to its martyrs is the basis for a more general burial duty: burial of the martyrs does not prefigure the organization of cemeteries for the

---

24. In Carthage, at the time of Cyprian, the place for celebrating martyrs' anniversaries seems to be the usual place for Christian gathering: see Cyprian, *Letters* 12.2.1, and the commentary of Clarke, *The Letters of St. Cyprian of Carthage*, 1:252–53. More broadly, see Yvette Duval, *Loca sanctorum Africae*, 2:456–57; and Paul-Albert Février, "Le culte des morts dans les communautés chrétiennes durant le IIIe siècle," in *Atti del IX Congresso internazionale di archeologia cristiana: Roma, 21–27 settembre 1975*, Studi di antichità cristiana 32 (Vatican City: Pontificio Istituto di archeologia cristiana, 1978), 1:269–72, reprinted in Paul-Albert Février, *La Méditerranée*, vol. 1, Collection de l'École française de Rome 225 (Rome: École française de Rome/Aix-en-Provence: Université de Provence, 1996).

faithful. Burying martyrs is not simply about fulfilling a pious duty, one due to every Christian: the martyrs' are clearly "very special dead" and the care taken to assure them a proper burial was in response to very particular needs. In the *Praeparatio evangelica,* Eusebius quotes, at the end of a series of extracts from Plato about the kind of death the wise man is ready to face in order to defend his beliefs, a passage from the *Republic* on the honor due to those who die for the fatherland, and adds, "That applies to the death of those who are friends of God, of whom it would be accurate to say that they represent the soldiers of the true religion. It is also our custom to gather at their tombs, to say prayers, to honor their blessed souls, certain that these gestures on our part are the right ones" (13.11.2). The martyr cult thus becomes a Christian version of the honors given to those who die for the fatherland.

Duty to remember the martyrs or duty to support the destitute, the duty to bury the dead played a significant role in the construction of a Christian identity throughout the third century and at the beginning of the fourth. We now need to see what becomes of it in Christian teaching during the fourth and fifth centuries.

Christian Piety and Burial Duty in the Fourth and Fifth Centuries

To justify burial duty, Lactantius notes that man is made in the image of God (*Divine Institutes* 6.12.30): "We will not therefore permit a creature made in God's image to fall prey to wild beasts and birds: we will return it to the earth whence it came...." He also insists that this duty be not given to one's relatives but to strangers and the poor. That is the condition for this work of compassion to be truly a sacrifice to God, since it involves neither affection, nor any hope of reward (6.12.18–19). According to the principle adopted in the *Divine Institutes,* Lactantius does not provide biblical authority for this teaching,[25] but his silence is not difficult to fill.

The model is above all that of Tobit, the indefatigable grave digger. In peacetime, he buried the bodies of his compatriots, who were abandoned behind the walls of Niniveh (Tob. 1:17). When King Sennacherib persecuted his family, Tobit risked his own life to bury them (1:18–20). He did not hesitate to leave the table and interrupt his meal to go take care of an

---

25. About this principle and its contradictions in the *Institutes,* see Pierre Monat, *Lactance et la Bible: une propédeutique latine à la lecture de la Bible dans l'Occident constantinien* (Paris: Études augustiniennes, 1982), 1:31–35.

abandoned corpse (2:4). These are all included among the good deeds enumerated by the angel who came to cure him (12:12–13). Other models are the two figures who care for the burial of Christ: Joseph of Arimathea, who went to find Pontius Pilate to ask him to turn over to him Christ's body and who gave him his own tomb (Matt 27:57–58; Mark 15:42–45; Luke 23:50–52), and Nicodemus who, according to John 19:38–42, helped Joseph lay Christ in the tomb "in accordance with Jewish burial customs." Finally, Abraham's purchase of a tomb for his wife Sarah (Gen. 23:8–9) is the model for the burial duty owed to the relatives.

What is the place of these different figures in Christian teaching? To answer that it is not enough simply to cite a few texts in which they appear; it is also necessary to determine the contexts in which they were used. I will focus on preaching and attempt to determine the frequency with which these figures were used, beyond the concrete examples that have come down to us.

Tobit

The book of Tobit "is not in the Canon, but it is used by ecclesiastical writers." Thus says Jerome in the preface of his *Commentary on Tobit*. It is true of both Greek and Latin ecclesiastical authors, as the patristic citations of the book of Tobit reveals.[26] Yet, the texts that deal with Tobit's funerary activities are relatively few, and exclusively in Latin.

We have seen above that Pontius compares the activity of Cyprian during the plague to that of Tobit (*Life of Cyprian* 8). Ambrose of Milan, in his *On Tobit*, does not actually stress this aspect of his activity. The treatise is entirely devoted to denouncing usury, and it is only in chapter 1 that Ambrose, rapidly summarizing the life of Tobit, says a few words about burying the dead: "There is no higher duty than to give to one who can no longer do so, than to protect from birds and beasts one like us in nature" (1.5). However, he does not call upon his readers to follow the example of Tobit.

The figure of Tobit was also known to the audience of Maximus of Turin, as is clear from sermon 41. Chapter 8 of the Gospel of Matthew on the requirements of the calling to follow Christ had just been read and Maximus explained why Christ chose the disciple who asked of him: "Lord, first let me go and bury my father." This disciple did not hesitate to abandon his dead or

---

26. See *Biblia patristica: index des citations et allusions bibliques dans la littérature patristique*, 7 vols. (Paris: Éditions du CNRS, 1975–1999); and Myla Perraymond, "Tobia e Tobiolo nell'esegesi della iconografia dei primi secoli," *Bessarione* 6 (1988): 141–54.

dying father, suggests Maximus, and joined Christ without having remained long enough to render his final filial duty, as indicated by the word *first*. This is where Tobit comes in: "Thus, as Tobit is justified because he abandons his meal for the sake of a burial, this man is approved because he abandons the burial of his father for the sake of Christ. For the one is not afraid to pass over his meal because some earthly work intervenes, while the other fears lest some delay cause him to omit the eating of heavenly bread. Hence, although in consideration of Christ we owe burial to everyone, this man forsook his father's burial out of love for Christ" (*Sermons* 41.2).

There is no call to follow Tobit here. Maximus evokes Tobit, but explains that we must distinguish between our priorities and that the greater love of Christ can legitimately cause one to neglect the final respect due to a father.

The figure of Tobit is mentioned by Augustine in *City of God* when he dispels the idea that because burial is not necessary for salvation, one can therefore neglect this duty to the dead: "This does not mean that the bodies of the departed are to be scorned and cast away, particularly not the bodies of the righteous and faithful...and Tobit is commended, as the angel testifies, for having done good service to God by giving burial to the dead" (1.13). Augustine is responding to pagan attacks following the sacking of Rome in 410. Pagans claimed that the lack of burial was an evil that God should have spared Christians. Augustine tries to show that the lack of burial was not the evil that pagans thought, and in particular that it was not an obstacle to resurrection. We have already met this charge of the pagans against Christians; like the writers of the *Acts of Martyrs* and the apologists, Augustine emphasizes the omnipotence of God. To better indicate the folly of the pagan critics, Augustine recalls that the philosophers preached scorn of burial (1.12.2). That is also why, in order to distance himself from such teaching, he is careful to specify later that providing a burial is the duty of every Christian and gives Biblical examples: Tobit; Joseph of Arimathia; the woman who poured precious perfume over the head of Christ in preparation for his burial (Matt. 26:10–12); and the Patriarchs of the Old Testament. In a similar series of exempla Tobit figures in the letter that Paulinus of Nola wrote to Pammachius to console him on the death of his wife.[27]

The only text in which Tobit is actually offered as an example to Christians is in a poem on funerals in the *Hymns for Every Day* of Prudentius (c. 348–410). In these verses, Prudentius explains that the greatest attention must be given to the tomb where the body lies waiting for the resurrection

---

27. Paulinus of Nola, *Epistulae* 13.

(*Cathemerinon* 10.37–48). Belief in the resurrection prompts Christians to take care of abandoned bodies:

> Enlightened by faith, devout Christians
> Thus the dead hold in reverence believing
> That the body enwrapt in cold slumber
> With new life will hereafter be quickened. (57–60)

Burial is not done with a view toward resurrection as if resurrection required it. But resurrection gives a Christian meaning to the attention to burial. To provide burial for abandoned corpses is thus a charitable work that serves the Lord (61–64). Hence the example of Tobit and the memory of the meal he did not hesitate to delay in order to take care of a body abandoned without burial (69–76) and of the compensation for his devotion (77–78), an allusion to the miraculous cure of his blindness (79–80). For Prudentius, therefore, the story of Tobit is a scriptural warrant that burying the dead is a good work.

The pietas of Tobit toward abandoned corpses is rarely offered as an example to Christians. To recognize Tobit in the features of the grave digger who is sometimes represented in Roman catacombs is totally gratuitous in the absence of any other evidence.[28]

Christ's Burial

It seems that the commentators on Christ's burial by Joseph and Nicodemus have been prone to consider what was exceptional about the episode rather than use it as an example.

In the *Divine Institutes* Lactantius does not speak of the burial of Christ except when he defends the "mystery of the cross." As a model of infamous death, the crucifixion was actually the preferred target of the mockeries of pagans. Lactantius answers these attacks saying there are two reasons for the death on the cross. First, Christ had to suffer a form of death that was common among the lowest of people. Second, he writes,

> His body had to be kept whole, since he was due to rise from the dead two days later. No one should be unaware of the fact that he himself

---

28. This hypothesis is proposed in Elena Conde Guerri, *Los 'fossores' de Roma paleocristiana: estudio iconografico, epigrafico y social*, Studi di antichità cristiana 33 (Vatican City: Pontificio istituto di archeologia cristiana, 1979), 109–15.

in speaking of his suffering had already made it known that he had the power of laying down and taking up his spirit when he wanted. Because he gave up his spirit while crucified, his executioners did not think it necessary to break his bones, as the custom was; instead, they merely pierced his side. Thus his body was taken down from the cross and carefully laid in its tomb still whole. That was all done so that his body should not be so wounded or damaged that it was unsuitable for resurrection. (*Divine Institutes* 4.26.31–33)

The special treatment reserved for Christ on the cross has already captured the attention of exegetes. Unlike the robbers crucified with him, his legs were not broken according to John 19:31–33. That is usually interpreted as proof of Christ's voluntary death,[29] and Lactantius, alluding to John 10:18, joined this tradition. He adds that his body had to be left intact for the resurrection and that is why it was "carefully enclosed in a tomb." Lactantius does not depart from straight exegesis: he understands every detail of the scene as proof that Christ fully intended to rise again as he had declared. What he says of the resurrection of Christ cannot be understood about the general resurrection, and we cannot conclude from this exegesis that Lactantius believed that burial is necessary for resurrection.[30]

In his *Commentary on the Gospel of Matthew*, Hilary of Poitiers notes that it was "necessary to entomb the one who would rise from the dead" (33.8) and quickly drops the literal meaning of the passage in order to explore what it might mean on a higher level. Similarly, in the *Treatise on the Gospel of Luke*, Ambrose explores what the passage might mean in relation to the figure of Christ and salvation. He exhorted Christians who were listening to him to clothe the "body of the Lord in glory" in other words to believe in his divinity, just as Joseph clothed the body of the Lord in a shroud, and then, referring to the late hour when Joseph went to Pilate, to come to Christ at any hour (10.136–44). However, he did not consider it opportune to invite Christians to take care of the burial of paupers and strangers. In the commentary on Psalm 61, entirely devoted to denouncing the assassination of Gratian in 386, Ambrose compares himself to another Joseph when he says that he recovered Gratian's body from Maximus (*In Psalmum 61 enarratio* 26). In the

---

29. See Origen, *Against Celsus* 2.16, and *Commentary on the Gospel of John* 19.102, with the note by Cécile Blanc, in Origène, *Commentaire sur Jean. 4, (Livres XIX et XX)*, ed. Cécile Blanc, Sources chrétiennes 290 (Paris: Éditions du Cerf, 1982), 372–74.

30. This is contra Yvette Duval, *Auprès des saints corps et âmes*, 43–44, and Edmond Le Blant, "Mémoire sur les martyrs chrétiens et les supplices destructeurs du corps," *Mémoires de l'Institut national de France, Académie des Inscriptions et Belles Lettres* 28 (1874): 83.

Commentary on Matthew, Jerome emphasizes that "the simplicity of the tomb of the Lord shames the pretensions of the wealthy who, even in their tombs, cannot forego their riches," but does not single out Joseph for any particular praise (27.59).

In the *Tractates on the Gospel of John,* the only lesson Augustine takes from the episode is the fact that Joseph and Nicodemus were following Jewish custom: "It does not seem to me that the Evangelist intended to say 'as the manner of the Jews is to bury' without a purpose, for indeed, if I am not mistaken, he thus advised that in duties of this sort that are performed for the dead, the custom of each nation ought to be preserved" (120.4). This is a recurring theme in his teaching on burial: the duties owed to the dead are determined by local custom.[31] In *De consensus euangelistarum* Augustine compares the different narratives of the Evangelists and finds no serious discrepancies, although in John there are significant variations on the role of Nicodemus. He points out, however, that John is not inconsistent in describing Joseph as being "secretly" a disciple of Christ, "because he feared the Jews" (John 19:38), whereas he had the courage to claim the body: "And we must suppose, further, that in the performance of that last burial duty, he cared less for the Jews, although he tried in ordinary circumstances, when hearing the Lord, to avoid exposing himself to their enmity" (3.22.59). The duty to bury is therefore sufficiently important for Joseph to run the risk of being denounced by the Jews as a disciple of Christ. Such reasoning is in any case implicit in Augustine's commentary.

If we turn to the collections of sermons of the fourth and fifth centuries, we cannot help noticing how little commentary there is on the burial of Christ. It seems that the liturgical readings of Easter week normally skip over the burial, stopping on the crucifixion and resuming with the resurrection. That is not the case at Hippo, but only Augustine's *Sermon 218* mentions Christ's tomb in an onomastic commentary on the names Joseph and Nicodemus.[32] In northern Italy, only Maximus of Turin has left a commentary on Christ's burial in his sermons 38 and 39, preached successively during the course of Easter week, in which he builds a parallel between Mary and Joseph of Arimathea. Just as Mary gave her womb for the birth of Christ, so Joseph gave his tomb for his rebirth; womb and tomb are both virginal, as Joseph's tomb was "a new tomb, never before used for burials" (John 19:41). Maximus goes so

---

31. On this topic, see Heikki Kotila, *Memoria mortuorum: Commemoration of the Departed in Augustine,* Studia Ephemeridis Augustinianum 38 (Rome: Institutum Patristicum Augustinianum, 1992), 95–98.

32. Augustine, *Sermons* 218.15. For the liturgical context, see Augustine of Hippo, *Sermons pour la Pâque,* ed. Suzanne Poque, Sources chrétiennes 116 (Paris: Éditions du Cerf, 1966), 71–73.

far as to say that with Joseph, the birth of Christ is even more "sacred": three days sufficed for Christ to rise and save the world, whereas his birth in the world had taken nine months! Maximus, at the beginning of his second sermon, given the next day, acts as if this comparison had shocked his audience. What better occasion to preach on the importance of burial duty? And yet he did not seize the opportunity and continued in the same vein; the bishop's attention was on Christ alone, as the means of salvation.

In a sermon on loving the poor, Gregory Nazianzen refers to Christ's tomb in a long speech:

> If you believe me at all, then, servants and brothers and sisters and fellow heirs of Christ, let us take care of Christ while there is still time; let us minister to Christ's needs, let us give Christ nourishment, let us clothe Christ, let us gather Christ in, let us show Christ honor—not just at our tables, as some do (Luke 7:36), nor just with ointment, like Mary (John 12:3), nor just with a tomb, like Joseph of Arimathea, nor just with the things needed for burial, like that half-hearted lover of Christ, Nicodemus (John 19:38), nor just with gold and frankincense and myrrh, like the magi (Matthew 2:11), who came to him before all the rest. But since the Lord of all things 'desires mercy and not sacrifice' (Matthew 9:13), and since 'a compassionate heart is worth more than tens of thousands of fat rams' (Daniel 3: 40), let us give this gift to him through the needy.... (*Orationes* 14.40)

Gregory contrasts sacrifice and pity, and puts the care of Joseph and Nicodemus to bury Jesus in the category of sacrifice. Therefore, for him they are not at all models of what must be done for the poor.

In sermon 88 of the *Homilies on Matthew*, John Chrysostom stresses Joseph's love for Christ but does not derive any lesson for his listeners. In sermon 85 of the *Homilies on John,* his comments are actually negative. Joseph and Nicodemus had great affection for Christ, but the grand funeral they performed show that they saw him merely as a man. The fact that Christ arose naked should be an invitation to cease the madness about funerals. The men who lavished attention on Christ's funeral did not yet believe in resurrection, and were following the custom of the Jews, as John 19:40 explicitly says. None of the twelve apostles was there. Finally, he adds, "And so you will know that he valued none of all that, Christ said; 'You saw me hungry, and you fed me; thirsty, and you gave me drink; naked, and you clothed me' (Matt. 25:35); but nowhere did he say, 'you saw that I was dead, and you buried me.'" (5) Although he is careful to stress that neither funerals nor burials were forbidden, he concludes, "It is not as sinful for a body to be cast aside unburied as for a soul to appear stripped of all virtue" (6). Therefore, the lack of burial does not pose any danger for salvation. Far from seeing the conduct of Joseph and Nicodemus as a model to be emulated, John Chrysostom uses the episode of the burial of Christ to preach on a familiar theme, the extravagance of funerals.

In the fourth and fifth centuries, Joseph and Nicodemus were therefore not being held up as examples for Christians to imitate, even if the negative interpretation of John Chrysostom was an isolated case. We must note, by contrast, the manner in which the example of Joseph was recalled at the beginning of the sixth century by Hypatios, the bishop of Ephesus:

> Jesus Christ our Lord, after being laid bare before us, willingly and without alteration, humbled himself, as the holy apostle tells us, unto his death upon the cross (Phil 2: 7–8). And after his crucifixion and his death, creative of life, as we are told by the Gospels, because of his ineffable love for mankind, he was cast off naked and unburied, was tended by Joseph and placed in his own tomb; that is how much and in how many ways he humbled himself to be as we are, yet without sin (Hebr 4:15). Whoever performs such holy service and (funerary) honor for his brothers who precede [him] in death, let him know that he does it for the Lord.[33]

This is an inscription regulating funerals for the inhabitants of Ephesus; the example of Joseph justifies here the provision of free funerals by the church. Whenever they felt the need—and in the beginning of the sixth century the context was entirely different—the bishops would recall biblical examples that served their purposes.

❧ The Burial of the Patriarchs

Although the burial of the Patriarchs is an important model for teaching about Christian burial in the Middle Ages,[34] it was of little interest to ancient commentators. Apart from the few general references we have already noted,

---

33. Henri Grégoire, *Recueil des inscriptions grecques-chrétiennes d'Asie mineure* (Paris: Leroux, 1922), no. 108, l.2–7, 35–37 (= *Die Inschriften von Ephesos*. 7.2, ed. H. Wankel (Bonn, Germany: Habelt, 1981), no. 4135). For a commentary, see Margherita Guarducci, *Epigrafia greca. 4, Epigrafi sacre pagane e cristiane* (Rome: Istituto poligrafico dello Stato, 1978), 401–4; and Gilbert Dagron, "'Ainsi rien n'échappera à la réglementation': État, Église, corporation, confréries: à propos des inhumations à Constantinople (IVe–Ve siècle)," in *Hommes et richesses dans l'Empire byzantin. 2, VIIe–XVe siècle*, Réalités byzantines (Paris: Lethielleux, 1991), 167–69.

34. See Michel Lauwers, "La sépulture des Patriarches (Genèse, 23): modèles scripturaires et pratiques sociales dans l'Occident médiéval ou Du bon usage d'un récit de fondation," *Studi Medievali* 37 (1996): 519–47.

Athanasius of Alexandria used their model to denounce certain Egyptian funerary practices, while Ambrose and Jerome took special note of Abraham's purchase of the cave of Mambre and discussed the question of the sale of tombs.

In the *Life of Antony*, Athanasius attributes a very special importance to Antony's burial.[35] Antony actually insisted absolutely that his body be buried in the ground, conforming to the practice he had defended over and over against the laity who followed traditional Egyptian practice. Athanasius thus presents one of these exhortations: "'It is neither lawful nor at all reverent to do this. The bodies of the patriarchs and the prophets are preserved even to this day in tombs, and the Lord's own body was put in a tomb, and a stone placed there hid it until he rose on the third day.' And in saying these things he showed that the person violates the Law who does not, after death, bury the bodies of the deceased, even though they are holy. For what is greater or holier than the Lord's body?" (90.4).

So the example of the Patriarchs of the Old Testament and above all that of Christ, legitimate the practice recommended by Antony. Burial is strictly associated here with the idea of hiding the body underground, for Antony feared above all that pious Christians would remove it. As he exhorts his followers at the moment of his death, "if you care for me and remember me as a father, do not permit anyone to take my body to Egypt, lest they set it in the houses.... Therefore, perform the rites for me yourselves, and bury my body in the earth. And let my word be kept secret by you, so that no one knows the place but you alone" (91.7). Athanasius is criticizing the traditional Egyptian practices: not only mummification, but the exposure of the body at home.[36] The Christians continued the traditional practice, in particular for the "very special dead" such as martyrs and ascetics.[37] Antony, and through him Athanasius, were opposing a form of relics cult.

Athanasius actually uses the same examples again in the festal letter of 369, in which he denounces the schismatic Melitians who followed these

---

35. See Monique Alexandre, "À propos du récit de la mort d'Antoine (Athanase, *Vie d'Antoine*. PG 26, 968–974, § 89–93): L'heure de la mort dans la littérature monastique," in *Le temps chrétien de la fin de l'Antiquité au Moyen Âge*, Colloques internationaux du CNRS 604 (Paris: Éditions du CNRS, 1984), 268–70.

36. See Barbara Borg, "The Dead as Guest at Table? Continuity and Change in the Egyptian Cult of the Dead," in *Portraits and Masks: Burial Customs in Roman Egypt*, ed. Morris L. Bierbrier (London: British Museum Press, 1997), 26–32.

37. See Theofried Baumeister, *Martyr invictus: der Martyrer als Sinnbild der Erlösung in der Legende und im Kult der frühen koptischen Kirche: zur Kontinuität des ägyptischen Denkens*, Forschung zur Volkskunde, 46 (Münster: Regensberg, 1972), 51–86; David Frankfurter, "The Cult of the Martyrs in Egypt before Constantine: The Evidence of the Coptic 'Apocalypse of Elijah,'" *Vigiliae Christianae* 48 (1994): 25–47, esp. 31–32.

practices on the pretext of honoring the martyrs: "They did not keep hidden in the earth the bodies of the martyrs who contested well, but they placed them on stretchers and boards so that those who want to can view them." He adds an additional reason for entombing the body: "In primitive times, God decided the case of Adam in one sentence: 'From earth you come, and to the earth you will return.' This applied to anyone who is descended from Adam, and everywhere, the dead are buried. Abraham acted in this way: he bought the cave of Ephron, and buried his wife Sarah there. And later Isaac buried Abraham; and in this same cave was buried the body of Jacob."[38]

Adam's punishment in Genesis 3:29 takes on a normative meaning here: "to earth you will return" is interpreted as a command to bury the body in the earth, where it will decompose. It is very easy for Athanasius to multiply the biblical examples for burial (he gives a long list in the festal letter of 369), but this usage of Genesis 3:29 underscores how difficult it is to find an explicit norm in Scripture.

In his final recommendations, Antony adds a commentary that has sometimes been misinterpreted: "Therefore, perform the rites for me yourselves, and bury my body in the earth. And let my word be kept secret by you, so that no one knows the place but you alone. For in the resurrection of the dead I shall receive my body incorruptible once again from the Savior. Distribute my clothing. To Bishop Athanasius give the one sheepskin and the cloak on which I lie, which he gave to me new, but I have by now worn out" (91.7–8).

The mention of the resurrection should not be read in relation to what precedes but instead to what follows: the distribution of Antony's clothing, his only authorized relics, as opposed to his body that Antony alone will regain at the resurrection. Athanasius does not say here that Antony insisted on being buried in order to receive his body at the resurrection, but he is keen to indicate that he himself possesses the only authentic relics of Antony: one of his sheepskin *melotes* (the other was willed by Antony to the bishop Serapion) and a cloak.[39] Although the context of these documents is quite specific, we recognize a now familiar theme: the difficulty of defining the piety Christians attached to burial duty.

---

38. Athanasius, *Letters* 41, ed. Louis-Théophile Lefort, Corpus scriptorum christianorum orientalium 151, Scriptores Coptici 20 (Louvain: Durbecq, 1955), 42, l.13–16 and l.28–34.

39. On the first point, I do not follow the interpretation of David Brakke, "'Outside the Place, within the Truth': Athanasius of Alexandria and the Localization of the Holy," in *Pilgrimage and Holy Space in Late Antique Egypt,* ed. David Frankfurter, Religions in the Graeco-Roman World 134 (Leiden: Brill, 1998), 461; but, for the second point, I follow him. See also Brian Brennan, "Athanasius' *Vita Antonii*: A Sociological Interpretation," *Vigiliae Christianae* 39 (1985): 223–24.

The commentaries of Ambrose and Jerome on Abraham's purchase of the cave of Mambre raise the question of the sale of tombs that later will be at the heart of medieval exegesis. Ambrose explains the verses from Genesis in *On Abraham*:

> The passage which follows contains the death of his wife, the mourning of the husband, the service of burial, whereby his marital affection is proven. 'And Abraham stood up from before his dead' (Gen. 23:3), so that we may not linger too long among the dead, but give what is due of respect. But Abraham hastened to pay the price of the burying place, although it was freely given (Gen. 23:4–9), so that we may build tombs for our parents and our kin, not on a stranger's land, but on our own: for often with the transfer of possessions, the graves in these same places are offered for sale. So Abraham acted thus, because there were as yet no temples of God in which could be laid the remains of those faithful to the Lord. (1.9.80)

Ambrose thinks that giving a proper funeral to a deceased spouse is one of the duties of marriage, but he insists more on the moderation that one should show in mourning. However, the location of the tomb is important: the one who builds it must own it. This is the first interpretation given by Ambrose of Abraham's insistence on purchasing the cave of Mambre: it is a precaution against conflicts that result from the presence of graves when lands or property are sold, conflicts widely attested to by numerous cases presented in the *Digesta*.[40] Ambrose adds a second explanation, of a historical nature: at that time, there were as yet no *templa dei*—in other words, churches where Christians could be buried. Ambrose was certainly thinking only of a very privileged form of burial, but there is no further clarification of his commentary.

Jerome denounces the sale of tombs, in the *Hebrew Questions on Genesis*, giving an exegesis on the name change of the owner of the land bought by Abraham. Scripture calls him first Efron, then Efran; one letter was removed from his Hebrew name, which, Jerome explains, means that he had not been of consummate virtue: "Therefore, let those who sell sepulchers without compulsion in order to receive money, and even extort it from those who are unwilling to pay, know that their name is to be changed and that some of their good name will perish. For even that man [i.e., Efran] who received the money unwillingly is tacitly held to blame" (23, 16).

---

40. See Yan Thomas, "*Corpus aut ossa aut cineres:* la chose religieuse et le commerce," *Micrologus* 7 (1999): 74–76.

It is difficult to know what Jerome had in mind in making these remarks, or even if he was really trying to apply this exegesis to the contemporary reality. Was he aiming these remarks at those who would refuse to give a burial to a family too poor to afford it? Nothing in the commentary encourages any such interpretation. The sale of tombs is also denounced by Gregory the Great at the end of the sixth century, in reference to the same incident in Genesis, but referring at that time to a very different custom, the sale of tombs in a church.

It was necessary to review these different texts to judge just how few of the patristic commentaries actually drew upon biblical examples for lessons on burial duty.[41] Each commentary encountered is different: burial duty had not become a commonplace with a fixed set of Scriptural references. It seems, moreover, that in the pastoral discourse the duty to bury strangers and the poor was scarcely mentioned after the text of Lactantius, for whom it was one of the cardinal Christian virtues at the beginning of the fourth century. The absence of this theme in Christian teaching has probably to do with the professionalization of the clergy between the second and fourth centuries. As Peter Brown has recently made clear, this was accompanied by a centralization in the hands of the bishop, if not a confiscation, of funds to redistribute to the poor.[42] It would then have fallen to the bishop to be responsible for the burial of Christians who could not pay for it themselves, and Christians would no longer be called upon for this service, except in their contributions to the church. So we must now turn to the documents concerning the bishops' responsibility for burial of the poor.

The Church and Burial of the Poor
The *Apostolic Tradition* and Its Various Witnesses

"Let there be no heavy charge for burial in the cemetery, for it belongs to all the poor; only the hire of the gravedigger and the cost of the tile shall be asked. The wages of the caretakers are to be paid by the bishop, lest any of those who go to that place be burdened."[43]

---

41. Some scattered allusions can be added: Zeno of Verona declares in a homily that "neither alive nor dead did they stay naked for long" in his city (1.14.8–9); Jerome mentions the duty to bury the dead as part of the good deeds done by Christians (*Ad Galatas* 2.14.18); to give a burial to the dead is presented as an effect of *humanitas* by Augustine in *De moribus ecclesiae catholicae* 27.

42. Peter Brown, *Poverty and Leadership in the Later Roman Empire* (Hanover, NH: University Press of New England, 2002).

43. Hippolytus, *Apostolic tradition* 40: *De locis sepulturae. Ne grauetur homo ad sepeliendum hominem in coemeteriis: res enim est omnis pauperis. Sed detur merces operarii ei qui effodit et pretium laterum. Qui sunt in loco illo et qui curam habent, episcopus nutriat eos ut nemo grauetur ex eis qui ueniunt ad haec loca.*

This chapter in the *Apostolic Tradition* is often offered as proof that caring for abandoned bodies traditionally fell to the church from the end of the second century onward. The *Apostolic Tradition* is a text attributed to Hippolytus and thought to describe the organization of the Roman Church at this time, but its authenticity poses a number of problems.[44] The attribution to Hippolytus of Rome is actually widely contested and the debate, first begun in 1947, continues; today there is still no consensus among specialists on the subject.[45] The stakes are high, involving the historical value of a text, and a Roman one, thought to be the oldest liturgical document.[46] Although the *Apostolic Tradition* appears to have been written at the end of the second century in Rome, it does not have the official status that some have wanted to attribute to it.[47] Moreover, the original Greek of the *Apostolic Tradition* has not survived. Bernard Botte has proposed a Latin reconstruction—that is, a Latin translation of translations or related texts thought to have come from the same archetype.[48] As a result, for every chapter it is necessary to check how it was reconstructed.

---

44. See Alexandre Faivre, "La documentation canonico-liturgique de l'Église ancienne," *Revue des sciences religieuses* 54 (1980): 204–19, 237–97 (see *Ordonner la fraternité: pouvoir d'innover et retour à l'ordre dans l'Église ancienne,* Histoire (Paris: Éditions du Cerf, 1992], 361–94); and Marcel Metzger, "Nouvelles perspectives pour la prétendue *Tradition apostolique,*" *Ecclesia Orans* 5 (1988): 241–59. See Elio Peretto's synthesis and bibliography in his edition of Pseudo-Hippolytus, *Tradizione Apostolica,* Collana di testi patristici 133 (Rome: Città Nuova, 1996); and Christoph Markschies, "Wer schrieb die sogenannte *Traditio Apostolica*?: neue Beobachtungen und Hypothesen zu einer kaum lösbaren Frage aus der altkirchlichen Literaturgeschichte," in *Tauffragen und Bekenntnis: Studien zur sogenannten 'Traditio Apostolica', zu den 'Interrogationes de fide' und zum 'Römischen Glaubensbekenntnis',* ed. Wolfram Kinzig, Christoph Markschies, and Markus Vinzent, Arbeiten zur Kirchengeschichte 74 (Berlin: De Gruyter, 1999), 1–74. Two recent English editions must now be considered: Hippolytus, *On the Apostolic Tradition,* ed. Alistair Stewart-Sykes (Crestwood, NY: St Vladimir's Seminar Press, 2001); and *The Apostolic Tradition: A Commentary,* ed. Paul F. Bradshaw, Maxwell E. Johnson, and L. Edward Phillips (Minneapolis: Fortress Press, 2002).

45. About Hippolytus's personality, see the present volume chapter 1, n. 4. See also the recent contribution of J. A. Cerrato, *Hippolytus between East and West: The Commentaries and the Provenance of the Corpus* (Oxford: Oxford University Press, 2003).

46. See Metzger, "Nouvelles perspectives," 249–50, about "the weakness of some discussions." For instance, Aimé-Georges Martimort, "Encore Hippolyte et la Tradition apostolique," *Bulletin de littérature ecclésiastique* 92 (1991): 137, concludes that it is important to recognize that it is a third-century text since it is the basis of current liturgy—in particular, Vatican II.

47. Manlio Simonetti, "Roma cristiana tra vescovi e presbiteri," in *Origine delle catacombe romane,* ed. Vincenzo Fiocchi Nicolai and Jean Guyon, Sussidi allo studio delle antichità cristiane 18 (Vatican City: Pontificio Istituto di archeologia cristiana, 2006), 40, goes as far as recommending no longer using the *Traditio* as a document on the Roman Church.

48. Bernard Botte, *La Tradition apostolique de saint Hippolyte: essai de reconstitution,* Liturgiewissenschaftliche Quellen und Forschungen 39 (Münster: Aschendorff, 1963). The other authoritative retroversion is Gregory Dix, *The Treatise on the Apostolic Tradition of St. Hippolytus of Rome, Bishop and Martyr,* 2nd ed., with corrections, preface, and bibliography by Henry Chadwick (London: SPCK, 1968). Steward-Sykes is still proposing a composite reconstruction, whereas Bradshaw, Johnson, and Philipps are giving in parallel an English translation of the different testimonies that have survived.

The chapter on burial has not survived in the *Fragments of Hauler,* or the collection of *Veronensis LV,* that Botte considers as an old Latin translation (end of the fourth century) of the *Apostolic Tradition*.[49] Thus he gave priority to what he considers to be a translation in Sahidic (a Coptic dialect of Upper Egypt) of the original Greek, as it was transmitted in the Egyptian canonico-liturgical collection of the fifth century, called *Alexandrian Synodos,* the original Greek of which did not survive. This Sahidic version, of which the oldest known manuscript dates from the eleventh century, would have been composed around 400.[50] Botte has also consulted Ethiopic and Arabic translations for certain details, although these were made from the Sahidic and not the Greek, and additions based on these are thus interpretations.[51]

The instructions regarding burial in the *Apostolic Tradition* have thus been reconstituted from documents that date from the sixth century at the earliest and that originate with the Egyptian Coptic Church. We cannot rule out the possibility that the original was adapted to correspond to a very different reality. Botte also called upon what he knew, or thought he knew, about the Christian funerary system in Rome at the end of the second century to direct his reconstruction. The decision to render the Greek word *koimeterion,* a singular noun in all translations, as a plural in the Latin reconstruction is a good example of this latter process. What in the original may have referred simply to the concrete case of a pauper's grave, became a description of the administration of cemeteries.

Along side the translations used by Botte in his reconstruction there are also adaptations of the *Apostolic Tradition* that are older and thus merit a separate consideration. The first of these texts has also been attributed to Hippolytus: it consists of thirty-eight canons written in Egypt during the second half of the fourth century,[52] from which we read,

> The sick are not to sleep in the dormitory, but rather the poor. That is why he who has a home, if he is sick, is not to be moved to the house of God. Rather he is only to pray and then return home.

---

49. Botte, *La Tradition apostolique de saint Hippolyte,* xvii–xx, xxxvi–xxxvii.
50. Ibid., xxi–xxii, xxxvii–xxxviii.
51. Ibid., xxxviii.
52. The original Greek text of the *Canons of Hippolytus* is lost, but there is a Sahidic translation from the beginning of the fifth century, edited and translated by René-Georges Coquin, Patrologia orientalis 31, no. 2 (Paris: Firmin-Didot, 1966). For the date, see Annick Martin, *Athanase d'Alexandrie et l'Église d'Égypte au IVe siècle (328–373),* Collection de l'École française de Rome 216 (Rome: École française de Rome, 1996), 163, n. 191.

> The steward is the one who has care of the sick. The bishop is to support them; even the vessel of clay necessary for the sick, the bishop is to give it to the steward.

The issue is certainly the poor and the *koimeterion,* but here the word is used in its earlier meaning of "dormitory." The text concerns the sick, not the dead: only the poor are allowed to sleep in the dormitory, apparently a building belonging to the church.

Two adaptations of the *Apostolic Tradition* that originated in Syria, most likely Antioch, are also known. In the *Apostolic Constitutions,* written around 380, there is no trace of our canon. The *Testamentum Domini,* which original Greek text dates from the fifth century, but which has come down to us only in Syriac, Ethiopic, and Arabic translations,[53] provides an interesting version of it. The Ethiopic and Syriac translations are very close:

> "If a poor man dies, let those who provide for each one provide for his clothing. If anyone who is a stranger dies and has no place to be buried, let those who have a place give [it]. But if the church has [a place], let it give [it]. And if he has no covering, let the church similarly give it. But if he does not have grave clothes, let him be shrouded. But if a man is found to have possessions, and does not leave them to the church, let them be kept for a time; and after a year do not let the church appropriate them, but let them be given to the poor for his soul. But if he desires to be embalmed, let the deacons provide for this, a presbyter standing by. If the church has a graveyard, and there is someone who lives there and keeps it, let the bishop provide for him from the church, so that he is no burden to those who come there.[54]

Three possibilities are considered for the burial of a stranger: either he has a tomb, or other believers provide him one, or the church has a burial place and provides him one. The possibility of the church owning a burial place is thus envisioned here unequivocally, but it is not set forth as a rule: there is also

---

53. See René-Georges Coquin, "Le 'Testamentum Domini': problèmes de tradition textuelle," *Parole de l'Orient* 5 (1974): 165–88.

54. English translation of the Syriac text by Bradshaw, in Bradshaw, Johnson, and Phillips, eds., *The Apostolic Tradition: A Commentary.* For the Syriac version, see *Testamentum Domini nostri Jesu Christi,* ed. Ignatius Rahmani (Mainz: Kirchheim, 1899; reprint, Hildesheim: Olms, 1968), 142–45. The Ethiopic text was edited by Robert Beylot (Louvain: Peeters, 1984). The Arabic text remains unpublished.

a call for charity to help bury the poor. Only the indigent and strangers seem to have had access to such a collective place. The rule was clearly for individuals to possess their own tombs.

Hence, it seems necessary to distinguish, in all of these different documents,[55] between the obligation to bury the poor and the administration of the church's burial place by the bishop. The obligation to provide a tomb for those who do not have one does not necessarily imply that the church possessed a burial place of its own: the faithful might also take charge of providing a tomb for the poor. However, if the church owned such a place, the bishop had to ensure that the poor were not required to pay to bury their dead in it.

The Duties of the Bishop according to Ambrose of Milan

We can compare these instructions in the canonico-liturgical documentation with a passage in the *De officiis* of Ambrose of Milan. This is also a normative text, but the relevant passage echoes the reality of the period and there are good arguments for suggesting that Ambrose here is reusing a sermon preached before the people.[56] In book 2, Ambrose praises at great length generosity, notably in the form of ransoming prisoners. This is a traditional theme, one that is found in Cicero's *De officiis*, but it is set off by the fact that Ambrose was criticized for having sold sacred vases for ransoming prisoners taken by the Goths after their victory over Valens in 378 at Hadrianopolis (today Edirne, Turkey). That provided an excellent example of conflicting

---

55. Two more texts should be considered. The first is the notice in the *Didascalia* in which the deacon must bury the foreigners. The original—written in Greek in the first half of the third century by a bishop from the region of Antioch—is lost, but the notice appears in a Syriac translation in the fourth century: see *Didascalia* 3.4, translated by Arthur Vööbus, Corpus scriptorum christianorum orientalium 402, Scriptores syri 176 (Louvain: Peeters, 1979), 30. The corresponding passage in the Latin translation has been lost. The second notice comes from the *Canons of Athanasius*, an Egyptian document prior to the Council of Chalcedon in 451; see Annick Martin, "L'image de l'évêque à travers les « Canons d'Athanase »: devoirs et réalités," in *L'évêque dans la cité du IVe au Ve siècle: image et autorité: actes de la table ronde organisée par l'Istituto patristico Augustinianum et l'École française de Rome (Rome, 1er et 2 décembre 1995)*, ed. Éric Rebillard and Claire Sotinel, Collection de l'École française de Rome 248 (Rome: École française de Rome, 1998), 59 and n. 2, but known only through an Arabic translation of the eleventh century. The canon 100 says that the church must take care of the dead when they are poor; see Wilhelm Riedel and Walter Ewing Crum, eds., *The Canons of Athanasius* (London: Williams and Norgate, 1904), 65.

56. See Rita Lizzi, *Vescovi e strutture ecclesiastiche nella città tardoantica: (l'Italia Annonaria nel IV–V secolo d.C.)*, Biblioteca di Athenaeum 9 (Como: New Press, 1989), 28–31.

usefulness. In a sort of peroration, Ambrose recapitulates different circumstances making the sale of the vases legitimate:

> Naturally, if someone siphons off profits for his own gain, it is a crime; but if he spends them on the poor and ransoms a prisoner, it is an act of mercy. No one can say: "Why is this poor man alive?" No one can complain if prisoners have been ransomed; no one can object if the temple of God has been built; no one can be upset if spare ground has been released for the burial of the faithful; no one can be sorry if the dead are being laid to rest in Christian tombs. For these three purposes, it is quite permissible to break up, melt down, or sell the church's vessels even when they have been consecrated. (2.142)

Ambrose considers it legitimate to sell liturgical vases in the context of acts of charity. That appears clearly from the opening lines, in which he contrasts personal profit and acts of mercy and mentions distributions to the poor and the ransoming of prisoners. This is followed by five sentences, identically constructed, that are presented as possible objections. Finally, Ambrose resumes his argument, saying that he has identified three legitimate purposes. The first two are distributions to the poor and ransoming of prisoners. The third one needs some elucidation. What exactly does "temple of God" (*templum dei*) mean? In several passages of book 2 of *De officiis*, *templum dei* designates the church as a building, but Ambrose recommends in every case to demonstrate the greatest moderation in expenses for ornamentation: it would seem unlikely therefore that here he is saying, with no explanation, that the building of churches is one of the legitimate uses for the sale of sacred vases. In the passage of *On Abraham* discussed above, *templum dei* designates a place to bury the remains of the faithful. This suggests actually a link between the last three propositions: the third purpose would thus refer to the burial of the dead, indicated by the expression "construct a temple of God," explained by (1) acquisition of land to expand the cemetery and (2) the costs of building the tombs.

In any case, Ambrose does explicitly refer to the purchase of land to enlarge burial grounds for believers. That seems to imply that such a place must have existed. The fifth and final proposition is less clear. Another possible translation would be, "No one should complain that deceased Christians are laid to rest in their tombs." Then the issue is not with the cost of burial, but it is given as a justification: just as one may not fault the poor for living, one may not reproach a dead Christian for lying in a tomb. The context of the whole passage is that of charitable works, and it is thus likely that

Ambrose had in mind only the case of burial of the poor, even if he does not say so explicitly.

 Bishops and Funerary Personnel

There is little concrete evidence about the funerary activities of bishops. The activity of the Melitian bishop of Alexandria, Georges, is known only because it was exceptional. In the biographical notice that Epiphanius devotes to him in the *Panarion,* we learn that he might have had a sort of monopoly on the burial of foreigners in Alexandria. Only his own personnel were entitled to be paid for burying foreigners; as Epiphanius notes, that was not done out of respect for the obligations of hospitality (3.76.1). Indirectly, we are able to deduce that Georges employed personnel responsible for burying the foreigners—the poor are not mentioned, because no income could be expected from their burials. The location of the burial is not discussed.

Evidence for the existence of such personnel is found in a few other documents. In Cirta, in 303, when the local authorities went to the house where Christians met to confiscate the Scriptures and other objects they kept there, they noted in their official report the presence of the bishop, two priests, two deacons and four subdeacons. Six grave diggers were named next, and the list ends with a reference to some other grave diggers whose names and exact number are not given (*Gesta apud Zenophilum consularem* 3). The idea that grave diggers were members of the lower clergy should be dropped.[57] But what was the purpose of their being there, grouped around the bishop, ready to assist the subdeacons to carry the objects confiscated by the local authorities? One cannot help being struck by their high number: more than six grave diggers, for a total number of Christians that cannot have been very great at this time. They were employed by the bishop as grave diggers and handymen, as their role in this episode demonstrates, but at least a few of them had another profession—as simple artisans, apparently—as one of them reveals during the course of his interrogation (14). We should also assume that they provided their service to others beside the bishop, and perhaps even to non-Christians.[58]

---

57. For a classical presentation, see Alexandre Faivre, *Naissance d'une hiérarchie: les premières étapes du cursus clérical,* Théologie historique 40 (Paris: Beauchesne, 1977), 284–87. We must also take into account the important analysis in Claire Sotinel, "Le personnel épiscopal: enquête sur la puissance de l'évêque dans la cité," in Rebillard and Sotinel, eds., *L'évêque dans la cité du IVe au Ve siècle,* 109–10 and n. 25, on the "lower orders." See also Yvette Duval, *Chrétiens d'Afrique,* 77–82.

58. See Claire Sotinel, "Le personnel épiscopal," 119.

At Vercellae (today Vercelli, Italy) in the second half of the fourth century, clerics did the work of grave diggers. This is evinced by Jerome's *Letter 1*. A Christian woman, who was unjustly accused of adultery, suffered a true martyrdom. After her execution, Jerome describes her burial: "Those of the clergy, whose duty it was to perform this office, wrapped the blood-stained corpse in a sheet, and then prepared to dig a grave and duly cover it over with stones" (12). But the innocent and brave woman was not dead! She showed signs of living on, and providence procured a substitute body: "In the meantime an aged female, who had been maintained at the expense of the church, rendered back her soul to heaven. So opportunely her corpse took the woman's place, and was buried in the tomb" (13). Her poverty, or her status as a widow supported by the church, explains why the church took charge of the funeral of the old woman. It was natural for the clergy, when they saw the accused woman become a new martyr by her manner of death, to take care of her burial, and it was also the local church that obtained the emperor's pardon for her. So, at Vercellae, the church did not seem to have the means of paying for the services of grave diggers and thus the task fell to the clergy.

In Egypt, documentary evidence allows us to highlight the continuity between the organization of the funerary professions in the service of Christians and non-Christians. A letter, dating from the second half of the third century or the beginning of the fourth, tells of a priest named Psenosiris, who was responsible for sending to the "Great Oasis" the mummified body of a certain Politiké and who entrusted it to some *necrotaphoi*.[59] From the records of the necrotaphoi of Kysis we are able to reconstruct precisely the organization of funerary professions in the Great Oasis. The position of necrotaphos, either sold or inherited, was a legal privilege that gave the holder the right to practice his trade in a given locality and to make use of one section of the necropolis.[60] The necrotaphoi who worked for the priest were apparently themselves Christians,[61] but they seem to have exercised their

---

59. P. Gren. II, 73 = P. Lond. 713; see Mario Naldini, *Il Cristianesimo in Egitto: lettere private nei papiri dei secoli II–IV*, new ed., Biblioteca patristica 32 (Fiesole, Italy: Nardini, 1998), no. 21, 131–35, 433. Deissmann's interpretation, which makes Politikè a Christian woman sent into exile to the Great Oasis because she refused to participate in the sacrifice (*Ein Original-Dokument aus der Diokletianischen Christenverfolgung: Papyrus 713 des British Museum*, ed. Adolf Deissmann (Tübingen: Mohr, 1902) must definitely be abandoned; see Guy Wagner, *Les Oasis d'Égypte à l'époque grecque, romaine et byzantine d'après les documents grecs*, Bibliothèque d'étude 100 (Cairo: Institut français d'archéologie orientale du Caire, 1987), 352, 355–56; and J. O'Callaghan, "Sobre PGrenf. II 73 (III/IVP)," *Zeitschrift für Papyrologie und Epigraphik* 67 (1987): 124–28.

60. See Wagner, *Les Oasis d'Égypte*, 350–55; and Françoise Dunand, "Les nécrotaphes de Kysis," *Cahiers de recherches de l'Institut de Papyrologie et d'Égyptologie de l'Université de Lille* 7 (1985): 117–27.

61. They are called *kaloi kai pistoi*: for parallels in the New Testament, see the commentary in Naldini, *Il Cristianesimo in Egitto*, 134.

profession in the same way as their non-Christian colleagues. This letter suggests that the church preferred to use the service of necrotaphoi who were Christians; but did the latter work exclusively for Christians? Papyri from Aphroditô seem to attest that, even after the Christianization of the entire country, the organization of the necrotaphoi remained unchanged.[62]

These examples show that no situation was typical and that the church did not have a uniform funerary organization everywhere in the Roman Empire.[63] The burial of the poor registered in the records of the church did not imply the same degree of organization everywhere. The imperial authority also continued to assume responsibility for abandoned corpses and provided funerals at a low cost for the inhabitants of some cities, even if the church, as we shall see now, was managing this service.

State, Church, and Funerary Assistance

The existence of an official body of undertakers and grave diggers working for the cities in the Late Roman Empire is not as well documented as Jean-Pierre Waltzing, by comparing them to the *collegiati* or *corporati* enrolled as firemen, suggested.[64] However, the constant effort by the city authorities to provide for the burial of abandoned corpses is well documented. John Bodel

---

62. See Jean Gascou, "La Vie de Patermouthios, moine et fossoyeur (*Historia monachorum X*)," in *Itinéraires d'Égypte: mélanges offerts au père Maurice Martin s.j.*, ed. Christian Décobert, Bibliothèque d'étude 107 (Cairo: Institut français d'archéologie orientale du Caire, 1992), 114.

63. I have already mentioned that the fossores of the Roman Catacombs are not members of the clergy. In large cities, workers involved with funerary activities are often associated with the bishops, whom they help in case of necessity. In that capacity they behave like other professional associations attracted by the authority of the bishop, who has become "a major urban patron"; see Peter Brown, *Power and Persuasion in Late Antiquity: Towards a Christian Empire* (Madison: University of Wisconsin Press, 1992), 101. See also Ramsay MacMullen, *Enemies of the Roman Order: Treason, Unrest, and Alienation in the Empire* (Cambridge, MA: Harvard University Press, 1966), 177–78. On the help the fossores brought to Damasius for his election in 366, see *Collectio Avellana, Ep. 1*, 7 and Charles Pietri, *Roma Christiana: recherches sur l'Église de Rome, son organisation, sa politique, son idéologie de Miltiade à Sixte III (311–440)*, Bibliothèque des Écoles françaises de Rome et d'Athènes 224 (Rome: École française de Rome, 1976), 1:413, for a narrative. On bishop Eulalius's dispatching of *dekanoi tôn martyriôn* (people attached to the service of *martyria*) against the Acemetes monks in 426 or 427, see Callinicos, *Life of Hypathios* 41.10. The role of funerary workers in Antioch at the time of the proclamation of the imperial edicts against Nestorius in 435 is narrated in the *Acts of the Second Council of Ephesus* 10.

64. Jean-Pierre Waltzing, *Étude historique sur les corporations professionnelles chez les Romains depuis les origines jusqu'à la chute de l'Empire d'Occident*, 4 vols. (Louvain: Peeters, 1895–1900), 2:130–32; François Martroye, "Les parabalani," *Bulletin de la Société Nationale des Antiquaires de France* (1923): 275–81. See also Jean-Michel Carrié, "Les associations professionnelles à l'époque tardive: entre *munus* et convivialité," in *Humana sapit: mélanges en l'honneur de Lellia Cracco Ruggini*, Bibliothèque de l'Antiquité tardive 3 (Turnhout: Brepols, 2001), 309–32.

has shown that in Rome and in other Italian cities, there were public areas called *lucus Libitinae* that were intended, notably, for paupers' graves.[65] The evidence he has gathered is primarily from the middle and late Republican periods, but, as Evelyne Patlagean has quite accurately written, "as soon as there is an organized space, most notably in cities, the community must see to the provision of such burial places."[66] One inscription from Bergamo, dated around the second century CE, proves that the Republican system was still in place.[67] The passage from the land-surveying treatise of Frontinus (at the end of the first century CE), which mentions loca publica outside the cities intended for paupers' graves and for public executions, is repeated by Agennius Urbicus in the fourth century.[68]

The imperial authorities' interest in trades involved in the transportation and burial of the dead is confirmed in the fourth century by a series of measures that gave them fiscal immunity. Two laws of Constantius, one in 356 and the other in 359, addressed to Taurus, the Praetorian prefect for Italy and Africa, deal with the exemption from *collatio lustralis* for the *copiatae*.[69] The word *copiatae* is a Latin transcription of the Greek *kopiatai*—literally, those who work hard—and one of the various words used to designate grave diggers. The *collatio lustralis,* or *chrysargyron,* was a tax on trades instituted by Constantine.[70] Funerary workers thus benefited from an exemption accorded, up to that time, to clergy and their dependents for charitable activities.[71] While considering the copiatae as lower members of the clergy must

---

65. John Bodel, "Graveyards and Groves: A Study of Lex Lucerina," *American Journal of Ancient History* 11 (1986). See also John Bodel, "Dealing with the Dead: Undertakers, Executioners and Potter's Fields in Ancient Rome," in *Death and Disease in the Ancient City,* ed. Valerie M. Hope and Eireann Marshall (London: Routledge, 2000), 128–51, esp. 128–35.

66. Evelyne Patlagean, *Pauvreté économique et pauvreté sociale à Byzance, 4e–7e siècles,* Civilisations et sociétés 48 (Paris: Mouton, 1977), 69.

67. Bodel, "Graveyards and Groves," 18.

68. Agennius Urbicus, *De controuersiis agrorum,* ed. Karl Thulin, Bibliotheca scriptorum Graecorum et Romanorum Teubneriana 47 (Stuttgart: Teubner, 1913): *Habent et res publica loca suburbana inopum funeribus destinata, quae loca culinas appellant. Habent et loca noxiorum poenis destinata.* See Bodel, "Graveyards and Groves," 81–83.

69. *Codex Theodosianus* 13.1.1 and 16.2.15. These laws have often been commented on in relation to immunities granted to the clergy; see Clémence Dupont, "Les privilèges des clercs sous Constantin," *Revue d'histoire ecclésiastique* 62 (1967): 729–52; Roland Delmaire, *Largesses sacrées et res privata: l'aerarium impérial et son administration du IVe au VIe siècle,* Collection de l'École française de Rome 121 (Rome: École française de Rome, 1989), 362–65; and Éric Rebillard, "Les formes de l'assistance funéraire dans l'Empire romain et leur évolution dans l'Antiquité tardive," *Antiquité tardive* 7 (1999): 275–76.

70. Delmaire, *Largesses sacrées et res privata,* 354–57.

71. See *Codex Theodosianus* 16.2.14, where Constantius recalls the privileges granted to the clerics by Constantine. See Dupont, "Les privilèges des clercs," 727, and Delmaire, *Largesses sacrées et res privata,* 362.

be rejected, it should be noted that clergy and funerary workers were closely associated in a law of Arcadius and Honorius that confirmed that they enjoyed certain advantages in exchange for their charitable activity.[72]

The involvement of the church in imperial measures facilitating burial for inhabitants of the empire is shown by Constantine's institution of free funerals for the people of Constantinople. Constantine's plan is known from later laws, particularly Justinian's *Novellae*, that retrace the history of the institution.[73] He appears to have given 950 workshops to the church, or at least the revenue from them, with each one expected to provide a grave digger in exchange for tax exemptions and relief from other typical financial burdens. Justinian's *Novellae* give no further detail on the beneficiaries of free funerals and it was not until the end of the ninth century that a *Novella* of Leon VI describes the measures of Constantine as being on behalf of the poor.[74] Gilbert Dagron, who studied the institution from the fourth to the tenth centuries, finds it anachronistic and suggests that Constantine's measures were an act of traditional civic evergetism and were thus intended for all the citizens and not only for the poor.[75] We should note that, while it may be difficult to confirm that Constantine entrusted this mission to the church from the beginning, it is confirmed, in any case, at the beginning of the fifth century by a law of Theodosius II (*Codex Justinianus* 1.2.4).

All these different laws show that the city was indeed traditionally responsible for the burial of abandoned corpses and that the bishops did not replace it in this role in the fourth century. However, the fact that the emperors turned to the bishops for providing these services in the capital of the empire explains that when the bishop became responsible for the city institutions—beginning in the second half of the fifth century, in varying degrees according to the area of the empire, and in a process that needs to be better understood[76]—it would be the bishops who took charge of burying

---

72. *Codex Theodosianus* 7.20.12. For copiatae and clergy, see Rebillard, "Les formes de l'assistance funéraire," 275–76.

73. See Piero Rasi, "Donazione di Costantino e di Anastasio alla chiesa di S. Sofia per le spese funeralizie a Constantinopoli," in *Festschrift für Leopold Wenger zu seinem 70. Geburtstag. 2,* Münchener Beiträge zur Papyrusforschung und antiken Rechtsgeschichte 35 (Munich: Beck, 1945), 269–282; Anna Maria Demicheli, *La ΜΕΓΑΛΗ ΕΚΚΛΗΣΙΑ nel lessico e nel diritto di Giustiniano,* Monografia del vocabulario di Giustiniano 3 (Milan: Giuffrè, 1990), 65–83; Dagron, "'Ainsi rien n'échappera à la réglementation,'" 155–82; and Rebillard, "Les formes de l'assistance funéraire," 274.

74. Leon, *Novellae* 12: "Constantine...thinking that taking care of the dead whose poverty followed all the way to the sepulture should be the responsibility of the emperor..."; on this text, see Anna Maria Demicheli, *La ΜΕΓΑΛΗ ΕΚΚΛΗΣΙΑ,* 82–83.

75. Dagron, "'Ainsi rien n'échappera à la réglementation,'" 169.

76. For the Orient, see Brown, *Power and Persuasion,* chap. 4. For the West, see the contrast between Augustine's world and that of Gregory the Great in Robert Markus, *Gregory the Great and*

the poor, whereas until that time they had probably been responsible only for the Christians.

The duty to provide burial is a form of piety that may have been an important part of the creation of a Christian identity in the third and fourth centuries, particularly because of the concern for giving martyrs a proper burial. But this duty, which was not an obligation of a religious nature (as we saw in chapter 4), is not given a prominent place in Christian pastoral literature, although it does not disappear entirely from the list of good deeds. None of the scriptural models for such a duty plays a significant role in Christian texts of the fourth and fifth centuries. It seems, then, that the burial duty cannot be seen as the source of the bishops' obligation to provide burial for Christians.

However, bishops made it their mission to provide graves for the poor. Peter Brown has provided us with a much better understanding of the role this could play in the bishops' strategy for gaining power.[77] The concern for providing tombs for the poor was not so much in response to a religious duty as it was an element of this strategy. It must be stressed, however, that the public authority, both civic and imperial, continued to take care of abandoned corpses in the empire, whether by granting fiscal privileges to the trades engaged in funerary work and/or in delegating the responsibility to bishops—again in exchange for some privileges.

The only categories that benefited from particular attention—those of the poor and foreigners—are the same ones that benefited from public solicitude generally, be it from humanitarian or hygienic motives. Care for the dead thus did not become the collective responsibility of the church or of Christians. Neither did the church claim a collective responsibility for the commemoration of the dead as we will now see in the final two chapters.

His World (Cambridge: Cambridge University Press, 1997). Now see J. H. W. G. Liebeschuetz, *The Decline and Fall of the Roman City* (Oxford: Oxford University Press, 2001).

77. See Brown, *Power and Persuasion*; Brown, *Poverty and Leadership in the Later Roman Empire*; and Éric Rebillard, "La conversion de l'Empire romain selon Peter Brown (note critique)," *Annales: histoire, sciences sociales* 54, no. 4 (1999), 813–23.

Chapter 6

Christian Funerals and Funerals of Christians

The Church and the Death Ritual in Late Antiquity

The notion that the church sought to assume collective responsibility for the relations between the living and the dead is closely linked to the idea that there was a Christian ritual for death and burial. However, there are only scattered data in the sources. Rather than reconstructing a ritual in hindsight, as liturgists continue to do in too many cases, we need to look at these scattered data in their proper context. It appears that the church was no more involved in developing rituals for death and burial than it was, for example, for marriage.[1] These issues are important because we know that mourning is a social process and that ritual plays an important part in it.[2] The role the church expected to play in this process is indicative of the one it intended to have in the lives of Christians generally.

Recent scholarship on the first proper liturgical documents has shown that they were the products of precise historical contexts, in which the relationships

---

1. See Louis Duchesne, *Christian Worship: Its Origin and Evolution*, 3rd English ed., translated by M. L. McClure (London: Society for Promoting Christian Knowledge, 1910), iii: "no mention will be found in these pages of funerary ritual, which is of an absolutely private nature, and which, with the exception of the special formularies for the Mass, has no very ancient features"; his position has remained very isolated. On marriage, see Philip L. Reynolds, *Marriage in the Western Church: The Christianization of Marriage during the Patristic and Early Medieval Periods*, Supplements to Vigiliae Christianae 24 (Leiden).

2. See Ian Morris, *Death-Ritual and Social Structure in Classical Antiquity*, Key Themes in Ancient History (Cambridge, MA: Cambridge University Press, 1992).

of the Christian church and society were different from what they were in Late Antiquity.³ It is therefore not a sound method to assume that an early and isolated evidence for one part of the death ritual is proof of the existence of the whole ritual. The best way to gain an understanding of the role the church expected to play in relations between the living and the dead in Late Antiquity is therefore an analysis of the documents in chronological order and a close study of the data they contain, in their own context.

Evidence from the Second and Third Centuries

The first document to consider is the *Acts of John,* an apocryphal text supposedly composed in Egypt in the second half of the second century.⁴ John was in Ephesus in the home of Andronicus when the latter's wife, Drusiana, chose suicide to escape the pursuit of one Callimachus. The burial itself is not mentioned in the narrative, but the *Acts of John* reports that the brothers gathered around John to hear his eulogy of the deceased woman (66). Two days later, they went to the tomb: "On the following day John and Andronicus and the brethren went at the break of day to the tomb in which Drusiana had been for three days, so that we might break bread there" (72). Liturgists have seen in this reference to a funerary Eucharist on the third day the proof that right from the origins Christians substituted the Eucharist for traditional sacrifices at the tomb. As the last editors of the text stressed, it is slightly ironic that the earliest evidence on a funerary Eucharist is found in a text that was an indirect criticism of it. Actually, as he was leaving, Andronicus found out that the keys to the tomb had been stolen by Callimachus, and John says, "It is right that they are lost, for Drusiana is not in the tomb. Nevertheless, let us go, that you do not appear neglectful" (72).⁵ The funerary ritual on the third day, even a Eucharist, is described simply as a consolation for Andronicus, not as something that was important to Drusiana's salvation. The apocryphal nature of the *Acts of John* ought not to make us dismiss this testimony. It is neither a Gnostic nor a popular text; it presents some literary qualities and seems to address an educated audience whether of pagans or of recent converts to Christianity. The tension caused by the attachment

---

3. See, in particular, Frederick Paxton, *Christianizing Death: the Creation of a Ritual Process in Early Medieval Europe* (Ithaca, NY: Cornell University Press, 1990).

4. Éric Junod and Jean-Daniel Kaestli, ed., *Acta Iohannis,* 2 vols., Corpus Christianorum. Series Apocryphorum 1–2 (Turnhout: Brepols, 1983); the first volume offers an excellent introduction to the literary and historical problems the text raises.

5. Ibid., 2:553–55.

to funerary rites, despite their being unnecessary from the point of view of salvation, is a constant one in all our evidence: it is not until Augustine's treatise *On the Care of the Dead* at the beginning of the fifth century that this tension finds a resolution.

It is important to note the active participation of the "brothers" in the funerals: they met at Andronicus's home, after the burial, to hear John; they all went together on the third day to the tomb. We find the same emphasis on the participation of the coreligionists in Aristides' *Apology*, a contemporary text:

> And if any righteous person of their number passes away from the world they rejoice and give thanks to God, and they follow his body, as if he were moving from one place to another: and when a child is born to any one of them, they praise God, and if again it chance to die in its infancy, they praise God mightily, as for one who has passed through the world without sins. And if again they see that one of their number has died in his iniquity or in his sins, over this one they weep bitterly and sigh, as over one who is about to go to punishment. (15.35)

The apologist mentions accompanying the body, a vague allusion to a funeral cortege in which the brothers participated, but he gives no description of the burial rites. What is important is to notice that Christians became involved when another Christian died, and that their main concern was for the salvation of the deceased.

Besides this solidarity toward each other, Christians seem to have wanted to demonstrate their difference from non-Christians. In the *Octavius*, written in Rome at the beginning of the third century, Minucius Felix reports the attacks of the pagan Caecilius: "You do not bind your head with flowers, you do not honor your body with perfumes; ointments you reserve for funerals, but even to your tombs you deny garlands; you anemic, neurotic creatures, you deserve to be pitied—but by our gods. The result is, you pitiable fools, that you have no enjoyment of life while you wait for the new life which you will never have" (12.6). In an elaborate chiasmus, Caecilius contrasts crowns, which Christians did not use either for the living or the dead, and perfumes, which they set aside for the dead. By stressing the rhetorical aspect of the passage, I want to indicate that the choice of elements discussed also followed literary imperatives. This text, beyond the literary artifice, makes it clear that Christians stood out for their specific funerary customs and/or by abstaining from certain traditional practices. The mortuary crown, which was customarily placed on the head of the deceased, had therefore apparently been rejected: Tertullian and Clement of Alexandria testify to this also, but primarily because the crown was also an attribute of the gods and symbolized idolatry.[6]

In his response, the Christian Octavius employs commonplaces borrowed from the philosophical arsenal, but it would be wrong to assume that Minicius Felix was doing so in order not to give away to his pagan readers the "true motive" behind Christian customs:[7]

> If you would be so kind, forgive us for not garlanding our heads; it is usual for us to inhale the pleasant scent of flowers with our noses, not to breathe it in with our hair or the backs of our heads. Neither do we place garlands on our dead. To my mind it is you who are the cause for wonderment here: how you can apply torches to the deceased (if they have sensation) or garlands (if they have none); if their state is blessed they have no need of flowers, if it is wretched they derive no joy from them. To our funerals the adornment we give is the same composure we show in our lives; neither do we bind a garland that withers, but from God we await a garland of flowers that blossom forever. Tranquil, moderate, confident in the generosity of our God, we enliven our hopes for happiness in the future by our faith in the majesty He manifests at present. And so, blessed is the state to which we rise again, blessed is the state in which we now live, by meditating on that future. (38.2)

Such a discussion is only relevant if it echoes a distinctively Christian practice. A Christian funeral should therefore have been recognizable as such to outside observers. Here the role of other Christians or of the clergy is not mentioned.

In the treatise *On the Soul*, Tertullian describes an interesting scene: "There was a woman born of Christian parents who died in her maturity and beauty after a brief but happy marriage. Before the burial the priest came to pray over her, and as soon as he uttered the first word of the prayer, she lifted her

---

6. For Tertullian, see the texts gathered and commented on in Victor Saxer, *Morts, martyrs, reliques en Afrique chrétienne aux premiers siècles: les témoignages de Tertullien, Cyprien et Augustin à la lumière de l'archéologie africaine,* Théologie historique 55 (Paris: Beauchesne, 1980), 39–42; see also Clement of Alexandria, *The Paidagogos* 2.8.73. For a traditional presentation of the topic, see Alfred Clement Rush, *Death and Burial in Christian Antiquity,* Studies in Christian Antiquity 1 (Washington, DC: Catholic University of America Press, 1941), 133–49.

7. See the note by Jean Beaujeu in Minucius Felix, *Octavius,* ed. Jean Beaujeu (Paris: Les Belles Lettres, 1974), 159–60.

hands and joined them together in a suppliant attitude; after the kiss of peace, she put her hands back at her sides" (51.6).

The exact circumstances of the prayer of the priest have been discussed extensively.[8] The scene takes place well before the placement of the body in the tomb, but does it occur at the graveside, or at the house of the deceased? In the first case, it could be used by liturgists as evidence for a funerary mass at the grave. In the second case, it would represent a funeral wake at the home of the deceased. Does the prayer conclude a celebration of the Eucharist? The mention of the kiss of peace might indicate as much. However, Tertullian notes only that which serves his argument and the data he provides are too vague to allow for a more detailed reconstruction of the scene. In any case, we must take note that a priest was present and that other people were in attendance, as the kiss of peace suggests.

One last document from the third century, the *Didascalia*, provides some data for the region around Antioch. The passage on the funerary cult is preserved in the Syriac translation of the fourth century, in the Latin of the fifth, and also appears in a compilation made in Antioch in the fourth century, the *Apostolic Constitutions*.[9] The context warrants particular attention, for, contrary to what one might expect from a canonico-liturgical document, no ritual is prescribed. The author's primary purpose was actually to dispel the idea that death constituted a pollution and to explain that, as a result, Christians were able to care for the dead without reservation. They could pray for the dead, gather around the tombs of the martyrs, even for the purpose of Eucharistic sacrifice. Latin and Syriac versions mention the possibility of a celebration "for the death of those who sleep"; the *Apostolic Constitutions* suggest that the dead be accompanied by the singing of psalms and insist on the fact that even the clergy may be in contact with the dead. The impression is the one already noted, that Christians participated in funerary rites even if an organized ritual cannot be reconstructed.

These documents, I reiterate, do not yield the earliest elements of a liturgy of death; however, they do raise certain questions relevant to this inquiry, most notably about the participation of fellow believers at the side of the family group, about the role of the clergy, and about the relative influence of individual initiative versus the intervention of the clergy.

---

8. See Jan Hendrik Waszink's commentary in *Quinti Septimi Florentis Tertulliani De Anima*, ed. Jan Hendrik Waszink (Amsterdam: Meulenhoff, 1947), 532–33, and a more recent update of the question in Saxer, *Morts, martyrs, reliques*, 65–68.

9. *Didascalia, versio latina* 61.1.9 ff.; *Didascalia, versio syriaca* 26; *Apostolic Constitutions* 6.30.

Funerals of Christians in the Fourth and Fifth Centuries

Three types of sources are available. The most frequently used are hagiographic texts: the death scene and funerals are always a high point in the narrative. Even if stereotypes of the genre were not yet fixed in the fifth century, these texts offer only an idealized description of a model for Christian funerals.[10] Moreover, these stories portray only people who belong to the church: bishops, ascetics, and virgins. The only description of the funeral of a layperson is that of Monica, the mother of Augustine, but we shall see that each detail was carefully chosen by the latter in keeping with his own pastoral concerns. Besides hagiographic texts there are some documents that refer to one custom or another and explain it. It is important here to consider the nature of the document in order to grasp its impact: a canon of a council cannot be put in the same category as a remark made in an aside in an exegetical commentary. Finally, pastoral literature, mostly in sermons, provides texts in which we glimpse the interaction between clergy and laymen, even if this is through the filter of the preacher's own agenda.[11] We must cross-examine these different sources in order to determine what made funerals of Christians Christian funerals, and to disclose the tensions between the clergy and Christians concerning funerary rites and customs.

Exemplary Funerals: Macrina and Monica

I choose to focus on the stories of the funerals of Macrina, told by her brother Gregory of Nyssa, and of Monica, told by her son Augustine in the *Confessions*. I do not claim that these are the best or the only choices. However, together these two examples provide a relatively wide social spectrum: at one end, Macrina, member of a rich family of Cappadocia and the

---

10. See Pierre Boglioni, "La scène de la mort dans les premières hagiographies latines," in *Essais sur la mort: travaux d'un séminaire de recherche sur la mort, Faculté de théologie, Université de Montréal*, ed. Guy Couturier, André Charron, and Guy Durand, Héritage et projet 29 (Montreal: Fides, 1985), 269–98. For Greek texts, see Monique Alexandre, "À propos du récit de la mort d'Antoine (Athanase, *Vie d'Antoine*. PG 26, 968–974, § 89–93): l'heure de la mort dans la littérature monastique," in *Le temps chrétien de la fin de l'Antiquité au Moyen Âge*, Colloques internationaux du CNRS 604 (Paris: Éditions du CNRS, 1984), 263–82. See also Siver Dagemark, "Funeral as a Hagiographic Motif in *Vita Augustini* and Some Other Biographies of Bishops," *Augustinianum* 40, no. 1 (2000): 255–89.

11. See Éric Rebillard, "Interaction between the Preacher and His Audience: The Case-Study of Augustine's Preaching on Death," in *Studia Patristica. 31*, ed. Elizabeth A. Livingstone (Louvain: Peeters, 1997), 86–96.

sister of two bishops,[12] and, at the other, Monica, wife of a modest African decurion.[13]

Macrina transformed her family estate into a double monastery, one for the women of the house under her direction and another for the men under the leadership of her brother Peter; she died there among her sisters, in the presence of her brother Gregory. The story of the death and funeral of Macrina is very important in Gregory of Nyssa's narrative.[14] When Macrina surrendered her soul, it was not necessary to close her eyes or to prepare her body with funerary toilet (*Life of Macrina* 25). When her death was announced, the virgins wept in grief and shouted Macrina's name in the midst of their cries, following the ancient custom of *conclamatio,* until Gregory called upon them to "turn their lamentations into psalming in the same strain" (26–27). Next, it was necessary to adorn the dead woman in preparation for the funerary wake that attracted a great crowd. The night was spent in singing hymns and psalms (32–33). The next morning, the bishop of the area arrived and the funeral procession began. The funeral bed was carried by the highest-ranking clergymen, led by the bishop and Gregory. The cortege, comparable to a liturgical procession with candles and singing, accompanied Macrina to the church where she was to be buried. Gregory noted that the crowd was so large, it took almost all day to traverse 1,500 meters from the monastery to the church. At the church a prayer was said; Gregory does not indicate whether or not the prayer was accompanied by the Eucharist (34). Macrina's body, lifted from the bed, was placed in the tomb beside her mother (35). Then the story moves quickly over "all the accustomed funerary rites" and recalls Gregory's last act, which was to kiss the dust of his sister's tomb (36).

Monica's funeral was closer to that of an ordinary Christian. She was a laywoman, and although her son held an important office, her obsequies did not bring out the entire city of Milan. Still, "many brethren and religious women assembled when they heard what was happening" (*Confessions* 9.12.31). Augustine gives few concrete details of the ritual that followed. When the death occurred, only the infant Adeodatus wept (29). Evodius

---

12. See Philip Rousseau, *Basil of Caesarea,* The Transformation of the Classical Heritage 20 (Berkeley and Los Angeles: University of California Press, 1994), chap. 1.

13. See Claude Lepelley, "*Spes saeculi:* le milieu social d'Augustin et ses ambitions séculières avant sa conversion," in *Congresso internazionale su s. Agostino nel XVI centenario della conversione, Roma, 15–20 settembre 1986,* Studia Ephemeridis Augustinianum 24 (Rome: Institutum Patristicum Augustinianum, 1987), 1:99–117.

14. Gregory of Nyssa, *Life of Macrina,* ed. Pierre Maraval, Sources chrétiennes 178 (Paris: Éditions du Cerf, 1971), 77–89, for a literary analysis.

began to chant Psalm 100 and was soon followed by the whole house. The ritual toilet and preparation of the body were left in the hands of specialists (31). Of the rest of the funeral, Augustine notes succinctly, "Now came the moment when the body was borne away. We followed it, and returned again dry-eyed." At the tomb, before placing the body, a Eucharist was celebrated (32). Augustine emphasizes two elements in the idealized funeral of his mother. First, as in Gregory's account, there is the absence of lamentation, tears and wailing, but without suggesting the absence of internal mourning, which Augustine expresses later (33). Second, the only arrangement Monica made for her funeral was to be remembered at the altar of the Lord: "On the day when her release was at hand she gave no thought to costly burial or the embalming of her body with spices, nor did she pine for a special monument or concern herself about a grave in her native land; no, that was not her command to us. She desired only to be remembered at your altar, where she had served you with never a day's absence" (36). Augustine does not say whether the Eucharistic sacrifice that was made before the body was placed in the tomb was the one Monica meant, or if she just wanted to be regularly commemorated at the altar by being included in the prayers. The principle, rather than the exact liturgical form, was what mattered to Augustine. As we shall see, the emphasis placed on Monica's attitude also matches his own pastoral concerns.

In considering these stories, it is important to point out that the death of a Christian did not have the sacramental dimension that has been familiar for a long time in Catholic countries. In antiquity, there was no equivalent of extreme unction, since up until the Carolingian era unction was a sacrament for the sick and not the dying,[15] and since the *viaticum,* the communion administered at the point of death, for a long time applied only to those penitents who were in urgent need of reconciliation.[16] Some documents describe a vigil at the church, but that was only for bishops or virgins: Ambrose was brought to the Cathedral Church of Milan; the vigil of Paula of Bethlehem took place in the Church of the Grotto of the Lord; for Macrina, a virgin and the sister of the bishop Gregory, the vigil was held in the vestibule of the local church.[17] Chanting of the Psalms was a central part of both the vigil and the funeral procession, offered as a Christian version of mourning dirges.

---

15. See Antoine Chavasse, *Étude sur l'onction des infirmes dans l'Église latine du IIIe au XIe siècle. 1, Du IIIe siècle à la réforme carolingienne* (Lyon: Librairie du Sacré-Coeur, 1942).

16. Éric Rebillard, *In hora mortis,* 199–224.

17. Paulinus, *Vita Ambrosii* 48.1; Jerome, *Epistulae* 108.29.1; Gregory of Nyssa, *Life of Macrina* 33.

The new meaning of death in Christianity completely transformed manifestations of mourning: joy and hope prevailed over sorrow and tears. This is the paradigmatic discourse illustrated in the death scenes of the earliest *Lives of the Saints*.[18] We will see that mourners did not entirely disappear from the funerals of Christians. The presence of the clergy and coreligionists is indicated in the same fashion as in the earliest documents. More important than the family or social connections were brothers in the faith, and simplicity and joy prevailed over opulence and tears. The celebration of the Eucharist, which is mentioned in the case of Monica, seems to have been absent for Macrina. It is far from being reported routinely in the *Lives of the Saints* and the fragmentary data we have on the subject is difficult to interpret, as we will see. However, we must contrast these stories with the testimony of the sermons, because the picture of the funerals of Christians that appears in them is very different.

Funerals of Christians in the Light of Sermons

Augustine, inspired by the parable of the rich man and Lazarus, often draws for examples of the earthly vanity of the wealthy Christians on their grand funerals. He usually gives concrete details that go beyond the mere stereotype.[19]

In a sermon in which he exhorts his audience to live a good life in order not to die a bad death, Augustine explains that dying badly must not be interpreted in a carnal sense, and refers to the parable in order to show that a good death, in the carnal sense, can lead directly to an eternal death: "Don't interrogate your eyes, but go back to the heart. I mean, if you interrogate your eyes, they will give you a false answer. A great deal of pomp and ceremony, after all, tarted up with worldly trimmings, could have been lavished on that rich man as he lay dying. What troops of ululating men-servants and maid-servants there could have been, what a procession of retainers, what a splendid funeral, what an expensive tomb! I presume he was smothered in aromatic spices" (*Sermons* 102.3). In another sermon, the reading of Psalm 48 suggests to him a similar development. With verses 10–12, "The imprudent person and the unwise will perish together, and will leave their wealth to strangers. Their tombs are their homes forever," he cannot help recalling the

---

18. For a classical presentation of this argument, see Johannes Quasten, *Music and Worship in Pagan and Christian Antiquity* 1930), trans. Boniface Ramsey, NPM Studies in Church Music and Liturgy (Washington, DC: National Association of Pastoral Musicians, 1983), 149–89, esp. 161–62.

19. See Saxer, *Morts, martyrs, reliques,* 153–56.

rich man of the parable, the cortege of those who mourn him, his expensive clothes, the perfumes and aromatics with which he was buried, and his sumptuous marble tomb (*Exposition 1 of the Psalms* 48.13).

There is no need to add to these examples: the funerals of the rich are far from reflecting the Christian ideal. Beyond the stereotype, Augustine's criticism is aimed at values widely shared in Roman society. A beautiful funeral implies a kind of remembering of the dead unrelated to whatever might have been said of him at the altar. The "memory" of him depends in fact upon the number of those who mourn him and on the beauty of his monument (*memoria,* in Latin). In another sermon, Augustine is more explicit: "So it is that funeral processions, crowds of mourners, expensive arrangements for burial, the construction of splendid monuments, can be some sort of consolation for the living, but not any assistance for the dead. It is not to be doubted, though, that the dead can be helped by the prayers of holy Church, and the Eucharistic sacrifice, and alms distributed for the repose of their spirits" (*Sermons* 172.2).

The contrast between these two kinds of *memoria* could not be greater. Augustine does not condemn what is not helpful for the salvation of the dead, for he recalls, at the end of his sermon, that Holy Scripture counts the proper care of the dead among good works (*Sermons* 172.3). Nor is he trying to substitute the communal commemorations of the church for private services. In the *De cura gerenda pro mortuis,* Augustine draws very helpful distinctions between the two spheres quite radically: funerals and other "concerns for the dead," presented as both a duty of the living and as a comfort to them, belong to the private, even secular, sphere; prayer, the Eucharist, and alms alone are useful for salvation and belong to the religious, or sacred, sphere. The bishops have nothing to say about whatever does not relate to salvation, except when they disagree—we shall see it with John Chrysostom—on the limits of the secular.

In several sermons, preached at Antioch or Constantinople, John Chrysostom denounced what he called "the madness about funerals" and recalled that faith in the resurrection should turn Christians away from traditional mourning.[20] Weeping, beating the breast, tearing the hair, requiring all the servants to mourn were all customs to be discarded by Christians. Calling upon professional mourners went even further, for those women were pagan.

Although in Antioch John simply condemned the use of professional mourners by Christians,[21] in Constantinople, perhaps because of his authority

---

20. The formula is found in John Chrysostom, *In Iohannem homiliae* 85.5. See Pietro Rentinck, *La cura pastorale in Antiochia nel IV secolo,* Analecta Gregoriana 178 (Rome: Università Gregoriana, 1970), 133–34.

21. See also John Chrysostom, *In Iohannem homiliae* 85.6.

as bishop, he made it an offense against ecclesiastical laws and threatened to excommunicate anyone who hired professional mourners. Thus in a sermon on Hebrews we read,

> If it should happen, and anyone should hire these mourning women, believe me when I say (I speak not without meaning but as I have resolved, let him who will, be angry), that I will exclude that person from the Church for a long time.... For, tell me, why do you invite both the priests and the singers?... We come, discoursing of the things concerning the resurrection, instructing all, even those who have not yet been smitten, through the honor shown to him, to bear it nobly if any such thing should happen, and you do bring those who overthrow our teachings? (*In epistulam ad Hebraeos homiliae* 4.7)

The presence of mourners, who were obviously not Christians, is incompatible with that of clergy. It actually mocked Christianity, and the deceased, to call on such people. In Constantinople, the competition among the different religious groups must not be overlooked: Chrysostom refers to pagans as well as Jews and heretics, who all might take advantage of these Christian contradictions.[22]

John clearly attests that there were Christians who brought a priest into their homes, after a death, in order to draw consolation from "Christian philosophy"; who invited the poor to sing Psalms, for which they gave them alms; and yet, at the same time, they hired the services of pagan women to mourn their dead in public.[23] These laypeople did not share, apparently, the opinion of their bishop about the boundaries between the sacred and secular.

Like Augustine, John Chrysostom contrasted what people expected from funerals—socially significant honors and some form of consolation—and the futility of these displays for salvation. In one of the *Homilies on John* he explains what to do in order to honor the dead: "But you, you disregard all these considerations; you call your servants, urge them to weep, as a way to honor the dead, and that is a shame and a great wrong.... You want to honor the dead? Do exactly the opposite of what you have been accustomed to doing; give alms, do good works, make oblations" (*In Iohannem homiliae* 62.5).

---

22. *In Epistulam ad Hebraeos homiliae* 4, 5. For Antioch, see John Chrysostom, *In Iohannem homiliae* 85.6, in which those who laugh are not identified by their belonging to a particular religious group.

23. See also John Chrysostom, *Homilies on Matthew* 31.4.

What is helpful to the dead are alms and prayers, especially the Eucharist. Like Augustine, John is careful to point out that he does not forbid funerals, nor urge people to neglect them, when he recalls the uselessness of their expense.[24] They are useless as a means of salvation, which is the church's sole concern and the only issue that relates to the authority of bishops. Chrysostom does not separate the two spheres, the secular sphere of funerals and the religious sphere of alms and prayer, as clearly as Augustine does, but the tensions between the laypeople and their bishop about the boundaries of the spheres are apparent.

Neither Augustine nor John Chrysostom recommend adopting a new liturgy of death when they mention prayers, offerings, or sacrifices. They do not suggest replacing traditional funerals with a Christian ceremony. They do not even prescribe the celebration of the Eucharist as a fixed element of a new ritual. Evidence on a funerary Eucharist suggest that the initiative remains in the hand of the family.

The Funerary Eucharist

Liturgists have tried to establish which type of celebration was known and when it was first attested. They have collected evidence on celebrations before and after the burial, in the presence or absence of the corpse, on the third day, on the seventh or the ninth, on the thirtieth or the fortieth day.[25] However, these practices were highly diverse and local, and bishops did not attempt to impose them on Christians.

A mass on the day of burial is mentioned in only two texts. At Ostia, the harbor of Rome, the Eucharist was celebrated at the grave and in the presence of the corpse when Monica, Augustine's mother, was buried (*Confessions* 9.12.32). At Hippo, for Augustine himself, "A sacrifice was offered to God in our presence to commend his bodily death, and then he was buried." Possidius, in his account, does not say where this celebration occurred (*Life of Augustine* 31.5). However, at Uzalis, not far from Hippo, for the funeral of the secretary of the bishop Evodius there was no sacrifice until the third day. Evodius describes the funeral he gave his secretary as an honorable funeral in a letter to Augustine (Augustine, *Epistulae* 158.2), thus suggesting a different local custom.

---

24. John Chrysostom, *In Iohannem homiliae* 85.5.
25. See Cyrille Vogel, "L'environnement cultuel du défunt durant la période paléochrétienne," in *La maladie et la mort du chrétien dans la liturgie: Conférences Saint-Serge: XXIe semaine d'études liturgiques*, Bibliotheca Ephemerides Liturgicae. Subsidia 1 (Rome: Edizioni Liturgiche, 1975), 381–413.

A canon from an African council is sometimes used to prove that the case of Augustine was an exception and that the celebration of the Eucharist at the time of the burial was forbidden in Africa.[26] Augustine himself notes in the *Confessions* that the sacrifice offered for his mother in Ostia was a local custom, thus different from the African tradition. What might explain Augustine's "exception"? It is true that he was a bishop and that the sacrifice was probably celebrated only in the presence of his priest.[27]

However, the African canon deserves closer examination. The following measures are adopted: fasting is required for celebrating the Eucharist and, as a result, when a death occurs in the afternoon, only prayers may be said if the priest has eaten; it is also forbidden to celebrate the Eucharist in the presence of a corpse and to give Communion to a lifeless body.[28] As we can see, the point was not to forbid the celebration of the Eucharist before the burial only to have it follow the burial. The appeal to the principle of Eucharistic fasting seems to have been related to a practice deemed abusive, in which the deceased was brought to the church for a celebration of the Eucharist immediately after his death and eventually took part in it. Two reasons are offered: the celebrant must fast, which might not be the case depending on when the deceased was brought in; the Eucharist could not be celebrated in the presence of a corpse. It is more in the nature of council legislation to forbid than to prescribe, but it must be noted that whereas Christians brought the deceased into church and expected a special service to which the deceased was closely associated, the church did not respond to that expectation. The body of the deceased should not be taken to the church; the Eucharist to commend the deceased's soul could be celebrated only if the priest had fasted, otherwise the latter would simply offer prayers. We will come upon similar conclusions again: the church did not seek to encourage the expectations of Christians about the care of the dead, as if the conditions that would satisfy the living could not be met. Mourning did not end with the funeral. The traditional

---

26. This is originally a canon of the Council of Hippo held in 393, but it was reproduced in the later collections of Hippo and of Carthage; see Charles Munier, "Cinq canons inédits du Concile d'Hippone du 8 octobre 393," *Revue de droit canonique* 12 (1968): 16–29.

27. See the discussion in Saxer, *Morts, martyrs, reliques,* 152.

28. *Concilium Hipponense* 4: *Aurelius episcopus dixit: Sicut frater et collega noster Saturninus salubri consideratione deprompsit, debent episcopi, non postquam pranderint, sed ieiuni cum populis ieiunis, quacumque hora, diuina celebrare mysteria. Si uero sumpserint cibos,* **pm** *cuiuscumque laici siue episcopi conmendantes, oratione eum tantummodo prosequantur. Illud autem quoniam praesentibus corporibus nonnulli audeant sacrificia celebrare et partem corporis sancti cum exanimi cadauere communicare arbitror prohibendum.* The abbreviation "pm" is difficult; here is the shorter version of the *Breuianum Hipponense* 28: *Ut sacramenta altaris nonnisi a ieiunis hominibus celebrentur, excepto uno die anniuersario quo cena domini celebratur. Nam si aliquorum postmeridiano tempore defunctorum siue episcoporum siue clericorum siue ceterorum commendatio facienda est, solis orationibus fiat, si illi qui faciunt iam pransi inueniantur.*

commemoration of the dead in the Greek world occurred on three days, the third, the ninth, and the thirtieth days after death; the Roman world observed only the ninth. Christians observed the same days, but the celebration of the Eucharist on them was not regularly scheduled.[29] The third day is mentioned in the West only by Evodius before it was included, along with the seventh and thirtieth days, in the Gelasian Sacramentaries (mid-eighth century).[30] Augustine explains, in an exegetical commentary written for his fellow bishops in 419, why the seventh day should be preferred over the ninth, which was traditional in the Roman world: "He [Joseph] mourned his father for seven days (Gen. 50:10). I do not know of any saint in Scripture whose mourning lasted nine days, which the Latins called the *novemdial*. So it seems to me that Christians should refrain from observing that number of days, because the custom is a pagan one. Moreover, the seventh day is supported by the authority of Scripture" (*Quaestiones in Heptateuchum* 1.172). Augustine has no difficulty finding Biblical examples for a mourning period of seven days. Nevertheless, he remains quite moderate in the advice he gives to discourage Christians from observing a period of nine days. It was on the seventh day that Ambrose returned to his brother's tomb, the day that recalls the Sabbath and symbolizes future rest (*De excessu fratris* 2.2). However it should be noted that the ninth day was the norm throughout the Eastern tradition.[31]

The day marking the end of the mourning period has, quite naturally, been the object of greatest attention. The Greek tradition, like the Jewish one, ended mourning on the thirtieth day, but Christians seem to have observed the fortieth day along with the thirtieth. According to Ambrose, both days were based upon Scripture: forty days of mourning was observed for Jacob, thirty for Moses. He misinterprets the forty days indicated in the case of Jacob, which were actually the time needed for embalming.[32] Augustine gives an accurate interpretation of the passage, but offers no commentary

---

29. Franz Cumont, "La triple commémoration des morts," *Comptes-rendus de l'Académie des Inscriptions et Belles Lettres* (1918): 278–94; Emil Freistedt, *Altchristliche Totengedächtnisstage und ihre Beziehung zum Jenseitsglauben und Totenkult der Antike*, Liturgiewiessenschaftliche Quellen und Forschungen 24 (Münster: Aschendorff, 1928); and Vogel, "L'environnement cultuel," 396–400.

30. On the testimony of Evodius, see Augustine, *Letters* 158.2. *Sacramentarium Gelasianum* 3.105, ed. Leo Cunibert Mohlberg, Rerum ecclesiasticarum documenta, Series maior, Fontes 4 (Rome: Herder, 1960), 246.

31. Franz Cumont, "La triple commémoration des morts," 285–86.

32. Ambrose, *On Emperor Theodosius* 3, with the commentary of Yves-Marie Duval, "Formes profanes et formes bibliques dans les oraisons funèbres de saint Ambroise," in *Christianisme et formes littéraires de l'Antiquité tardive en Occident: huit exposés suivis de discussions*, Entretiens sur l'antiquité classique 23 (Geneva: Fondation Hardt pour l'étude de l'Antiquité classique, 1977), 280–82.

on commemorative customs (*Locutionum in Heptateuchum libri septem* 1.207). John Chrysostom, who makes the same misinterpretation as Ambrose about Jacob, uses a version of the Septuagint in which the mourning period for Moses was also forty days. However, he stigmatizes the length of this mourning, as incompatible with the Christian conception of death. It is difficult to see it as evidence for the forty days' observance in Antioch (*De sanctis Bernice et Prosdoce* 3). The *Apostolic Constitutions,* written in the area of Antioch at the end of the fourth century, refer to the third, ninth, and thirtieth days.[33] Aside from Milan, where Ambrose observed it for Theodosius, there is evidence of forty days of mourning in Dalmatia, at Constantinople, and at Alexandria.[34] According to Franz Cumont, the forty days was a Semitic tradition that originated in Syria.[35] In any case, it is important to mention here the great variety of customs followed and to point out that these practices were part of very longstanding local traditions to which the church accommodated itself with relatively good grace.

The explicit references to a Eucharist in connection with the third, seventh, ninth, thirtieth, or fortieth days are rare and there is no reason to think that it was an established and systematic practice. Evodius's testimony on a celebration at the grave on the third day has already been cited several times. Ambrose had the Eucharist celebrated on the seventh day for his brother Satyrus, and on the fortieth for the Emperor Theodosius. Yves-Marie Duval convincingly showed that allusions to those liturgical celebrations, at least in part, structured the funerary orations Ambrose pronounced on these occasions. However, he adds this commentary: "such recourse to the ordinary liturgy is highly instructive. Neither Ambrose's own brother, nor Theodosius the victorious Emperor, was entitled to a 'special' liturgy. They were treated the same as ordinary Christians, which they were especially."[36] The difficulty is that we have no evidence on this "ordinary liturgy" and the way Ambrose talks about one of the biblical readings done on the celebration of the seventh

---

33. *Apostolic Constitutions* 8.42.1–3. Some manuscripts give a duration of forty days: see Marcel Metzger, in *Les Constitutions apostoliques. 3, Livres VII et VIII*, ed. Marcel Metzger, Sources chrétiennes 330 (Paris: Éditions du Cerf, 1987), 260–61, and the note of Louis Canet about the *tessarakonta* and Lucian's recension of the *Septuaginta* in *Comptes-rendus de l'Académie des Inscriptions et Belles Lettres* (1918): 294–97.

34. For Dalmatia, see Jerome, *Epistulae* 118.4, where Iulianus, of whom we know nothing else, ends the mourning for his two daughters on the fortieth day. Melania remains in Constantinople for the mourning period of his uncle—that is, forty days (*Life of Melania* 56). For Alexandria, see Palladius, *Historia Lausiaca* 21.15.

35. Cumont, "La triple commémoration des morts," 287–88.

36. Duval, "Formes profanes et formes bibliques," 280; Duval also speaks of the "ordinary liturgy of the fortieth day" (282).

day in honor of Satyrus does not support such an interpretation: "Hence, not unmeetly has the Holy Spirit declared today through the voice of the little reader what a splendid man my brother was.... I recognize the voice of God: what no testamentary disposition provided for, the Spirit has revealed" (*On His Brother Satyrus* 1.61). The reference to the voice of God does not suggest that Ambrose did not himself choose these readings or that they were required by the liturgy. Actually, not only was it quite common to consider the voice in the Psalms to be that of the Holy Spirit,[37] but Psalm 14 might also have been read in a different liturgical circumstance, the ceremony of the fortieth day rather than the seventh, for the funeral of Theodosius. That would suggest that we see in this psalm one of several possible funeral readings, rather than the one required for a specific occasion. This argument holds also for other readings to which there are allusions, even if they eventually became fixed elements of the funeral service.[38] In order to justify the choice of the fortieth day rather than the thirtieth, since he knows and recalls that the two customs are founded on the authority of Scripture, Ambrose stresses the parallel between Jacob and Joseph on one side and Theodosius and Honorius on the other (*De obitu Tbheodosii* 3–4).

This does not necessarily mean that the ceremonies for Satyrus and Theodosius were exceptional, but there is still nothing to suggest that they were conform to a common liturgy. There was no such thing: the first choice made was to have a funeral service; the second was to select components among a repertoire still in the process of becoming the closed list of readings of the later liturgy. Our evidence is not sufficient to determine how much lay Christians were asking their church for such services, but the funerary Eucharist does not appear to have been the norm nor even specifically recommended.

The distinction between funerals of Christians and Christian funerals adopted by Paul-Albert Février from the epigraphists is still a useful one, although the underlying idea of a progressive transformation of funerals of Christians into Christian funerals is debatable.[39] From this point of view, Christian funerals were an ideal not only formulated but sought after from

---

37. See Ambrose, *Explanation on Psalm 61* 1.1 and 3.
38. Duval, "Formes profanes et formes bibliques," 278 and n. 3, cites Psalms 14, 23, and 114, and Wisdom 4:7–11 (see *De obitu Valentinian* 51, 57; *De excessus fratris* 1.30), attested by Augustine as well; see Anne-Marie La Bonnardière, *Biblia Augustiniana. A. T., Le livre de la Sagesse* (Paris, Études Augustiniennes, 1970), 75–78, about Sermon 396, given for the funeral of a bishop).
39. See Paul-Albert Février, "La mort chrétienne," in *Segni e riti nella chiesa altomedievale occidentale: XXXIII Settimana di studio del Centro italiano sull'alto medioevo, 11–17 aprile 1985,* Settimane di studio del Centro italiano di studi sull'alto medioevo 33 (Spoleto: Centro italiano di studi sull'alto medioevo, 1987), 881–952.

the beginning, and the time taken to attain that ideal can be explained by accidents and obstacles that slowed down the process. I do not think that we have evidence to support this point of view. In the fourth and fifth centuries, there was no "Christian ritual" that the church attempted to impose for lay Christians: the family remained the principal player in funerals. The expectations of Christians, as revealed in African canonical documentation and in the sermons of John Chrysostom, were quite real however. Christians called upon the clergy when a death occurred within their families. The clergy was able to offer consolation and prayers, but, as we are going to see, these prayers did not respond to the expectations of the laypeople.

CHAPTER 7

The Church, Christians, and the Dead

Commemoration of the Dead in Late Antiquity

In recent years, medievalists have shown how the Christian cult of the dead was woven into, and evolved with, social institutions, even though doctrine itself did not necessarily change.[1] The relationship between doctrine and practice is a complex one, and several points of funerary doctrine were not yet established by the mid-fifth century.[2] It is not my intention to define the stages of development of the Christian cult of the dead. I wish here to reexamine the evidence in the pastoral context in which they were produced in order to reconstruct both sides of a dialogue that has often been approached only as the confrontation of elite and popular cultures.[3]

---

1. See in particular, Frederick Paxton, *Christianizing Death: The Creation of a Ritual Process in Early Medieval Europe* (Ithaca, NY: Cornell University Press, 1990); Jean-Claude Schmitt, *Ghosts in the Middle Ages: The Living and the Dead in Medieval Society,* trans. Teresa Lavender Fagan (Chicago: University of Chicago Press, 1998); Michel Lauwers, *La mémoire des ancêtres, le souci des morts: morts, rites et société au moyen âge (Diocèse de Liège, XIe–XIIIe siècles),* Théologie historique 103 (Paris: Beauchesne, 1997).

2. This is particularly true of an essential element of the medieval "system": the status of the dead between the moment of death and resurrection. See Claude Carozzi, *Le voyage de l'âme dans l'au-delà d'après la littérature latine (Ve–XIIIe siècle),* Collection de l'École française de Rome 189 (Rome: École française de Rome, 1994); and Peter Brown, "*Gloriosus obitus*: The End of the Ancient Other World," in *The Limits of Ancient Christianity: Essays on Late Antique Thought and Culture in Honor of R. A. Markus,* ed. William E. Klingshirn and Mark Vessey, Recentiores (University of Michigan Press, 1999), 289–314.

3. This is usually how Augustine's *De cura gerenda pro mortuis* is read; see Yvette Duval, *Auprès des saints corps et âme: l'inhumation "ad sanctos" dans la chrétienté d'Orient et d'Occident du IIIe au VIIe*

The Church and the Cult of the Dead

All Souls Day, or the Commemoration of All the Faithful Departed, on November 2, was only introduced into the Christian liturgical calendar at the beginning of the eleventh century by Odilon, abbot of Cluny from 994 to 1049.[4] Was a feast of the dead observed by the early church as well?

The Early Church and the Feast of the Dead

The traditional Roman calendar included a feast of the dead during the month of February that concluded on February 22 with the solemnity of the *Caristia*. The oldest calendar of the Roman Church, transmitted in the Codex-Calendar of 354, indicated a celebration on February 22 called *natale Petri de cathedra*.[5] This has led specialists of liturgy to think that the Christian ceremony arose as a substitute for the pagan feast. As Louis Duchesne explains it, "The reason will be clear if we glance at the ancient calendars of pagan Rome, wherein we see that the 22nd of February was devoted to the celebration of a festival, popular above all others, in memory of the dead of each family.... It was very difficult to uproot such ancient and cherished habits. It was, doubtless, to meet this difficulty that the Christian festival of the 22nd of February was instituted."[6] This hypothesis of the moderns actually dates back to the twelfth century. Jean Beleth (d. 1182) had already connected the feast of the *Cathedra Petri* to the pagan custom of bringing food to the tombs of the dead on that day (*Rationale diuinorum officiorum* 83). After provoking numerous discussions, the question of the origin of the celebration has been resolved.[7] The day was observed by the Church of Rome, but little known in the provinces. It was not a banquet to observe the anniversary of St. Peter that paralleled banquets commemorating the dead; nor was

---

siècle (Paris: Études Augustiniennes, 1988), and Vincenza Zangara, *Exeuntes de corpore: discussioni sulle apparizioni dei morti in epoca agostiniana*, Biblioteca della Rivista di storia e letteratura religiosa. Studi 1 (Florence: Olschki, 1990).

    4. Lauwers, *La mémoire des ancêtres, le souci des morts*, 140–46.

    5. Michele Renee Salzman, *On Roman Time: The Codex-Calendar of 354 and the Rhythms of Urban Life in Late Antiquity*, The Transformation of the Classical Heritage 17 (Berkeley and Los Angeles: University of California Press, 1990), 47.

    6. Louis Duchesne, *Christian Worship: Its Origin and Evolution*. 3rd English ed., trans. M. L. McClure (London: Society for Promoting Christian Knowledge, 1910), 278.

    7. Paul-Albert Février, "Natale Petri de cathedra," *Comptes rendus de l'Académie des Inscriptions et Belles Lettres* (1977): 514–31; Charles Pietri, *Roma christiana: recherches sur l'Église de Rome, son organisation, sa politique, son idéologie de Miltiade à Sixte III (311–440)*, Bibliothèque des Écoles françaises de Rome et d'Athènes 224 (Rome: École française de Rome, 1976), 381–89.

it a celebration of the founding of the episcopacy. Paul-Albert Février has noted that February 22, the day of the *Caristia,* was a celebration of Concord, related to the cult of the Lares and not, like the days that preceded, to that of the Manes. The Roman Church would therefore have celebrated its own feast of the Concord on February 22, with Peter as its patron saint. Charles Pietri also rejects the funerary nature of the feast, but maintains that it was introduced deliberately to replace pagan funerary banquets, as evinced in some of the sources on that celebration. In any case, the Church of Rome did not institute a Christian feast of the dead as a substitute for a pagan feast.

There is a reference in a sermon of Augustine to a "day of our dead brothers" (*Sermons* 173.1), but that sermon shows every sign of being truncated. It is possible that the opening phrase was the addition of the copyist who incorporated it into the short series of three sermons relating to the dead that have come to us as an appendix of the medieval collection *De verbis Apostoli.* Without further evidence, therefore, this sermon cannot be held as proof that the church in Africa celebrated a feast of the dead in the fourth and fifth centuries.[8]

✣ The Church and the Parentalia

In the Roman Empire, the cult of the dead was basically a family cult. Relatives and friends gathered at the tomb and shared with the deceased a meal, albeit a symbolic one.[9] Christians, whose tombs were found among non-Christian ones, often those of parents and friends, did the same.[10] They also gathered together to celebrate in the same way the memory of their "very special dead," the martyrs. From early on, bishops objected to these practices at the tombs of the martyrs. Peter Brown has studied the multiple motivations

---

8. Anne-Marie La Bonnardière, *Biblia Augustiniana. N. T., Les Épîtres aux Thessaloniciens, à Tite et à Philémon* (Paris: Études Augustiniennes, 1964), 9–10, and Victor Saxer, *Morts, martyrs, reliques en Afrique chrétienne aux premiers siècles: les témoignages de Tertullien, Cyprien et Augustin à la lumière de l'archéologie africaine* Théologie historique 55 (Paris: Beauchesne, 1980), 160–61, do not take into account the way the text was transmitted. On the collection *De verbis Apostoli,* see Gert Partoens, "La collection de sermons augustiniens 'De verbis apostoli': introduction et liste des manuscrits les plus anciens," *Revue Bénédictine* 111 (2001): 320. On "truncated" sermons, see François Dolbeau, "Nouveaux sermons de saint Augustin pour la conversion des païens et des donatistes (VI)," *Revue des études augustiniennes* 39 (1993): 421–23, reprinted in Augustine of Hippo, *Vingt-six sermons au peuple d'Afrique,* ed. François Dolbeau, Collection des études augustiniennes, Série antiquité 147 (Paris: Institut d'études augustiniennes, 1996), 471–523.

9. See John Scheid, *Quand faire, c'est croire: les rites sacrificiels des Romains,* Collection historique (Paris: Aubier, 2005), 161–88.

10. See Ramsay MacMullen, *Christianity and Paganism in the Fourth to Eighth Centuries* (New Haven, CT: Yale University Press, 1997), 92–94, 153–57.

for and consequences of the bishops' control over the cult of the saints.[11] The bishops' attitude toward the cult of the ordinary dead is, most of the time, considered together with their attitude toward the martyr cult.[12] However, the implications of an attempt at controlling the cult of the ordinary dead would prove very different and warrant closer examination. We need to review evidence on the cult of the dead in Christian texts and pay particular attention to the distinction between martyrs and the ordinary dead.[13]

In *De spectaculis,* Tertullian explains that Christians renounce two kinds of idolatry when they are baptized: "So on that account, since both kinds of idol stand on the same footing (dead men and gods are one and the same thing), we abstain from both kinds of idolatry. Temples or tombs, we abominate both equally; we know neither sort of altar; we adore neither sort of image; we pay no sacrifice; we pay no funeral rite. No, and we do not eat of what is offered in sacrificial or funeral rite, because 'we cannot eat of the Lord's supper and the supper of demons' (1 Cor 10: 21)" (13.3–4). In order to denounce idolatry, Tertullian often borrows from the Hellenistic philosopher Euhemerus the theory that gods are men who became divine after their death. The fact that identical practices are found in the cult of gods and the cult of the dead is presented as proof that gods are simply men who have died. Thus, the funerary cult is rarely the direct object of Tertullian's attacks.[14] In this text, however, Tertullian implies that Christians should not participate in the cult of the dead, bring offerings to the tombs, or consume food from such offerings at banquets given to celebrate the dead.

This passage is sometimes cited as evidence that at the beginning of the third century Christians did not participate in funerary banquets, contrary to what they did in the fourth century according to Augustine's testimony.[15] Yet such an interpretation is difficult to sustain in the context of the treatise: Tertullian was not describing something Christians did not do, but stating what it was they were not supposed to do. In *De idololatria,* in which, as we

---

11. Peter Brown, *The Cult of the Saints: Its Rise and Function in Latin Christianity* (Chicago: University of Chicago Press, 1981).

12. Such absence of distinction is characteristic in Peter Karpinski, *Annua die dormitionis: Untersuchungen zum christlichen Jahrgedächtnis der Toten auf dem Hintergrund antiken Brauchtums,* Europäische Hochschulschriften. Reihe 23, Theologie 300 (Frankfurt am Main: Lang, 1987).

13. For a more thorough study, especially of the testimony of Augustine, see Éric Rebillard, "*Nec deserere memorias suorum:* Augustine and the Family-Based Commemoration of the Dead," *Augustinian Studies* 36, no. 1 (2005): 99–111.

14. See a list of texts in Saxer, *Morts, martyrs, reliques,* 36–39. At times, Saxer underestimates the difficulty of drawing information about funerary rites from texts that only allude to those rites, but aim at denouncing idolatry or polytheism.

15. Saxer, *Morts, martyrs, reliques,* 148–49.

have already seen, he discusses the banquets in which Christian participation was permissible, he does not refer explicitly to funerary rites or commemorative celebrations. Nevertheless, he leaves the door wide open for the passive attendance by Christians at funerary banquets, since taking part could be considered a family or social obligation.[16] Tertullian's ambivalent attitude notwithstanding, Février has shown convincingly that in Rome archeological evidence—the only evidence that clearly comes from third century monuments—attests to the practice of Christian funerary meals in the catacombs or nearby.[17]

An early council, held at Elvira in Spain between 295 and 314, contains two canons that are sometimes understood in relation to the cult of the dead. The first forbids the lighting of candles in daylight *in cimiterio;* the second forbids women from going there at night, because, under the pretext of praying, they could indulge in all kinds of debauchery.[18] *Cimiterium* does not mean "cemetery," but a monument where one or more martyrs are buried, a fact that explains the bishop's authority over the place. In order to justify the ban on candles, the canon actually mentions the tranquility of the *sanctorum spiritus,* the souls of the saints, who can only be martyrs. The council, therefore, addressed forms of worship at martyrs' tombs.

Zeno, bishop of Verona in Northern Italy (c. 350–80), mentions banquets offered to the dead in terms reminiscent of those of Tertullian. This mention appears in a sermon Zeno preached to newly baptized Christians during Easter week on the three types of sacrifice: pagan, Jewish, and Christian.[19] He includes funerary banquets, or *refrigeria,* in an enumeration of pagan forms of sacrifice that Christians were to avoid: "Also displeasing to God are those who are wandering among the tombs, who are offering sacrificial meals (*prandia...sacrificant*) to the rotting corpses of the dead, who, because of their passion for debauchery and drunkenness, have suddenly produced

---

16. See Tertullian, *De Idololatria* 16.4–5.

17. Paul-Albert Février, "Le culte des morts dans les communautés chrétiennes durant le IIIe siècle," in *Atti del IX Congresso Internazionale di archeologia cristiana, Roma, 21–27 settembre 1975. 1, I monumenti cristiani precostantiniani,* (Vatican City: Pontificio Istituto di archeologia cristiana, 1978), 211–74. For recent discoveries, see Anna Maria Giuntella, Giuseppina Borghetti, and Daniela Stiaffini, *Mensae e riti funerari in Sardegna: la testimonianza di Cornus,* Mediterraneo tardoantico medievale. Scavi e ricerche 1 (Taranto: Scorpione, 1985).

18. Council of Elvira, canons 34 and 35; on the authenticity and the date of the composite collection of the Council of Elvira, see Reinhart Herzog, ed., *Nouvelle histoire de la littérature latine. 5, Restauration et renouveau: la littérature latine de 284 à 374 après J.-C.,* French version under the direction of Gérard Nauroy (Turnhout: Brepols, 1993), 493 and bibliography.

19. Zeno, *Tractatus* 1.25. About the liturgical context, see Gordon P. Jeanes, *The Day Has Come! Easter and Baptism in Zeno of Verona,* Alcuin Club Collection 73 (Collegeville, MN: Litugucal Press, 1995), 141–42.

martyrs for their own purpose in infamous places, with carafes and chalices" (*Tractatus* 1.25.6.11). Zeno asks the newly baptized to renounce practices he presents as forms of sacrifice. It seems that, in order to justify themselves in the eyes of their dissatisfied bishop, Christians had "invented" martyrs: they did not observe the *parentalia* as pagans did, they claimed, but honored the martyrs.[20]

Gaudentius, bishop of Brescia in the same area of Italy (c. 390–410), warned the neophytes about the different paths leading to idolatry, addressing them as follows:

> Consider as idolatry poisons, incantations, amulets, fate, auguries, oracles, omens, *parentalia;* the *parentalia,* I say, from which the evil of idolatry has reared its sinful head. At first, indeed, men began to prepare meals for the dead to satisfy their own gluttony, in order to feed themselves, but then they dared to celebrate sacrilegious sacrifices as well in honor of the dead, although it cannot be said that those who celebrate the *parentalia* are honoring their dead with a sacrifice when, using tombs as tables and so drunk their hands shake as they pour their wine, they stammer about the soul's thirst. (*Tractatus* 4.14–15)

Like Zeno, Gaudentius stresses the fact that these meals in honor of the dead were actually a form of cult, a sacrifice. The inclusion of the parentalia among practices that manifestly were of a magical and superstitious nature was not obvious to his listeners, for Gaudentius himself paused to explain it. Unless they were acting entirely in bad faith, it does seem that Christians saw in the banquets of the parentalia merely an opportunity to share a meal and honor their dead.

These two texts are revealing of a tension between bishops and Christians on the subject of traditional practices linked to the cult of the dead. While the former condemned them as a form of sacrifice, the latter defended their actions as merely remembering the dead or honoring the martyrs. What these sermons teach us about the pastoral context in which the bishops denounced traditional forms of cults of the dead is that Christians were attached to the memory of their dead. The fact that the bishops combined

---

20. We must abandon the idea that Zeno was condemning Donatist practices, as claimed in Jean Doignon, "Refrigerium et catéchèse à Vérone au IVe siècle," in *Hommages à Marcel Renard,* ed. Jacqueline Bibauw, Collection Latomus 102 (Brussel: Latomus, 1969), 2:220–39. See Carlo Truzzi, *Zeno, Gaudenzio e Cromazio: testi e contenuti della predicazione cristiana per le chiese di Verona, Brescia e Aquileia (360–410 ca.),* Testi e ricerche di scienze religiose 22 (Brescia: Paideia, 1985), 219–20, n. 79.

moral considerations with religious ones regarding these idolatrous practices shows that they thought that a simple ban would have been useless.

Ambrose adopted a more active policy: in Milan, when Augustine lived there, the celebration of the parentalia at the martyrs' tombs was forbidden. According to the *Confessions,* his mother Monica was actually refused access to the martyrs' tombs when she went there with offerings. Monica immediately renounced this African custom: "Once she had ascertained, however, that Ambrose, illustrious preacher and exemplar of piety as he was, had forbidden the celebration of these rites even by those who conducted them with restraint, lest any opportunity might be given to drunkards to indulge in excess, and also because the custom resembled the parentalia and so was close kin to the superstitious practices of the pagans, she most willingly gave it up" (*Confessions* 6.2.2). According to Augustine, Ambrose offered two reasons for the ban: the risk of intemperance and the similarity to the pagan rite of the parentalia.

Ambrose's own allusions to funerary banquets are brief. In a treatise on fasting, deriving from a Lenten predication, Ambrose denounces the various pretexts set forth for drinking: "They say, 'Let us drink to the health of the emperors!... Let us drink to the health of the armies, to our companions' strength, the health of our children.' And they think that these wishes reach God, as do those who bring the chalices to the martyrs' tombs, drink all night and believe that otherwise their prayers will not be answered. O foolish men who believe that drunkenness is a sacrifice, who think that their drunkenness is pleasing to those who showed them how to endure martyrdom through fasting!" (*De Helia et ieiuno* 17.62). The example of banquets to honor martyrs is mentioned in passing. Ambrose does not even say that they are forbidden, but speaks ironically about appealing to the good graces of the martyrs. In book 7 of the *Commentary on Luke,* the reference is even briefer. Ambrose, about Luke 9:60, "Let the dead bury the dead" writes, "As we know that burial is a religious duty, why is this man forbidden to bury his own father?" (7.34). He explains at length that it is a question of priority and concludes: "Thus it is not forbidden to mourn and bury a father, but the piety of duty to God is placed above familial duty" (7.41). Then he imagines other interpretations and ends with the prophetic meaning: "There is also, in the prophetic sense, the burial that consists in laying on the tombs of our ancestors what you know reader which the infidel cannot understand: not that food or drink is ordered, but the reverent participation in the holy offering is revealed. It is thus not about forbidding a gift, but the religious mystery is that there will not be communion between us and dead pagans; for as the sacraments are of the living, those who have life are not dead" (7.43).

The arcane discipline forces Ambrose to be allusive, but he seems to be referring to laying out the Eucharist on the tombs (*supra sepulcra maiorum quaedam ponamus*). Here "elders" (*maiores*) are not necessarily the martyrs, but could be all who have died in the faith. Luke's verse means, in that case, that pagans, who are dead in the moral sense, cannot participate in this "mystery" and that this "holy offering" can be made only on the tombs of the faithful. It is interesting to point out that Ambrose felt the need to clarify an ambiguity and added specifically that he is not speaking of "bringing food or drink"—in other words, the traditional offerings of parentalia. But the context is too vague to suggest that the Eucharist is presented as a substitute for the traditional offerings of the parentalia.

These two texts are Ambrose's only references to funerary meals. They do not refer to the ban on the parentalia at the martyrs' tombs, either because it had succeeded entirely or because it was not for him a major issue. The importance given to it in the *Confessions* actually owes a great deal to Augustine's own pastoral concerns at the time he was writing. Augustine describes quite precisely the manner in which Monica was accustomed to celebrating the parentalia in Africa:

> She would bring her basket containing the festive fare which it fell to her to taste first and then distribute; but she would then set out no more than one small cup, mixed to suit her abstemious palate, and from that she would only sip for courtesy's sake. If it happened that there were many shrines of the dead to be honored in this manner she would carry round the same single cup and set it forth in each place. She thus served to her fellow-worshipers extremely sparing allowances of the wine which was not only heavily diluted but by this time no more than lukewarm. What she sought to promote at these gatherings was piety, not intemperance. (6.2.2)

We should not assume that Monica visited only the tombs of martyrs. The presence of relatives suggests that she intended also to honor the memory of her family's dead.

Augustine, for his part, mounted a veritable campaign in Africa to forbid banquets in honor of the martyrs. He was still a priest when he enlisted Aurelius, the bishop of Carthage, in a reform of the martyr cult (*Epistulae* 22). Augustine described funerary banquets as drunken parties that should no longer be tolerated in Africa, as Italy and the East had already condemned them (*Epistulae* 22.4). He used the words of Paul in Romans 13:13, in order to justify the condemnation "Not in feasting and drunkenness": "At least let this great disgrace be kept from the tombs of the bodies of the saints; at least let it be kept from the places for the sacraments, from the houses of prayer. For who dares to forbid privately what is called the honor of the martyrs when it is celebrated in public?" (*Epistulae* 22.2) Augustine favored a total ban on funerary banquets at the tombs of the martyrs, as well as in churches during the celebration of their feasts. His campaign met with local resistance, as he describes, but the clergy in Africa followed his lead and a council soon forbade the clergy from organizing banquets in churches.[21] The distinction between what fell within the private sphere and that of the church is clearly indicated.

Augustine actually specifies a different attitude for ordinary dead, as he explains to Aurelius:

> But since carnal and ignorant folks often regard these drinking bouts and dissolute banquets in the cemeteries as not merely honors paid to the martyrs, but also as consolations for the dead, it seems to me to be easier to dissuade them from this foul and shameful practice if it is also forbidden by the Scriptures and if sacrifices for the spirits of the dead, which we should believe can truly help them, are at their tombs not sumptuous and are offered, not sold, without pride and with readiness to all who ask. But should some wish to offer some money out of devotion, let them give it immediately to the poor. In that way they will not seem to abandon the commemorations of their own dear ones, something that can produce no slight sadness of heart, and they will celebrate in the church what they celebrate with piety and goodness. (*Epistulae* 22.6)

It seemed important to Augustine that Christians not be under the impression that the church required them to abandon the tombs of their relatives. That is why he suggests that meals at the tombs be tolerated. They could be considered as alms if the poor who were present were to be fed and all ostentation were avoided. The Eucharist has to be celebrated in church. As alms, banquets could be offered as a way of comforting the dead.

---

21. On this dossier, see James J. O'Donnell in Augustine, *Confessions*, vol. 2, *Commentary on Books 1–7* (Oxford: Clarendon Press, 1992), 334–39. See also Frederik Van der Meer, *Augustine the Bishop: The Life and Work of a Father of the Church* (1949), trans. Brian Battershaw and G. R. Lamb (London: Sheed and Ward, 1962), 520–25; Saxer, *Morts, martyrs, reliques*, 133–49; and Heikki Kotila, *Memoria mortuorum: Commemoration of the Departed in Augustine*, Studia Ephemeridis Augustinianum 38 (Rome: Institutum Patristicum Augustinianum, 1992), 62–77.

Augustine explains on several occasions that the Eucharist, prayer, and alms are three forms of aid for the dead recommended by the church. This trio appears, for instance, at the end of *De cura gerenda pro mortuis*:[22] "We should not think that any aid comes to the dead for whom we are providing care, except what we solemnly pray for in their behalf at the altars, either by sacrifices of prayers or of alms" (18.22). We should not hastily view this "system" as an attempt to substitute for a family cult of the dead a community cult directed by the church, for these banquets remained a family initiative, therefore an individual one.[23]

Two of Augustine's sermons, preached between 410 and 412, attest to the continuing celebration of the parentalia and confirm Christians' attachment to it. A commentary on Psalm 48 railed against the dying rich who, giving little thought to salvation, rejoiced to be surrounded by children and grandchildren, for, according to verse 12 of the Psalm, "they will remember his name":

> "These will invoke their names in their own lands." What does that mean? They will carry bread and wine to the tombs, and there call upon the names of the dead. Just think how fervently the name of that rich man in the gospel must have been invoked after his death! People would have been getting drunk at his grave-cults, yet not a drop found its way below to his burning tongue. The celebrants are providing a treat for their own bellies, not for the spirits of their ancestors. Nothing reaches the spirits of the dead except what they did for themselves while they were alive; if they did no good in their lifetime, nothing will avail them when they are dead. (*Explanation 1 on Psalm 48* 15)

The parable of the rich man (Luke 16:19–31) was mentioned by Augustine earlier in his sermon to emphasize the vanity of funerals. The reference to the impossibility of the rich man to quench his thirst may refer to beliefs about the refrigerium. Augustine wants only to recall the futility of hoping for any solace, after death, other than that which was earned while living. He does not denounce the parentalia strictly speaking except as a false aid for the dead.

The theme of sermon 361 is the resurrection and, like Paul (1 Cor. 15:32), Augustine cites the verse of Isaiah 22:3: "Let us eat and drink, for tomorrow we may die!" These are the words of those who do not believe in the

---

22. See Kotila, *Memoria mortuorum*, 98–107, for a list of texts.
23. This is contra Kotila, *Memoria mortuorum*.

resurrection. The parentalia are among the things they mock: "When we're dead, even if our parents, or dear ones, or relatives bring things along to our graves, they will bring them for themselves, the living, not for us, the dead. Scripture too, in fact, has mocked such practices, when it says about people who are insensible to good things that are presented to them, 'As if you were to lay a banquet,' it says, 'around a dead person'" (Sir 30:18) (*Sermons* 361.6.6).

It is rather paradoxical for Augustine to put in the mouths of those who deny an afterlife the same words he used to criticize the parentalia, specifically that only the living can benefit from them. The recourse to Scripture by these adversaries of resurrection should not be surprising. In his response, Augustine firmly rejects any suggestion that Scripture refers in any way to the parentalia:

> And it's obvious that this doesn't benefit the dead, and that it's a custom of the pagans, and that it doesn't flow from the channel of justice derived from our fathers the patriarchs; we read about their funerals being celebrated; we don't read of funeral sacrifices being offered for them. And as for the objection some people bring from the Scriptures: "Break your bread and pour out your wine on the tombs of the just, but do not hand it over to the unjust" (Tb 4:17), this is not the occasion, indeed, to expatiate on it; but still I will say that the faithful can understand what is being said. It is well known, after all, to the faithful how the faithful do these things out of a religious respect for their dear departed; and that such rites are not to be granted to the unjust, that is to unbelievers, because "the just man lives by faith" (Rom. 1:17), this too is known to the faithful. (*Sermons* 361.6.6)

While the verse from Sirach may have been used by some people who denied the resurrection, the quote from Tobit seems to have been used by others seeking to show that Scripture referred to the parentalia without criticism. Augustine in fact shifted his target momentarily, as indicated by the conclusion of the passage, "So nobody should try to turn a remedy into a hurt, and attempt to twist a rope from the Scriptures, and with it lob a deadly noose over his own soul" (*Sermons* 361.6.6). Those who are twisting a rope from Scripture are those who seek to defend the parentalia by citing the verse from Tobit: "Break your bread and pour out your wine on the tombs of the just." Augustine rejects the literal interpretation and explains, in veiled terms—because not all of his listeners were baptized—that the bread and wine had to be understood allegorically as the body and blood of Christ. He finds support for his interpretation in the mention of the just, meaning the faithful, as opposed to non-Christians who were barred from participating in the Eucharist. The parentalia thus had some defenders among Christians who cited Scripture in defense of a traditional practice that, to them, was not an offense against their Christian faith. Augustine rejected that interpretation, but seems not to condemn the practice explicitly, although he had noted earlier that it was a pagan practice shunned even by Jews. This is not the major theme of his sermon on resurrection, but the brief digression is worth noting as evidence that the *parentalia*, a private ritual, was the object of tension between Christians and their bishop.

Augustine, like Ambrose, mentioned the opportunity available to Christians to commemorate their dead with the Eucharist on their tombs. Would that have been a Eucharistic service, or a nonliturgical Communion? There is, in fact, some evidence that believers took home the Eucharist and kept it there on reserve.[24] Thus it is not impossible that they reserved it with the intention of sharing it with their family and friends at the tomb of an ancestor. Although the context of the parentalia lends itself to such an interpretation, there is reason for some skepticism. In Augustine's letter to Aurelius examined above, the celebration of the Eucharist is explicitly placed at the church. Celebrations of the anniversary of a death are mentioned, but they generally involved only martyrs and bishops and were not usually performed at the tomb.[25]

The Eastern ecclesiastical sources appear to have been less averse to family commemorations of the dead.[26] The *Apostolic Constitutions* devote one chapter (8.44) to the restraint that members of the clergy ought to show when they are invited to commemorations of the dead. They may drink wine, but in moderation, if they hope to intercede for the departed. Other texts refer to banquets honoring the martyrs, and Gregory Nazianzen wrote several epigrams against "men with wide backs" who gave feasts at the martyrs' tombs.[27] To honor martyrs Christians brought to their tombs "silver, wine,

---

24. See Henri Leclercq, *Dictionaire d'archéologie chrétienne et de liturgie*, s. v. "Réserve eucharistique"; see also Otto Nussbaum, *Die Aufbewahrung der Eucharistie,* Theophaneia 29 (Bonn: Hanstein, 1979).

25. See Saxer, *Morts, martyrs, reliques,* 157, which indicates that there is no allusion to an anniversary of ordinary dead in Augustine or other contemporary sources, and adds that it comes from the "private character of celebrating the anniversary of the dead," in contrast to the martyrs' which are officially celebrated by the church.

26. See Pierre Maraval, *Lieux saints et pèlerinages d'Orient: histoire et géographie des origines à la conquête arabe,* Histoire (Paris: Éditions du Cerf, 1985), 218–19, for a collection of texts on banquets to celebrate the martyrs.

27. See Claude Mossay, *La mort et l'au-delà dans saint Grégoire de Naziance,* Recueil de travaux d'histoire et de philologie. 4ᵉ série 34 (Louvain: Publications universitaires de Louvain, 1966),

food" and, Gregory adds, "belching" (*Epigrams* 166). In one epigram, he imagines the following dialogue: "Assert not falsely that martyrs are commenders of the belly. This is the law of your gullets, good people. But I know one way of honoring the martyrs, to drive away wantonness from the soul, and decrease your fatness by weeping" (168).

In another epigram, he addresses the martyrs directly: "I testify, you martyrs. The belly-lovers have made your worship into wantonness. You desire no sweet-smelling table, nor cooks. But they honor you with belching rather than righteousness" (169).

This kind of dialogue belongs to the literary genre of the epigram, but these texts confirm that Christians saw banquets at martyrs' tombs as a way of honoring them. In one epigram Gregory claims to believe that Christians had ended this kind of parentalia: "In honor of the demons those who wished formerly to gain the favor of the demons celebrated impure banquets. This we Christians renounced, and instituted spiritual meetings for our martyrs. But now I am in some dread. Listen to me, you revelers: you desert us for daimonic rites" (175).

In a certain way he presents the cult of the martyrs as a Christian version of the cult of the dead, in which spiritual assemblies have replaced the frenzied festivities of funerary banquets.

These festivities are frequently criticized, but generally without allusion to demons and as essentially profane. Marguerite Harl, who has studied this commonplace in Greek preaching at the end of the fourth century, suggests that it arose in part from a reaction on the part of bishops who were trained in the ascetic tradition and had to face popular celebrations in which the religious element seemed secondary.[28]

Was it in order to control the cult of the martyrs that the church left the cult of the dead outside its sphere? The texts examined here show that Christians continued to celebrate the parentalia in the fourth and fifth centuries, despite the hostility they encountered from their bishops. The latter presented commemorative banquets as a form of sacrifice, whereas lay Christians saw these as a way of honoring the dead. While the bishops sought to reform traditional forms of remembering the dead, they did not ban them. In the East, the clergy even appear to have participated. Augustine points out

---

244–46; and Frank R. Trombley, *Hellenic Religion and Christianization, c. 370–529*, 2nd ed. (Leiden: Brill, 2001), 29–30.

28. Marguerite Harl, "La dénonciation des festivités profanes dans le discours épiscopal et monastique, en Orient chrétien, à la fin du IVe siècle," in *La fête, pratique et discours: d'Alexandrie hellénistique à la mission de Besançon*, Annales littéraires de l'Université de Besançon 262. Centre de recherches d'histoire ancienne 42 (Paris: Les Belle Lettres, 1981), 123–47.

that it was impossible for the church to appear to urge Christians to neglect the memory of their ancestors. There was no specific Christian substitute: allusions to a Eucharistic celebration are vague, and not simply because of the arcane. It seems, as I shall show, that the prayer for the dead offered during the Eucharist did not meet the expectations of believers.

The Church's Prayer for the Dead and the Expectations of Christians

Our sources, which are not liturgical documents, are necessarily vague, but they provide insights about what was at stake with the status of the dead in the church. In the fourth and fifth centuries, the utility of the prayer for the dead was at the center of a debate that has been studied, typically, in terms of the theological significance of the prayer. However, it seems that the form of the prayer was also a major issue.[29]

Offerings in the Name of the Dead

Tertullian mentions the commemoration of the dead several times, but his allusions are rather difficult to place in their liturgical context.[30] In the treatise *On the Crown*, in a listing of liturgical uses that have no basis in Scripture, Tertullian gives the following example: "We make offerings (*oblationes facimus*) on behalf of the dead every year for their (actual) birth" (3.3). In two treatises in which he addresses problems linked to remarriage, Tertullian comments in the same terms the obligation to observe the anniversary of the death of a husband or wife:

> Here a man's reason for shame is doubled, since after a second marriage he has two wives by his side, one in the flesh, the other in the spirit. Your affection for your first wife will become even more devoted, now that she is secure in the Lord. You certainly will not be able to hate her.

---

29. For a *status quaestionis*, see Joseph Ntedika, *L'évocation de l'au-delà dans la prière pour les morts: étude de patristique et de liturgie latine (IVe-VIIIe s.)*, Recherches africaines de théologie 2 (Louvain: Nauwelaerts, 1971); and Brian E. Daley, *The Hope of the Early Church: A Handbook of Patristic Eschatology* (Cambridge: Cambridge University Press, 1991).

30. See the texts collected and commented on in Saxer, *Morts, martyrs, reliques*, 69–73; and Karpinski, *Annua dies dormitionis*, 79–116, with the reservations of Pierre Petitmengin, "Chronica Tertullianea et Cyprianea. 1988," *Revue des études augustiniennes* 35 (1989): 315–45.

You pray for her soul. You offer the annual sacrifice for her. (*Exhortation to Chastity* 11)

To be sure, she prays for his soul. She asks that, during the interval, he may find rest and that he may share in the first resurrection. She offers the sacrifice each year on the anniversary of his falling asleep. (*On Monogamy* 10)

Given the strict parallelism of these three texts, the three expressions, *oblationes facere, oblationes reddere* and *offere,* can designate only the same form of commemoration. They refer explicitly to the offerings brought for a Eucharistic sacrifice: bread and wine. One part of them is consecrated at the time of the celebration, but the remainder is distributed to the poor or eaten after the service.[31] When the offering is made on behalf of one departed, he is named in the Eucharistic prayer. Tertullian could be alluding to a "special Mass" held for a death anniversary, as there was no daily service at this time. According to another hypothesis the offerings are prepared on the anniversary day, perhaps even taken to the church on that day, but are not used until the following Sunday. Such a practice is attested in the *Dialogues* of Gregory the Great, but these are almost four centuries later than Tertullian's text.[32]

This form of commemoration of the dead is also evinced for the third century in a letter of Cyprian. The clergy of Furnos wrote to Cyprian to ask what they should do about their bishop Geminius Victor who, upon his death, nominated in his will a presbyter as guardian.[33] This practice seemed to have actually been condemned by a previous council: "The bishops who preceded us after holy deliberation on this question decreed the following salutary provisions for the future: no brother should nominate on his death one of the clergy as guardian or trustee, and should anyone do this the offering should not be made on his behalf nor should the sacrifice be celebrated for his repose. For he does not deserve to be named at the altar of God in the prayer of the bishop seeing that he was prepared to distract away from that altar bishops and ministers of religion" (*Epistulae* 1.2.1).

---

31. See Rupert Berger, *Die Wendung "offere pro" in der römischen Liturgie,* Liturgiewissenschaftliche Quellen und Forschungen 41 (Münster: Aschendorff, 1964), 29–32, 42–60.

32. See Eoin de Bhaldraithe, "*Oblationes pro defunctis, pro nataliciis annua die facimus:* What Did Tertullian Mean?" in *Studia Patristica. 20,* ed. Elizabeth A. Livingstone (Louvain: Peeters, 1989), 346–51.

33. Cyprian, *Epistulae* 1; for the historical circumstances and a commentary, see *The Letters of St. Cyprian of Carthage,* vol. 1, ed. Graeme Wilber Clarke, Ancient Christian Writers 43 (New York: Newman Press, 1984), 147–61; Victor Saxer, "La date de la lettre 1 (66) de Cyprien au clergé et au peuple de Furni," *Revue des Études Augustiniennes* 23 (1977): 56–62; and Saxer, *Morts, martyrs, reliques,* 102–4.

The punishment that is called for confirms the association between making the offering on behalf of the deceased and naming him in the prayer. In this case, a special service "for his repose" was celebrated not on the tomb but in the church, as the reference to the "altar of God" would suggest. The punishment had to be applied to their bishop by the clergy and the people of Furnos: "It is not right that in your community the offering should be made for his repose or that any prayers of supplication should be made on his behalf in your church" (*Epistulae* 1.2.2). The first proposition repeats the ban on making the offering on behalf of Geminius Victor, while the second suggests that prayers of supplication were offered for some time after death.

These texts provide only fragmentary information on these commemorative practices, but it is clear that the initiative was in the hands of the relatives of the departed. Relatives brought offerings on behalf of the departed to the church to be consecrated during the celebration so that he will be named in the prayers. The process remained a private one, even though associated with the community.

Fourth- and fifth-century documents refer only rarely to the practice, though it continued. It is alluded to in the letter the bishop of Rome, Innocent I, wrote in 416 to Decentius, the bishop of Gubbio in Umbria, who had consulted him on a number of liturgical issues. The question was about the moment at which it was proper to name those who provided the offerings, thus suggesting, only implicitly, the possibility of offerings made on behalf of a deceased.[34]

Two texts from Jerome are often cited in connection with this practice. In the first, he is commenting upon the reproaches of Jeremiah (11:15–16) to the people in the temple: "Can consecrated meat avert your punishment? When you engage in your wickedness, then you rejoice." This verse, he claims, could be addressed to the rich who expected to receive clemency from the judge because of their wealth, and adds, "Now the names of those who give are publicly recited, and what is given in redemption of sin is turned to their praise. They no longer remember the poor widow from the Gospel, who by putting two very small copper coins in the temple treasury surpassed all the offerings of the wealthy" (*In Hieremiam* 2.108.5). Jerome considered that the naming of donors was a sign of pride, but did not specifically mention offerings on behalf of the dead. His biblical example seems to imply that he was thinking about the reading of a sort of subscription list rather than the

---

34. See Robert Cabié, ed., *La lettre du pape Innocent Ier à Décentius de Gubbio (9 mars 416)*, Bibliothèque de la Revue d'histoire ecclésiastique 58 (Louvain: Publications universitaires de Louvain, 1973), 22–23 (for the text), 40–41 (for the commentary).

naming of those who bring offerings for the Eucharistic sacrifice. This is clearly the case in the second text, a passage of his *Commentary on Ezekiel,* in which he also criticizes the rich: "In churches, the deacon names publicly those who give; 'this one gave so much, that one promises this much,' and they enjoy the applause of the people even as they are tortured by their conscience" (6.18.5–9). The context is not at all that of the Eucharist. Jerome is criticizing the new or—at least, according to the first text—recent custom of reading the names of those who make or promise gifts to churches. Jerome is thus critical of an entirely different practice from that of naming those who bring the offering or those on whose behalf it is brought, and his testimony should not be used to explain the loss of interest in this practice, even though it is not evinced anywhere else in the West throughout the fourth and fifth centuries.[35]

Indeed, the practice did not end, and there are references to it in the sixth century. Gregory of Tours (c. 538–594) tells of a widow who brought a daily offering of fine wine from Gaza to the church on behalf of the memory of her husband "because she never doubted that through the mercy of the Lord her deceased husband would repose [in paradise] on the day that she made an offering to the Lord on behalf of his soul." The rest of the story shows that this offering was used the same day: an unscrupulous subdeacon took the wine for his own drinking; the husband told his widow about it in a vision and she got confirmation of the fraud the next day during the Eucharist (*In gloria confessorum* 64). Gregory does not say the deceased was named during the celebration, but bringing offerings certainly allowed for a specific prayer to be made on his behalf.

Evidence from the East is no more abundant.[36] The *Testamentum Domini,* an original Greek version of which circulated in Syria during the fifth century, is the only evidence of a comparable practice. This document describes a church arrangement near the entrance where "the priest writes down the names of those who offer oblations, or of those for whom they have been offered: when the holy things are offered by the bishop, the reader, or even the proto-deacon names in commemoration those for whom the priests and the people offer in supplication."[37]

---

35. See Martin Klöckener, "Die *recitatio nominum* im Hochgebet nach Augustins Schriften," in *Gratias agamus: Studien zum eucharistischen Hochgebet: für Balthasar Fischer,* ed. Andreas Heinz und Heinrich Rennings, Pastoralliturgische Reihe (Freiburg: Herder, 1992), 191–93.

36. See Robert F. Taft, "Toward the Origins of the Offertory Procession in the Syro-Byzantine East," *Orientalia Christiana Periodica* 36 (1970): 73–107.

37. *Testamentum Domini* 1.19, trans. Robert F. Taft, *A History of the Liturgy of St. John Chrysostom,* vol. 4, *The Diptychs,* Orientalia Christiana Analecta 238 (Rome: Pontificium Institutum Studiorum Orientalium, 1991), 40.

What would explain the relative silence of our sources from the fourth and fifth centuries? It may be due to the very fragmentary nature of the documentation, but it also seems that bishops did not recommend such practice and were more interested in the issue of remembering the dead during the Eucharistic prayer itself.

The Departed in the Eucharistic Prayer

The church, independent of those individuals who wished to remember their relatives on a particular day, commemorated collectively the departed during the course of each Eucharistic service. This practice has been studied in terms of the development of the canon of the Roman Mass, or of the liturgical diptychs of the Orthodox Mass, a perspective that has obscured somewhat the evidence of the fourth and fifth centuries.

THE ROMAN MASS

The *Memento* of the dead that is included among the prayers of intercession said by the priest after the consecration was introduced in the canon of the Roman Mass after the eighth century.[38] Before it was introduced, the departed were mentioned in the universal prayer, which includes all believers and occurs after the readings. This prayer, which disappeared during the sixth century, before being reinstated by Vatican II, was not originally intended for the departed. The first mention of the departed appears in a prayer attributed to Pope Gelasius (492–496) "for the refreshment [*refrigerium*] of the souls of the faithful and especially of the holy bishops of the Lord who have been at the head of our Catholic Church." The evocation of the departed was reduced to a rapid and general reference. We do not know if the departed were mentioned elsewhere in the mass before the end of the fifth century and it is extremely risky to interpret these changes in the absence of contemporary liturgical commentary.[39]

AUGUSTINE'S TESTIMONY

According to Victor Saxer, in Africa at the time of Augustine, the names of the dead were recited during the celebration of the Eucharist from lists

---

38. See Bernard Botte, ed., *Le canon de la messe romaine: édition critique*, Textes et études liturgiques 2 (Louvain: Abbaye de Mont César, 1962), 67–69.

39. See Paul De Clerck, *La "prière universelle" dans les liturgies latines anciennes: témoignages patristiques et textes liturgiques*, Liturgiewissenschaftliche Quellen und Forschungen 62 (Münster: Aschendorff, 1977).

kept up to date in every community: the diptychs.[40] This term designated both the tablets on which the names were inscribed (twofold and attached at a hinge—hence their name, derived from the Greek words for "two" and "fold"), and the liturgical act of reading them aloud. The issue is important enough to require a detailed examination of the evidence.

In a sermon preached shortly after the Conference of Carthage in 411, Augustine returns to Petilianus's complaint concerning the fact that the memory of Caecilianus, the bishop whose election to the see of Carthage in 312 had led to the Donatist schism, was commemorated in Hippo. We eventually learn that his name was read at the altar along with the names of the bishops considered "faithful and innocent" (*Sermons* 359.6). Were these all dead bishops? In any case, churches also kept lists of the living members of their clergy. When the priest Bonifatius was suspected of having had illicit relations with a monk at the monastery of Hippo named Spes, Augustine, who did not believe he was guilty, refused to remove his name from the list of priests of his Church while awaiting judgment.[41] He left the responsibility to the clergy:

> And now, if you do not want his name to be read out in the list of priests for fear that we give a pretext to those who do not want to enter the Church—as the apostle says, to those who are looking for a pretext—that action will not be due to us, but to those because of whom it was done. For what harm does it do a man if human ignorance does not want his name to be read out from that list, provided a bad conscience does not remove him from the book of the living? (*Epistulae* 78.4)

The custom was, therefore, not only to maintain a list of the members of the clergy but also to have their names read out of the list during the Eucharist. This recitation is unrelated, however, to the commemoration of the dead, of which no mention is made.

In several texts Augustine also mentions that the names of the martyrs were read during the Eucharist, but he contrasts the commemoration of the martyrs with that of the dead:

> That's why, as the faithful know, Church custom has it that at the place where the names of the martyrs are recited at God's altar, we don't pray

---

40. Saxer, *Morts, martyrs, reliques*, 162–65; see also Klöckener, Die *recitatio nominum*, 196–199, with updated bibliography.

41. See *Prosopographie chrétienne du Bas-Empire. 1, Prosopographie de l'Afrique chrétienne* (Paris: Éditions du CNRS, 1982), 148 (Bonifatius 5).

for them, while we do pray for the other departed brothers and sisters who are remembered there. (*Sermons 159*.1)

So it's not surprising, my brothers and sisters—you know the place in the Mass where the martyrs' names are recited? The Church doesn't pray for them. Yes, the Church is quite right to pray for the other departed who have fallen asleep; but for the martyrs it does not pray, but instead commends itself to their prayers. (*Sermons 284*.5)

Why is it, as the faithful know, that the martyrs names are recited in their own place, quite distinct from the faithful; and that the Church doesn't pray for them, but commends itself to their prayers? (*Sermons 297*.2.3)

Notice, please; in the recitation of names at the altar of Christ, their names are recited in the most honored place; but for all that, they are not worshiped instead of Christ. (*Sermons 273*.7)

It is obvious from these texts that the martyrs and the other dead are not commemorated in the same way: one prays for the dead, one asks for the prayers of the martyrs,[42] and this is indicated in the liturgy of the Eucharist by invoking them at two different times. Although the reading of the names of the martyrs is mentioned specifically, that of the dead is at best simply implied in the last two texts.[43] We should add that there is no mention of lists or tablets containing names and kept up to date in every church. Moreover, these would quickly have become too long to be read during the Eucharist. A few other texts contain more precise information about the commemoration of the dead.

The first text to consider and the earliest chronologically is the narrative of the death of Monica in the *Confessions*. One day during her illness she lapsed into unconsciousness, and when she awoke she addressed her sons: "Lay this body anywhere, and take no trouble over it. One thing only do I ask of you, that you remember me at the altar of the Lord wherever you may be" (9.11.27). Augustine refers to her request again in the long prayer that concludes book 9 of the *Confessions*, before inviting his readers to join him: "Inspire others, my Lord, my God, inspire your servants who are my brethren, your children who are my masters, whom I now serve with heart

---

42. See Augustine, *Homily on the Gospel of John* 84.1, but with no allusion to the reading of the names.
43. William Chatterley Bishop, "The African Rite," *Journal of Theological Studies* 13 (1912): 257, excludes the existence of lists of names for ordinary dead.

and voice and pen, that as many of them as read this may remember Monica, your servant.... So may the last request she made of me be granted to her more abundantly by the prayers of many, evoked by my confessions, than by my prayers alone" (9.12.30). "Remember her at the altar": this expression does not imply the mention of Monica's name during the Eucharist but instead that she be kept in mind, with loving devotion, as Augustine says, at the time when the departed are collectively commemorated. Monica's request that her sons, wherever they may be, remember her at the altar, and Augustine's subsequent appeal to his readers, proves that prayers for the dead are not linked to the actual writing of the names on diptychs in each church.

The contrast drawn by Monica between her lack of concern for the disposition of her body and her concern that she be remembered in the prayers of the church reappears in *De cura pro mortuis gerenda*. In that work, Augustine describes quite precisely the form of the prayer for the dead, writing, "Those supplications in behalf of the dead are not to be passed over. The Church undertakes such prayers that are to be made for all the dead in a Christian and Catholic society, in the general commemoration even though there be no mention of their names. In this way commemoration is made by one devoted mother for those who lack such prayers, whether parents, or sons, or any relations whatsoever, or friends" (4.6). It is quite clear that commemoration of the dead during the Eucharist did not include the reading of names. Augustine says this twice: the commemoration is "general" as opposed to that of a single individual, and there is no mention of the names of the dead.[44] Why is Augustine emphatic about this? Is he attempting to impose a collective commemoration in place of the traditional familial one? He suggests, rather, that relatives or friends of the departed are in charge of a more individual commemoration and that the church offers a commemoration by default in case individual prayers are lacking. Similarly, he explicitly associates the church and the relatives in the care for the dead when he says that "the Church nor the care of relatives does not render in vain what religious service it can for the departed."[45] If he is being emphatic, it may also be because anonymity in the commemoration of the dead did not satisfy the expectations of relatives and friends about the departed.

---

44. Augustine, *De cura pro mortuis gerenda* 4.6: ... *non sunt praetermittendae supplicationes pro spiritibus mortuorum. Quas faciendas pro omnibus in christiana et catholica societate defunctis etiam tacitis nominibus eorum sub generali commemoratione suscepit ecclesia, ut quibus ad ista desunt parentes aut filii aut quicumque cognati uel amici ab una eis exhibeantur pia matre communi.*

45. Augustine, *De cura pro mortuis gerenda* 1.2: *Ita fit ut neque inaniter ecclesia uel suorum cura pro defunctis quod potuerit religionis impendat;* see *City of God* 21.24).

In any case, these texts allow us to reject the hypothesis of tablets, kept current by the churches and containing the names of the departed for reading during the Eucharist. The commemoration of the dead by the church is general and anonymous and therefore could not claim to be a substitute for traditional and familial practices without seeming to recommend that Christians "abandon the commemoration of their own dear ones."

Eastern Sources

Eastern sources have been the object of an exhaustive inventory in a recent study by Robert Taft devoted to diptychs in the Byzantine liturgy.[46] According to his conclusions, diptychs appeared at the end of the fourth century. Originally, the churches would have maintained complete lists of names of the living and the dead, read by the deacon during the service at a moment that could vary from place to place, but that was directly linked to the prayers of intercession preceding the Eucharistic prayer. The reading of names by a deacon is different from the mention of various categories of departed by the bishop; its inclusion during the prayers of intercession distinguishes it from the reading of the names of those who bring the offering. However, the custom of reading the names would very quickly have been limited to a list of officials and would become an issue of ecclesiastical politics. A difficulty arises from this reconstruction of the history of the diptychs, because while the second stage is clearly documented, there is little documentation of the first.

Only one document explicitly refers to the reading of names during the prayer of intercession. This is the anaphora, or Eucharistic prayer, which has come down to us under the name of Sarapion, bishop of Thmuis in Egypt before 350. This document, of which the only extant Greek text is contained in an eleventh-century manuscript, was believed to be the oldest liturgical book after the *Apostolic Tradition,* but its authenticity had been seriously challenged. Unable to confirm the attribution to Sarapion, the last editor of the text nevertheless argued strongly for identifying the document as a mid-fourth century Egyptian collection of prayers.[47] After the consecration, the prayers of intercession for the living begin, followed by those for the departed: "And we call out also for all who have fallen asleep, for whom also the menial (is made). After the announcement of the names: Sanctify these souls for you know them all. Sanctify all who have fallen asleep in the Lord.

---

46. See Taft, *The Diptychs.*
47. See Maxwell E. Johnson, *The Prayers of Sarapion of Thmuis: A Literary, Liturgical, and Theological Analysis,* Orientalia Christiana Analecta 249 (Rome: Pontificio Istituto Orientale, 1995).

Number them with all your holy powers, and give them a place and a mansion in your kingdom." The repetition of "Sanctify these souls" (whose names have just been read) in "Sanctify all who have fallen asleep in the Lord" seems to suggest that the list included only a few names, as does the comparison with another ancient Egyptian anaphora, from the papyrus of Strasbourg Gr. 254: "To the souls of those who have fallen asleep give rest; remember those whom we make mention today, both those whose names we say and whose names we do not say."[48] The wording here is unambiguous: only some names are read, but all the dead are remembered at the altar. One might think that these are the names of those who have died in the preceding days or weeks, depending upon the size of the community. If the rubric is not an interpolation,[49] Sarapion's anaphora should be considered as evidence of the reading of the names of the dead.

However, all the other documents, which are nonliturgical in nature but explain liturgy or refer to it, describe a general commemoration, including the mention of different categories of the departed in the prayers of intercession. This is the case in the *Apostolic Constitutions,* compiled at Antioch around 380. There are three prayers of intercession: the first precedes the consecration, and the second is spoken by the bishop following the consecration; the third, very like the first, is said by the deacon during the breaking of bread. It is only during the third that the dead are mentioned: "Let us remember the holy martyrs, that they may consider us worthy of carrying on their struggle; let us pray for those who have died in the faith" (1.13.6). There is no rubric, however, that would lead one to suppose that the names of the dead were read during the prayer of the deacon.

In the *Mystagogic Catecheses,* preached by Cyril of Jerusalem (c. 350–87) and by his successor John II (387–417) during Holy Week and addressed to the newly baptized,[50] the departed are mentioned in the prayers of intercession that follow the consecration: "Then we commemorate those who have gone to their rest, first of all the patriarchs, prophets, apostles and martyrs, so that God may receive our petitions in answer to their prayers and intercessions. Then we pray for our holy ancestors and bishops who have gone to their rest, and in general for all who have gone to their rest before us, for we believe that great benefit will result for the souls for whom prayer is offered when the holy and most awesome sacrifice lies on the altar" (23.9).

---

48. Ibid., 258. See also the English translation in Taft, *The Diptychs,* 35, n. 42.
49. See Gregory Dix, *The Shape of Liturgy* (Westminster: Dacre Press, 1947), 499.
50. Cyril of Jerusalem, *Mystagogic Catecheses,* ed. Auguste Piédagnel and Pierre Paris, 2nd rev. ed., Sources chrétiennes, 126bis (Paris: Éditions du Cerf, 1988), 177–87, for the question of authorship.

The departed are the subject of a general commemoration, without the reading of names, at a particularly significant moment in the service.

In the *Catechetical Homilies,* Theodore of Mopsuestia (c. 350–428) mentions a commemoration of the dead at two points in the liturgy of the Eucharist. The first comes before the consecration and is accompanied by the reading of a list of names: "Then all rise, according to the signal given them by the deacon, and look at what is taking place. The names of the living, and of the dead who have passed away in the faith of Christ, are then read from the tablets of the church" (15.43). To this description, Theodore adds, "And it is clear that in the few of them who are mentioned now, all the living and the departed are [implicitly] mentioned." He is very clear: only a small number of names are read, and thus written on the tablets. No criteria for selection is indicated, but the moment in the liturgy when this reading occurs recalls the practice of mentioning the names of the living who have brought offerings and of the dead in whose name gifts are made. The second mention of the departed, after the consecration, occurs during the prayers of intercession and takes the form of a general commemoration of all those who have passed away (16.14).

Two sermons of John Chrysostom mention, verbatim apparently, the phrase that introduces the commemoration of the dead during the liturgy of the Eucharist. One was a sermon preached at Antioch in 392–93, the second at Constantinople in 400–401, but they present a very similar text:

> For these things were not devised to no purpose, nor is it in vain that we make commemoration of the departed during the divine mysteries, and come forward on their behalf praying to the Lamb who is lying there, who takes away the sin of the world, but in order that from this some relief might come to them. Not in vain does he who stands at the altar cry out when the fearsome mysteries are accomplished: "for all those who have fallen asleep in Christ, and for those who make commemorations of them." (*Homilies on 1 Corinthians* 41.2–5)

> It is not in vain that the deacon cries out: "For those who have fallen asleep in Christ, and for those who make commemorations of them." It is not the deacon who utters this sound, but the Holy Spirit—I mean the charism. What do you say? The sacrifice is at hand and everything is set out in due order. (*Homilies on the Acts of the Apostles* 21.4)

Scholars argue about whether the prayers of intercession John Chrysostom refers to are part of the anaphora itself, or actually belong to the litany spoken by the deacon during the fractionating of the bread.[51] To John Chrysostom, what mattered was that the prayers follow the consecration and precede the distribution of communion; the church, the priests, and the martyrs are remembered at the same time as the dead. The formula quoted verbatim by John makes no reference to a list of individual names or to the reading of the diptychs.

Finally, we need to consider the section of the *Panarion* of Epiphanius of Salamis devoted to a critique of the prayer for the dead given by Aerius of Pontus (c. 380). Epiphanius attributes to Aerius the expression *onomazein onomata*, "to name the names" and uses himself the phrase *legein onomata*, "to read the names" (*Panarion* 75.3.5 and 75.7.1), but there it refers to the "category" of the dead rather than the individual names of the departed. When he tries to explain the need for these prayers, Epiphanius refers only to categories and says nothing to indicate that the dead are remembered individually (*Panarion* 75.7.4). The testimony about Aerius has therefore nothing to do with the use of the diptychs.

Eastern documents before the sixth century do not confirm that the names of the dead were read in connection with the consecration during Eucharist. The commemoration of the dead seems, in both East and West, to have been general and anonymous: the category of the dead is mentioned, usually, among others: bishops, martyrs, and the like. The church, in late antiquity, did not assume responsibility for the individual commemoration of the departed that was so important to Christians, and, as the discussions on the utility of the prayer for the dead will show, it does not appear to have intended to substitute collective or communal commemorations for individual ones.

❧ The Controversies about the Prayer for the Dead

While it does not seem that the commemoration of the dead during the Eucharist was a new practice at that time, the question of its value and meaning was raised during the second half of the fourth century.

In the *Mystagogic Catecheses,* Cyril of Jerusalem provides a long commentary on the value of praying for the dead that has sometimes been interpreted

---

51. See Taft, *The Diptychs,* 41–46; Frans van de Paverd, *Zur geschichte der Messliturgie in Antiocheia und Konstantinopel gegen Ende des vierten Jahrhunderts: Analyse der Quellen bei Johannes Chrysostomos,* Orientalia Christiana Analecta 187 (Rome: Pontificum Institutum Orientalium Studiorum, 1970), 348–55, 501–7; and Frans van de Paverd, "Anaphoral Intercessions, Epiclesis and Communion-Rites in John Chrysostom," *Orientalia Christiana Periodica* 49 (1983): 322–28, in which a different reconstitution is offered about the question of the diptychs.

as an indication that this was a liturgical novelty.[52] But why would the bishop have chosen to explain this to his listeners who presumably had no had direct knowledge of earlier usages? Yet Cyril was responding explicitly to those who questioned the value of the commemoration of the dead:

> I know many people say: "what good does it do for a soul to be commemorated in the offering once it has departed from this world, with or without sins?" Well then, suppose a king had banished some citizens who had offended him, and then their friends wove a garland and presented it to the king on behalf of the exiles. Wouldn't he grant them a remission of their punishment? In the same way, when we offer our petitions to God on behalf of the departed, even if they were sinners, instead of weaving a garland we offer Christ who was immolated for our sins, and thus, on their behalf and our own, we propitiate the God who loves mankind. (5.10)

The commemoration of the dead following the consecration is thus, in Cyril's view, a way of obtaining divine indulgence for them: Christ sacrificed himself for their sins. Cyril does not specify the kind of sins that can be atoned for in this way.

Epiphanius had to face objections that threaten the economy of salvation. Here are Aerius's objections to the cult of the dead: "Why do you mention the names of the dead after their deaths? If the living prays or has given alms, how will this benefit the dead? If the prayer of the people here has benefited the people there, no one should practice piety or perform good works! He should get some friends any way he wants, either by bribery or by asking friends on his deathbed, and they should pray that he may not suffer in the next life, or be held to account for his heinous sins" (*Panarion* 75.3.5). According to Aerius, who preached a rigorous asceticism, the prayer for the dead might encourage the living to be lax by allowing them to hope that the sins they have committed can be expiated after their death by the prayer of the living. Epiphanius, in his refutation, remains very cautious on the utility of the prayer:

> And then, as to naming the dead, what could be more helpful? What could be more opportune or wonderful than that the living believe that the departed are alive and have not ceased to be, but are with the Lord and live with him—and that the most sacred doctrine should declare

---

52. See Taft, *The Diptychs*, 38.

that there is hope for those who pray for their brethren as though they were off on a journey? And even though the prayer we offer for them cannot root out all their faults—how could it, since we often slip in this world, inadvertently and deliberately—it is still useful as an indication of something more perfect. (*Panarion* 75.7.1–3)

The prayers for the dead are primarily useful for the living. They are a lesson about death: it is not nothingness, but life in the Lord. And if perfection is possible for the dead, it is all the more so for the living. But it is ultimately in Christological terms that Epiphanius interprets the commemoration of the dead: "For we commemorate both righteous and sinners. Though we pray for sinners, for God's mercy, and for the righteous, the fathers, the patriarchs, prophets, apostles, evangelists, martyrs and confessors, for bishops and anchorites and the whole band of saints, we worship our Lord Jesus Christ to distinguish him from the whole of humanity by our honor of him, remembering that the Lord is not on a level with any man—even though each man has performed a million righteous deeds and more" (*Panarion* 75.7.4–5). All humans, even saints, need God's mercy, for only Christ is without sin. Hence, to pray for sinners, the ordinary dead, as well as for the virtuous—in particular, the martyrs—is a lesson in Christology.

Theodore of Mopsuestia presents the same kind of argument in the *Catechetical Homilies* when he comments upon the first mention of the dead, before the consecration:

And it is clear that in the few of them who are mentioned now, all the living and the departed are implicitly mentioned. This is done for the teaching of what took place in the economy of Christ our Lord, or which the present service, which is divine help for all, living and dead alike, is the commemoration. Indeed the living look to the future hope, while the dead are not really dead but cast in a sleep in which they remain in the hope, for which our Lord received his death, which we are commemorating in this sacrament. (15.43)

Theodore, like Epiphanius, gives a Christological reading of the liturgy: the dead are mentioned because Christ's death, remembered in the service of the Eucharist, had the effect of transforming death into sleep in anticipation of the resurrection. Of the second mention that follows the consecration, he notes, "and later he begins to make mention of those who have departed, as if to show that this sacrifice keeps us in this world, and grants also after death, to those who have died in the faith, that ineffable hope which all the children of the sacrament of Christ earnestly desire and expect" (16.14). The commemoration of the dead in the prayer of intercession has the same value as their mention before the consecration: it confirms that they share in the hope of resurrection. Theodore thus gives an interpretation that relates the prayer for the dead to the remembrance of Christ rather than to its benefits for the dead.

Eustratius, a priest at Constantinople in the sixth century, has transmitted several fragments from a homily of Cyril of Alexandria (c. 380–444) titled "Against Those Who Deny that the Sacrifice Should Be Offered for the Dead" in a treatise on the status of the soul after death. Cyril provides little information on the motives of his adversaries, but it appears that they had opposed the celebration of the Eucharist for the salvation of a particular individual on his tomb: "It is not right, they say, that we should go to the tombs of those who have fallen asleep in order to pray for them and even celebrate the Eucharist, Christ being present through the mystery of the holy sacrifice."[53]

What was troubling to these Christians was the association of the dead with Christ, through the Eucharist. To defend its legitimacy, Cyril had no better argument than the liturgical tradition of commemorating the dead during the Eucharistic service, and thus in the presence of the body and blood of Christ. The value of praying for the salvation of the dead is not the issue in this homily.

The controversies over the prayer for the dead reveal that while its usefulness was sometimes contested and therefore also its place in the Eucharistic service, bishops who defended the liturgical practice did not insist so much on its usefulness for the salvation of the dead as on its usefulness as a teaching for the living. As we will see with Augustine and John Chrysostom, the prayer for the dead generally did not seem to correspond to the expectations of the Christians.

Augustine and the Prayer for the Dead

Augustine's position on the prayer for the dead is clearly laid out in *De cura pro mortuis gerenda,* written around 420–21.[54] Paulinus of Nole questioned

---

53. Eustratius Constantinopolitanus, *De statu animarum post mortem* (CPG 7522), 28, in Leone Allacci, *De utriusque ecclesiae occidentalis atque orientalis perpetua in dogmate de purgatorio consensione* (Rome: Luna, 1655), 319–580; Allacci's Latin translation is published in Jacques-Paul Migne, *Theologiae cursus completus,* vol. 18 (Paris: Migne, 1865). Passages from the homely *Adversus eos qui negant offerendum esse pro defunctis* (CPG 5234.2) of Cyril are republished in *PG* 76, 1424–25. For a critical edition with the Syriac fragment, see Philip Edward Pusey, ed., *Sancti patris nostri Cyrilli Archiepiscopi Alexandrini In D. Joannis Evangelium* (Oxford: Clarendon, 1872), 3:542, l.2–6.

54. See Joseph Ntedika, *L'évolution de la doctrine du purgatoire chez saint Augustin,* Publications de l'Université Lovanium de Léopoldville 20 (Paris: Études Augustiniennes, 1966), esp. 33–36. The notion of purgatory is not relevant to our present discussion.

him on the apparent contradiction between the church's universal practice of praying for the dead and the words of the Apostle in 2 Corinthians 5:10, that men will be judged according to how they have lived their lives. The response is brief: "according to what they have done through the body they are aided by what has been done religiously in their behalf after the body" (1.2). This means that the prayer for the dead is of no advantage to a man after death, or, as Augustine clarifies later, that it helps only those who were not entirely good, and therefore saved, or entirely evil, and therefore damned, but rather those who were not wholly evil.

The way in which Augustine refers to the book of the Maccabees suggests that Paulinus had also questioned the authority of this liturgical practice: "We read in the books of the Maccabees that sacrifice is offered for the dead. Yet, even if it were read nowhere in the Old Testament, the authority of the universal Church which clearly favors this practice is of great weight, where in the prayers of the priest which are poured forth to the Lord God at his altar the commemoration of the dead has its place" (1.3). The custom of the universal church of commemorating the dead during the Eucharist suffices to legitimize the practice.[55] In fact, Augustine makes only a brief reference to the second book of the Maccabees, which contains a long justification for the sacrifice offered for the dead.[56] The same lesson is repeated in the manual Augustine wrote at the request of Laurentius, the *Enchiridion*. The development of the argument is identical: one should not deny the utility of the prayer for the dead, but it benefits only those who were worthy during their lives (29.110). He repeats these pages as well as the ones written in *De cura* when he replies to the questions of Dulcitius, Laurentius's brother (*De octo Dulcitii quaestiones* 2).

Joseph Ntedika and others have emphasized that Augustine's position was in part dictated by a reaction to some opinions about mercy (*De ciuitate Dei* 21), and to the millenarian views found in the *Apocalypse of Paul* or espoused by some Spanish Christians.[57] This approach gives a lot of weight to the

---

55. See Bernard Capelle, "Autorité de la liturgie chez les Pères," *Recherches de théologie ancienne et médiévale* 21 (1954): 5–22; and Konrad Federer, *Liturgie und Glaube: Eine theologiegeschichtliche Untersuchung*, Paradosis 4 (Fribourg: Paulusverlag, 1950).

56. This is the case in the Vulgate, but it has been proven that the commentaries about the prayer for the dead were actually marginal notes. Augustine (in the early fifth century in the West) and Eustratius of Constantinople (in the sixth century in the East) are actually the first authors who quote the text of 2 Maccabees as proof of the value of the prayer for the dead. See Ntedika, *L'évocation de l'au-delà dans la prière pour les morts*, 1–7.

57. Ntedika, *L'évolution de la doctrine du purgatoire*, 16–17. On the "miséricordieux," see the note of Gustave Bardy in *Œuvres de saint Augustin*, vol. 37, Bibliothèque augustinienne (Paris: Desclée de Brouwer, 1960), 806–9.

doctrinal aspect of the question and minimizes perhaps the pastoral aspects. It seems, actually, that Christians did not so much doubt the efficacy of the prayer for the dead as they expected more from them. Laurentius and Dulcitius were both laypersons, and their questions show the interest this issue held for Christians.[58]

Further evidence of this is found in Augustine's discussion, at roughly the same period, with another layperson, Vincentius Victor, on the nature of the soul and on the possibility for children who died unbaptized to be aided by prayers and sacrifices at the altar of God.[59] Vincentius Victor found support for his position in 2 Maccabees: "We find," he says, "that the priests adopted this plan that the offering of sacrifices should restore to purity the souls of those who were bound by guilt from the forbidden act" (*De anima et eius origine* 2.11.15). To which Augustine responds, "He says this as though he read in Scripture that sacrifices were offered for the uncircumcised, just as he decreed that these sacrifices of ours be offered for the unbaptized. Circumcision was, of course, the sacrament of that era which prefigured the baptism of ours" (*De anima et eius origine* 2.11.15). The issue is not the utility of the prayer for the dead generally, but for someone who is not baptized. Augustine rejects the possibility—which, he stresses, is contrary to the universal practice of the church: to pray for the departed who belonged to the fellowship of Christians (in other words, the baptized). In terms of typological interpretation, the example of the Maccabees only confirms this, as the soldiers were circumcised.

In a recently discovered text, Augustine responds to the request from a local bishop he visited in 404 or 407, to use his authority to reconfirm the prohibition against burying a catechumen in a church because of the celebration of the Eucharist.[60] He concludes this brief address, given after the sermon itself, with these words: "Each one of you, dear catechumens, while you're still alive, may beware of perishing when you're dead, and of neither your own families nor mother Church herself finding means by which they can come to your aid" (*Sermons 142*.4).

---

58. On Laurentius et Dulcitius, see *La prosopographie chrétienne du Bas-Empire. 1, Afrique (303–533)*, 330–33 (Dulcitius 2), 629 (Laurentius 2).

59. This controversy is presented by Albert de Veer in *Œuvres de saint Augustin*, vol. 22, Bibliothèque augustinienne (Paris: Desclée de Brouwer, 1975), 273–320.

60. Augustine, *Sermons Dolbeau 7*. See François Dolbeau, "Nouveaux sermons de saint Augustin pour la conversion des païens et des donatistes (II)," *Revue des études augustiniennes* 37 (1991): 289–95; and Augustin d'Hippone, *Vingt-six sermons au peuple d'Afrique*, ed. François Dolbeau, Collection des études augustiniennes. Série antiquité 147 (Paris: Institut d'études augustiniennes, 1996), 297–303.

As he does in *On the Care of the Dead,* Augustine closely associates Mother Church and the relatives in his *post tractatum* on the burial of catechumens. Rather than trying to substitute Mother Church for the family, Augustine sets limits on what the living can do for the dead. This text, much earlier than the questions raised by Vincentius Victor, shows that Christians expected the prayer of the church to be an aid, even for the unbaptized, and that for them, in order to benefit from this prayer, the best place to be buried was at the site of the celebration itself.[61]

In another sermon, the precise context for which is lost, we are able to assess the expectations of Augustine's audience.[62] He affirms that only the prayers of the church, the Eucharist, and alms made on their behalf, and not funerals and monuments, benefit the dead. Then he adds, "The whole Church, I mean, observes this tradition received from the Fathers, that prayers should be offered for those who have died in the communion of the body and blood of Christ, whenever their names are mentioned at the sacrifice in the usual place" (*Sermons 172.2.2*). Thus he uses again a liturgical argument: if the universal church commemorates the dead during the Eucharist, it means that prayer is beneficial. But he sets two limits: "For those, you see, who have departed from their bodies without the faith that works through love (Gal. 5:6) and its sacraments, acts of piety of this sort are performed in vain.... So no new merits are won for the dead when their good Christian friends do any work on their behalf, but these things are credited to them as a consequence of their preceding merits" (*Sermons 172.2.2*).

In order for the departed to benefit from the prayers of the church and of their families, they must be baptized and not be "all evil," according to the categories of *On the Care of the Dead*. The need for continuity between the good works done by the departed while he lived and those performed for him by his relatives is a central notion for Augustine. This sermon shows that more than doubts about the utility of prayers for the dead Augustine's audience had expectations that these prayers could not, in his opinion, meet.[63]

---

61. See Paul-Albert Février, "Quelques aspects de la prière pour les morts," *Senefiance* 10 (1981): 255–82, which proposes this explanation as an alternative to the search for an ad sanctos burial in order to understand the phenomenon of church burials.

62. Augustine, *Sermons* 172. This sermon belongs to the same group of sermons on the dead that are mentioned in note 8.

63. The dossier from Augustine's predication could be larger. François Dolbeau showed me a working edition of a fragment of an Augustinian sermon discovered by Raymond Etaix, mentioned in Gert Partoens, "Nouvelle collection de sermons rassemblée par saint Césaire," *Revue bénédictine* 37 (1977): 17, where the same themes are developed, but within a context of which we know nothing.

What was at stake was not to impose upon Christians attached to traditional commemorative practices a more spiritual conception of the cult of the dead but to set limits on what the living were able to do for the dead.

John Chrysostom and the Prayer for the Dead

John Chrysostom's sermons confirm this, even though his response is not the same. When he refers to commemoration of the dead during the liturgy of the Eucharist, he is always talking about what Christians can do for relatives who died in a state of sin or without having been baptized.

In a sermon on 1 Corinthians, John Chrysostom criticizes, as he was in the habit of doing, the traditional manifestations of mourning and reminds Christians that they should welcome death. Then he recalls a possible objection: do we not have reason to tremble for the fate of those who died in a state of sin? He writes, "'Nay, on this very account I lament,' say you, 'because he departed being a sinner.' This is a mere pretext and excuse.... But grant that he departed with sin upon him, even on this account one ought to rejoice, that he was stopped short in his sins and added not to his iniquity; and help him as far as possible, not by tears, but by prayers and supplications and alms and offerings. For not unmeaningly have these things been devised" (*Homilies on 1 Corinthians* 41.4).

Chrysostom's first argument is a liturgical one: "Nor do we in vain make mention of the departed in the course of the divine mysteries, and approach God in their behalf, beseeching the Lamb who is before us, who takes away the sin of the world; not in vain, but that some refreshment may thereby ensue to them. Not in vain does he that stands by the altar cry out when the tremendous mysteries are celebrated, 'For all that have fallen asleep in Christ, and for those who perform commemorations on their behalf'" (*Homilies on 1 Corinthians* 41.4). When the dead are remembered during the Eucharist, it cannot be in vain.

The second argument is from Scripture. "God is wont to grant the petitions of those who ask for others," he writes, giving the example of Job making offerings for his sons (Job 1:5) and citing 2 Corinthians 1:11 ("As you help us by your prayers then many will give thanks on our behalf for the gracious favor granted us in answer to the prayers of many"). He may then call for prayers to be offered for the dead:

> Let us not then be weary in giving aid to the departed, both by offering on their behalf and obtaining prayers for them; for the common expiation of the world is even before us. Therefore with boldness do we then entreat for the whole world, and name their names with those

of martyrs, of confessors, of priests. For in truth one body are we all, though some members are more glorious than others; and it is possible from every source to gather pardon for them, from our prayers, from our gifts in their behalf, from those whose names are named with theirs. (*Homilies on 1 Corinthians* 41.5)

The value of the prayer for the departed depends upon the whole church—both earthly and celestial—joining forces, as shown by prayers of intercession, to which John Chrysostom refers again.

He returns to the same themes in a sermon on the Epistle to the Philippians, in which he explains that death belongs to the class of indifferent things and that it is not dying that is sad, but the suffering of a just punishment after death. As a result, two categories of death should be mourned: death of sinners and of the unbaptized. But they should be mourned with dignity, without external manifestation of grief such as crying, the tearing of hair, and the like: "Let us weep for these; let us assist them according to our power; let us think of some assistance for them, small though it be, yet still let us assist them. How and in what way? By praying and entreating others to make prayers for them, by continually giving to the poor on their behalf" (*Homilies on Philippians* 3.4). Chrysostom is prudent and does not promise salvation to sinners or the unbaptized, yet he confirms that it is possible to help them. He recalls again the example of Job making offerings for his children (Job 1:5), after citing God's promise to Ezekias (2 Kings 20:6: "I will defend this city for my own sake and for my servant David's sake"), and he adds, "If the remembrance only of a just man had so great power when deeds are done for one, how great power will it not have?" (*Homilies on Philippians* 3.4). Once more, he uses an example in which God shows mercy to someone because of the merit of another. That is when commemoration of the dead is mentioned: "Not in vain did the Apostles order that remembrance should be made of the dead in the dreadful mysteries. They know that great gain results to them, great benefit; for when the whole people stands with uplifted hands, a priestly assembly, and that awful Sacrifice lies displayed, how shall we not prevail with God by our entreaties for them?" (*Homilies on Philippians* 3.4).

Like Augustine, Chrysostom excludes the unbaptized from the benefit of the commemoration of the dead: "And this we do for those who have departed in faith, while the catechumens are not thought worthy even of this consolation, but are deprived of all means of help save one. And what is this? We may give to the poor on their behalf" (*Homilies on Philippians* 3.4). There is still hope for the catechumens who are not remembered in the prayers with the baptized and all those who died in communion with the church; alms made in their name may benefit them.

However, in no way are they participating in the Eucharist after their death, just as they were not during their lives. The principle organizing the aid that can come from the prayer for the dead is the same principle that governs the relations among the living, as Chrysostom indicates with a wordplay on the figurative meaning of cadavers (for sinners): "For God wills that we should be mutually assisted; why else has he ordered us to pray for peace and the good estate of the world? Why on behalf of all men? Since in this number are included robbers, violators of tombs, thieves, men laden with untold crimes; and yet we pray on behalf of all; perchance they may turn. As then we pray for those living, who differ not from the dead, so too we may pray for them" (*Homilies on Philippians* 3.4). A reciprocal relationship is established here among the living in which the dead participate through their shared membership in the church.

While Chrysostom likes stressing this reciprocity, he does not try to impose a communal model of the cult of the dead. In a sermon on the Acts of the Apostles he returns to what is more appropriate for sinners than simply mourning their deaths: "Shall we not try to snatch him from his perils? For it is, yes, it is possible, if we will, to mitigate his punishment, if we make continual prayers for him, if for him we give alms. However unworthy he may be, God will yield to our importunity" (*Homilies on the Acts of the Apostles* 21.4).

John Chrysostom reaffirms God's power to show mercy to someone on the basis of the merit of another. Unable to boast of his own good deeds, the sinner can be aided by good deeds done in his name. Here, Chrysostom is more specific about the usefulness of alms. The beneficiaries of such alms will pray for the dead:

> Let us not busy ourselves about monuments, not about memorials. This is the greatest memorial: set widows to stand around him. Tell them his name: bid them all make for him their prayers, their supplications: this will overcome God: though it have not been done by the man himself, yet because of him another is the author of the almsgiving. Even this pertains to the mercy of God: widows standing around and weeping know how to rescue, not indeed from the present death, but from that which is to come. Many have profited even by the alms done by others on their behalf: for even if they have not got perfect (deliverance), at least they have found some comfort thence. (*Homilies on the Acts of the Apostles* 21.4)

Widows, whose names are entered in the church registers in order to receive its aid, clearly substitute for the mourners. In exchange for the alms they receive, they pray for the departed in whose name charity was shown. It is interesting to note the reference to the name. The rest of the text can be compared to what Augustine says about the role of the church when parents or relatives are not able to care for the departed.

Chrysostom then raises two issues: What about the poor? What about those who die alone? The response to the first is classic: it is the thought that counts, more than the amount of the alms. The response to the second is more surprising: "And why, I ask, did he know no one? That is punishment in itself." Knowing how to keep friends, a spouse, children is a essential component to a good life. The Mother Church is not mentioned here. Comforting the dead may be the work of the church as a whole through mention of them during the Eucharist. But more individual comfort has to come from relatives if one dies in a state of sin or unbaptized. Relatives request that the name of the departed be mentioned in the prayers of the poor or of widows to whom they give alms. To the anonymous commemoration by the church there is added an individual commemoration organized by the family or friends that is of particular necessity according to the status of the departed when he left this world.

Unlike Augustine, Chrysostom responds more positively to the expectations of the faithful. He proposes a mediation of the church, through its widows and its poor, but he does not suggest substituting the aid of the universal church for that which each Christian can offer the dead by his own initiative. The universal Church prays only for baptized Christians who did not die in a state of sin; John Chrysostom is less incisive on this point than Augustine, but very clear nevertheless. All others—and Augustine's listeners like those of Chrysostom believed themselves to be among this category—must count upon the help of their relatives. Chrysostom gives Christians more to hope for from this aid, but he, too, emphasizes that these hopes depend entirely upon what their families will care to provide.

Setting limits on what the living are able to do for the dead was a major issue for the development of a Christian cult of the dead.[64] In this chapter we have shown that in Late Antiquity, even if it offered no single response, the church remained cautious. In particular, bishops did not promise salvation to those who were not baptized or to sinners. They did not discourage

---

64. See Jean-Claude Schmitt, *Ghosts in the Middle Ages: The Living and the Dead in Medieval Society*, trans. Teresa Lavender Fagan (Chicago: University of Chicago Press, 1998), esp. chap. 1, on what must change before a Christian liturgy for the dead can develop.

Christians from praying for them, or from having widows and the poor pray for special intercession for them. On the other hand, they also did not discourage Christians from their traditional banquets at the tombs for fear, as Augustine said, that they would appear to be asking them to neglect their dead. Everything was done as though, by not taking responsibility for the salvation of all the dead, the church had left the responsibility for commemorating the dead to the family and friends of the departed.[65] Although it is possible to sketch, particularly with the sermons of John Chrysostom, the main lines of the subsequent development of the Christian cult of the dead, historians should not leap ahead and ignore several centuries during which the church, in the Roman Empire, left the cult of the dead outside of its sphere.

---

65. The same ambivalence is to be found in the question of ad sanctos burial. While the practice was not recommended by the church, it was not forbidden either. The success of ad sanctos burial, well described in Yvette Duval, *Auprès des saints corps et âmes,* is also in part the Christians' response to the fact that the church does not take responsibility for the cult of the dead.

Conclusion

The initial question regarding the existence of cemeteries in the third century—by *cemeteries,* I mean, spaces that were administered by the church for the communal burial of Christians—now seems a distant one. This book does not by any means answer all the questions raised about archaeological evidence on Christian burial. Its only claim regarding archaeological evidence is to suggest new questions. Nothing that we know about the structural organization of the church or that we find in the theological and the liturgical sources, provided we avoid teleological interpretations, supports the traditional position according to which the Late Antique church was concerned with providing a communal burial place for all Christians.

Only a fresh look at the primary sources, with no assumption about their meaning, can advance our knowledge and understanding. As Charles Pietri has written, referring specifically to the work of Giovanni Battista De Rossi, "knowledge cannot progress by repeating, with a rather non critical attitude, the early syntheses that the greatest writers offered as a hypothesis, as though they were a definitive vulgate."[1] The passage in the *Apostolic Tradition* on the

---

1. Charles Pietri. "Régions ecclésiastiques et paroisses romaines," in *Actes du XIe Congrès International d'Archéologie Chrétienne,* Collection de l'École française de Rome 123 (Rome: École française de Rome, 1989), 2:1037.

burial of the poor, for instance, can no longer be cited as evidence for the existence of cemeteries organized by the church in Rome in the third century, when all the philological work that led to its reconstruction was guided by the very idea that such cemeteries were organized. Augustine's treatise *On the Care of the Dead* might surprisingly be found to provide a theological justification to the human concern for the body once we discard our prejudices about popular belief and theological teaching.

Beyond these limited results, whatever their methodological importance, I believe that this book raises two sets of questions. The first is about the interaction between Christians and non-Christians in a society that did not undergo major structural changes in either the third century (with its "crisis") or the second half of the fourth century (when Christianity became the religion of the emperor). A new study of the representation of these interactions in ecclesiastical sources is needed. Through the prism of the funerary practices, it seems that Christians, starting in the third century, were not organized in such solid and hostile groups as have often been described. The attitude toward the collegia is one good example: the silence of ecclesiastical sources on such a basic form of social practice in the Roman Empire has led many to assume that for Christians the church took the place of the collegia, whereas it actually appears that the church had to accept Christians' membership in collegia, which had Christian members but were not necessarily Christian collegia.

The second set of questions regards the authority of the church and its limits. Burial of Christians lay outside the control of the church, as did the organization of places where Christians were buried, even though the presence of martyrs' tombs, whose appeal we know sometimes involved the church. The church did not claim any such control, and an analysis of pastoral themes related to the commemoration of the dead shows that power and authority were not the only issues. The idea that Christian beliefs about the afterlife imply the church's control over burial should be abandoned. In any case we cannot just say that ideas about the purification of sin after death and the communion of saints—this concept that we have not encountered in our evidence supposes a perfect reciprocity between Christians both living and dead, and thus implies both the duty of the living to pray for the dead and the martyrs' intercessions—were not sufficiently formed, as if they were inscribed in the essence of Christianity. Such a perspective, while legitimate for a theologian, is not so for the historian.

Rather, the historian must consider a different form of Christianity than what emerged in the Middle Ages. In Late Antiquity, Christianity was not concerned with the burial of the dead nor even, to a great extent, with their memory. Thus it tolerated, to keep a negative formulation, a large secular sphere—one that covered even aspects of Christian life as important as their relationship to the dead. The limits of this secular sphere, the process of its formation, and the social interactions that it implies, all remain to be explored.

 Primary Sources

Acts of John

Acta Iohannis. Edited by Éric Junod and Jean-Daniel Kaestli. Corpus christianorum. Series Apocryphorum 1–2. Turnhout: Brepols, 1983. English translation: *The Apocryphal New Testament.* Translated by J. K. Elliott. Oxford: Clarendon Press, 1993.

Acts of Martyrs

The Acts of the Christian Martyrs. Edited and translated by Herbert Musurillo. Oxford: Clarendon Press, 1972.

Atti e passioni dei martiri. Edited by A. A. R. Bastiaensen. Scrittori greci e latini. Rome: Fondazione Lorenzo Valla/Milan: Mondadori, 1987.

Agennius Urbicus

De controuersiis agrorum. In *Corpus agrimensorum Romanorum.* Edited by Carl Thulin. Bibliotheca scriptorum Graecorum et Romanorum Teubneriana. Stuttgart: Teubner, 1913.

Alciphron

The Letters of Alciphron, Aelian and Philostratus. Edited and translated by Allen Rogers Benner and Francis H. Fobes. Loeb Classical Library 383. Cambridge, MA: Harvard University Press, 1949.

Ambrose of Milan

De Abraham. In *Sancti Ambrosi Opera,* vol. 1. Edited by Karl Schenkl. Corpus scriptorum ecclesiasticorum latinorum 32, no. 1. Vienna: Tempsky, 1897. English translation: *On Abraham.* Translated by Theodosia Tomkinson. Etna, CA: Center for Traditionalist Orthodox Studies, 2000.

De excessus fratris. In *Sancti Ambrosi Opera,* vol. 7. Edited by Otto Faller. Corpus scriptorum ecclesiasticorum latinorum 73. Vienna: Tempsky, 1955. English translation: *Funeral Orations by Gregory Nazianzen and Saint Ambrose.* Translated by Leo P. McCauley, John J. Sullivan, Martin R. P. McGuire, and Roy J. Deferrari. Fathers of the Church. New York: Fathers of the Church, 1953.

De Helia et ieiunio. In *Sancti Ambrosi Opera,* vol. 2. Edited by Karl Schenkl. Corpus scriptorum ecclesiasticorum latinorum 32, no. 2. Vienna: Tempsky, 1897. English translation: *De Helia et ieiunio.* Translated by Sister Mary Joseph Aloysius Buck. Patristic Studies 19. Washington, DC: Catholic University of America, 1929.

De obitu Theodosii. In *Sancti Ambrosi Opera,* vol. 7. Edited by Otto Faller. Corpus scriptorum ecclesiasticorum latinorum 73. Vienna: Tempsky, 1955. English translation: *Funeral Orations by Gregory Nazianzen and Saint Ambrose.* Translated by Leo P. McCauley, John J. Sullivan, Martin R. P. McGuire, and Roy J. Deferrari. Fathers of the Church. New York: Fathers of the Church, 1953.

De officiis. Edited with introduction, translation, and commentary by Ivor J. Davidson. Oxford: Oxford University Press, 2001.

De Tobia. In *Sancti Ambrosi Opera,* vol. 2. Edited by Karl Schenkl. Corpus scriptorum ecclesiasticorum latinorum 32, no. 2. Vienna: Tempsky, 1897.

Expositio in evangelium S. Lucae. Edited by George Tissot. Sources chrétiennes 45bis and 52bis. Paris: Éditions du Cerf, 1971–76. English translation: *Exposition of the Holy Gospel according to Saint Luke.* Translated by Theodosia Tomkinson. Etna, CA: Center for Traditionalist Orthodox Studies, 1998.

In Psalmum 61 enarratio. In *Sancti Ambrosi Opera,* vol. 6. 2nd ed. Edited by Monica Zelzer. Corpus scriptorum ecclesiasticorum latinorum 64. Vienna: Verlag der österreichischen Akademie der Wissenschaften, 1999.

Aristides

Apologia. Edited by Bernard Pouderon and Marie-Joseph Pierre. Sources chrétiennes 470. Paris: Éditions du Cerf, 2003. English translation: *The Apology of Aristides.* Translated by J. Rendel Harris. Texts and Studies 1. Cambridge: Cambridge University Press, 1891.

Athanasius

Epistulae festales. Edited by Louis-Théodore Lefort. Corpus scriptorum christianorum orientalium 151. Scriptores Coptici 20. Louvain: Durbecq, 1955.

Vita Antonii. Edited by G. J. M. Bartelink. Sources chrétiennes 400. Paris: Éditions du Cerf, 1994. English translation: *The Life of Antony and the Letter to Marcellinus.* Translated by Robert C. Gregg. New York: Paulist Press, 1980.

Augustine

Confessiones. Edited by James J. O'Donnell. Oxford: Clarendon Press, 1992. English translation: *The Confessions.* Translated by Maria Boulding. The Works of Saint Augustine: A Translation for the 21st Century 1. New York: New City Press, 1997.

De ciuitate Dei. Edited by Bernhard Dombart and Alfons Kalb. Corpus Christianorum. Series Latina 47–48. Turnhout: Brepols, 1955. English translation: *Concerning the City of God against the Pagans.* Translated by Henry Bettenson. Harmondsworth, UK: Penguin, 1972.

De consensu euangelistarum. Edited by Franz Weihrich. Corpus scriptorum ecclesiasticorum latinorum 43. Vienna: Tempsky, 1904.

De cura pro mortuis gerenda. Edited by Joseph Zycha. Corpus scriptorum ecclesiasticorum latinorum 61. Vienna: Tempsky, 1900. English translation: Saint Augustine, *Treatises on Marriage and Other Subjects.* Edited by Roy J. Deferrari. Fathers of the Church 15. New York: Fathers of the Church, 1955.

De moribus ecclesiae catholicae. Edited by Johannes Baptist Bauer. Corpus scriptorum ecclesiasticorum latinorum 90. Vienna: Tempsky, 1992. English translation: J. K. Coyle, *Augustine's De moribus ecclesiae catholicae: A Study of the Work, Its Composition and Its Sources.* Paradosis 25. Fribourg: The University Press, 1978.

De natura et origine animae. Edited by Carl Franz Urba and Joseph Zycha. Corpus scriptorum ecclesiasticorum latinorum 60. Vienna: Tempsky, 1913. English translation: *Answers to the Pelagians.* Vol. 1. Translated by Roland Teske. The Works of Saint Augustine: A Translation for the 21st Century 1, no. 23. New York: New City Press, 1997.

De octo Dulcitii quaestiones. Edited by Almut Mutzenbecher. Corpus christianorum. Series latina 44A. Turnhout: Brepols, 1975.

Enarrationes in psalmos. Edited by Eligius Dekkers and Johannes Fraipont. Corpus Christianorum. Series Latina 38–39. Turnhout: Brepols, 1990. English translation: *Expositions on the Psalms.* Translated by Maria Boulding. The Works of Saint Augustine: A Translation for the 21st Century 3, nos. 15–20. New York: New City Press, 2000–2004.

Enchiridion. Edited by Ernest Evans. Corpus Christianorum. Series Latina 46. Turnhout: Brepols, 1969. English translation: *Faith, Hope and Charity.* Translated by Louis A. Arand. Ancient Christian Writers 3. Westminster: Newman, 1955.

Epistulae. Edited by Alois Goldbacher. Corpus scriptorum ecclesiasticorum latinorum 34, nos. 1–2; 44, 57–58. Vienna: Tempsky, 1895–1923; *Œuvres de saint Augustin. 46B, Lettres 1*–29*.* Edited by Johannes Divjak. Bibliothèque augustinienne. Paris: Études augustiniennes, 1987. English translation: *Letters.* Translated by Roland Teske. 4 vols. The Works of Saint Augustine: A Translation for the 21st Century 2, nos. 1–4. New York: New City Press, 2001–5.

In Iohannis euangelium tractatus. Edited by R. Willems. Corpus christianorum. Series latina 36. Turnhout: Brepols, 1954. English translation: *Tractates on the Gospel of John 112–24.* Translated by John W. Rettig. Fathers of the Church. Washington, D.C: Catholic University of America Press, 1995.

Locutiones in Heptateuchum; Quaestiones in Heptateuchum. Edited by Johannes Fraipont. Corpus christianorum. Series latina 33. Turnhout: Brepols, 1958.

Sermones. In *Patrologiae cursus completus. Patrologia Latina* Vols. 38–39. Paris: 1841–1855; *Patrologiae cursus completus. Series Latina, Supplementum.* Vol. 2. Edited by Adalbert Hamman. Paris: Garnier, 1961; Augustin d'Hippone, *Vingt-six sermons au peuple d'Afrique.* Edited by François Dolbeau. Collection des études augustiniennes. Série antiquité 147. Paris: Institut d'études augustiniennes, 1996. English translation: *Sermons.* Translated by Edmund Hill. 11 vols. The Works of Saint Augustine: A Translation for the 21st Century 3, nos. 1–11. New York: New City Press, 1990–97.

Callinicus

Vita sancti Hypatii. Edited by G. J. M. Bartelink. Sources chrétiennes 177. Paris: Éditions du Cerf, 1971.

Cicero

De Legibus. Edited with an English translation by Clinton Walker Keyes. Loeb Classical Library 213. Cambridge, MA: Harvard University Press, 1928.

Tusculanae dissertationes. Edited with an English translation by J. E. King. Loeb Classical Library 141. Cambridge, MA: Harvard University Press, 1945.

Commodianus

Instructiones. Edited by J. Martin. Corpus christianorum. Series latina 128. Turnhout: Brepols, 1960.

Collectiones Iuris Canonici

Concilia Africae. Edited by Charles Munier. Corpus christianorum. Series latina 149. Turnhout: Brepols, 1974.

Concilia Galliae. A. 511–a. 695. Edited by Charles de Clercq. Corpus Christianorum. Series Latina 148A. Turnhout: Brepols, 1963.

Concilia Hispaniae. Edited by Juan Vives. España cristiana. Textos 1. Barcelona: Instituto Enrique Flórez, 1963.

Collectio Avellana. Edited by Otto Guenther. Corpus scriptorum ecclesiasticorum latinorum 35. Vienna: Tempsky, 1895.

Gesta collationis Carthagini habitae anno 411. Edited by Serge Lancel. Corpus Christianorum. Series Latina 149A. Turnhout: Brepols, 1974.

Innocentius I, *Epistula 25.* Edited by Robert Cabié. Bibliothèque de la Revue d'histoire ecclésiastique 58. Louvain: Publications universitaires de Louvain, 1973.

Sententiae LXXXVII Episcoporum. Edited by Hermann von Soden. In *Nachrichten von der Königlichen Gesellschaft der Wissenschaften zu Göttingen, Phil.—hist. Klasse,* 1909, 247–307.

Cyprian

Epistulae. Edited by G. F. Diercks. Corpus Christianorum. Series Latina 3B–C. Turnhout: Brepols, 1994–1996. English translation: *The Letters of St. Cyprian of Carthage.* 4 vols. Translated by G. W. Clarke. Ancient Christian Writers 43–44. New York: Newman Press, 1984–89.

Cyril of Jerusalem

Mystagogiae. Edited by Auguste Piédagnel. Sources chrétiennes 126bis. Paris: Éditions du Cerf, 1988. English translation: Edward Yarnold, *Cyril of Jerusalem.* London: Routledge, 2000.

Epiphanius

Panarion. Edited by Karl Holl. 2nd ed. by Jürgen Dummer. Die griechischen christlichen Schriftsteller der ersten Jahrhunderte 25, 31, 37. Berlin: Akademie Verlag, 1980–85. English translation: *The Panarion of Epiphanius of Salamis.* 3 vols. Translated by Frank Williams. Leiden, Netherlands: Brill, 1987–1994.

Eusebius

Historia Ecclesiastica. 2 vols. Edited with an English translation by Kirsopp Lake and J. E. L. Oulton. Loeb Classical Library 153, 265. Cambridge, MA: Harvard University Press, 1980.

Praeparatio evangelica. Edited by Karl Mras. Die griechischen christlichen Schriftsteller der ersten Jahrhunderte 43. Berlin: Akademie Verlag, 1954–56.

Fontes Iuris

Codex Theodosianus. 2nd ed. Edited by Theodor Mommsen and P. M. Meyer. Berlin: Weidmann, 1954. English translation: *The Theodosian Code and Novels, and the Sirmondian Constitutions.* Translated by Clyde Pharr. Princeton, NJ: Princeton University Press, 1952.

Digesta. Latin text edited by Theodor Mommsen with the aid of Paul Krueger; English translation by Alan Watson. Philadelphia: University of Pennsylvania Press, 1985.

"Edict of Nazareth." In *Textes de droit romain,* vol. 2, *Les lois des romains.* 7th ed. by Paul Frédéric Girard and Félix Senn. Naples: Jovene, 1977. English translation: *Ancient Roman Statutes.* Edited by Clyde Pharr. Austin: University of Texas Press, 1961.

Leo VI, *Novellae.* Edited by P. Noailles and A. Dain. Nouvelle collection de textes et documents. Paris: Les Belles Lettres, 1944.

Sententiae Pauli. In *Textes de droit romain,* vol. 1, 7th ed. Edited by Paul Frédéric Girard and Félix Senn. Paris: Dalloz, 1967.

Valentinianus, *Novellae.* 2nd ed. Edited by Theodor Mommsen and P. M. Meyer. Berlin: Weidmann, 1954. English translation: *The Theodosian Code and Novels, and the Sirmondian Constitutions.* Translated by Clyde Pharr. Princeton, NJ: Princeton University Press, 1952.

Gaudentius of Brescia

Tractatus. Edited by Ambrosius Glück. Corpus scriptorum ecclesiasticorum latinorum 58. Vienna: Tempsky, 1936.

Gesta apud Zenophilum consularem

In J.-L. Maier, *Le dossier du Donatisme,* vol. 1, *Des origines à la mort de Constance II (303–361).* Texte und Untersuchungen zur Geschichte der altchristlichen Literatur 134. Berlin: Akademie Verlag, 1987.

Gregory of Nazianzus

Epitaphia. In *Greek Anthology.* Vol. 2. Edited with an English translation by W. R. Paton. Loeb Classical Library 68. Cambridge, MA: Harvard University Press, 1919.

Oratio 14. In *Patrologiæ Græcæ.* Vol. 35. Paris: J.-P. Migne, 1885. English translation: In *Gregory of Nazianzus.* Edited by Brian E. Daley. London: Routledge.

Gregory of Nyssa

Epistola canonica. 2nd ed. Edited by Georgius Pasquali. Gregorii Nysseni Opera 8, no. 2. Leiden: Brill, 1959. English translation: *The Letters.* Translated by Anna M. Silvas. Supplements to Vigiliae Christianae 83. Leiden: Brill, 2007.

Vita Macrinae. Edited by Pierre Maraval. Sources chrétiennes 178. Paris: Éditions du Cerf, 1971. English translation: Gregory of Nyssa, *Ascetical Works.* Translated by Virginia Woods Callaghan. Fathers of the Church 58. Washington, DC: Catholic University of America Press, 1967.

Gregory of Tours

In gloria confessorum. Edited by Bruno Krusch. Monumenta Germaniae historica. Scriptorum rerum merovingicarum 1, no. 2. Hannover: Hahn, 1885. English translation: *Glory of the Confessors.* Translated by Raymond Van Dam. Translated Texts for Historians. Liverpool: Liverpool University Press, 1988.

Hilary of Poitiers

In Matthaeum. Edited by Jean Doignon. Sources chrétiennes 254, 258. Paris: Éditions du Cerf, 1978–79.

Hippolytus

Commentarii in Danielem. Edited by M. Lefèvre. Sources chrétiennes 14. Paris: Éditions du Cerf, 1947.

Refutatio omnium haeresium. Edited by Miroslav Marcovich. Patristische Texte und Studien 25. Berlin: De Gruyter, 1986. English translation: *The Refutation of All Heresies.* Translated by J. H. MacMahon. Ante-Nicene Christian Library 6. Edinburg: T. and T. Clark, 1868.

Traditio Apostolica. Edited by Bernard Botte. Sources chrétiennes 11bis. Paris: Éditions du Cerf, 1968. English translation: *On the Apostolic Tradition.* Edited by Alistair Stewart-Sykes. Crestwood, NY: St. Vladimir's Seminary Press, 2001; *The Apostolic Tradition: A Commentary.* Edited by Paul F. Bradshaw, Maxwell E. Johnson, and L. Edward Phillips. Minneapolis, MN: Fortress Press, 2002.

Iamblichus

De vita Pythagorica. Edited by Edouard des Places. Collection des Universités de France. Paris: Les Belles Lettres, 1982. English translation: *On the Pythagorean Life.* Translated by Gillian Clark. Translated Texts for Historians. Liverpool: Liverpool University Press, 1989.

Jerome

Commentarii in Euangelium Matthaei Edited by Émile Bonnard. Sources chrétiennes 242, 259. Paris: Éditions du Cerf, 1978–1979.

Commentarius in Ionam. Edited by Yves-Marie Duval. Sources chrétiennes 323. Paris: Éditions du Cerf, 1985.

Epistulae [Letters]. Edited by Isidorus Hilberg. Corpus scriptorum ecclesiasticorum latinorum 54–56. Vienna: Tempsky, 1910–18. English translation: *Select Letters of St. Jerome.* Translated by F. A. Wright. Loeb Classical Library 262. Cambridge, MA: Harvard University Press, 1933.

Hebraicae quaestiones in libro Geneseos. Edited by Paul de Lagarde. Corpus christianorum. Series latina 72. Turnhout, Belgium: Brepols, 1959.

John Chrysostom

De coemeterio et de cruce. In *Patrologiæ Græcæ*. Vol. 49. Paris: J.-P. Migne, 1862.

In Acta apostolorum homiliae 1–55. In *Patrologiæ Græcæ*. Vol. 60. Paris: J.-P. Migne, 1862. English translation: in *A Select Library of the Nicene and Post-Nicene Fathers of the Christian Church.* Vol. 11. Edited by Philip Schaff. New York: Christian Literature Company, 1888.

In epistulam ad Hebraeos homiliae 1–34. In *Patrologiæ Græcæ*. Vol. 63. Paris: J.-P. Migne, 1862. English translation: in *A Select Library of the Nicene and Post-Nicene Fathers of the Christian Church.* Vol. 14. Edited by Philip Schaff. New York: Christian Literature Company, 1888.

In epistulam ad Philippenses homiliae 1–15. In *Patrologiæ Græcæ*. Vol. 62. Paris: J.-P. Migne, 1862. English translation: in *A Select Library of the Nicene and Post-Nicene Fathers of the Christian Church.* Vol. 13. Edited by Philip Schaff. New York: Christian Literature Company, 1888.

In epistulam i ad Corinthios homiliae 1–44. In *Patrologiæ Græcæ*. Vol. 61. Paris: J.-P. Migne, 1862. English translation: in *A Select Library of the Nicene and Post-Nicene Fathers of the Christian Church.* Vol. 12. Edited by Philip Schaff. New York: Christian Literature Company, 1888.

In Iohannem homiliae 1–88. In *Patrologiæ Græcæ*. Vol. 59. Paris: J.-P. Migne, 1862. English translation: in *A Select Library of the Nicene and Post-Nicene Fathers of the Christian Church.* Vol. 14. Edited by Philip Schaff. New York: Christian Literature Company, 1888.

In Mattheum homiliae 1–99. In *Patrologiæ Græcæ*. Vol. 57. Paris: J.-P. Migne, 1862. English translation: in *A Select Library of the Nicene and Post-Nicene Fathers of the Christian Church.* Vol. 10. Edited by Philip Schaff. New York: Christian Literature Company, 1888.

Julian

The Works of the Emperor Julian. Edited with an English translation by Wilmer Cave Wright. Loeb Classical Library. Cambridge, MA: Harvard University Press, 1913–23.

Justin

Apologiae. Edited by Charles Munier. Sources chrétiennes 507. Paris: Éditions du Cerf, 2006. English translation: *The First and Second Apologies.* Translated by Leslie William Barnard. Ancient Christian Writers 56. New York: Paulist Press, 1997.

Lactantius

Divinae Institutiones. Edited by Samuel Brandt. Corpus scriptorum ecclesiasticorum latinorum 19. Vienna: Tempsky, 1890. English translation: *Divine Institutes.*

Translated by Anthony Bowen and Peter Garnsey. Translated Texts for Historians. Liverpool: Liverpool University Press, 2003.

Liber Pontificalis

Edited by Louis Duchesne. 2 vols. 2nd ed. Paris: De Boccard, 1955–57.

Liturgica

The Canons of Athanasius. Edited by W. Riedel and W. E. Crum. London: Williams and Norgate, 1904.
Constitutiones apostolicae. Edited by Marcel Metzger. Sources chrétiennes, 320, 329, 336. Paris: Éditions du Cerf, 1986–87.
Didascalia, versio latina. Edited by Erik Tidner. Texte und Untersuchungen zur Geschichte der altchristlichen Literatur 75. Berlin: Akademie Verlag, 1963.
Didascalia, versio syriaca. Edited and translated by Arthur Vööbus. Corpus scriptorum christianorum orientalium 402. Scriptores syri 176. Louvain, Belgium: Peeters, 1979.
The Prayers of Sarapion of Thmuis. Edited by Maxwell E. Johnson. Orientalia Christiana Analecta 249. Rome: Pontificio Istituto Orientale, 1995.
Sacramentarium Gelasianum. Edited by L. C. Mohlberg. Rerum ecclesiasticarum documenta. Series maior, Fontes 4. Rome: Herder, 1960.
Testamentum Domini. Edited by Ignatius Rahmani. Mainz, Germany: Kirchheim, 1899.
Testamentum Domini éthiopien. Edited by Rémi Beylot. Louvain, Belgium: Peeters, 1984.

Macrobius

Saturnalia. 2nd ed. Edited by Johannes Willis. Bibliotheca scriptorum Graecorum et Romanoru Teubneriana. Leipzig, Germany: Teubner, 1970.

Maximus of Turin

Sermones. Edited by Almut Mutzenbecher. Corpus christianorum. Series latina 23. Turnhout, Belgium: Brepols, 1962. English translation: *The Sermons of St. Maximus of Turin.* Translated by Boniface Ramsey. Ancient Christian Writers 50. New York: Newman Press, 1989.

Minucius Felix

Octavius. Edited by Jean Beaujeu. Collection des Universités de France. Paris: Les Belles Lettres, 1974. English translation: *The Octavius of Marcus Minucius Felix.* Translated by G. W. Clarke. Ancient Christian Writers 39. New York: Newman Press, 1974.

Origen

Contra Celsum. 5 vols. Edited by Marcel Borret. Sources chrétiennes 132, 136, 147, 150, 227. Paris: Éditions du Cerf, 1967–76. English translation: Translated by Henry Chadwick. Cambridge: Cambridge University Press, 1953.

Palladius

Historia Lausiaca. In *Vite dei santi*. Vol. 2. Edited by G. J. M. Bartelink. Scrittori greci e latini. Milan: Mondadori/Rome: Fondazione Lorenzo Valla, 1974. English translation: *Lausiac History*. Translated by Robert T. Miller. Ancient Christian Writers 34. Westminster: Newman Press, 1965.

Paulinus

Vita Ambrosii. In *Vite dei Santi*. Vol. 3. Edited by A. A. R. Bastiaensen. Scrittori greci e latini. Milan: Fondazione Lorenzo Valla/Mondadori, 1975.

Paulinus of Nola

Epistulae. Edited by Willem von Hartel. Corpus scriptorum ecclesiasticorum Latinorum 29. Vienna: Tempsky, 1894. English translation: 2 vols. Translated by P. G. Walsh. Ancient Christian Writers 35–36. Westminster: Newman Press, 1966–67.

Philo

De ebrietate. In *Les œuvres de Philon d'Alexandrie*. 2 vols. Edited by Jean Gorez. Paris: Éditions du Cerf, 1962.

Philostratus

Lives of the Sophists. Edited with an English translation by W. C. Wright. Loeb Classical Library 134. Cambridge, MA: Harvard University Press, 1921.

Pliny the Elder

Natural History. 11 vols. Edited with an English translation by H. Rackham. Loeb Classical Library. Cambridge, MA: Harvard University Press, 1938–63.

Pontius

Vita Cypriani. In *Vite dei Santi*. Vol. 3. Edited by A. A. R. Bastiaensen. Scrittori greci e latini. Milan: Fondazione Lorenzo Valla/Mondadori, 1975.

Possidius

Vita Augustini. In *Vite dei Santi*. Vol. 3. Edited by A. A. R. Bastiaensen. Scrittori greci e latini. Milan: Fondazione Lorenzo Valla/Mondadori, 1975. English translation: *The Life of Saint Augustine*. Edited by John E. Rotelle. Villanova, PA: Augustinian Press, 1988.

Prudentius

Cathemerinon liber. Edited by Maurice Lavarenne. Collection des universités de France. Paris: Les Belles Lettres, 1943. English translation: *The Poems of Prudentius*. 2 vols. Translated by M. Clement Eagan. Ancient Christian Writers 43, 52. Washington, DC: Catholic University of America Press, 1962.

(Pseudo-)Quintillian

Declamationes XIX maiores Quintiliano falso ascriptae. Edited by Lennart Hakanson. Bibliotheca scriptorum Graecorum et Romanorum Teubneriana. Stuttgart: Teubner, 1982. English translation: *The Major Declamations Ascribed to Quintilian.* Translated by Lewis A. Sussman. Frankfurt: Lang, 1987.

Scriptores Historiae Augustae

3 vols. Edited with an English translation by David Magie. Loeb Classical Library 139, 140, 263. Cambridge, MA: Harvard University Press, 1979–82.

(Pseudo-)Seneca

De remediis fortuitorum. In *De Senecae philosophi librorum recensione et emendatione.* Edited by Otto Rossbach. Hildesheim: Olms, 1969.

Servius

Servii grammatici qui feruntur in Vergilii carmina commentarii. Edited by G. Thilo. Hildesheim: Olms, 1961.

Sidonius Apolinaris

Poems and Letters. 2 vols. Edited with an English translation by W. B. Anderson. Loeb Classical Library. Cambridge, MA: Harvard University Press, 1936–65.

Tatian

Oratio ad Graecos. Edited and translated by Molly Whittaker. Oxford Early Christian Texts. Oxford: Clarendon Press, 1982.

Tertullian

Ad Scapulam. Edited by Emil Dekkers. Corpus Christianorum. Series Latina 2. Turnhout: Brepols, 1954.
Apologeticum. Edited with an English translation by T. R. Glover. Loeb Classical Library 250. Cambridge, MA: Harvard University Press, 1934.
De anima. Edited by J. H. Waszing. Corpus Christianorum. Series Latina 2. Turnhout: Brepols, 1954.
De corona. Edited by Jacques Fontaine. Érasme. Paris: Presses universitaires de France, 1966.
De exhortatione castitatis. Edited by Claudio Moreschini and Jean-Claude Fredouille. Sources chrétiennes 319. Paris: Éditions du Cerf, 1985. English translation: *Treatises on Marriage and Remarriage.* Translated by William P. Le Saint. Ancient Christian Writers 13. Westminster: Newman Press, 1951.
De idololatria. Edited and translated by J. H. Waszink and J. C. M. Van Winden. Supplements to Vigiliae Christianae 1. Leiden: Brill, 1987.
De monogamia. Edited by Paul Mattei. Sources chrétiennes 343. Paris: Éditions du Cerf, 1988. English translation: *Treatises on Marriage and Remarriage.* Translated by William P. Le Saint. Ancient Christian Writers 13. Westminster: Newman Press, 1951.

De resurrectione mortuorum. Edited by J. G. Ph. Borleffs. Corpus Christianorum. Series Latina 2. Turnhout: Brepols, 1954.

De spectaculis. Edited with an English translation by T. R. Glover. Loeb Classical Library 250. Cambridge, MA: Harvard University Press, 1934.

Theodore of Mopsuestia

Catechetical Homilies. Edited and translated by Alphonse Mingana. Woodbrooke Studies 6. Cambridge: Heffer, 1933.

Zeno of Verona

Tractatus. Edited by Bengt Löfstedt. Corpus christianorum. Series latina 22. Turnhout: Brepols, 1971.

Secondary Sources

Albertario, Emilio. "A proposito di un nuovo studio sulle multe sepolcrali." *Zeitschrift der Savigny-Stiftung für Rechtsgeschichte. Romanistische Abteilung* 32 (1911): 386–90.

——. *Studi di diritto romano. 2, Cose, diritti reali, possesso.* Milan: Guiffrè, 1941.

Alexandre, Monique. "À propos du récit de la mort d'Antoine (Athanase, *Vie d'Antoine.* PG 26, 968–974, § 89–93): l'heure de la mort dans la littérature monastique." In *Le temps chrétien de la fin de l'Antiquité au Moyen Âge*, 263–82. Colloques internationaux du CNRS 604. Paris: Éditions du CNRS, 1984.

Alföldi, Andreas. "Der Rechtsstreit zwischen der römischen Kirche und dem Verein der Popinarii: (Ein Beitrag zur Beurteilung der 'Historia Augusta')." *Klio* 31 (1938): 249–53.

Applebaum, Shimon. "The Jewish Community of Hellenistic and Roman Teucheira in Cyrenaica." *Scripta Hierosolymitana* 7 (1961): 27–52.

——. *Jews and Greeks in Ancient Cyrene.* Studies in Judaism in Late Antiquity 28. Leiden: Brill, 1979.

Ascough, Richard S. "Translocal Relationships among Voluntary Associations and Early Christianity." *Journal of Early Christian Studies* 5 (1997): 223–41.

Ausbüttel, Frank M. *Untersuchungen zu den Vereinen im Westen des römischen Reiches.* Frankfurter althistorische Studien 11. Kallmünz: Lassleben, 1982.

Avigad, Nahman, ed. *Beth She'arim.* Volume 3, *The Archaeological Excavations during 1953–1958: The Catacombs 12–13.* New Brunswick, NJ: Rutgers University Press, 1976.

Barnes, Timothy David. *Tertullian: A Historical and Literary Study.* Oxford: Clarendon Press, 1982.

Baumeister, Theofried. *Martyr Invictus: der Martyrer als Sinnbild der Erlösung in der Legende und im Kult der frühen koptischen Kirche: zur Kontinuität des ägyptischen Denkens.* Forschung zur Volkskunde 46. Münster: Regensberg, 1972.

Bavel, Tarsicius J. van. "'No One Ever Hated His Own Flesh': Eph. 5:29 in Augustine." *Augustiniana* 45 (1995): 45–93.

Beard, Mary, John North, and Simon Price. *Religions of Rome.* Cambridge: Cambridge University Press, 1998.

Berger, Rupert. *Die Wendung "offere pro" in der römischen Liturgie.* Liturgiewissenschaftliche Quellen und Forschungen 41. Münster: Aschendorff, 1964.

Bertrand-Dagenbach, Cécile. *Alexandre Sévère et l'Histoire Auguste.* Collection Latomus 208. Brussels: Latomus, 1990.

Bidez, Joseph. *La vie de l'empereur Julien.* Collection d'études anciennes. Paris: Les Belles Lettres, 1930.

Bidez, Joseph, and Franz Cumont. *Les mages hellénisés: Zoroastre, Ostanès et Hystaspe d'après la tradition grecque.* Paris: Les Belles Lettres, 1938.

Bisconti, Fabrizio. "L'ipogeo degli Aureli in viale Manzoni: un esempio di sincresi provata." *Augustinianum* 25 (1985): 889–903.

Bishop, William C. "The African Rite." *Journal of Theological Studies* 13 (1912): 250–77.

Bodel, John. "Graveyards and Groves: A Study of Lex Lucerina." *American Journal of Ancient History* 11 (1986): 1-133.

Bodel, John. "Dealing with the Dead: Undertakers, Executioners and Potter's Fields in Ancient Rome." In *Death and Disease in the ancient city,* edited by Valerie M. Hope and Eireann Marshall, 128–51. New York: Routledge, 2000.

———. "From *Columbaria* to Catacombs: Collective Burial in Pagan and Christian Rome." In *Commemorating the Dead: Texts and Artifacts in Context: Studies of Roman, Jewish and Christian Burials,* edited by Laurie Brink and Deborah Green, 177–242. Berlin: De Gruyter, 2008.

Boffo, Laura. *Iscrizioni greche e latine per lo studio della Bibbia.* Biblioteca di storia e storiografia dei tempi biblici 9. Brescia: Paideia, 1994.

Boglioni, Pierre. "La scène de la mort dans les premières hagiographies latines." In *Essais sur la mort: travaux d'un séminaire de recherche sur la mort, Faculté de théologie, Université de Montréal,* edited by Guy Couturier, André Charron, and Guy Durand, 269–98. Héritage et projet 29. Montréal: Fides, 1085.

Boissier, Gaston. *La religion romaine d'Auguste aux Antonins.* Paris: Hachette, 1878.

Bollmann, Beate. *Römische Vereinshäuser: Untersuchungen zu den Scholae der römischen Berufs-, Kult—und Augustalen-Kollegien in Italien.* Mainz: Von Zabern, 1998.

Bonfioli, Mara, and Silvio Panciera. "Della cristianità del *collegium quod est in domo Sergiae Paullinae.*" *Atti della Pontificia Academia Romana di Archeologia. Rendiconti* 44 (1971–72): 185–201.

———. "In domo Sergiae Paullinae. Nota Aggiuntiva." *Atti della Pontificia Academia Romana di Archeologia. Rendiconti* 45 (1972–73): 137–38.

Borg, Barbara. "The Dead as Guest at Table? Continuity and Change in the Egyptian Cult of the Dead." In *Portraits and Masks: Burial Customs in Roman Egypt,* edited by Morris L. Bierbrier, 26–32. London: British Museum Press, 1997.

Borgen, Peder. *Early Christianity and Hellenistic Judaism.* Edinburgh: T and T Clark, 1996.

———. "'Yes' 'No' 'How far?' The Participations of Jews and Christians in Pagan Cults." In *Paul in His Hellenistic Context,* edited by Troels Engberg-Pedersen, 30–59. Edinburgh: T and T Clark, 1994.

Botte, Bernard. *La Tradition apostolique de saint Hippolyte: essai de reconstitution.* Liturgiewissenschaftliche Quellen und Forschungen 39. Münster: Aschendorff, 1963.

Bottini, Angelo. *Archeologia della salvezza: l'escatologia greca nelle testimonianze archeologiche.* Biblioteca di archeologia 17. Milan: Longanesi, 1992.

Bouffartigue, Jean. "L'authenticité de la Lettre 84 de l'empereur Julien." *Revue de philologie* 79, no. 2 (2005): 231–242

Bowes, Kim. *Private Worship, Public Values, and Religious Change in Late Antiquity.* Cambridge: Cambridge University Press, 2008.

Brakke, David. "'Outside the Place, within the Truth': Athanasius of Alexandria and the Localization of the Holy." In *Pilgrimage and Holy Space in Late Antique*

Egypt, edited by David Frankfurter, 445–81. Religions in the Graeco-Roman World 134. Leiden: Brill, 1998.

Brandenburg, Hugo. "*Coemeterium:* der Wandel des Bestattungswesen als Zeichen des Kulturumbruchs der Spätantike." *Laverna* 5 (1994): 206–32.

———. "Überlegungen zu Ursprung und Entstehung der Katakomben Roms." In *Vivarium: Festschrift Th. Klauser zum 90. Geburtstag,* 11–49. Jahrbuch für Antike und Christentum. Ergänzungsband 11. Münster: Aschendorff, 1984.

Brelich, Angelo. *A halálszemlélet formái a római birodalom sírfeliratain = Aspetti della morte nelle iscrizioni sepolcrali dell'Impero romano.* Dissertationes Pannonicae 7. Budapest: Magyar Nemzeti Múzeum, 1937.

Brennan, Brian. "Athanasius' *Vita Antonii:* A Sociological Interpretation." *Vigiliae Christianae* 39 (1985): 209–27.

Brent, Allen. *Hippolytus and the Roman Church in the Third Century: Communities in Tension before the Emergence of a Monarch-Bishop.* Supplements to Vigiliae Christianae 31. Leiden: Brill, 1995.

Brown, Peter. *The Body and Society: Men, Women and Sexual Renunciation in Early Christianity.* New York: Columbia University Press, 1988.

———. *The Cult of the Saints: Its Rise and Function in Latin Christianity.* Chicago: Chicago University Press, 1981.

———. "*Gloriosus obitus:* The End of the Ancient Other World." In *The Limits of Ancient Christianity: Essays on Late Antique Thought and Culture in Honor of Robert A. Markus,* edited by William E. Klingshirn and Mark Vessey, 289–314. Recentiores. Ann Arbor: University of Michigan Press, 1999.

———. *Power and Persuasion in Late Antiquity: Towards a Christian Empire.* Madison: University of Wisconsin Press, 1992.

———. *Poverty and Leadership in the Later Roman Empire.* Menahem Stern Jerusalem Lectures. Hanover, NH: University Press of New England, 2001.

———. *The Rise of Western Christendom: Triumph and Diversity, 200–1000 A.D.* 2nd ed. Oxford: Blackwell, 2003.

Brunt, John C. "Rejected, Ignored, or Misunderstood? The fate of Paul's Approach to the Problem of Food Offered to Idols in Early Christianity." *New Testament Studies* 31 (1985): 113–24.

Bullough, Donald. "Burial Community and Belief in the Early Medieval West." In *Ideal and Reality in Frankish and Anglo-Saxon Society,* edited by Patrick Wormald, Donald Bullough, and Roger Collins, 177–201. Oxford: Blackwell, 1991.

Burkert, Walter. *Ancient Mystery Cults.* Cambridge, MA: Harvard Univeristy Press, 1987.

Buschmann, Gerd. *Martyrium Polycarpi: eine formkritische Studie: ein Beitrag zur Frage nach der Entstehung der Gattung Märtyreakte.* Beihefte zur Zeitschrift für die neutestamentliche Wissenschaft und die Kunde der älteren Kirche 70. Berlin: De Gruyter, 1994.

Butti, Ignazio. "La *cognitio extra ordinem:* da Augusto a Diocleziano." In *Aufstieg und Niedergang der römischen Welt: (ANRW): Geschichte und Kultur Roms im Spiegel der neueren Forschung. 2, Principat. 14, Recht,* 29–59. Berlin: De Gruyter, 1982.

Bynum, Caroline W. *The Resurrection of the Body in Western Christianity.* Lectures on the history of religions, new series 15. New York: Columbia University Press, 1995.

Cafissi, Anna. "Contributo alla storia dei collegi romani: i *collegia funeraticia.*" *Studi e ricerche dell'Istituto di Storia, Facoltà di Lettere e Filosofia, Università di Firenze* 2 (1983): 89–111.

Caillet, Jean-Pierre. "L'amende funéraire dans l'épigraphie chrétienne de Salone." *Vjesnik za arheologiju i historiju dalmatinsku* 81 (1988): 33–45.

Capelle, Bernard. "Autorité de la liturgie chez les Pères." *Recherches de théologie ancienne et médiévale* 21 (1954): 5–22.

Capocci, Valentino. "Sulla concessione e sul divieto di sepoltura nel mondo romano ai condamnati a pena capitale." *Studia et documenta historiae et iuris* 22 (1956): 266–310.

Carletti, Carlo. "L'arca di Noè overro La chiesa di Callisto e l'uniformità della 'morte scritta'." *Antiquité tardive* 9 (2001): 97–102.

Carozzi, Claude. *Le voyage de l'âme dans l'au-delà d'après la littérature latine (Ve–XIIIe siècle).* Collection de l'École française de Rome 189. Rome: École française de Rome, 1994.

Carrié, Jean-Michel. "Les associations professionnelles à l'époque tardive: entre *munus* et convivialité." In *Humana sapit: mélanges en l'honneur de Lellia Cracco Ruggini*, edited by Jean-Michel Carrié and Rita Lizzi Testa, 309–32. Bibliothèque de l'Antiquité tardive 3. Turnhout: Brepols, 2002.

Carrié, Jean-Michel, and Rousselle, Aline. *Nouvelle histoire de l'antiquité. 10, L'Empire romain en mutation: des Sévères à Constantin (192–337).* Points. Histoire 221. Paris: Seuil, 1999.

Cerrato, J. A. *Hippolytus between East and West: The Commentaries and the Provenance of the Corpus.* Oxford: Oxford University Press, 2003.

Chavasse, Antoine. *Étude sur l'onction des infirmes dans l'Église latine du IIIe au XIe siècle. 1, Du IIIe siècle à la réforme carolingienne.* Lyon: Librairie du Sacré-Coeur, 1942.

Clermont-Ganneau, Charles Simon. "L'antique nécropole juive d'Alexandrie." *Comptes rendus de l'Académie des Inscriptions et Belles-Lettres* (1907): 236–39, 375–76.

Colafemmina, Cesare. "Saggio di scavo in località Collina della Maddalena a Venosa." *Vetera Christianorum* 18 (1981): 443–51.

Conde Guerri, Elena. *Los fossores de Roma paleocristiana: estudio iconografico, epigrafico y social.* Studi di antichità cristiana 33. Vatican City: Pontificio istituto di archeologia cristiana, 1979.

Cooper, Kate. *The Fall of the Roman Household.* Cambridge: Cambridge University Press, 2007.

Coquin, René-Georges. "Le *Testamentum Domini:* problèmes de tradition textuelle." *Parole de l'Orient* 5 (1974): 165–88.

Covolo, Enrico dal. "Una *domus ecclesiae* a Roma sotto l'impero di Alessandro Severo?" *Ephemerides Liturgicae* 102 (1988): 64–71.

Cracco Ruggini, Lelia. "Le associazioni professionali nel mondo romano-byzantino." In *Artigianato e tecnica nella società dell'alto Medioevo occidentale,* 59–193. Settimane internazionale di studio del Centro italiano di studi sull'Alto Medioevo 18. Spoleto: Centro italiano di studi sull'Alto Medioevo, 1971.

Creaghan, John S. "Violatio sepulcri: An Epigraphical Study." PhD diss., Princeton University, 1951.

Cumont, Franz. *After-Life in Roman Paganism.* New Haven, CT: Yale University Press, 1922.

———. *Lux perpetua*. Paris: Geuthner, 1949.

———. *The Mysteries of Mithra*. Translated by Thomas McCormack. New York: Dove, 1956.

———. "Un rescrit impérial sur la violation de sépulture." *Revue historique* 163 (1930): 241–66.

———. *Textes et monuments figurés relatifs aux mystères de Mithra*. 2 vols. Brussels: Lamertin, 1896–99.

———. "La triple commémoration des morts." *Comptes-rendus de l'Académie des Inscriptions et Belles Lettres* (1918): 278–94.

Dagemark, Siver. "Funeral as a Hagiographic Motif in *Vita Augustini* and some other Biographies of Bishops." *Augustinianum* 40, no. 1 (2000): 255–89.

Dagron, Gilbert. "Ainsi rien n'échappera à la réglementation: État, Église, corporation, confréries: à propos des inhumations à Constantinople (Ive–Ve siècle)." In *Hommes et richesses dans l'Empire byzantin. 2, VIIe–XVe siècle*, 155–82. Réalités Byzantines. Paris: Lethielleux, 1991.

Daley, Brian E. *The Hope of the Early Church: A Handbook of Patristic Wschatology*. Cambridge: Cambridge University Press, 1991.

De Bhaldraithe, Eoin. "*Oblationes pro defunctis, pro nataliciis annua die facimus*: What Did Tertullian Mean?" In *Studia Patristica* vol. 20, edited by E. A. Livingstone, 346–51. Louvain: Peeters, 1989.

De Clerck, Paul. *La "prière universelle" dans les liturgies latines anciennes: témoignages patristiques et textes liturgiques*. Liturgiewissenschaftliche Quellen und Forschungen 62. Münster: Aschendorff, 1977.

De Rossi, Giovanni Battista. "Esame archeologico e critico della storia di s. Callisto narrata nel libro nono dei Filosofumene." *Bullettino di archeologia cristiana* 4 (1866): 1–14, 17–33, 77–99.

———. "Le iscrizioni trovate nei sepolcri all'aperto cielo nella villa Patrizi." *Bullettino di archeologia cristiana* 3 (1865): 53–54.

———. *La Roma sotterranea cristiana*, vol. 1. Rome: Cromo-litografia pontificia, 1864.

———. "Dei sepolcreti cristiani non sotterranei." *Bullettino di archeologia cristiana* 2 (1864): 25–32.

———. "Le varie e successive condizioni di legalità dei cemeteri, il vario grado di libertà dell'arte cristiana, e la legalità della medesima religione nel primo secolo verificate dalle recenti scoperte nel cemetero di Domitilla." *Bullettino di archeologia cristiana* 3 (1865): 89–99.

Dehandschutter, Boudewijn. "The *Martyrium Polycarpi*: A Century of Research." In *Aufstieg und Niedergang der römischen Welt (ANRW): Geschichte und Kultur Roms im Spiegel der neueren Forschung. 2, Principat. 27, Religion. 1*, 485–522. Berlin: De Gruyter, 1993.

Delattre, Alfred Louis. *Gamart ou la nécropole juive de Carthage*. Lyon: Mougin-Rusand, 1895.

Delehaye, Hippolyte. *Les origines du culte des martyrs*. Subsidia hagiographica 20. Brussels: Société des Bollandistes, 1933.

Delmaire, Roland. *Largesses sacrées et res privata: l'aerarium impérial et son administration du IVe au VIe siècle*. Collection de l'École française de Rome 121. Rome: École française de Rome, 1989.

Demicheli, Anna Maria. *La ΜΕΓΑΛΗ ΕΚΚΛΗΣΙΑ nel lessico e nel diritto di Giustiniano*. Monografia del vocabulario di Giustiniano 3. Milan: Giuffrè, 1990.

Digeser, Elizabeth DePalma. *The Making of a Christian Empire: Lactantius and Rome.* Ithaca, NY: Cornell University Press, 2000.

Dix, Gregory. *The Treatise on the Apostolic Tradition of St. Hippolytus of Rome, Bishop and Martyr.* 2nd ed. with corrections, preface, and bibliography by Henry Chadwick. London: SPCK, 1968.

Doignon, Jean. "*Refrigerium* et catéchèse à Vérone au IVe siècle" In *Hommages à Marcel Renard,* edited by Jacqueline Bibauw, 2:220–39. Collection Latomus 102. Brussels: Latomus, 1969.

Dondin-Payre, Monique. *Exercice du pouvoir et continuité gentilice: les Acilii Glabriones du IIIe siècle av. J.-C. au Ve siècle ap. J.-C.* Collection de l'École française de Rome 180. Rome: École française de Rome, 1993.

Duchesne, Louis. *Christian Worship: Its Origin and Evolution.* 3rd English ed. Translated by M. L. McClure. London: Society for Promoting Christian Knowledge, 1910.

———. *Histoire ancienne de l'Église.* 3rd ed. 3 vols. Paris: Fontemoing, 1907–1908.

Dunand, Françoise. "Les nécrotaphes de Kysis." *Cahiers de recherches de l'Institut de Papyrologie et d'Égyptologie de l'Université de Lille* 7 (1985): 117–127.

Dupont, Clémence. "Les privilèges des clercs sous Constantin." *Revue d'histoire ecclésiastique* 62 (1967): 729–52.

Duquenne, Luc. *La chronologie des lettres de S. Cyprien: le dossier de la persécution de Dèce.* Subsidia Hagiographica 54. Brussels: Société des Bollandistes, 1972.

Duval, Noël. "Études d'architecture chrétienne nord-africaine. 1, Les monuments chrétiens de Carthage: études critiques." *Mélanges de l'École française de Rome. Antiquité* 84 (1972): 1071–1125.

———. *Les églises africaines à deux absides: recherches archéologiques sur la liturgie chrétienne en Afrique du Nord.* Bibliothèque des Écoles françaises d'Athènes et de Rome 218 and 218 bis. Rome: École française de Rome, 1973.

Duval Yves-Marie. "Formes profanes et formes bibliques dans les oraisons funèbres de saint Ambroise." In *Christianisme et formes littéraires de l'Antiquité tardive en Occident: huit exposés suivis de discussions,* 235–91. Entretiens sur l'antiquité classique 23. Geneva: Fondation Hardt pour l'étude de l'Antiquité classique, 1977.

Duval, Yvette. *Auprès des saints corps et âme: l'inhumation "ad sanctos" dans la chrétienté d'Orient et d'Occident du IIIe au VIIe siècle.* Paris: Études Augustiniennes, 1988.

———. *Chrétiens d'Afrique à l'aube de la paix constantinienne: les premiers échos de la grande persecution.* Collection des études augustiniennes. Série Antiquité 164. Paris: Institut d'Études Augustiniennes, 2000.

———. *Loca Sanctorum Africae: le culte des martyrs en Afrique du IVe au VIIe siècle.* Collection de l'École française de Rome 58. Rome: École française de Rome, 1982.

Effros, Bonnie. *Caring for Body and Soul: Burial and the Afterlife in the Merovingian World.* University Park: Pennsylvania State University Press, 2002.

———. "*De partibus Saxoniae* and the Regulation of Mortuary Custom: A Carolingian Campaign of Christianization or the Suppression of Saxon Identity?" *Revue belge de philologie et d'histoire* 75, no. 2 (1997): 267–86.

Ennabli, Liliane. *Carthage: une métropole chrétienne du IVe à la fin du VIIe siècle.* Études d'Antiquités africaines. Paris: Éditions du CNRS, 1997.

Étaix, Raymond. "Nouvelle collection de sermons rassemblée par saint Césaire." *Revue bénédictine* 37 (1977): 7–33.

Faivre, Alexandre. "La documentation canonico-liturgique de l'Église ancienne." *Revue des sciences religieuses* 54 (1980): 204–19, 237–97.

———. *Naissance d'une hiérarchie: les premières étapes du cursus clérical*. Théologie historique 40. Paris: Beauchesne, 1977.

———. *Ordonner la fraternité: pouvoir d'innover et retour à l'ordre dans l'Église ancienne*. Histoire. Paris: Éditions du Cerf, 1992.

Federer, Konrad. *Liturgie und Glaube: eine theologiegeschichtliche Untersuchung*. Paradosis 4. Fribourg: Paulusverlag, 1950.

Fédou, Michel. *Christianisme et religion païenne: dans le Contre Celse d'Origène*. Théologie historique 81. Paris: Beauchesne, 1988.

Feissel, Denis. "Notes d'épigraphie chrétienne. 2." *Bulletin de correspondance hellénique* 101 (1977): 224–28.

———. "Notes d'épigraphie chrétienne. 4." *Bulletin de correspondance hellénique* 104 (1980): 459–72.

———. *Recueil des inscriptions chrétiennes de Macédoine du IIIe au VIe siècle*. Bulletin de Correspondance Hellénique. Supplément 8. Paris: De Boccard, 1983.

Ferrua, Antonio. "Gli anatemi dei padri di Nicea." *Civiltà cattolica* 108 (1957): 378–97.

———. "Il Cimitero dei nostri morti." *Civiltà Cattolica* 109 (1958): 273–85. Reprinted in *Scritti vari di epigrafia e antichità cristiane*, 284–96. Inscriptiones Christianae Italiae. Subsidia 3. Bari: Edipuglia, 1991.

———. *Note al Thesaurus linguae latinae: addenda et corrigenda*. Bari: Edipuglia, 1986.

———. *Le pitture della nuova catacomba di via Latina*. Monumenti di antichità cristiana 2, no. 8. Vatican City: Pontificio Istituto di Archeologia Cristiana, 1960.

Février, Paul-Albert. "Le culte des morts dans les communautés chrétiennes durant le IIIe siècle." In *Atti del IX Congresso Internazionale di archeologia cristiana, Roma, 21–27 settembre 1975*, 1:211–74. Studi di antichità cristiana 32, no. 1. Vatican City: Pontificio Istituto di archeologia cristiana, 1978.

———. *La méditerranée de Paul-Albert Février*. Collection de l'École française de Rome 225. Rome: École française de Rome/Aix-en-Provence: Université de Provence, 1996.

———. "La mort chrétienne." In *Segni e riti nella chiesa altomedievale occidentale: XXXIII Settimana di studio del Centro italiano sull'alto medioevo, 11–17 aprile 1985*, 881–952. Settimane di studio del Centro italiano di studi sull'alto medioevo 33. Spoleto: Centro italiano di studi sull'alto medioevo, 1987.

———. "Natale Petri de cathedra." *Comptes rendus de l'Académie des Inscriptions et Belles Lettres* (1977): 514–31.

———. "Quelques aspects de la prière pour les morts." *Senefiance* 10 (1981): 255–82.

Fiocchi Nicolai, Vincenzo. "Strutture funerarie ed edifici di culto paleocristiani di Roma dal III al VI secolo." In *Le iscrizioni dei cristiani in Vaticano*, 121–41. Inscriptiones Sanctae Sedis 2. Vatican City: Monumenti, Musei e Gallerie Pontificie, 1997.

Fiocchi Nicolai, Vincenzo, and Jean Guyon. "Relire Styger: les origines de l'*area* I du cimetière de Calliste et la crypte des papes." In *Origine delle catacombe romane*, edited by Vincenzo Fiocchi Nicolai and Jean Guyon, 121–61. Sussidi allo studio delle antichità cristiane 18. Vatican City: Pontificio Istituto di archeologia cristiana, 2006.

Flambart, Jean-Marc. "Éléments pour une approche financière de la mort dans les classes populaires du Haut-Empire: analyse du budget de quelques collèges funéraires de Rome et d'Italie." In *La mort, les morts et l'au-delà dans le monde romain: actes du colloque de Caen, 20–22 novembre 1985,* edited by F. Hinard, 209–244. Caen: Université de Caen, 1987.

Foucault, Michel. *History of Sexuality,* vol. 3, *The Care of the Self.* Translated by Robert Hurley. New York: Vintage, 1990.

Franchi de' Cavalieri, Pio. "Il κοιμητηρίον di Antiochia." In *Note agiografiche.* 7, 146–53. Studi e testi 49. Rome: Tipografia Vaticana, 1928.

Frankfurter, David. "The Cult of the Martyrs in Egypt before Constantine: The Evidence of the Coptic Apocalypse of Elijah." *Vigiliae Christianae* 48 (1994): 25–47.

Freistedt, Emil. *Altchristliche Totengedächtnisstage und ihre Beziehung zum Jenseitsglauben und Totenkult der Antike.* Liturgiewiessenschaftliche Quellen und Forschungen 24. Münster, Germany: Aschendorff, 1928.

Frend, William H. C. *Martyrdom and Persecution in the Early Church: A Study of Conflict from the Maccabees to Donatus.* Oxford: Oxford University Press, 1965.

Frugoni, Arsenio. *Arnaud de Brescia nelle fonti del secolo XII.* Rome: Nella sede dell'Istituto, 1954.

Gafni. Isaiah. "Reinterment in the Land of Israel: Notes on the Origin and Development of the Custom." *Jerusalem cathedra* 1 (1981): 96–104.

Gagé, Jean. *Les classes sociales dans l'Empire romain.* 2nd ed. Bibliothèque historique. Paris: Payot, 1971.

Gaiffier, Baudouin de. "La lecture des Actes de martyrs dans la prière liturgique en Occident: à propos du passionnaire hispanique." *Analecta Bollandiana* 73 (1954): 134–66.

Gaiffier, Baudouin de. "La lecture des Passions de martyrs à Rome avant le IXe siècle." *Analecta Bollandiana* 87 (1969): 63–78.

Galinié, Henri, and Elizabeth Zadora-Rio, eds. *Archéologie du cimetière chrétien: actes du 2e colloque A.R.C.H.E.A. (Orléans, 29 septembre–1er octobre 1994).* Revue archéologique du Centre de la France. Supplément 11. Tours: Féracf/Simarre, 1996.

Gascou, Jean. "La Vie de Patermouthios, moine et fossoyeur (*Historia monachorum* X)." In *Itinéraires d'Égypte: mélanges offerts au père Maurice Martin s. j.,* edited by Christian Décobert, 107–14. Bibliothèque d'étude 107. Cairo: Institut français d'archéologie orientale du Caire, 1992.

Gaudemet, Jean. *Les sources du droit de l'Église en Occident du IIe au VIIe siècle.* Initiations au christianisme ancien. Paris: Éditions du Cerf/Éditions CNRS, 1985.

Giorgi, Giuseppe. *Le multe sepolcrali in diritto romano.* Bologna: Beltrami, 1910.

Giovannini, Adalberto, and Marguerite Hirt. "L'inscription de Nazareth: nouvelle interprétation." *Zeitschrift für Papyrologie und Epigraphik* 124 (1999): 107–32.

Giuntella, Anna Maria, Giuseppina Borghetti, and Daniela Stiaffini. *Mensae e riti funerari in Sardegna: la testimonianza di Cornus.* Mediterraneo tardoantico e medievale. Scavi e ricerche 1. Taranto: Scorpione, 1985.

Goffart, Walter. *Barbarian Tides: The Migration Age and the Later Roman Empire.* Middle Ages Series. Philadelphia: University of Pennsylvania Press, 2006.

Goodenough, Erwin Ramsdell. *Jewish Symbols in the Greco-Roman Period*, vol. 2, *The Archaeological Evidence from the Diaspora*. Bollingen series 37. New York: Pantheon, 1953.

Goodman, Martin, ed. *Jews in a Graeco-Roman World*. Oxford: Clarendon Press, 1998.

Gregg, Robert C. "Marking Religious and Ethnic Boundaries: Cases from the Ancient Golan Heights." *Church History* 69, no. 3 (2000): 519–57.

Grégoire, Henri. *Recueil des inscriptions grecques-chrétiennes d'Asie mineure*. Paris: Leroux, 1922.

Grzybek, Erhard, Marta Sordi. "L'Édit de Nazareth et la politique de Néron à l'égard des chrétiens." *Zeitschrift für Papyrologie und Epigraphik* 120 (1998): 279–91.

Gsell, Stéphane. *Les monuments antiques de l'Algérie*. Paris: Fontemoing, 1901.

Guarducci, Margherita. *Epigrafia greca. 4, Epigrafi sacre pagane e cristiane*. Rome: Istituto poligrafico dello Stato, 1978.

Guyon, Jean. *Le cimetière aux deux lauriers: recherches sur les catacombes romaines*. Bibliothèque des Écoles françaises d'Athènes et de Rome 264. Rome: École française de Rome, 1987.

———. "La vente des tombes à travers l'épigraphie de la Rome chrétienne (IIIe–VIIe siècles): le rôle des *fossores, mansionarii, praepositi* et prêtres." *Mélanges de l'École française de Rome. Antiquité* 86 (1974): 549–96.

Guzzo, Pier Giovanni. "Altre note tarantine." *Taras* 12 (1992): 135–41.

Hachlili, Rachel. *Ancient Jewish Art and Archaeology in the Diaspora*. Handbuch der Orientalistik. 1, Nahe und Mittlere Osten 35. Leiden: Brill, 1998.

Hamman, Adalbert. *La vie quotidienne des premiers chrétiens (95–197)*. Paris: Hachette, 1971.

Harl, Marguerite. "La dénonciation des festivités profanes dans le discours épiscopal et monastique, en Orient chrétien, à la fin du IVe siècle." In *La fête, pratique et discours: d'Alexandrie hellénistique à la mission de Besançon*, 123–47. Annales littéraires de l'Université de Besançon 262. Centre de recherches d'histoire ancienne 42. Paris: Les Belle Lettres, 1981.

Harland, Philip A. *Associations, Synagogues, and Congregations: Claiming a Place in Ancient Mediterranean Society*. Minneapolis: Fortress Press, 2003.

———. "Honouring the Emperor or Assailing the Beast: Participation in Civic Life among Associations (Jewish, Christian and Other) in Asia minor and the Apocalypse of John." *Journal for the Study of the New Testament* 77 (2000): 99–121.

Harnack, Adolf von. *Die Mission und Ausbreitung des Christentums in den ersten drei Jahrhunderten*. Leipzig: Hinrichs, 1902.

Harries, Jill. "Death and the Dead in the Late Roman West." In *Death in Towns: Urban Responses to the Dying and the Dead, 100–600*, edited by Steven Bassett, 56–67. Leicester: Leicester University Press, 1993.

———. *Law and Empire in Late Antiquity*. Cambridge: Cambridge University Press, 1998.

Henten, Jan Willem van, Abraham Bij de Vaate. "Jewish or Non-Jewish? Some Remarks on the Identification of Jewish Inscriptions from Asia Minor." *Bibliotheca Orientalis* 53 (1996): 16–28.

Hermann-Mascard, Nicole. *Les reliques des saints: formation coutumière d'un droit.* Collection d'histoire institutionnelle et sociale 6. Paris: Klincksieck, 1975.

Herzog, Reinhart, ed. *Nouvelle histoire de la littérature latine. 5, Restauration et renouveau: la littérature latine de 284 à 374 après J.-C.* French version under the direction of Gérard Nauroy. Turnhout, Belgium: Brepols, 1993.

Hettner, Felix. "De Iove Dolicheno." Inaug.-diss., Bonn, 1877.

Hörig, Monica. *Corpus Cultus Iovis Dolicheni: (CCID).* Études préliminaires aux religions orientales dans l'Empire romain 106. Leiden: Brill, 1987.

Jeanes, Gordon P. *The Day Has Come! Easter and Baptism in Zeno of Verona.* Alcuin club collection 73. Collegeville, MN: Litugucal Press, 1995.

Johnson, Mark J. "Pagan-Christian Burial Practices of the Fourth Century: Shared Tombs?" *Journal of Early Christian Studies* 5, no. 1 (1997): 37–59.

Johnson, Maxwell E. *The Prayers of Sarapion of Thmuis: A Literary, Liturgical, and Theological Analysis.* Orientalia Christiana Analecta 249. Rome: Pontificio Istituto Orientale, 1995.

Jungmann, Josef A. *The Place of Christ in Liturgical Prayer.* London: Chapman, 1989.

Juster, Jean. *Les juifs dans l'Empire romain: leur condition juridique, économique et sociale.* Paris: Geuthner, 1914.

Karpinski, Peter. *Annua die dormitionis: Untersuchungen zum christlichen Jahrgedächtnis der Toten auf dem Hintergrund antiken Brauchtums.* Europäische Hochschulschriften. Reihe 23, Theologie 300. Frankfurt am Main: Lang, 1987.

Kaser, Max. *Das römische Zivilprozessrecht.* 2. Aufl. neu bearb. von Karl Hackl. Handbuch der Altertumswissenschaft. 10, Rechtsgeschichte des Altertums. 3, 4. Munich: Beck, 1996.

———. "Zum römischen Grabrecht." *Zeitschrift der Savigny-Stiftung für Rechtsgeschichte. Romanistische Abteilung* 95 (1978): 15–92.

Keretztes, Paul. *Imperial Rome and the Christians,* vol. 2, *From the Severi to Constantine the Great.* Lanham, MD: University Press of America, 1989.

Klingshirn, William E. *Caesarius of Arles: The Making of a Christian Community in Late Antique Gaul.* Cambridge Studies in Medieval Life and Thought 22. Cambridge: Cambridge University Press, 1994.

Klöckener, Martin. "Die *recitatio nominum* im Hochgebet nach Augustins Schriften." In *Gratias agamus: Studien zum eucharistischen Hochgebet: für Balthasar Fischer,* edited by Andreas Heinz und Heinrich Rennings, 183–210. Pastoralliturgische Reihe. Freiburg: Herder, 1992.

Kloppenborg, John S. "Edwin Hatch, Churches and Collegia." In *Origins and Method: Towards a New Understanding of Judaism and Christianity: Essays in Honour of John C. Hurd,* edited by Bradley H. McLean, 212–238. Journal for the Study of the New Testament. Supplement series 86. Sheffield: JSOT Press, 1993.

Kloppenborg, John S., and Steven G. Wilson, eds. *Voluntary Associations in the Graeco-Roman World.* London: Routledge, 1996.

Koch, W. "Comment l'empereur Julien tacha de fonder une église païenne." *Revue belge de philologie et d'histoire* 6 (1927): 123–46; 7 (1928): 49–82, 511–50, 1363–85.

Kontorini, Vassa. *Inscriptions inédites relatives à l'histoire et aux cultes de Rhodes au IIe et au Ier s. av. J.-C.,* vol. 1, *Rhodiaka.* Archaeologia transatlantica 6. Publications d'histoire de l'art et d'archéologie de l'Université catholique de Louvain 42.

Louvain-la-Neuve: Institut supérieur d'archéologie et d'histoire de l'art, Collège Erasme, 1983.

Kotila, Heikki. *Memoria mortuorum: Commemoration of the Departed in Augustine*. Studia Ephemeridis Augustinianum 38. Rome: Institutum Patristicum Augustinianum, 1992.

Kraemer, Ross Shepard. "Jewish Tuna and Christian Fish: Identifying Religious Affiliation in Epigraphic Sources." *Harvard Theological Review* 84 (1991): 141–62.

Krammer, Josef. "Was bedeutet κοιμητηρίον in den Papyri?" *Zeitschrift für Papyrologie und Epigraphik* 80 (1990): 269–72.

Kyle, Donald G. *Spectacles of Death in Ancient Rome*. London: Routledge, 1998.

La Bonnardière, Anne-Marie. *Biblia Augustiniana. N. T., Les Épîtres aux Thessaloniciens, à Tite et à Philémon*. Paris: Études Augustiniennes, 1964.

———. *Biblia Augustiniana. A. T., Le livre de la Sagesse*. Paris: Études Augustiniennes, 1970.

Labriolle, Pierre de. *La réaction païenne: étude sur la polémique antichrétienne du Ier au VIe siècle*. 9th ed. Edited by Jean Zeiller. Paris: L'artisan du livre, 1948.

Lane, Eugene E., ed. *Corpus cultus Iovis Sabazii*. Études préliminaires aux religions orientales dans l'Empire romain 100. Leiden: Brill, 1985.

Lantier, Raymond. "Notes de topographie carthaginoise: cimetières romains et chrétiens de Carthage." *Comptes rendus de l'Académie des Inscriptions et Belles-Lettres* (1922): 22–28.

Lattimore, Richmond A. *Themes in Greek and Latin Epitaphs*. Illinois Studies in Language and Literature 28, nos. 1–2. Urbana: University of Illinois Press, 1942.

Lauwers, Michel. "Le cimetière dans le Moyen Âge latin: lieu sacré, saint et religieux." *Annales: histoire, sciences sociales* 54, no. 5 (1999): 1047–72.

———. *La mémoire des ancêtres, le souci des morts: morts, rites et société au Moyen Âge (Diocèse de Liège, XIe–XIIIe siècles)*. Théologie historique 103. Paris: Beauchesne, 1996.

———. *Naissance du cimetière: lieux sacrés et terre des morts dans l'Occident medieval*. Collection historique. Paris: Aubier, 2005.

———. "La sépulture des Patriarches (Genèse, 23): modèles scripturaires et pratiques sociales dans l'Occident médiéval ou Du bon usage d'un récit de fondation." *Studi Medievali* 37 (1996): 519–47.

Lazzarini, Sergio. "Tutela legale del sepolcro familiare romano." *Antichità altoadriatiche* 43 (1997): 83–97.

Le Blant, Edmond. "Mémoire sur les martyrs chrétiens et les supplices destructeurs du corps." *Mémoires de l'Institut national de France, Académie des Inscriptions et Belles Lettres* 28 (1874): 75–95.

Le Bohec, Yves. "Inscriptions juives et judaïsantes de l'Afrique romaine." *Antiquités africaines* 17 (1981): 165–207.

Lemerle, Paul. *Philippes et la Macédoine orientale à l'époque chrétienne et Byzantine*. Bibliothèque des Écoles françaises de Rome et d'Athènes 158. Paris: De Boccard, 1945.

Lenel, Otto. *Das Edictum perpetuum: ein Versuch zu seiner Wiederherstellung*. Aalen, Germany: Scientia Antiquariat, 1956.

Leon, Harry J. *The Jews of Ancient Rome* (1960). Updated ed. Peabody: Hendrickson, 1995.

———. "The Jews of Venusia." *Jewish Quarterly Review* 44 (1954): 267–84.

Lepelley, Claude. *Les cités de l'Afrique romaine au Bas-Empire*. Paris: Études augustiniennes, 1979.

———. "*Spes saeculi:* le milieu social d'Augustin et ses ambitions séculières avant sa conversion." In *Congresso internazionale su s. Agostino nel XVI centenario della conversione, Roma, 15–20 settembre 1986*, 1:99–117. Studia Ephemeridis Augustinianum 24. Rome: Institutum Patristicum Augustinianum, 1987.

Leveau, Philippe. "Une area funéraire de la nécropole occidentale de Cherchel." *Antiquités Africaines* 5 (1971–74): 73–152.

———. *Caesarea de Maurétanie: une ville romaine et ses campagnes*. Collection de l'École française de Rome 70. Rome: École française de Rome, 1984.

———. "Fouilles anciennes sur les nécropoles antiques de Cherchel." *Antiquités africaines* 12 (1978): 89–108.

———. "Nécropoles et monuments funéraires à Caesarea de Maurétanie." In *Römische Gräberstrassen: Selbstdarstellung—Status—Standart (Kolloquium in München vom 28. bis 30 Oktober 1985)*, edited by Henner von Hesberg and Paul Zanker, 281–90. Abhandlungen/Bayerische Akademie der Wissenschaften, Philosophisch-Historische Klasse. n. F. 96. Munich: Verlag der Bayerischen Akademie der Wissenschaften, 1987.

Liebeschuetz, J. H. W. G. *The Decline and Fall of the Roman City*. Oxford: Oxford University Press, 2001.

Lieu, Judith. "The Forging of a Christian Identity." *Mediterranean archaeology* 11 (1998): 72–82.

———. *Image and Reality: The Jews in the World of the Christians in the Second Century*. Edinburgh: T and T Clark, 1996.

Lieu, Judith, John North, and Tessa Rajak, eds. *The Jews among Pagans and Christians in the Roman World*. London: Routledge, 1992.

Lizzi, Rita. *Vescovi e strutture ecclesiastiche nella città tardoantica: (l'Italia Annonaria nel IV–V secolo d.C.)*. Biblioteca di Athenaeum 9. Como: New Press, 1989.

Longo, Giannetto. *Ricerche romanistiche*. Milan: Giuffrè, 1966.

———. "La sepoltura dei cristiani giustiziati." *Annali della Facoltà di Lettere e Filosofia, Università di Macerata* 22 (1958): 75–98.

MacMullen, Ramsay. *Christianity and Paganism in the Fourth to Eighth Centuries*. New Haven, CT: Yale University Press, 1997.

———. *Enemies of the Roman Order: Treason, Unrest, and Alienation in the Empire*. Cambridge, MA: Harvard University Press, 1966.

———. *Paganism in the Roman Empire*. New Haven, CT: Yale University Press, 1981.

Mancini, Gioacchino. "Scoperta di un antico sepolcreto cristiano nel territorio veliterno, in località Solluna." *Notizie degli scavi di antichità* (1924): 341–53.

Mandouze, André, ed. *Prosopographie chrétienne du Bas-Empire. 1, Prosopographie de l'Afrique chrétienne*. Paris: Éditions du CNRS, 1982.

Maraval, Pierre. *Lieux saints et pèlerinages d'Orient: histoire et géographie des origines à la conquête arabe*. Histoire. Paris: Éditions du Cerf, 1985.

Markschies, Christoph. "Wer schrieb die sogenannte Traditio Apostolica? neue Beobachtungen und Hypothesen zu einer kaum lösbaren Frage aus der altkirchlichen Literaturgeschichte." In *Tauffragen und Bekenntnis: Studien zur sogenannten 'Traditio Apostolica,' zu den 'Interrogationes de fide' und zum 'Römischen Glaubensbekenntnis,'* edited by Wolfram Kinzig, Christoph Markschies, and

Markul Vinzent, 1–74. Arbeiten zur Kirchengeschichte 74. Berlin: De Gruyter 1999.

Markus, Robert. *The End of Ancient Christianity.* Cambridge: Cambridge University Press, 1990.

———. *Gregory the Great and His World.* Cambridge: Cambridge University Press, 1997.

Martimort, Aimé-Georges. 1991. "Encore Hippolyte et la 'Tradition apostolique.'" *Bulletin de littérature ecclésiastique* 92 (1990): 133–44.

Martin, Annick. *Athanase d'Alexandrie et l'Église d'Égypte au IVe siècle (328–373).* Collection de l'École française de Rome 216. Rome: École française de Rome, 1996.

———. "L'image de l'évêque à travers les 'Canons d'Athanase': devoirs et réalités." In *L'évêque dans la cité du IVe au Ve siècle: image et autorité: actes de la table ronde organisée par l'Istituto patristico Augustinianum et l'École française de Rome (Rome, 1er et 2 décembre 1995),* edited by Éric Rebillard and Claire Sotinel, 59–70. Collection de l'École française de Rome 248. Rome: École française de Rome, 1998.

Martin, Dale B. "The Construction of the Ancient Family: Methodological Considerations." *Journal of Roman studies* 86 (1996): 40–60.

Martin, Susan D. *The Roman Jurists and the Organization of Private Building in the Late Republic and the Early Empire.* Collection Latomus 204. Brussels: Latomus, 1989.

Martroye, François. "Les parabalani." *Bulletin de la Société Nationale des Antiquaires de France* (1923): 275–81.

Mathieu, Jean-Marie. "Horreur du cadavre et philosophie dans le monde romain: le cas de la patristique grecque du IVe siècle." In *La mort, les morts et l'au-delà dans le monde romain: actes du colloque de Caen, 20–22 novembre 1985,* edited by François Hinard, 311–20. Caen: Université de Caen, 1987.

Matthews, John F. *Laying Down the Law: A Study of the Theodosian Code.* New Haven, CT: Yale University Press, 2000.

Mazar, Benjamin, ed. *Beth She'arim,* vol. 1, *Catacombs 1–4.* Jerusalem: Massada.

Mazzarino, Santo. *Il pensiero storico classico,* 2 vols. Collezione storica. Bari: Laterza, 1968.

McCready, Wayne O. "Ekklesia and Voluntary Association." In *Voluntary Associations in the Graeco-Roman World,* edited by John S. Kloppenborg and Steven G. Wilson, 59–73. London: Routledge, 1996.

McLean, Bradley H. "The Agrippinilla Inscription: Religious Associations and Early Church Formation." In *Origins and Method: Towards a New Understanding of Judaism and Christianity: Essays in Honour of John C. Hurd,* edited by Bradley H. McLean, 239–70. *Journal for the Study of the New Testament.* Supplement series 86. Sheffield: JSOT Press, 1993.

McNeill, William H. *Plagues and Peoples.* New York: Doubleday, 1989.

Meeks, Wayne A. *The First Urban Christians: The Social World of the Apostle Paul.* New Haven, CT: Yale University Press, 2003.

Mercati, Giovanni. "D'alcuni nuovi sussidi per la critica del testo di S. Cipriano." *Studi e documenti di storia e diritto* 19 (1898): 321–63; 20 (1899): 61–88.

———. *Opere minori.* Vatican City: Biblioteca apostolica vaticana, 1937.

Merlat, Pierre. *Jupiter Dolichenus: essai d'interprétation et de synthèse.* Publications de l'Institut d'art et d'archéologie de l'Université de Paris 5. Paris: Presses universitaires de France, 1960.

Metzger, Marcel. "Nouvelles perspectives pour la prétendue *Tradition apostolique.*" *Ecclesia Orans* 5 (1988): 241–59.

Meyers, Eric M. "Report on the Excavations at the Venosa Catacombs 1981." *Vetera Christianorum* 20 (1983): 445–59.

Miles, Margaret. *Augustine on the Body.* Dissertation Series, American Academy of Religion 31. Missoula, MT: Scholars Press, 1979.

Millet, Gabriel. "Recherches au Mont-Athos." *Bulletin de correspondance hellénique* 29 (1905): 55–141.

Miranda, Elena. "La comunità giudaica di Hierapolis di Frigia." *Epigraphica Anatolica* 31 (1999): 109–55.

Momigliano, Arnaldo. "Severo Alessandro *archisynagogus:* una conferma alla *Historia Augusta.*" *Athenaeum* 12 (1934): 151–53.

Mommsen, Theodor. *De collegiis et sodaliciis Romanorum.* Kiel, Germany: Libraria Schwersiana, 1843.

Monat, Pierre. *Lactance et la Bible: une propédeutique latine à la lecture de la Bible dans l'Occident constantinien.* Paris: Études augustiniennes, 1982.

Monceaux, Paul. *Histoire littéraire de l'Afrique chrétienne: depuis les origines jusqu'à l'invasion arabe,* 7 vols. Paris: Leroux, 1901–3.

Morris, Ian. *Death-Ritual and Social Structure in Classical Antiquity.* Key Themes in Ancient History. Cambridge: Cambridge University Press, 1992.

Mossay, Claude. *La mort et l'au-delà dans Saint Grégoire de Nazianze.* Louvain, Belgium: Publications universitaires de Louvain, 1996.

Mrozek, Stanislaw. "À propos de la répartition chronologique des inscriptions latines sous le Haut-Empire." *Epigraphica* 35 (1973): 113–18.

Munier, Charles. "Cinq canons inédits du Concile d'Hippone du 8 octobre 393." *Revue de droit canonique* 12 (1968): 16–29.

Münz, Dr. "Anatheme und Verwünschungen auf altchristliche Monumenten." *Annalen des Vereins für Nassauische Altertumskunde und Geschichtsforschung* 14 (1877): 169–81.

Nautin, Pierre. *Hippolyte et Josippe: contribution à l'histoire de la littérature chrétienne du IIIe siècle.* Paris: Éditions du Cerf, 1947.

Newton, Derek. *Deity and Diet: The Dilemma of Sacrificial Food at Corinth.* Journal for the Study of the New Testament. Supplement series 169. Sheffield: Sheffield Academic Press, 1998.

Nicholson, Oliver. "The 'Pagan Churches' of Maximinus Daia and Julian the Apostate." *Journal of Ecclesiastical History* 45 (1994): 1–10.

Nicolet, Claude, Robert Ilbert, and Jean-Claude Depaule, eds. *Mégapoles méditerranéennes: géographie urbaine retrospective. Actes du colloque organisé par l'École française de Rome et la Maison méditerranéenne des sciences de l'homme (Rome, 8–11 mai 1996).* Collection de l'École française de Rome 261. L'atelier méditerranéen. Paris: Maisonneuve et Larose/Rome: École française de Rome, 2000.

Nock, Arthur D. "Cremation and Burial in the Roman Empire." *Harvard Theological Review* 25 (1932): 321–59.

———. *Essays on Religion and the Ancient World,* edited by Zeph Stewart. Cambridge, MA: Harvard University Press, 1972.

———. "Tomb Violations and Pontifical Law." *Journal of Biblical Literature* 60 (1941): 88–95.

Noethlichs, Karl L. "Spätantike Jenseitsvorstellungen im Spiegel des staatlichen Gräberschutzes: zur Novelle 23 Kaiser Valentinians III." In *Jenseitsvorstellungen in Antike und Christentum: Gedenkschrift für Alfred Stuiber*, 47–54. Jahrbuch für Antike und Christentum. Ergänzungsband 9. Münster, Germany: Aschendorff, 1982.

North, John. "The Development of Religious Pluralism." In *The Jews among pagans and Christian in the Roman World*, edited by Judith Lieu, John North, and Tessa Rajak, 174–93. London: Routledge, 1992.

Noy, David. "Where Were the Jews of the Diaspora Buried?" In *Jews in a Graeco-Roman World*, edited by Martin Goodman, 75–89. Oxford: Clarendon Press, 1998.

———. "Writing in Tongues: The Use of Greek, Latin and Hebrew in Jewish Inscriptions from Roman Italy." *Journal of Jewish Studies* 48 (1997): 300–311.

Ntedika, Joseph. *L'évocation de l'au-delà dans la prière pour les morts: étude de patristique et de liturgie latine (IVe–VIIIe s.)*. Recherches africaines de théologie 2. Louvain: Nauwelaerts, 1971.

———. *L'évolution de la doctrine du purgatoire chez saint Augustin*. Publications de l'Université Lovanium de Léopoldville 20. Paris: Études Augustiniennes, 1966.

Nuove Ricerche su Ippolito. Studia Ephemeridis Augustinianum 30. Rome: Institutum patristicum Augustinianum, 1989.

Nussbaum, Otto. *Die Aufbewahrung der Eucharistie*. Theophaneia 29. Bonn: Hanstein, 1979.

O'Callaghan, José. "Sobre PGrenf. II 73 (III/IV P)." *Zeitschrift für Papyrologie und Epigraphik* 67 (1987): 124–28.

Ogle, Marbury Bladen. "The Sleep of Death." *Memoires of the American Academy in Rome* 11 (1933): 81–117.

Pailler, Jean-Marie. "'Sépulture interdite aux non bachisés': dissidence orphique et vêture dionysiaque." In Jean-Marie Pailler, *Bacchus: figures et pouvoirs*, 111–26. Histoire. Paris: Les Belles Lettres, 1995.

Parrot, André. *Malédictions et violations de tombes*. Paris: Geuthner, 1939.

Partoens, Gert. "La collection de sermons augustiniens 'De verbis apostoli': introduction et liste des manuscrits les plus anciens." *Revue Bénédictine* 111 (2001): 318–52.

Patlagean, Evelyne. *Pauvreté économique et pauvreté sociale à Byzance, 4e–7e siècles*. Civilisations et sociétés 48. Paris: Mouton, 1977.

Patterson, John R. "Patronage, Collegia and Burial in Imperial Rome." In *Death in Towns: Urban Responses to the Dying and the Dead, 100–600*, edited by Steven Bassett, 15–27. Leicester, England: Leicester University Press, 1993.

Paverd, Frans van de. "Anaphoral Intercessions, Epiclesis and Communion-Rites in John Chrysostom." *Orientalia Christiana Periodica* 49 (1983): 303–39.

———. *Zur geschichte der Messliturgie in Antiocheia und Konstantinopel gegen Ende des vierten Jahrhunderts: Analyse der Quellen bei Johannes Chrysostomos*. Orientalia Christiana Analecta 187. Rome: Pontificium Institutum Orientalium Studiorum, 1970.

Paxton, Frederick. *Christianizing Death: The Creation of a Ritual Process in Early Medieval Europe*. Ithaca, NY: Cornell University Press, 1990.

Pergola, Philippe. *Le catacombe romane: storia e topografia*. Edited by P. M. Barbini. Argomenti 8. Rome: Carocci, 1998.

Pergola, Philippe. *Les cimetières chrétiens de Rome depuis leurs origines jusqu'au neuvième siècle: le cas du 'praedium Domitillae' et de la catacombe homonyme sur la "Via Ardeatina."* PhD diss., Univeristy of Aix-en-Provence, 1992.

———. "*Mensores frumentarii christiani* et annone à la fin de l'Antiquité (relecture d'un cycle de peintures)." *Rivista di archeologia cristiana* 66 (1990): 167–84.

Perraymond, Myla. "Formule imprecatorie ('APAI) nelle iscrizioni funerarie paleocristiane." *Quaderni dell'Istituto di lingue e letteratura latina* 2–3 (1980–81): 115–45.

———. "Tobia e Tobiolo nell'esegesi della iconografia dei primi secoli." *Bessarione* 6 (1988): 141–154.

Perrin Michel-Yves. "L'invention du cimetière: le cas romain." *Communio* 20 (1995): 99–113.

Perry, Jonathan S. *A Death in the Familia: The Funerary Colleges of the Roman Empire.* Unpublished diss., University of North Carolina–Chapel Hill, 1999.

———. *The Roman Collegia: The Modern Evolution of an Ancient Concept.* Mnemosyne Supplements 277. Leiden: Brill, 2006.

Petitmengin, Pierre. "Le *Codex Veronensis* de saint Cyprien: philologie et histoire de la philology." *Revue des études latines* 46 (1968): 330–78.

Pétré, Hélène. *Caritas: étude sur le vocabulaire latin de la charité chrétienne.* Études et documents 22. Louvain: Spicilegium Sacrum Lovaniense, 1948.

Petzl, Georg. "Die epigramme des Gregor von Nazianz über Grabräuberei und das Hierothesion des kommagenischen Königs Antiochos I." *Epigraphica Anatolica* 10 (1987): 117–29.

Pietri, Charles. "Appendice prosopographique à la Roma Christiana (311–440)." *Mélanges de l'École française de Rome. Antiquité* 89 (1977): 371–415.

———. "Régions ecclésiastiques et paroisses romaines." In *Actes du XIe Congrès International d'Archéologie Chrétienne*, 1035–62. Collection de l'École française de Rome 123. Rome: École française de Rome, 1989.

———. *Roma Christiana: recherches sur l'Église de Rome, son organisation, sa politique, son idéologie de Miltiade à Sixte III (311–440).* Bibliothèque des Écoles françaises de Rome et d'Athènes 224. Rome: École française de Rome, 1976.

Poe, Alison C. *The Third-Century Mausoleum ("Hypogeum") of the Aurelii in Rome: Pagan or Mixed-Religion Collegium Tomb.* Unpublished diss., Brown University, 2007.

Poinsotte, Jean-Michel. "Commodien dit de Gaza." *Revue des études latines* 74 (1996): 270–281.

Porton, Gary G. *Goyim: Gentiles and Israelites in Mishnah-Tosefta.* Brown Judaic Studies 155. Atlanta: Scholars Press, 1988.

Pjrinz, Friedrich. "Die Bischöfliche Stadtherrschaft im Frankenreich vom 5. bis zum 7. Jahrhundert." *Historische Zeitschrift* 217 (1974): 1–35.

Quasten, Johannes. *Music and Worship in Pagan and Christian Antiquity* (1930). Translated by B. Ramsey. NPM studies in Church Music and Liturgy. Washington, DC: National Association of Pastoral Musicians, 1983.

———. "*Vetus superstitio et nova religio:* The Problem of *refrigerium* in the Ancient Church of North Africa." *Harvard Theological Review* 33 (1940): 253–66.

Raepsaet-Charlier, Marie-Thérèse. *Prosopographie des femmes de l'ordre sénatorial (Ier–IIe siècle).* Louvain: Peeters, 1987.

Rajak, Tessa. "Archisynagogoi: Office, Title and Social Status in the Greco-Jewish Synagogue." *Journal of Roman Studies* 83 (1993): 75–93.
———. "Inscription and Context: Reading the Jewish Catacombs of Rome." In *Studies in Early Jewish Epigraphy*, edited by Jan Willem van Henten and Pieter Willem van der Horst, 226–41. Arbeiten zur Geschichte des antiken Judentums und des Urchristentums 21. Leiden: Brill, 1994.
———. "The Jewish Community and Its Boundaries." In *The Jews among Pagans and Christians in the Roman World*, edited by Judith Lieu, John North, and Tessa Rajak, 9–21. London: Routledge, 1992.
———. "The Rabbinic Dead and the Diaspora Dead at Beth She'arim." In *The Talmud Yerushalmi and Graeco-Roman culture*, edited by Peter Schäfer, 349–66. Texte und Studien zum Antiken Judentum 71. Tübingen: Mohr Siebeck, 1998.
Rasi, Pietro. "Donazione di Costantino e di Anastasio alla chiesa di S. Sofia per le spese funeralizie a Constantinopoli." In *Festschrift für Leopold Wenger zu seinem 70. Geburtstag*, 2:269–82. Münchener Beiträge zur Papyrusforschung und antiken Rechtsgeschichte, 35. Munich: Beck, 1945.
Raubitschek, Antony Erich. "Early Christians Epitaphs from Athens." *Hesperia* 16 (1947): 1–54.
Reasoner, Mark. *The Strong and the Weak: Romans 14.1–15.13 in Context*. Monograph Series, Society for New Testament Studies 103. Cambridge: Cambridge University Press, 1999.
Rebillard, Éric. "Les *areae* carthaginoises (Tertullien, *Ad Scapulam* 3, 1): cimetières communautaires ou enclos funéraires de chrétiens?" *Mélanges de l'École française de Rome. Antiquité* 108, no. 1 (1996): 175–89.
———. "La conversion de l'Empire romain selon Peter Brown (note critique)." *Annales: histoire, sciences sociales* 54, no. 4 (1999): 813–23.
———. "L'Église de Rome et le développement des catacombes: à propos de l'origine des cimetières chrétiens." *Mélanges de l'École française de Rome. Antiquité* 109, no. 2 (1997): 741–63.
———. "Église et sépulture dans l'Antiquité tardive (Occident latin, 3e–6e siècles)." *Annales: histoire, sciences socials* 54, no. 5 (1999): 1027–46.
———. "Les formes de l'assistance funéraire dans l'Empire romain et leur évolution dans l'Antiquité tardive." *Antiquité tardive* 7 (1999): 269–82.
———. *In hora mortis: évolution de la pastorale chrétienne de la mort aux IVe et Ve siècles dans l'Occident latin*. Bibliothèque des Écoles françaises d'Athènes et de Rome 283. Rome: École française de Rome, 1994.
———. "Interaction between the Preacher and His Audience: The Case-Study of Augustine's Preaching on Death." In *Studia Patristica. 31*, edited by Elizabeth A. Livingstone, 86–96. Louvain, Belgium: Peeters, 1997.
———. "KOIMHTHRION et COEMETERIUM: tombe, tombe sainte, nécropole." *Mélanges de l'École française de Rome. Antiquité* 105, no. 2 (1993): 975–1001.
———. "*Nec deserere memorias suorum*: Augustine and the Family-Cased Commemoration of the Dead." *Augustinian Studies* 36, no. 1 (2005): 99–111.
Rentinck, Pietro. *La cura pastorale in Antiochia nel IV secolo*. Analecta Gregoriana 178. Rome: Università Gregoriana, 1970.
Reseghetti, Silvia. "Il provvedimento di Settimio Severo sui collegia 'religionis causa' e i cristiani." *Rivista di Storia della Chiesa in Italia* 42 (1988): 357–64.

Reynolds, Philip L. *Marriage in the Western Church: The Christianization of Marriage during the Patristic and Early Medieval Periods.* Supplements to Vigiliae Christianae 24. Leiden: Brill, 1994.
Ricerche su Ippolito. Studia Ephemeridis Augustinianum 13. Rome: Istituto Patristico Augustinianum, 1977.
Ritti, Tullia. "Nuovi dati su una nota epigrafe sepolcrale con stefanotico da Hierapolis di Frigia." *Scienze dell'antichità* 6–7 (1992–93): 41–68.
Robert, Louis. "Les inscriptions de Thessalonique." *Revue de philologie* 100 (1974): 180–246.
Robertis, Francesco Maria de. *Storia delle corporazioni e del regime associativo nel mondo romano.* Bari, Italy: Adriatica, 1973.
Rohde, Erwin. *Psyche: The Cult of Soul and Belief in Immortality among the Greeks.* Freeport, NY: Books for Libraries Press, 1928.
Rordorf, Willy. "Aux origines du culte des martyrs." *Irenikon* 65 (1972): 315–31.
Rossi, Anna Maria. "Ricerche sulle multe sepolcrali romane." *Rivista di storia dell'antichità* 5 (1975): 111–59.
Rousseau, Philip. *Basil of Caesarea.* Transformation of the Classical Heritage 20. Berkeley and Los Angeles: University of California Press, 1994.
Rousselle, Aline. "La persécution des chrétiens à Alexandrie au IIIe siècle." *Revue historique du droit français et étranger* 52 (1974): 222–51.
———. *Porneia: On Desire and Body in Antiquity.* Translated by Felicia Pheasant. Oxford: Blackwell, 1988.
Rush, Alfred Clement. *Death and Burial in Christian Antiquity.* Studies in Christian Antiquity 1. Washington, DC: Catholic University of America Press, 1941.
Rutgers, Leonard Victor. "Archeological Evidence for the Interaction of Jews and Non-Jews in Late Antiquity." *American Journal of Archeology* 96 (1992): 101–18.
———. "Dating the Jewish Catacombs of Ancient Rome." In *The Hidden Heritage of Diaspora Judaism,* 45–71. Contributions to Biblical Exegesis and Theology 20. Louvain: Peeters, 1998.
———. *The Jews in Late Ancient Rome: Evidence of Cultural Interaction in the Roman Diaspora.* Religions in the Graeco-Roman World 12. New York: Brill, 1995.
———. "Überlegungen zu den jüdischen Katakomben Roms." *Jahrbuch für Antike und Christentum* 33 (1990): 140–57.
Salamito, Jean-Marie. "La christianisation et les nouvelles règles de la vie sociale." In *Histoire du christianisme des origines à nos jours. 2, Naissance d'une chrétienté (250–430),* edited by Charles and Luce Pietri, 675–717. Paris: Desclée/Fayard, 1995.
———. "Les dendrophores dans l'Empire chrétien: à propos de Code Théodosien, XIV, 8, 1 et XVI, 10, 20, 2." *Mélanges de l'École française de Rome. Antiquité* 99 (1987): 991–1018.
Saller, Richard, and Brent D. Shaw. "Tombstones and Roman Family Relations in the Principate: Civilians, Soldiers and Slaves." *Journal of Roman Studies* 74 (1984): 124–56.
Salzman, Michele R. *On Roman Time: The Codex-Calendar of 354 and the Rhythms of Urban Life in Late Antiquity.* Transformations of the Classical Heritage 17. Berkeley and Los Angeles: University of California Press, 1990.

Saxer, Victor. "La date de la lettre 1 (66) de Cyprien au clergé et au peuple de Furni." *Revue des Études Augustiniennes* 23 (1977): 56–62.

———. *Morts, martyrs, reliques en Afrique chrétienne aux premiers siècles: les témoignages de Tertullien, Cyprien et Augustin à la lumière de l'archéologie africaine.* Théologie historique 55. Paris: Beauchesne, 1980.

———. *Vie liturgique et quotidienne à Carthage vers le milieu du IIIe siècle: le témoignage de saint Cyprien et de ses contemporains d'Afrique.* 2nd ed. Studi di antichità cristiana 29. Vatican City: Pontificio Istituto di archeologia cristiana, 1984.

Scheid, John. "Communauté et communauté: réflexions sur quelques ambiguïtés d'après l'exemple des thiases de l'Égypte romaine." In *Les communautés religieuses dans le monde gréco-romain. Essai de définition,* edited by Nicole Belayche and Simon C. Mimouni, 61–74. Bibliothèque de l'École des Hautes Études. Sciences Religieuses 117. Paris: Brepols, 2003.

———. "Le délit religieux dans la Rome tardo-républicaine." In *Le délit religieux dans la cité antique: (Table ronde, Rome, 6–7 avril 1978),* 117–71. Collection de l'École française de Rome 48. Rome: École française de Rome, 1981.

———. *Quand faire, c'est croire: les rites sacrificiels des Romains.* Collection historique. Paris: Aubier, 2005.

———. *religion et piété à Rome.* Textes à l'appui. Paris: Éditions La Découverte, 1985.

Schmitt, Jean-Claude. *Ghosts in the Middle ages: The Living and the Dead in Medieval Society.* Translated by Teresa Lavender Fagan. Chicago: University of Chicago Press, 1998.

Schöllgen, Gregor. *Die Anfänge der Professionalisierung des Klerus und das kirchliche Amt in der Syrischen Didaskalie.* Jahrbuch für Antike und Christentum. Ergänzungsband 26. Münster: Aschendorff, 1998.

Schrumpf, Stefan. *Bestattung und Bestattungswesen in Römischen Reich: Ablauf, soziale Dimension und ökonomische Bedeutung der Totenfürsorge in lateinischen Westen.* Göttingen: Bonn University Press, 2006.

Schwabe, Moshe, and Baruch Lifschitz, eds. *Beth She'arim,* vol. 2, *The Greek Inscriptions.* Jerusalem: Massada, 1974.

Seland, Torrey. "Philo and the Clubs and Associations of Alexandria." In *Voluntary Associations in the Graeco-Roman world,* edited by John S. Kloppenborg and Steven G. Wilson, 110–27. London: Routledge, 1996.

Shaw, Brent D. "Latin Funerary Epigraphy and Family Life in the Later Roman Empire." *Historia* 33 (1984): 457–97.

Simonetti, Manlio. "Una nuova proposta su Ippolito." *Augustinianum* 36 (1996): 13–46.

———. "Roma cristiana tra vescovi e presbiteri." In *Origine delle catacombe romane,* edited by Vincenzo Fiocchi Nicolai and Jean Guyon, 29–40. Sussidi allo studio delle antichità cristiane 18. Vatican City: Pontificio Istituto di archeologia cristiana, 2006.

Sirks, Adrian J. B. *Food for Rome: The Legal Structure of the Transportation and Processing of Supplies for the Imperial Distributions in Rome and Constantinople.* Studia Amstelodamensia ad epigraphicam, ius antiquum et papyrologicam, pertinentia 31. Amsterdam: Gieben, 1991.

Smith, Roland B. E. *Julian's Gods: Religion and Philosophy in the Thought and Action of Julian the Apostat.* London: Routledge, 1995.

Sokolowski, Franciszek. *Lois sacrées des cités grecques. Supplément.* École française d'Athènes. Travaux et mémoires 11. Paris: De Boccard, 1962.

Sordi, Marta. *I cristiani e l'Impero romano.* Milan: Jaca, 1984.

Sordi, Marta, and Maria Luisa Cavigiolo. "Un'antica 'chiesa domestica' di Roma? (*Il collegium quod est in domo Sergiae L. F. Paullinae*)." *Rivista di Storia della Chiesa in Italia* 25 (1971): 369–74.

———. "Sergia Paulina e il suo *collegium.*" *Rendiconti dell'Istituto Lombardo, Scienze e Lettere* 113 (1979): 14–20.

Sotinel, Claire. "Le personnel épiscopal: enquête sur la puissance de l'évêque dans la cité." In *L'évêque dans la cité du IVe au Ve siècle: image et autorité: actes de la table ronde organisée par l'Istituto patristico Augustinianum et l'École française de Rome (Rome, 1er et 2 décembre 1995),* edited by Éric Rebillard and Claire Sotinel, 105–26. Collection de l'École française de Rome 248. Rome: École française de Rome, 1998.

Souza, Manuel de. *Religiosus ou les métamorphoses du "religieux" dans le monde romain, de la fin de la République à l'Empire chrétien (IIe siècle av. J.-C.-début du Ve siècle apr. J.-C.).* PhD diss., Université François Rabelais, Tours, 2001.

Stark, Rodney. "Epidemics, Networks, and the Rise of Christianity." In *Social Networks in the Early Christian Environment: Issues and Methods for Social History.* Edited by L. M. White, 159–75. Semeia 56. Atlanta: Scholars Press, 1992.

———. *The Rise of Christianity: A Sociologist Reconsiders History.* Princeton, NJ: Princeton University Press, 1996.

Stern, Karen B. *Inscribing Devotion and Death: Archaeological Evidence for Jewish Populations of North Africa.* Religions in the Graeco-Roman World 161. Leiden: Brill, 2008.

Straub, Johannes. *Heidnische Geschichtsapologetik in der christlichen Spätantike: Untersuchungen über Zeit und Tendenz der Historia Augusta.* Antiquitas. 4, Beiträge zur Historia-Augusta-Forschung 1. Bonn: Habelt, 1963.

Strubbe, Johan H. M. *Arai epitymbioi: Imprecations against Desecrators of the Grave in the Greek Epitaphs of Asia Minor: A Catalogue.* Inschriften griechischer Städte aus Kleinasien 52. Bonn: Habelt, 1997.

———. "Cursed Be He that Moves My Bones." In *Magika Hiera: Ancient Greek Magic and Religion,* edited by Christopher A. Faraone and Dirk Obbink, 33–59. New York: Oxford University Press, 1991.

———. "Curses against Violation of the Grave in Jewish Epitaphs of Asia Minor." In *Studies in Early Jewish Epigraphy,* edited by Jan Willem van Henten and Pieter Willem van der Horst, 70–128. Arbeiten zur Geschichte des antiken Judentums und des Urchristentums 21. Leiden: Brill, 1994.

Suchecki, Zbigniew. "La cremazione nella legislazione della chiesa." *Apollinaris* 66 (1993): 653–728.

Taft, Robert F. *A History of the Liturgy of St. John Chrysostom,* vol. 4, *The Diptychs.* Orientalia Christiana Analecta 238. Rome: Pontificium Institutum Studiorum Orientalium, 1991.

———. "Toward the Origins of the Offertory Procession in the Syro-Byzantine East." *Orientalia Christiana Periodica* 36 (1970): 73–107.

Tam Tinh Tran, Vincent. *Le culte des divinités orientales en Campanie en dehors de Pompéi, de Stabies et d'Herculanum.* Études préliminaires aux religions orientales dans l'Empire romain 27. Leiden: Brill, 1972.

Testini, Pascquale. *Le catacombe e gli antichi cimiteri cristiani in Roma.* Roma cristiana 2. Bologna: Cappelli, 1966.

Theissen, Gerd. *The Social Setting of Pauline Christianity: Essays on Corinth*. Edited and translated with an introduction by John H. Schütz. Philadelphia: Fortress Press, 1982.

———. "Die Starken und die Schwaren in Korinth: soziologische Analyse eines theologischen Streites." *Evangelische Theologie* 35 (1975): 155–72.

Thomas, Yan. "*Corpus aut ossa aut cineres:* la chose religieuse et le commerce." *Micrologus* 7 (1999): 73–112.

Tosi, Massimo. "*Multae, comminationes, dirae* nelle iscrizioni funerarie transpadane pagane e cristiane." *Rivista archeologica dell'antica provincia e diocesi di Como* 175 (1993): 189–241.

Toynbee, Jocelyn M. C. *Death and Burial in the Roman World*. Baltimore: John Hopkins University Press, 1996.

Tran, Nicolas. *Les membres des associations romaines: le rang social des collegiati en Italie et en Gaules sous le Haut-Empire*. Collection de l'Ecole française de Rome 367. Rome: Ecole française de Rome, 2006.

Trebilco, Paul R. *Jewish Communities in Asia Minor*. Monograph Series, Society for New Testament Studies 69. New York: Cambridge University Press, 1991.

Treffort, Cécile. *L'Église carolingienne et la mort: christianisme, rites funéraires et pratiques commemoratives*. Collection d'histoire et d'archéologie médiévales 3. Lyon: Presses Universitaires de Lyon, 1996.

Trombley, Frank R. *Hellenic Religion and Christianization, c. 370–529*. 2nd ed. Leiden: Brill, 2001.

Truzzi, Carlo. *Zeno, Gaudenzio e Cromazio: testi e contenuti della predicazione cristiana per le chiese di Verona, Brescia e Aquileia (360–410 ca.)*. Testi e ricerche di scienze religiose 22. Brescia: Paideia, 1985.

Turcan, Robert. "Bacchoi ou bacchants? de la dissidence des vivants à la ségrégation des morts." In *L'association dionysiaque dans les sociétés anciennes*, 227–46. Collection de l'École française de Rome 89. Rome: École française de Rome, 1986.

———. "Origines et sens de l'inhumation à l'époque impériale." *Revue des études anciennes* 60 (1958): 323–47.

Turner, Victor. *The Ritual Process: Structure and Anti-Structure*. Chicago: Aldine, 1969.

Uhalde, Kevin. *Expectations of Justice in the Age of Augustine*. Philadelphia: University of Pennsylvania Press, 2007.

Van der Meer, Frederik. *Augustine the Bishop: the Life and Work of a Father of the Church*. Translated by Brian Battershaw and G. R. Lamb. London: Sheed and Ward, 1962.

Van Nijf, Onno M. *The Civic World of Professional Associations in the Roman East*. Dutch Monographs on Ancient History and Archaeology 17. Amsterdam: Gieben, 1997.

Vermaseren, Maarten Jozef. *Corpus cultus Cybelae Attidisque*. 2 vols. Études préliminaires aux religions orientales dans l'Empire romain 50. Leiden: Brill, 1977–89.

———. *Corpus inscriptionum et monumentorum religionis Mithriacae*. The Hague: Nijhoff, 1960.

Vidal, Michel, ed. *Incinérations et inhumations dans l'Occident romain aux trois premiers siècles de notre ère: actes du Colloque international de Toulouse-Montréjeau (IVe Congrès archéologique de Gaule méridionale), 7–10 octobre 1987*. Toulouse: Association pour la promotion du patrimoine archéologique et historique en Midi-Pyrénées, 1991.

Vismarra, Cinzia. "L'apport des textes antiques." In *Incinérations et inhumations dans l'Occident romain aux trois premiers siècles de notre ère: actes du Colloque international de Toulouse-Montréjeau (IVe Congrès archéologique de Gaule méridionale), 7–10 octobre 1987,* edited by Michel Vidal, 107–47. Toulouse: Association pour la promotion du patrimoine archéologique et historique en Midi-Pyrénées, 1991.

Vismarra, Cinzia. "I cimiteri ebraici di Roma." In *Società romana e impero tardoantico. 2. Le merci. Gli insediamenti,* edited by Andrea Giardina, 351–89. Collezione storica. Bari: Laterza, 1986.

———. "L'inscription funéraire dite de Nazareth." *Revue internationale des droits de l'antiquité* 2 (1953): 285–321.

Visscher, Fernand de. *Le droit des tombeaux romains.* Milan: Giuffrè, 1963.

Vogel, Cyrille. "L'environnement cultuel du défunt durant la période paléochrétienne." In *La maladie et la mort du chrétien dans la liturgie: Conférences Saint-Serge: XXIe semaine d'études liturgiques,* 381–413. Bibliotheca Ephemerides Liturgicae. Subsidia 1. Rome: Ediciones Liturgiche, 1975.

Volp, Ulrich. *Tod und ritual in den christlichen Gemeinden des Antike.* Supplements to Vigiliae Christianae 65. Leiden: Brill, 2002.

Wagner, Guy. *Les Oasis d'Égypte à l'époque grecque, romaine et byzantine d'après les documents grecs.* Bibliothèque d'étude 100. Cairo: Institut français d'archéologie orientale du Caire, 1987.

Waltzing, Jean-Pierre. *Étude historique sur les corporations professionnelles chez les Romains depuis les origines jusqu'à la chute de l'Empire d'Occident.* 4 vols. Louvain: Peeters, 1895–1900.

———. "La thèse de J.-B. De Rossi sur les collèges funéraires chrétiens." *Bulletin de l'Académie royale de Belgique (Classe des lettres, etc.)* 6 (1912): 387–401.

Williams, Margaret H. "The Jews and Godfearers Inscription from Aphrodisias: A Case of Patriarcal Interference in Early 3rd Century Caria?" *Historia* 41 (1992): 297–310.

———. "The Jews of Corycus: A Neglected Diasporan Community from Roman Times." *Journal for the Study of Judaism* 25 (1994): 274–86.

———. "The Meaning and Function of *Ioudaios* in Graeco-Roman Inscriptions." *Zeitschrift für Papyrologie und Epigraphik* 116 (1997): 249–62.

———. "The Organisation of Jewish Burials in Ancient Rome in the Light of Evidence from Palestine and the Diaspora." *Zeitschrift für Papyrologie und Epigraphik* 101 (1994): 165–82.

Wilpert, Josef. "Ein unbekanntes Gemälde aus der Katakombe der hl. Domitilla und die coemeterialen Fresken mit darstellungen aus dem realen Leben." *Römische Quartalschrift* 1 (1887): 20–41.

Wischmeyer, Wolfgang. *Von Golgatha zum Ponte Molle: Studien zur Sozialgeschichte der Kirche im dritten Jahrhundert.* Forschungen zur Kirchen—und Dogmengeschichte 49. Göttingen: Vandenhoeck and Ruprecht, 1992.

Wood, Ian. *The Merovingian Kingdoms, 450–751.* New York: Longman, 1993.

Wuilleumier, Pierre. *Tarente des origines à la conquête romaine.* Bibliothèque des Écoles françaises d'Athènes et de Rome 148. Paris: Ed. De Boccard, 1939.

Zangara, Vincenza. *Exeuntes de corpore: discussioni sulle apparizioni dei morti in epoca agostiniana.* Biblioteca della Rivista di storia e letteratura religiosa. Studi 1. Firenze: Olschki, 1990.

INDEX

Abthugni (North Africa), 10
Achilles (Roman martyr), tomb of, 33
Acilii Glabriones, family of, 43
Acmetes monks, 119n63
Acmonia (Asia Minor), epitaphs from, 21, 22
Acts of the Apostles 13, 43
Acts of Felix of Abthugni, 10
Acts of John, 124–25
Acts of Martyrs, 95, 96, 102
"Ad duos lauros" catacomb, 35
ad sanctos burial, 175n65
Adeodatus (son of Augustine of Hippo), 129
Aeneid, Servius' commentary on, 81, 91
Aerius of Pontus, 164–66
Against Celsus (Origen), 44n24, 84–85, 104n29
Agennius Urbicus, 120
Agrigento (Sicily), burials in, 20
Alciphron, 90–91
Alexandria (Egypt), 23, 94, 137
Ambrose of Milan
 on duty to bury the dead, 101, 104, 110, 115–17
 on funerals and funeral rites, 136–38
 on parentalia, 146–47
Ampliatus, hypogeum of, 33
anathemas on tombs, 21–22, 73–75
annona, 55
Antioch, burials in, 6–7, 119n63, 127, 132, 137
Antiochus I of Commagene, tomb of, 76
Antony the Hermit, 108–9
Aphroditô (Egypt), undertakers from, 119
Apocalypse of Paul, 168
Apollonius of Athens (rhetor), 80
Apologeticum (Tertullian), 10, 43–45, 49–50, 93
Apology (Aristides), 91–93, 125
Apostolic Constitutions, 114, 127, 137, 151, 162

Apostolic Tradition, 111–15, 176–77
Applebaum, Shimon, 22
Arca (in modern Lebanon), burials in, 47
Arcadius (Roman emperor), 121
Archytas, tomb of, 16
areae in Carthage, 7–12
Aristides, 91–93, 125
Asia Minor, burials in, 19–22, 71, 73–74
associations, Greco-Roman. *See* collegia
Athanasius of Alexandria, 108–9
Attis, cult of, 17
Augustine of Hippo
 on burial of catachumens, 169–70
 on commemoration of the dead
  in Eucharistic service, 157–61, 170
  parentalia, 146–53
  prayers for the dead, position on, 167–71
 on duty to bury the dead, 102, 105
 feast of the dead in sermon of, 142
 funeral of, 134
 on funerals and funerary rites
  Eucharist, funerary, 134–35
  Monica (mother), funeral of, 128–31, 134–35
  mourning period, 136
  sermons, funerary, 131–34
 on love of the body and care of the dead, 85–88
 Monica (mother) and. *See* Monica
 on salvation and burial, ix, 86, 102, 125, 133–34
Augustus (Roman emperor), 59, 60, 61, 62
Aurelius (bishop of Carthage), 147–48, 151
Aurelius Aristeas, epitaph of, 22
Ausbüttel, Frank M., 38

Bacchus, cult of, 15
banquets, funerary. *See* parentalia
Basil of Caesarea, 68–69
Basilides (bishop), 28
Beleth, Jean, 141

213

Bergamo (Italy), 120
Beth She'Arim, Palestine, catacombs of, 19, 24
Bible cited in defense of parentalia, 150–51
biblical citations. *See individual books of the Bible*
biblical Patriarchs
   burials of, 26, 107–11
   mourning periods of, 136–37
Bidez, Joseph, 65
bishops
   care of the dead, authority over, ix–x, xii–xiii, 2–3, 8, 35–36, 174–75, 177–78
   Eucharistic commemoration of, 158
   funerals and funerary rites, lack of involvement in, 132–33, 134
   grave diggers, control over/employment of, 35–36, 70, 111, 117–19, 121–22
   martyrs, burial of, 98–99
   parentalia (funerary banquets)
      Eastern Church's greater tolerance of, 151–52
      Western Church's attempts to curtail, 142–51
   plagues of 251 and 266, on burial of dead during, 93–94
   poor, responsibility for burying
      Ambrose of Milan on, 115–17
      Apostolic Tradition on, 111, 115
      funerary activities, evidence of, 117
      imperial authority, Church involvement in, 121–22
      origins of, 111, 122
   professionalization of clergy and, 49, 111
   violation of tombs, enforcement of laws regarding, 69, 70
Bodel, John, 119–20
body, changing attitudes towards, xi, 10, 57
   Augustine on love of the body and care of the dead, 85–88
   cremation versus inhumation
      cadavers, laws against profanation of, 79, 85
      Christianity's influence on shift towards inhumation, 82–85
      first century, cremation as norm in, 79–80
      religious objections to cremation, 80–82
      replacement of cremation by inhumation, xi, 79–80
      vulnerability to tomb violation, 79

resurrection, burial practice and belief in, xi, 10, 57, 82–85, 87
soul, body's retention of, 81–82
violation of tombs, rules regarding, 78–79. *See also* violation and protection of tombs
Bonifatius (priest of Hippo), 158
Botte, Bernard, 112–13
Brandenburg, Hugo, 8
Brown, Peter, ix*n*1, xii, 111, 119n63, 122, 142
burial associations. *See* collegia
burial duties. *See* duty to bury the dead
Burkert, Walter, 14, 18
Bynum, Caroline W., 83–84

cadavers, profanation of
   Gregory of Nazianzen's epigrams on, 77–78
   inhumation, change to preference for, 79, 85
   in late Roman law, 59, 61–63
Caecilianus (bishop of Carthage), 158
Caesarea of Mauritania (modern Cherchel, Algeria), burial grounds of, 9, 11, 12, 31, 32
Callixtus and catacomb of Callixtus, x–xi*n*5, 2–7, 12
canon law
   on cemeteries, 144
   on Church's duty to bury the poor, 115n55
   on funerary Eucharist, 135
   on tomb violation, 68–70
Capitulatio de Partibus Saxoniae, 29
care of the dead in Late Antiquity, ix–xiii, 176–78
   by Christians. *See* Christianity
   collective burial. *See* collective burial and religious identity
   collegia, funerary. *See* collegia
   commemoration. *See* commemoration of the dead
   duty to bury. *See* duty to bury the dead
   family responsibility for. *See* family responsibility for care of the dead
   funerals. *See* funeral and funeral rites, Christian
   by Jews. *See* Jews
   limits on Church authority over, 174–75, 177–78
   non-Christians, Christian interaction with, 177
   sources used to study, x–xi

tomb violations, rule regarding. *See* violation and protection of tombs
Caristia, 141–42
Carrié, Jean-Michel, 55
Carthage
  areae in, 7–12
  Conference of, 158
  Jewish burial sites in, 23
catachumens, burial of/prayers for, 169–70, 172–73
catacombs, Roman. *See also names of individual catacombs*
  collective burial of Christians, evidence of, 30, 32–36
  collegia, ownership of sections by, 55–56
  fossores, 35–36, 119n63
  Jewish catacombs, 19, 23–24, 27
  origins of Christian cemeteries and cemetery organization, x, 2–7, 12
catacombs of Beth She'Arim, Palestine, 19, 24
Catechetical Homilies (Theodore of Mopsuestia), 163, 166
Celsus, 84-85
cemeteries and cemetery organization, Christian, origins of, 1–12, 176–77
  Carthage, areae in, 7–12
  etymology of cemetery, 3–7
  martyrs' tombs, koimeteria as, 6–7, 97, 144
  poor, obligation of Church to bury, 115
  rest or sleep, cemetery as meaning a place of, 3, 113–14
  Roman catacombs, x, 2–7, 12
Chaeremon (deacon), 99
Charlemagne, 29
Christ
  burial of, 96, 101, 103–7
  resurrection as occasion of Edict of Nazareth, 60
Christianity
  body, view of. *See* body, changing attitudes towards
  clergy. *See* bishops; clergy; deacons
  collective burial and religious identity of, 27–36
    burial practices of, 30–32
    Church teaching of, 27–29
    Roman catacombs, evidence of, 30, 32–36
  collegia. *See under* collegia
  commemoration. *See* commemoration of the dead
  duty to bury. *See* duty to bury the dead
  funerals and funeral rites. *See* funerals and funeral rites, Christian

groups and communities formed by Christians, 48–50
inhumation, shift to, 82–85
limits on Church authority over care of dead, 174–75, 177–78
mystery cults, supposed influence of, 14–15
non-Christians, Christian interaction with, 177
origins of cemeteries and cemetery organization, 1–12
  Carthage, areae in, 7–12
  etymology of cemetery, 3–7
  Roman catacombs, x, 2–7, 12
Roman knowledge of, 45
Severus Alexander, philo-Christianity of, 45–47
violation of tombs and
  Church canons on tomb violation, 68–70
  epitaphs. *See* epitaphs, protective
  late imperial constitutions concerning, 65–68
Cicero, 58, 91n7, 115
Cirta, 117
City of God (*De ciuitate Dei;* Augustine of Hippo), 85, 102, 168
CJ (*Codex Justinianus*), 54, 61, 64, 121
Clement of Alexandria, 126
clergy. *See also* bishops; deacons
  Eucharistic commemoration of, 158
  at funerary rites, 126–27, 133, 139
  as grave diggers, 117, 118, 120–21
  professionalization of, 49, 111
Cn. Cornelius Severus, 43
Codex Justinianus (*CJ*), 54, 61, 64, 121
Codex Theodosianus, 62–65, 120–21n71–72, 120n69
collective burial and religious identity, x–xi, 23–36
  of Christians, 27–36
    burial practices of, 30–32
    Church teaching of, 27–29
    Roman catacombs, evidence of, 30, 32–36
  of Jews. *See under* Jews
  of mystery cults, 14–18, 27
  religious pluralism of Late Roman empire and, 23–24
collegia, xi, 37–56
  Christianity and, 47–56
    churches organized as collegia, concept of, 41–47
    groups and communities formed by Christians, 48–50

collegia *(continued)*
   Christianity and *(continued)*
      membership of Christians in collegia with pagan membership, 28–29, 50–56
      Roman catacomb sections owned by collegia, 55–56
   corpora and, 55
   disappearance/development of, 53–55
   familial interactions with, 40–41
   Jewish involvement in, 22
   mensores, 55
   purposes of, 37–41
   Severan legislation dealing with, 2–3, 54
   social importance of, 39–40, 56
   supposed types of, 37–39, 44–45, 55
   Tertullian's defense of Christians forming illegal associations, 2, 43–45
commemoration of the dead, xii, 140–75
   Church's responsibility for, limits on, 174–75
   offerings, Eucharistic, 153–57
   parentalia (funerary banquets). *See* parentalia
   prayers. *See* prayers for the dead
   Roman feast of the dead, no Church adaptation of, 141–42
Commodianus, 51
Commodus (Roman emperor), 45
community/communitas, as terms, 48–49
Como (Italy), church of St. Julian at, 75
conclamatio, 129
Concordia Sagittaria (Dalmatia), 73
Conference of Carthage, 158
Confessions (Augustine of Hippo), 128, 129, 134, 146, 159
Constantine, Peace of, 3, 8
Constantine the Great (Roman emperor), 120, 121
Constantinople, burial at, 121, 132–33, 137
Constantius (Roman emperor), 63–64, 79, 120
copiatae, 120–21
1 Corinthians
   5:10, 53
   8–10, 28, 51, 52n61
   8:4, 51
   8:7, 51
   10:21, 143
   10:25, 51
   10:32–33, 53
   15:32, 149
2 Corinthians
   1:9, 31n77
   1:11, 171
   5:10, 168

Cornelii, family of, 79
corpora, 55
Corycus (Asia Minor), 21
Councils
   Elvira, 144
   Hippo, 135n26
   Laodicea, 6
   Mâcon, 69
   Marseille, 69
   Vatican II, 157
cremation
   inhumation replacing, xi, 79–80
   religious objections to, 80–82
   violation of tombs, vulnerability to, 79
cult groups, pagan, collective burial for, 14–18, 27
cult of the dead, xii, 140–75
   parentalia (funerary banquets). *See* parentalia
   prayers. *See* prayers for the dead
   Roman feast of the dead, no Church adaptation of, 141–42
cult of fire, 80
cult of martyrs, 96–97, 99–100, 144, 152
Cumae (modern Cuma, Italy), inscription from, 15
Cumont, Franz, 14–16, 59, 60, 80, 137
Cure of Greek Maladies (Theodoret of Cyrus), 29
curses on tombs, 21–22, 73–75
Cybele, cult of, 17, 30
Cyprian of Carthage
   collective burial and religious identity, 28–29
   collegia, 50
   duty to bury the dead and, 94, 96, 98, 99
   on offerings for the dead, 154–55
   origins of cemeteries and cemetery organization, 11
Cyril of Alexandria, 167
Cyril of Jerusalem, 162

Dagron, Gilbert, 121
Dalmatia, burial in, 73, 137
Damasius (bishop of Rome), 119n63
Daniel 3:40, 106
Daphne, martyrium of (Antioch), 7
De anima (*On the Soul*; Tertullian), 4, 81, 84, 126–27
De anima et eius origine (Augustine of Hippo), 169
De ciuitate Dei (*City of God*; Augustine of Hippo), 85, 102, 168
De Corona (*On the Crown*; Tertullian), 84, 153

De cura pro mortuis gerenda (*On the Care of the Dead;* Augustine of Hippo), 85–88, 125, 132, 140n3, 160, 167, 168, 170, 177
De ebrietate (Philo of Alexandria), 52
De idolatria (Tertullian), 28, 52–53, 143–44
De legibus (Cicero), 58
De officiis (Ambrose of Milan), 115–17
De officiis (Cicero), 115
De remediis fortuitorum (Pseudo-Seneca), 91n7
De resurrectione mortuorum (Tertullian), 84
de Robertis, Francesco Maria, 44, 54
De Rossi, Giovanni Battista
  on collective burial, 30, 33, 35
  on collegia, 43–45
  on origins of Christian cemeteries and cemetery organization, 1–3, 7, 176
De spectaculis (Tertullian), 143
De verbis Apostoli (collection of sermons), 142
de Visscher, Fernand, 59, 60, 61, 64
deacons
  burial responsibilities of, 98–99, 115n55
  Callixtus as archdeacon, 2, 3
  cemetery administration, supposed responsibility for, 2, 3
dead, care of. *See* care of the dead in Late Antiquity
Decentius (bishop of Gubbio), 155
Decius (Roman emperor), 28
Delattre, Alfred Louis, 11, 23n50
Delehaye, Hippolyte, 13
dendrophori, 54
Denis (bishop of Alexandria), 94, 99
Deuteronomy 21:18-21, 52
Dianae et Antinoi, cult of, 38
Didascalia, 115n55, 127
Digesta
  on collegia, 38, 44, 54
  duty to bury the dead and, 90, 110
  on violation and protection of tombs, 58, 59, 61–64
Dionysius (bishop of Rome), 3
Dionysius, cult of, 15
Dioscorides, 80
Discourse to the Greeks (Tatian), 83n75
Divine Institutes (Lactantius), 91, 97, 100, 103–4
Divus Augustus (Suetonius), 44n25
Dolbeau, François, 170n63
Doliché (modern Dülück, Turkey), burial at, 18
Domitian (Roman emperor), 33

Domitilla, catacomb of, 30, 33–34, 55
Donatism, 145n20, 158
Duchesne, Louis, 141
Dulcitius (tribune), 168–69
duty to bury the dead, xi–xii, 89–122
  Augustine on, 85–88
  Christ, burial of, 96, 101, 103–7
  construction of early Christian identity via, 90–100
    martyrs, burial of, 95–100
    during plagues of 251 and 266, 93–95
    poor, burial of, 91–93
  foreigners, 115n55, 117, 122
  fourth and fifth century models of, 100–111
    Christ's burial, 101, 103–7
    Patriarchs, burials of, 107–11
    Tobit, 100–103
  grave diggers, Church control over/employment of, 117–19
  in Greco-Roman society generally, 90–91
  Julian's letter not shedding light on, 89–90
  the poor. *See* poor, burial for
  Tobit as model of, 98, 100–103
Duval, Yvette, 7–8, 12, 87n81

Eastern Church
  parentalia (funerary banquets), tolerance of, 151–52
  prayers for the dead in Eucharistic service, 161–64
Eastern cults, collective burial, and religious identity, 14–18, 27
Ecclesiastical History (*Historia Ecclesiastica;* Eusebius of Caesarea), 3n8, 4n12, 6n20, 6n22, 83, 94–95, 99
Edict of Antioch (Edict of Julian), 64–65
Edict of Nazareth, 59–61
Edict of the praetor, 58
Elvira, Council of, 144
Enchiridion (Augustine of Hippo), 168
Ephesians 5:29, 86, 87n80
Epiphanius of Salamis, 117, 164–66
episcopal responsibilities. *See* bishops
epitaphs, protective, 70–79
  fines listed in, 72–73
  Gregory of Nazianzen, epigrams of, 75–78
  on Jewish tombs, 21–22, 70–71, 73, 74
  maledictions and anathemas, 21–22, 73–75
  restricting use of tomb, 71–72

Eucharist
  catachumens, burial of, 169
  offerings for the dead at, 153–57
  parentalia and, 147, 148–49, 151, 153
  as part of funeral rite, 124, 127, 130–32, 134–39
  prayers for the dead at Eucharistic services. *See under* prayers for the dead
Euhemerus, 143
Eulalius (bishop), 119n63
Eusebius (martyr), 99
Eusebius of Caesarea
  Ecclesiastical History (*Historia Ecclesiastica*), 3n8, 4n12, 6n20, 6n22, 83, 94–95, 99
  on duty to bury the dead, 97, 100
Eustratius Constantinopolitanus, 167
Evodius (bishop), 129–30, 134, 136, 137

Fabian (bishop of Rome), 3
factiones, 44
Faltonia Hilaritas, tomb of, 31, 32
family responsibility for care of the dead, x, xii
  in Christian community, 30
  collegia, interaction with, 40–41
  epitaphs restricting use of tomb to family, 71–72
  funerals and funerary rites, 124–25, 134, 139
  in Jewish community, 20–21, 26–27
  martyrs, burial of, 99
  mystery cults and, 14, 18, 27
  parentalia (funerary banquets), 142, 147–50
  prayers for the dead, 160–61, 174–75
  in Western Roman empire, 14
Faustus (deacon), 99
Ferrua, Antonio, 5, 34
Février, Paul-Albert, 138, 142, 144
fines, funerary, 72–73
fire, cult of, 80–81
Flambart, Jean-Marc, 39
Flavia Domitilla, and catacomb of Domitilla, 33
Flavii Aurelii, hypogea of, 33–34
foreigners, duty to bury, 115n55, 117, 122
fossores of Roman catacombs, 35–36, 119n63. *See also* grave diggers
frater/fraternitas, as Christian terms, 49–50
Fröhner, Wilhelm, 60
Frontinus, 120
Fructuosus (martyr), 96
Frugoni, Arsenio, 1
funeral associations. *See* collegia

funerals and funeral rites, Christian, xii, 123–29
  Augustine of Hippo, funeral of, 134
  Christian funerals versus funerals for Christians, 138–39
  clergy, role of, 126–27, 133, 139
  elaborate ceremonies, condemnation of, 125–26, 131–34
  Eucharist, funerary, 124, 127, 130–32, 134–39
  family responsibility for, 124–25, 134, 139
  fourth and fifth century evidence of, 128–38
  in hagiographic texts, 128
  lamentation, discouragement of, 125, 126, 129–33
  liturgical evidence, 123–24
  Macrina (sister of Gregory of Nyssa), funeral of, 128–29, 130
  Monica (mother of Augustine of Hippo), 128–31, 134–35
  mortuary crown and flower garlands, rejection of, 125–26
  mourners, presence of, 125, 129–31, 133
  mourning period, 135–37
  professional mourners, ban on hiring, 132–33
  psalms sung at, 129, 130, 133, 138
  second and third century evidence of, 124–27
  sermons, funerary, 128, 131–34
funerary banquets. *See* parentalia
funerary fines, 72–73

Gaius Julius Aquilinus, portico built by, 17
Gaius Marius, 79
Galatians 5:6, 170
Galerius (Roman emperor), 97
Gallienus (Roman emperor), 3, 6, 97
Gammarth necropolis (Carthage), 23
Gaudentius (bishop of Brescia), 145
Gelasian Sacramentaries, 136
Gelasius (pope), 157
Geminius Victor (bishop of Furnos), 154–55
Genesis
  3:29, 109
  23, 26
  23:3, 110
  23:4-9, 110
  23:8-9, 101
  49:29-31, 26
  50:10, 136
  50:25, 26

INDEX

Georges (Melitian bishop of Alexandria), 117
Giovannini, Adalberto, 61
Gnostics, 83
Gordian (Roman emperor), 61
Gratian (Roman emperor), 65, 79, 104
grave diggers, 117–19
    Church control over/employment of, 35–36, 70, 111, 117–19, 121–22
    civil authority's control over/employment of, 35–36, 119–21
    clergy as, 117, 118, 120–21
    martyrs, burial of, 98, 99
    Roman catacombs, fossores responsible for developing, 35–36, 119n63
    Tobit, representations of, 101
    violation of tombs by, 70
Great Oasis (Egypt), undertakers in, 118
Gregory of Nazianzen, 75–78, 89n1, 106, 151–52
Gregory of Nyssa, 68–69, 128–29, 130
Gregory of Tours, 156
Gregory the Great (pope), 111, 121n76, 154
Gross-Krotzenburg (Germany), burials at, 16
Grzybek, Erhard, 60
Gsell, Stéphane, 8
Guyon, Jean, 35

Harl, Marguerite, 152
Hatch, Edwin, 42
Hebrews 4:15, 107
Heinrici, Carl Friedrich Georg, 42
Herodotus, 80
Hettner, Felix, 18
Hierapolis (Asia Minor), epitaphs from, 21, 22
Hilarianus (governor of Carthage), 8
Hilary of Poitiers, 29, 104
Hippo, Council of, 135n26
Hippolytus of Rome
    Apostolic Tradition attributed to, 112, 113
    on Callixtus, 2, 12
    cemetery as term, use of, 4
    Refutation of All Heresies recognized as work of, 2
    Severus Alexander, treatise dedicated to mother of, 46
Hipponium (modern Vibo Valentia, Italy), burials at, 16
Hirt, Marguerite, 61
Historia Augusta, 45–47
Historia Ecclesiastica (Eusebius of Caesarea). *See Ecclesiastical History*
Histories (Herodotus), 80
homilies
    on funerals and funeral rites, 128, 131–34
    on parentalia, 142, 144, 145, 149, 150, 151
    on prayers for the dead, 158, 159, 163, 169–73, 175
Honorius (Roman emperor), 121, 138
Hypatios (bishop of Ephesus), 107

identity, religious. *See* religious identity
In Aeneid (Servius), 81, 91
inhumation
    ancient Roman custom of, 79
    cadavers, laws against profanation of, and change to, 79, 85
    within city limits, 66
    cremation, replacing, xi, 79–80
    violation of tombs, vulnerability to, 79
Innocent I (bishop of Rome), 155
Instructions (Commodianus), 51
Isaiah 22:3, 149
Isis, cult of, 27, 30
ius sepulcri, 71

Jeremiah 11:15–16, 155
Jerome
    on duty to bury the dead, 101, 105, 110–11, 118
    on funerals and funeral rites, 137n34
    on offerings for the dead, 155–56
Jerusalem Talmud, 25–26
Jews
    Aristides on, 92
    collective burial, supposed practice of, 18–27
        Asia Minor, burials in, 19–22
        family responsibility for care of the dead, 20–21, 26–27
        Italy outside of Rome, burials in, 19–22
        in major Jewish population centers, 22–24
        purchasing of tombs by Jews, 24–25
        rabbinical/biblical teaching on, 25–26
        Roman catacombs, 19, 23–24, 27
        social integration of, 18–19
    epitaphs, protective, 21–22, 70–71, 73, 74
    Severus Alexander, philo-Judaism of, 46–47
    Tobit, as model of duty to bury the dead, 98, 100–103

INDEX

Job 1:5, 171, 172
John, Gospel of
  10:18, 104
  11:11, 4n11
  12:3, 106
  19:31–33, 104
  19:38, 105, 106
  19:38–42, 101
  19:40, 106
  19:41, 105
John Chrysostom
  cemetery as term, use of, 6
  on Christ's burial, 106–7
  on funerals and funerary rites, 132–34, 137, 139
  on prayers for the dead, 163–64, 171–74
John Damascene, 92
John II (patriarch of Jerusalem), 162
John II (pope), 69
Joseph of Arimathea, 96, 101–7
Judges
  8:32, 26
  16:31, 26
Julia Mammaea, 46
Julian (Roman emperor), 64–65, 79, 89–90
Julian, Edict of, 64–65
Julius Africanus, 46
Julius Caesar (Roman emperor), 64
Julius I (bishop of Rome), 5
Jupiter Dolichenus, cult of, 18
Jupiter Heliopolitanus, cult of, 17–18
Juster, Jean, 25
Justin Martyr, 93
Justinian
  CJ (Codex Justinianus), 54, 61, 64, 121
  Novellae, 121

1 Kings 13:22, 86
2 Kings
  20:6, 172
  23:17–18, 86

Lactantius
  on duty of burial, 91, 97, 100, 103–4, 111
  on protective epitaphs, 75n57
Lanuvium (modern Lanuvio, Italy), burials at, 38, 44
Laodicea, Council of, 6
Late Antiquity, care of dead in. *See* care of the dead in Late Antiquity
Laurentius (dedicatee of the *Enchiridion*), 168–69
Lemnos (Greek island), epitaph from, 72–73

Leon, Harry J., 24, 47
Leon VI (byzantine emperor), 121
Letter of the Churches of Lyons and Vienna, 83, 84
Leucius of Theveste (martyr), 11
Leveau, Philippe, 9n34
lex Iulia, 44, 61
Liber Pontificalis, 3, 5
Liberian Catalog, 5
Liberius (bishop of Rome), 5
Libosus of Vaga (martyr), 11, 12
Life of Barlaam and Joasaph (John Damascene), 91–92
Lucian, 49
Luke, Gospel of
  7:36, 106
  9:60, 146
  19:17, 99
  23:50–52, 101

2 Maccabees, 168, 169
Macedonia, 73
Macer (jurist), 61
MacMullen, Ramsay, xii–xiii
Mâcon, Council of, 69
Macrina (sister of Gregory of Nyssa), funeral of, 128–29, 130
Macrobius, 79
maledictions on tombs, 21–22, 73–75
Manlius Acilius Glabrio (consul), 43
Marcia (concubine of Commodus), 45
Marcianus (jurist), 52
Marcus Antonius Restitutus, tomb of, 30
Mark, Gospel of, 15:42–45, 101
Markus, Robert, 50
Marseille, Council of, 69
Martialis (bishop), 28, 50
martyrs
  Augustine on utility for salvation of burial next to martyr, ix, 86
  cult of, 96–97, 99–100, 144, 152
  duty to provide burial for, 95–100
  Eucharistic commemoration of, 158–59
  koimeteria as tombs of, 6–7, 97
  parentalia (funerary banquets), 142–48, 151–52
  relics, 66–67, 97
  violation of tombs, laws regarding, 66–67
Matthew, Gospel of
  2:11, 106
  8, 101
  8:25, 27n69
  18:22, 29
  25:35, 106

26:10–12, 102
27:57–58, 101
27:57–61, 96
28:12–15, 60
Maximinus Daia (Roman emperor), 6, 94
Maximus (bishop of Turin), 101–2, 105–6
Maximus (Roman emperor), 104
Mazzarino, Santo, 46
meals, funerary. *See* parentalia
Meeks, Wayne A., 42, 49
Melitians (schismatic group), 108–9, 117
mensores, collegium of, 55
Milan (Italy), 64
Millet, Gabriel, 73
Minucius Felix, 82–83, 125–26
Mishna, 26
Mithras, cult of, 15, 16
Momigliano, Arnaldo, 46
Mommsen, Theodor, 37, 38, 44, 72
Monica (mother of Augustine of Hippo)
  funeral of, 128–31, 134–35
  parentalia, celebration of, 146, 147
  prayers for the dead and death of, 159–60
Montanism, 52
Monteverde, catacomb of, 23
Morris, Ian, 80
Mrozek, Stanislaw, 53
mummification, 108, 118
Mystagogic Catecheses (Cyril of Jerusalem), 162, 164
mystery cults, 14–18, 27

Natural History (Pliny the Elder), 79
Nazareth, Edict of, 59–61
necrotaphoi. *See* grave diggers
Nemrod Dag (Turkey), 76
Neoplatonism, 65
Nereus (Roman martyr), tomb of, 33
Nero (Roman emperor), 59, 60
Nestorius, 119n63
Nicholas of Damas, 80
Nicodemus, 101, 103, 105–7
Nock, Arthur Darby, 80
North, John, 24
Novellae
  Justinian, 121
  Leon VI, 121
  Valentinian III, 66–69, 79
Ntedika, Joseph, 168
Numidicius (martyr), 99

Octavius (Minucius Felix), 82–83, 125–26
Odilon (abbot of Cluny), 141

Opinions of Paul, 62, 63
oriental cults, 14–18, 27
Origen, 2, 4, 44n24, 84–85, 104n29
origins of Christian cemeteries and cemetery organization, 1–12
  Carthage, areae in, 7–12
  etymology of cemetery, 3–7
  Roman catacombs, x, 2–7, 12
Orphic cults, 15, 16
Ostia (Italy), 20, 134, 135

pagan mystery cults, 14–18, 27
Pailler, Jean-Marie, 15
Pammachius, 102
Panaetius (stoic), 81
Panarion (Epiphanius of Salamis), 117, 164–66
parentalia (funerary banquets), 142–53
  Christians' continuing celebration of, 143–49, 152–53
  debauchery, as potential occasion for, 144–49, 152
  Eastern Church's greater tolerance of, 151–52
  Eucharist and, 147, 148–49, 151, 153
  as family cult or practice, 142, 147–50
  for martyrs versus the ordinary dead, 142–48, 151–52
  Scripture cited in defense of, 150–51
  Western Church's attempts to curtail, 142–51
Patlagean, Evelyne, 120
Patriarchs
  burials of, 26, 107–11
  mourning periods of, 136–37
Patterson, John R., 39
Paul (jurist), 62
Paul and Pauline writings
  collegia, concept of Christian churches organized as, 42
  on eating meat from a sacrifice, 51
  on groups and communities formed by Christians, 48
  on relationships between Christians and pagans, 28, 51
  Sergia Paulina, house church of, 42
  Sergius Paulus, conversion of, 43
Paulinus (author of *Vita Ambrosii*), 130n17
Paulinus of Nola, ix, 102, 167–68
Peace of Constantine, 3, 8
Pergamum, church at, 51–52
Pergola, Philippe, 33, 55
Perpetua (martyr), 8–9
Persian cult of fire, 80

Petilianus (Donatist bishop), 158
Pétré, Hélène, 49–50
Petzl, Georg, 76
Philippians 2:7–8, 107
Philo of Alexandria, 52
philologico-combinatory method, 1, 2n3
Philostratus, 80
Pietri, Charles, 35, 142, 176
plagues of 251 and 266, burial of dead during, 93–95
Plato, *Republic*, 100
Pliny the Elder, 79
Pliny the Younger, 45n29
pluralism, religious, of Late Roman empire, 23–24
Politiké, mummy of, 118
Polycarp of Smyrna, 96–97
Pontius (author of *Life of Cyprian*), 94, 95, 100
poor, burial for, xii, 111–22
    Ambrose of Milan on, 115–17
    Apostolic Tradition on, 111–15
    civil authority's responsibility for, 119–22
    in early Christian apologetics, 91–93
    as episcopal responsibility. *See under* bishops
    grave diggers, Church control over/employment of, 117–19
Possidius (bishop of Calama), 134
Pozzuoli (Italy), 17–18
Praeparatio evangelica (Eusebius of Caesarea), 100
prayers for the dead, 153–75
    alms given for, 172–73
    Augustine's position on, 167–71
    catachumens, 169–70, 172–73
    controversies over, 164–67
    in Eucharistic service
        Augustine on, 157–61, 170
        controversies over, 167
        Eastern Church, 161–64
        individual names, recitation of, 158–59, 160–64
        offerings, 153–57
        Roman Mass, 157–61
    family responsibility for, 160–61, 174–75
    John Chrysostom's position on, 163–64, 171–74
professional associations, development of, 55
professional mourners, ban on hiring, 132–33
professionalization of clergy, 49, 111

protection of tombs, rules regarding. *See* violation and protection of tombs
Prudentius, 102–3
Psalms
    14, 138
    48, 149
    48:10-12, 131
    61, 104
    100, 130
    at funerary rites, 129, 130, 133, 138
Psenosiris (priest), 118
Pseudo-Quintilian, 90n6
Pseudo-Seneca, 91n7
Pythagorism, 16, 81

Quintilian, 90

Rajak, Tessa, 19
Ravenna (Italy), church of San Vitale in, 75
refrigeria (funerary banquets). *See* parentalia
Refutation of All Heresies (Hippolytus), 2, 4
relics, 66–67, 97, 108–9
religious identity
    collective burial and. *See* collective burial and religious identity
    duty to bury the dead, construction of early Christian identity via, 90–100
    martyrs, burial of, 95–100
    during plagues of 251 and 266, 93–95
    poor, burial of, 91–93
    pluralism of Late Roman empire, 23–24
Republic (Plato), 100
Reseghetti, Silvia, 44
resurrection
    Christian burial practice and belief in, xi, 10, 57, 82–85, 87, 109
    Christ's resurrection as occasion of Edict of Nazareth, 60
Revelation 2:12–14, 18–20, 52n58
Rhodes (Greek island), 16
Robert, Louis, 76
Roman catacombs. *See* catacombs, Roman
Roman Mass, prayers for the dead in Eucharistic service of, 157–61
Romans
    1:17, 150
    13:13, 147
    14:1–15, 51n57
    14:13, 51n57
Rutgers, Leonard V., 19, 26n66

Sabazians, 16–17
Salamito, Jean-Marie, 54

sale of tombs, 24–25, 110–11
Salona (Dalmatia), 73
2 Samuel 21:12–14, 26
Sarapion (bishop of Thmuis), 161–62
Satyrus (brother of Ambrose of Milan), 137–38
Saxer, Victor, 157
Saxons, burials of, 29
Scheid, John, 47, 57
scriptural citations. *See individual books of the Bible*
Scripture cited in defense of parentalia, 150–51
segregation of burials by religious groups. *See* collective burial and religious identity
Semahot, 25
Septimius Severus (Roman emperor), 44, 59, 61, 80
Serapion (bishop), 109
Sergia Paulina, house church/collegium of, 42–43
Sergius Paulus (proconsul of Cyprus), 43
sermons
    on funerals and funeral rites, 128, 131–34
    on parentalia, 142, 144, 145, 149, 150, 151
    on prayers for the dead, 158, 159, 163, 169–73, 175
Servius, 81, 91
Severianus, funerary enclosure of, 31–32
Severus Alexander (Roman emperor), 45–47
Sidonius Apollinaris, 70
Sirach 30:18, 150
Smith, Rowland, 65
Smyrna (Asia Minor), burials at, 10n37, 20–21, 96–97
Solluna (Rome), funerary basilica at, 31
Sordi, Marta, 42–43, 46, 60
soul, body's retention of, 81–82
Spes (monk of Hippo), 158
Stephen (bishop of Rome), 28
Strubbe, Johan, 73
Successus of Abbir Germaniciana (martyr), 11
Suetonius, 44n25
Sulla the dictator, 79

Taft, Robert, 161
Tarentum (modern Taranto, Italy), 16, 20
Tatian, 83n75
Taurus (Praetorian prefect), 120
Teos (modern Sigacik, Turkey), 17

Tertullian
    attack on retention of part of soul in body, 81
    on Carthaginian areae, 8–10
    cemetery as term, use of, 4
    collective burial, supposed comment on, 28
    on cremation versus inhumation, 84, 85
    defense of Christians forming illegal collegia, 2, 43–45
    fraternitas, defense of, 49–50
    on funerals and funerary rites, 125–27
    on offerings for the dead, 153–54
    on parentalia, 143–44
    poor, on burial of, 93
    on relationships between Christians and pagans, 52–53
Tertullus (martyr), 11, 98
Testamentum Domini, 114
Teucheira, Cyrenaica (modern Tukrah, Libya), burials at, 22
Theodore of Mopsuestia, 163, 166
Theodoret of Cyrus, 29
Theodosian Code, 62–65, 120–21n71–72, 120n69
Theodosius I (Roman emperor), 65, 79, 137–38
Theodosius II (Roman emperor), 121
1 Thessalonians 4:13f, 4n11
Thomas, Yan, 58, 59, 62
Thrace, burials at, 73
Thyatira, church at, 52
Tiberius (Roman emperor), 53
Tlos (Lycia), 20
To Scapula (Tertullian), 8
Tobit
    1:17, 100
    1:18–20, 100
    2:4, 100
    4:17, 150
    12:12–13, 101
    duty to bury the dead, as model of, 98, 100–103
Tosefta, 25–26
Trajan (Roman emperor), 45n29
True Doctrine (Celsus), 84–85
Turcan, Robert, 80, 81
Turner, Victor, 48–49, 50
Twelve Tables, 58

Uzalis (North Africa), 134

Valentinian III (Roman emperor), 65–69, 79

INDEX

Valerian (Roman emperor), 3, 6, 11, 45, 97
Valerius Mercurius, epitaph of, 30
Van Nijf Onno M., 39–40
Vatican II, 157
Venosa (Italy), burials at, 20
Vercellae (modern Vercelli, Italy), 118
Via Latina, catacomb of, 34
Via Livenza, hypogea of, 34
Victor (bishop of Rome), 45
Victor (priest of Caesarea), epitaph of, 32
Vigna Cimarra, catacomb of, 23
Villa Labicana, catacomb of, 23
Villa Patrizi (Rome), inscriptions at, 30
Villa Randanini, catacomb of, 23–24
Villa Torlonia, catacombs of, 23
Vincentius Victor, 169
violation and protection of tombs, xi, 57–79
  body, changing attitudes towards, 78–79
  cadavers, profanation of
    Gregory of Nazianzen's epigrams on, 77–78
    inhumation, change to preference for, 79, 85
    in late Roman law, 59, 61–63
  Christianity
    Church canons on tomb violation, 68–70
    epitaphs. *See* epitaphs, protective
    late imperial constitutions concerning, 65–68
  cremation vs. inhumation, 79
  epitaphs. *See* epitaphs, protective
  funerary fines, 72–73
  Gregory of Nazianzen, epigrams of, 75–78
  in late Roman law, 58–68
    cadavers, specific rules about profanation of, 59, 61–63
    civil and religious protections, 58, 63–64
    Edict of Nazareth, 59–61
    Edict of the praetor, 58
    imperial constitutions of 4th and 5th centuries, 63–68
    public offense (crimen), tomb violation as, 59–61
  peacefulness of the tomb, Roman devotion to, 10
Volp, Ulrich, ix

Waltzing, Jean-Pierre, 55, 119
Western Church
  family responsibility for care of the dead in, 14
  parentalia (funerary banquets), attempts to curtail, 142–51
  prayers for the dead in Eucharistic service of Roman Mass, 157–61
Williams, Margaret H., 24–25
Wilpert, Josef, 55

Zeno (bishop of Verona), 144–45
Zephyrinus (bishop of Rome), x–xi n5, 2

www.ingramcontent.com/pod-product-compliance
Lightning Source LLC
Chambersburg PA
CBHW061346300426
44116CB00011B/2019